Creaturely Theology

On God, Humans and Other Animals

Celia Deane-Drummond
and David Clough

scm press

© Celia Deane-Drummond and David Clough 2009

Published in 2009 by SCM Press
Editorial office
13–17 Long Lane,
London, EC1A 9PN, UK

SCM Press is an imprint of Hymns Ancient and Modern Ltd
(a registered charity)
St Mary's Works, St Mary's Plain,
Norwich, NR3 3BH, UK
www.scm-canterburypress.co.uk

British Library Cataloguing in Publication data

A catalogue record for this book is available
from the British Library

978 0 334 04189 4

Typeset by Regent Typesetting, London
Printed and bound by
CPI William Clowes Ltd, Beccles, Suffolk

Contents

Acknowledgements   v

Contributors   vii

Introduction   I
Celia Deane-Drummond and David Clough

Part One   Historical Approaches

  I Towards a Thomistic Theology of Animality   21
     John Berkman

  2 The Anxiety of the Human Animal: Martin Luther on
     Non-human Animals and Human Animality   41
     David Clough

  3 Animals in Orthodox Iconography   61
     Esther D. Reed

Part Two   Systematic Approaches

  4 The Redemption of Animals in an Incarnational
     Theology   81
     Denis Edwards

  5 The Way of All Flesh: Rethinking the *Imago Dei*   100
     David S. Cunningham

Part Three   Hermeneutical Approaches

  6 The Question of the Creature: Animals, Theology and
     Levinas' Dog   121
     Aaron S. Gross

7 The Animals We Write On: Encountering Animals in
   Texts   138
   Rachel Muers

8 Elves, Hobbits, Trolls and Talking Beasts   151
   Stephen R. L. Clark

Part Four   The Moral Status of Animals

9 Slouching Towards Jerusalem? An Anti-human Theology
   of Rough Beasts and Other Animals   171
   Peter Manley Scott

10 Are Animals Moral? Taking Soundings through Vice,
   Virtue, Conscience and *Imago Dei*   190
   Celia Deane-Drummond

11 Humans, Animals, Evolution and Ends   211
   Neil Messer

Part Five   Ecological Perspectives

12 'They shall not hurt or destroy in all my holy mountain'
   (Isaiah 65.25): Killing for Philosophy and a Creaturely
   Theology of Non-violence   231
   Michael Northcott

13 The New Days of Noah? Assisted Migration as an
   Ethical Imperative in an Era of Climate Change   249
   Christopher Southgate

Postscript   266
David Clough and Celia Deane-Drummond

Bibliography   270
Index of Names and Subjects   289

Acknowledgements

This book could not have happened without the support of the University of Chester in facilitating the work of the Centre for Religion and the Biosciences, which held a series of public lectures and a one-day conference on the theme of non-human animals in 2005–06. We are grateful to the Revd Canon Judy Hunt, Dr Mary Midgley, Professor Stephen Clark and Dr Margaret Atkins for their generous contributions to these public events. Their presentations provided the occasion for further reflection on the theological significance of animals and resulted in the collaboration of Celia Deane-Drummond and David Clough, which led to the colloquium that formed the basis of this book. The colloquium title was 'Towards a Theology of the Animal: Systematic, Scientific and Ethical Perspectives' and was held in the magnificent and unique surroundings of St Deiniol's Library, Hawarden, 2–4 November 2007. The working party at St Deiniol's discussed short papers, which were refined and developed to form the various chapters in this volume. All the contributors took part in this colloquium and each benefited from face-to-face discussion and feedback on our developing ideas. We therefore owe a special debt of gratitude, not only to the contributors who were prepared to give of their time generously in this way, but also to the library, whose hospitality provided a comfortable and scholarly environment in which to thrash out our ideas in conversation with one another. The editors are also particularly grateful for the assistance of Margaret Atkins in the editorial review process. When the idea of this colloquium was first conceived, Dr David Clough was based at Cranmer Hall in Durham, but subsequently the University of Chester, in its wisdom, recruited David for the Theology and Religious Studies Department. The editors have therefore been in the happy position of being able to collaborate on this project as colleagues in the same department, and hope this will provide a platform for further projects in this area. We are also grateful for the assistance of Lynne Cumisky in preparation of the index. Special thanks also to Natalie Watson of SCM

Press for sharing our vision for this book and her support throughout the process.

Contributors

John Berkman is Associate Professor of Theology and Philosophy at The Dominican School of Philosophy and Theology and The Graduate Theological Union, Berkeley, California. He is author of 'The Consumption of Animals and the Catholic Tradition' in *Food for Thought: The Debate over Eating Meat* (2004), 'Prophetically Pro-Life: John Paul II's Gospel of Life and Evangelical Concern for Animals' (1999), 'The Chief End of All Flesh' (with Stanley Hauerwas, 1992), and numerous other articles in scholarly books and journals.

Stephen R. L. Clark is Professor of Philosophy at the University of Liverpool. His books include *The Moral Status of Animals* (1977), *The Nature of the Beast* (1982), *How to Think about the Earth* (1993), *Animals and their Moral Standing* (1997), *The Political Animal* (1999), *Biology and Christian Ethics* (2000) and *G. K. Chesterton: Thinking Backward, Looking Forward* (2006). He is currently working on the late antique philosopher Plotinus, and on the role of faith in civil society.

David Clough is Senior Lecturer in Theology at the University of Chester. He has written on Karl Barth's ethics in *Ethics in Crisis* (2005) and on Christian pacifism in a twenty-first-century context in a book co-authored with Brian Stiltner: *Faith and Force: A Christian Debate about War* (2007). His current research interest is the place of non-human animals in Christian theology and ethics, on which he has written several articles and is currently working on a monograph.

David S. Cunningham is Professor of Religion at Hope College in Holland, Michigan, USA. He is the author of five books and numerous essays and articles on various topics in Christian theology and ethics; he has also edited two book collections. His most recent book is *Christian Ethics: The End of the Law* (2008).

Celia Deane-Drummond is Professor of theology and the biological sciences at the University of Chester. She has developed a particular focus on contemporary theology and ethics in relation to environmental, medical and, more recently, non-human animals. More recent books include *The Ethics of Nature* (2004), *Wonder and Wisdom: Conversations in Science, Spirituality and Theology* (2006), *Genetics and Christian Ethics* (2006), *Ecotheology* (2008). Edited collections include *Re-Ordering Nature: Theology, Society and the New Genetics* (2003), edited with Bronislaw Szerszynski, *Future Perfect: God, Medicine and Human Identity*, edited with Peter Scott (2006) and *Teilhard de Chardin on People and Planet* (2006). She is also Director of the Centre for Religion and the Biosciences at the University of Chester.

Denis Edwards is Senior Lecturer in Systematic Theology in the School of Theology at Flinders University. He teaches for the Catholic Theological College within the ecumenical consortium of the Adelaide College of Divinity and is a priest of the Roman Catholic Archdiocese of Adelaide. He has been involved in setting up the Flinders University and Adelaide College of Divinity Centre for Theology, Science and Culture and conferences on science and theology co-sponsored by the Center for Theology and the Natural Sciences (Berkeley) and the Vatican Observatory. In 1992 he was invited to become a founding member of the International Society for Science and Religion. Recent publications include *Ecology at the Heart of Faith* (2006), *Breath of Life: A Theology of the Creator Spirit* (2004), *The God of Evolution: A Trinitarian Theology* (1999) and, as editor, *Earth Revealing – Earth Healing: Ecology and Christian Theology* (2001) and with Mark Worthing, *Biodiversity and Ecology: An Interdisciplinary Challenge* (2004). His current research is exploring the theology of divine action in the light of the costs of evolution.

Aaron S. Gross is a historian of religions who specializes in modern Jewish traditions. His forthcoming dissertation theorizes the significance of 'the question of the animal' for the study of religion, grounding this theorization in an examination of Jewish and South Asian dietary practices pertaining to animal food. Gross holds a Masters of Theological Studies from Harvard Divinity School and is a PhD candidate at the University of California, Santa Barbara. He is co-editor of a forthcoming interdisciplinary volume entitled *Animal Others and the Human Imagination*.

Neil Messer is Senior Lecturer in Christian Theology at the University of Wales, Lampeter. A specialist in theological ethics with a research training in the biomedical sciences, his current research is focused on the engagement of Christian theology with ethical issues in biology, biotechnology and medicine. His recent publications include *Selfish Genes and Christian Ethics: Theological and Ethical Reflections on Evolutionary Biology* (2007) and *SCM Study Guide to Christian Ethics* (2006).

Rachel Muers is Lecturer in Christian Studies at the University of Leeds. She is the author of *Keeping God's Silence: Towards a Theological Ethics of Communication* (2004) and *Living for the Future: Theological Ethics for Coming Generations* (2008), and editor with David Grumett of *Eating and Believing: Interdisciplinary Perspectives on Vegetarianism and Theology* (2008). She is the principal investigator on the research project 'Vegetarianism as Spiritual Choice in Historical and Contemporary Theology', funded by the Arts and Humanities Research Council.

Michael Northcott is Professor of Ethics at the University of Edinburgh, a priest in the Scottish Episcopal Church and author of many books and papers in ecological ethics and theology, including *A Moral Climate: The Ethics of Global Warming* (2007). He is currently working on a research project on the extinction of species.

Esther D. Reed is Associate Professor of Theological Ethics at the University of Exeter. She teaches topics that include God, Sex and Money; The Ethics of Dietrich Bonhoeffer; Body and Society; and Health-Care Issues in Christian Perspective. She delivered the 2007 Sarum Lectures at Salisbury Cathedral and her latest book is *The Ethics of Human Rights: Contested Doctrinal and Moral Issues* (2007). She is a member of the Methodist Church and serves on its Faith and Order Committee.

Peter Manley Scott is Senior Lecturer in Christian Social Thought and Director of the Lincoln Theological Institute at the University of Manchester. He is author of *Theology, Ideology and Liberation* (1994), *A Political Theology of Nature* (2003) and numerous articles. He is co-editor of the *Blackwell Companion to Political Theology* (2004), *Future Perfect? God, Medicine and Human Identity* (2006), *Nature, Space and Sacred* (2009) and *Re-moralising Britain?* (2009), and is co-editor of a special issue of the *International Journal of Public Theology*, on the theme of theology and the urban. He has lectured widely, and is currently writing a book on the politics of nature for an ecological, global age.

Christopher Southgate is Research Fellow in Theology at the University of Exeter. He is the co-ordinating editor of *God, Humanity and the Cosmos* (2005), a companion to the science and religion debate, now in its second edition. In 2008 he published a monograph, *The Groaning of Creation: God, Evolution and the Problem of Evil*. He is currently working on the use of the Bible in environmental ethics, and philosophical and theological issues relating to the origin of life.

Introduction

CELIA DEANE-DRUMMOND AND
DAVID CLOUGH

Since we have good reason to believe that only a very few of God's creatures – human beings, and perhaps angels – engage in theology, the term 'creaturely theology' may seem problematically broad, perhaps giving the impression that the authors gathered here indulge in the hope of finding some chimpanzee equivalent to St Augustine. And since we also believe that God does not engage in theology, theology must be an activity particular to God's creatures, making the term 'creaturely theology' tautologous or redundant. What led us to adopt 'Creaturely Theology' as the title for this collection, despite these disadvantages, was a collective sense that the term had the virtue of gesturing towards a starting point for theology notable only in its comparative rarity. By 'creaturely theology' we mean to indicate something simple: engaging in the theological task conscious of one's creatureliness. The importance of this consciousness became clear to us when considering appropriate ways to think and speak of those of God's non-human creatures with which we have most in common. First, doing theology conscious of one's creatureliness forces on the theologian a certain humility: to be a creature is to be finite, possessed for a short time of a knowledge that is incomplete, and fallible even in the use of this inadequate resource. Such awareness will usefully guard against making poorly grounded and over-confident assertions of God's preferential purposes for the species to which one belongs, or its relative merit in relation to the rest of God's creation. Second, doing theology remembering that one is a creature makes clear that when the objects of one's theologizing are other creatures of God, we recognize those other creatures as, at the most fundamental level, like us: one creature reflecting on another. Such a recollection makes clear that the first word in this theological task must be of our connection to, relationship with and solidarity alongside others of God's creatures, rather than of differentiation from them, which has been the more common starting point (and frequently the ending point too). Third, doing theology in awareness of being one of God's creatures encourages attentiveness to the many attempts that have been made to build a high boundary wall between *Homo sapiens* and every other species of creature within creation. Such attending leads quickly to critical questions concerning the multiple and contradictory foundations of this barrier, and the motives of the architects for attempting the construction of such an unpromising structure.

Early in the attempt to do theology in this creaturely mode, animals have a tendency to creep in. The word 'animal' has an informative etymology, referring at its root to a creature with the breath of life. It is a comparative newcomer, not used in the King James translation of the Bible, and hardly in use at all until the end of the sixteenth century. The difficulty with 'animal' is that from its earliest usage, and despite its etymological roots, it has been ambiguous about whether it includes human beings: it is used to refer to all living creatures of a given kingdom (Animalia), or sometimes in a more restrictive sense to refer to warm blooded mammals, as a collective term to refer to Animalia or mammals apart from human beings. While this radical ambiguity in modern terminology might well be considered an apt representation of a radical modern ambivalence about the relationship between human beings and other creatures also designated as mammals, it presents something of a problem when, as frequently in this volume, the subject matter is precisely the nature of this relationship. In modern English usage, while biologists attempt to resolve the ambiguity inclusively, the binary opposition has largely prevailed: one goes to the zoo to see the animals, and one expects to find them looking through the bars from within rather than without. To accept this usage, however, and use the term 'animal' consistently to exclude human beings seems to concede from the outset that the most significant relationship between *Homo sapiens* and all other animate living creatures is one of binary opposition. To hold out, on the other hand, for a consistently inclusive usage of 'animal', is both historically unjustified and, in all probability, doomed to failure. For these reasons we have opened this volume to all kinds of animals, that is, understood in an inclusive or exclusive sense to include or exclude humans, though hope, at least at points, to help the reader to attend to which is which.

Creaturely theology in the sense we are attempting is clearly no novelty: such concerns bring to mind an image of St Francis of Assisi preaching to the birds, or, in a British context, St Columba's white horse shedding tears at the passing of this great saint and lover of animals. The inclusion of such stories in the lives of these early saints points to something fundamental about earlier conceptions of other animate creatures, namely, that they were not radically separate from the human community, but creatures like us, not only dependent on each other, but also on God. If we compare this view with modern practices in contemporary society – replete with industrial farming, in which, for example, layer upon layer of battery hens are crammed into confined spaces – we may be excused for wondering if perhaps our own perception has gone awry, rather than dismissing earlier hagiography as romantic effervescence.

Given the rupture with these earlier memories and its consequences, it is hardly surprising that the first modern efforts to name a philosophy and theology of non-human animals sought to persuade others that animals do matter and need to be taken seriously. At this stage the most prominent concern was *ethical*, namely, trying to change particular practices that were cruel towards animals, either through industrialized farming, some forms of medical experimentation or careless pet ownership. Peter Singer is perhaps best known in this camp, seeking to persuade his readers of the validity of taking a broader view that takes into account the sum total of suffering, and includes all creatures with interests.[1] As a utilitarian, he combines consequentialism with a sum ranking that totals all utilities, along with a substantive theory of the good, which in his case is the satisfaction of preferences. Although he has sometimes been dubbed an animal rights campaigner, this is actually a misnomer, since his perspective still allows for some cruel treatment of animals, as long as it is outweighed by other benefits, viewed in terms of preference satisfaction. Perhaps the most radical aspect of his philosophy was his charge of 'speciesism' towards those who gave greater attention to human communities. Instead, satisfaction of preferences was all that counts, so that a human being may be deemed to have a lower level of preference satisfaction in some situations than, for example, other animals. More explicit attention to animal rights became established through the work of Tom Regan, who argued for the value of individual animals as 'subjects of a life'.[2] He restricts his attention to mammalian life in particular as that which is

---

1 Peter Singer, *Animal Liberation: A New Ethic for Our Treatment of Animals*, London: Jonathan Cape, 1990 [1975]. For a more detailed discussion of Singer, Regan and Linzey, see C. Deane-Drummond, *The Ethics of Nature*, Oxford: Blackwell, 2004, pp. 54–85. Drawing on Thomist thought, Deane-Drummond argues for a virtue approach to animal ethics, over against the utilitarian approach of Singer or the rights approach of Regan and Linzey.

2 Tom Regan and Peter Singer (eds), *Animal Rights and Human Obligations*, Englewood Cliffs: Prentice Hall, 1976; Tom Regan, *The Case for Animal Rights*, London: Routledge, 1988 [1984].

worthy of most attention. Regan extends the consideration of rights understood in terms of the basic dignity of individual (mammalian) creatures, and in this sense parts company from the sum calculus of Singer. In this sense his clarion call for the total abolition of all commercial agriculture, not just intensive rearing, alongside a ban on hunting, a ban on medical use of animals and all meat-eating goes further than Singer in its practical implications.[3]

Andrew Linzey is perhaps the best-known author writing from a Christian perspective on the topic of non-human animals, arguing with Singer for the liberation of animals and with Regan for the recognition of rights for animals.[4] He attempts to illuminate links between Christianity and the philosophy of Regan by attaching to it a particular theological rationale that he finds upon re-examination of the tradition.[5] His main concern is to persuade other Christian believers of the imperative in caring about what happens to animals, and that other considerations, including broader tendencies towards earth-keeping, need to be resisted if they have a negative impact on animal suffering.[6] He finds theological justification of his view by turning to the incarnation, God incarnate in *flesh*, so that all animals are subjects of inherent value to God. Adapting Bonhoeffer's notion of theos-rights in order to include animals, he argues that animal rights flow directly from the rights given by God; that is, God establishes the specific value of some living beings. In this sense, humans do not bestow rights on animals, rather, they recognize their rights as already given by God. Filling out this view, he adds the idea of generosity; interpreted as giving moral priority to the weak, in this case the animals, so that they are analogous to children in terms of human responsibility. Indeed, he does not simply equate the two, but seeks to give even *higher* priority to

---

3 See, for example, Tom Regan, *The Thee Generation*, Philadelphia: Temple University Press, 1991.

4 See, for example, A. Linzey, *Animal Rights: A Christian Assessment*, London: SCM Press, 1976; *Christianity and the Rights of Animals*, London: SPCK, 1987; *Animal Theology*, London: SCM Press, 1994; *Animal Gospel: Christian Faith as if Animals Mattered*, London: Hodder & Stoughton, and Louisville: Westminster John Knox Press, 1999. In the 1987 work, Linzey prefers language of 'theos-rights': other animals have claims on us on the basis of their inherent value as God's creatures.

5 The jointly authored texts speak of the close relationship between Regan and Linzey. See, for example, A. Linzey and T. Regan (eds), *Animals and Christianity: A Book of Readings*, London: SPCK, 1989.

6 The ethical priority is clear in, for example, his rather more recent *Animal Theology*, which devotes the bulk of attention to ethical issues, rather than theological discussion. On the latter point, see A. Linzey, 'The Conflict between Ecotheology and Animal Theology', in *Creatures of the Same God: Explorations in Animal Theology*, Winchester: Winchester University Press, 2007, pp. 49–71.

animals; so that, 'animals, like children, should be seen as having not equal claim, but even greater claim upon us precisely because of their vulnerability and relative powerlessness'.[7] Linzey is strident in his rejection of animal experimentation, meat-eating, hunting and all practices that infringe such rights. He also seeks to find ancient spiritual resources that support his views, and in pastorally oriented texts speaks of recovering liturgies of animal care that welcome animals into the human community.[8] Perhaps the most interesting volume in this vein is the jointly authored text *After Noah: Animals and the Liberation of Theology*, with Dan Cohn-Sherbok, in which they argue for the celebration of animals in place of their exploitation, where animals become agents of justice in Jewish rabbinic literature, and Jesus' identification with animals in the apocryphal literature raises questions about human creaturely relationships.[9]

The work of the Christian philosopher Stephen R. L. Clark on non-human animals has received less notice than that of Linzey, especially from theologians, but is impressive in its scope, depth and engagement over time. His books on the topic include *The Moral Status of Animals* (1977), *The Nature of the Beast* (1982), *Animals and their Moral Standing* (1997), *The Political Animal* (1999) and *Biology and Christian Ethics* (2000).[10] He distances himself from both utilitarianism and rights-based models and draws eclectically and often lyrically on classical traditions to argue for a revolution in our regard for animals and the corresponding implications of this for our thinking about the human. Of particular relevance to this volume is his contention that human 'superiority' to other animals, insofar as it is real at all, consists only in 'the possibility that we may (and the corresponding duty that we should) allow our fellow creatures their part of the action'.[11] While the main thrust of his arguments is philosophical, rather than theological, his interrogation of theological issues brings new insights that serve to challenge presuppositions about theology and ethics. This is particularly evident in *How to Think about the Earth* (1993), which, while it dealt

---

7 A. Linzey, 'Animal Rights', in Paul Barry Clarke and Andrew Linzey (eds), *Dictionary of Ethics, Theology and Society*, London: Routledge, 1996, pp. 29–33.

8 A. Linzey, *Animal Rites: Liturgies of Animal Care*, London: SPCK, 1999.

9 A. Linzey and D. Cohn-Sherbok, *After Noah: Animals and the Liberation of Theology*, London: Mowbray, 1997.

10 S. R. L. Clark, *The Moral Status of Animals*, Oxford: Clarendon Press, 1977; *The Nature of the Beast*, Oxford: Oxford University Press, 1982; *Animals and their Moral Standing*, London: Routledge, 1997; *The Political Animal*, London: Routledge, 1999; *Biology and Christian Ethics*, Cambridge: Cambridge University Press, 2000.

11 Clark, *Moral Status of Animals*, p. 168.

with environmental issues more broadly, was also set in the context of his earlier discussion of animal issues.[12]

Martha Nussbaum is representative of what the philosopher David DeGrazia has dubbed the new generation of thinkers on non-human animals.[13] She argues for the flourishing of animal species according to their capabilities, drawing on the economic philosophy of Amartya Sen.[14] Nussbaum recognizes clearly that trying to judge what might be the norm for a given species is an evaluative matter, that is, it cannot simply be read off the way nature is. Indeed, drawing on Aristotle, she argues that the capacity for humans to wonder at a given life form 'at least suggests the idea that it is good for that being to flourish as the kind of thing it is'.[15] DeGrazia argues that while the first generation of thinkers on animals, such as Singer and Regan, argued simply *that* animals matter, the new generation argue for much deeper consideration of *how* they matter. He includes Mary Midgley in this new wave, who, in *Animals and Why They Matter*, was writing on such issues considerably before many others had begun to grasp their significance.[16] Midgley raises, in particular, the issue of the importance of symbolism in human deliberation of animals, the sociability of animals in their ability to bond with humans, and boundary considerations of environmental ethics. Stephen Webb has also turned his attention to pets in particular as a basis for developing a theology of compassion for animals, eschewing animal rights discourse, and viewing pets as gifts rather than objects of our consumption.[17] Yet apart from the edited collection *Animals on the Agenda*, in which a range of scholars wrote short essays on topics ranging from scriptural interpretation, through to theological questions about whether animals have souls or are redeemed, there is relatively little discussion among theologians about *why* and *how* animals matter.[18] Further, in the latter volume it soon becomes clear that particular readings of tradition are such in order to set

---

12 S. R. L. Clark, *How to Think about the Earth*, London: Mowbray, 1993.

13 D. DeGrazia, *Taking Animals Seriously*, Cambridge: Cambridge University Press, 1996. See Aaron Gross in this volume for further comment.

14 M. Nussbaum, 'Beyond Compassion and Humanity: Justice for Non-Human Animals', in Cass R. Sunstein and Martha Nussbaum (eds), *Animal Rights: Current Debates and New Directions*, Oxford: Oxford University Press, 2005, pp. 299–320. For longer discussion, see M. Nussbaum, *Frontiers of Justice: Disability, Nationality, Species Membership*, Cambridge: Belknap/Harvard University Press, 2006, pp. 325–407.

15 Nussbaum, 'Beyond Compassion', p. 306.

16 Mary Midgley, *Animals and Why They Matter*, London: Routledge, 1983.

17 Stephen Webb, *Of God and Dogs: A Christian Theology of Compassion for Animals*, Oxford: Oxford University Press, 1997.

18 A. Linzey (ed.), *Animals on the Agenda*, London: SPCK, 1998.

up certain theologians as instigators and culprits of a negative attitude towards animals. Such a view reinforces the belief of philosophers such as John Gray, that Christianity's cardinal error is in its assumption that humans are different from animals.[19] Aquinas is top of this list. Yet, for all the more obvious ethical views towards animals that Aquinas shared with his cultural contemporaries, there is implicit in his thinking a far more sympathetic and sensitive treatment of non-human creatures.[20]

It is appropriate that this volume begins with a historical section, and a challenge to such stereotypes, in John Berkman's critical, but far more sensitive, reading of Aquinas. He explores not just Aquinas' understanding of the purpose or end of humans and non-human animals, but significantly raises the issue of ensoulment understood in terms of animal capabilities and the kinds of appetites found in humans and non-humans. Furthermore, he grasps the nettle so often ranged against Aquinas' association of rationality as uniquely endowed on human animals. His essay is representative of the book as a whole in as much as it seeks to penetrate more deeply than ever the roots of the tradition, and in this sense is *radical* in its orientation.

Continuing this detailed engagement with the Christian tradition, David Clough engages Martin Luther on the relationship between humans and other animals, noting that Luther found the close association between human beings and non-human animals problematic long before Darwin had brought this to the attention of his associates in his *Origin of Species*. Clough argues that the tension between Luther's emphasis on human salvation and his recognition of the immanence of God in creation must be seen in the context of his sympathy for birds and other creatures, seen most clearly in his attempted sabotage of a hunt by hiding a rabbit from the hounds. He suggests that this tension cannot be resolved within Luther's corpus, but that one route might be to use the anagogical method Luther employs to resolve an analogous tension concerning the animality of Christ.

Esther Reed's treatment of Orthodox icons pushes us to look at other ways of considering non-human animals in the tradition that have also been largely neglected, at least in Western theological reflection. Her chapter opens up a world that is suggestive of a much deeper theological and spiritual tradition in inclusion of animals, while recognizing at the

---

19 J. Gray, *Straw Dogs: Thoughts on Humans and Other Animals*, London: Granta Books, 2002, p. 4.

20 Judith Barad discusses this issue in her J. Barad, *Aquinas on the Nature and Treatment of Animals*, San Francisco: Scholars Press, 1995. For discussion of this and primary texts, see Deane-Drummond, *The Ethics of Nature*, 2004, pp. 73–7.

same time the anthropocentrism that hovers in the background. Yet she also considers that the overall direction of these icons works towards animals becoming truer to themselves as animals, rather than becoming like humans as knowing subjects. In this sense, the uncertainty that surrounds any supposed separation of animals from humans is the place where we learn to accommodate both kinds.

While the historical approach is suggestive of a rather different, systematic approach to non-human animals than has hitherto been recognized, the possibility of further development of traditions in contemporary theology is advanced in the second section of this book, dedicated to more systematic approaches. As in the last section, there is no attempt to be fully comprehensive in this respect, but rather to offer representative chapters that show something of what is possible through a rereading of tradition towards a theology of the animal.

Denis Edwards' chapter in particular retrieves Athanasius' classic theology of redemption through incarnation so that redemption is widened out to include non-human animals. While Athanasius talks more generally of creation, rather than animals as such, Edwards argues for lines of extension towards a contemporary theology of redemption of all animals. His essay is also of significance in that it points to a possible theological approach to the interminable debate between environmental and animal ethics. His theology is a theology of inclusion, not just a fragile joining of animals with human communities, but one that sets the boundary of community wider than this as well, including all creaturely beings. This immediately raises the issue of how far and to what extent humans might be considered different from other creatures, named in the tradition as bearing the image of God.

David Cunningham develops the theme of the image of God in his chapter in order to argue for an extension of the idea of image-bearing to creatures beyond the human community. He interrogates the supposed distinctions between human beings and other animals that theologians have used to add content to the *imago Dei* and shows that the grammar of the concept of image makes clear that considerations of degree rather than absolute difference are inescapable. In the final section of his essay he examines a range of implications of using 'flesh' rather than 'image of God' to think about theological anthropology, noting its abundant usage in the Bible, its function in establishing relationship with God and commonality between creatures, its incarnational import, and eschatological resonance.

Such considerations raise important questions about how we are interpreting the place of non-human animals in the tradition, that is, hermeneutics. The third section begins with a robust chapter by the Jewish scholar Aaron Gross, who argues for a reconsideration of precisely *how* we think religiously about animals, in conversation with the Jewish thinker Emmanuel Levinas. Gross lays out three interpretive orientations or, as he describes them, 'rigours': a pragmatic rigour that attends to day-to-day experience, science and political issues; an ontological rigour that attends to symbolic meanings of animals and the role they play in defining human being; and a structural rigour that attends to the many-layered meanings of animals and the intersections between these meanings. For him, animal questions are not merely *additional* to other reflections, but require a critical rethinking of core religious beliefs, including our understanding of, for example, the meanings of divinity and humanity.[21] He also challenges some interpreters of Levinas: he finds in Levinas' attitude towards animals rather more ambiguity than previous readings have suggested. Further, Gross suggests that Levinas' ambiguous engagement with the idea that humankind 'is responsible for the universe, the hostage of the creature . . .' has profound implications for how we might perceive animals more generally.

Rachel Muers takes us deeper into problematic questions associated with the representation of animals in scriptural texts. Beginning with the provocative critique of Carol Adams, that non-human animals are not simply marginalized but, rather, never come into view, and are then subsequently marginalized, Muers asks the reader to consider other aspects of the sacred text that regularly resist our attention, namely the appearance of animals in the margins. In particular, such marginalia invite readers to pause in a way that goes further than simply reflecting instrumental use in the manner Adams suggests. Indeed, she finds very little evidence in biblical texts of the symbolic portrayal of animals as beastly in the negative sense that Midgley finds in the classic tradition more generally. Instead, drawing on the book of Job, animals are represented as creatures, qualified by their common dependence on God as creator. While it is possible in traditional texts, such as Augustine, to see evidence for a self-conscious reading of, for example, lambs and pigs beyond their

---

21 There are certain parallels here with ecotheology, inasmuch as many ecotheologians also believe that environmental questions are not merely ethical, but demand a critical reinterpretation of core traditions and beliefs. Both are also grounded in particular practical issues to hand, and both are contextual inasmuch as they start from concerns facing particular communities. The systematic work in this respect, as for animals, has barely begun. For overview, see C. Deane-Drummond, *Ecotheology*, London: Darton, Longman & Todd, 2008.

literal meaning – which has significance in the history of relations with Judaism – this does not necessarily amount to a form of instrumentalization of animals in general, for animals are drawn in as much as written on.

Stephen Clark's entertaining and thought-provoking essay pushes us further back into the meaning of symbol-making that emerged in the context of consideration of our earliest origins as hominid ancestors, that is, an exploration of the meaning of the boundary between the human and non-human in evolutionary terms. He challenges the largely unexamined views of evolutionary archaeologists in their assumption that our own species *Homo sapiens* must, in the course of pre-history, have violently outwitted its hominid neighbours. He also believes that stories about creatures like us tell us as much about ourselves as our earliest ancestors. Our fantasies about Neanderthals, Indonesian 'hobbits' and the like tell us about our own particular fears and preoccupations. Further, just because they were different from humans today does not necessarily mean that coexistence was impossible. Clark suggests that the way we are inclined to interpret such history points to alternative futures for human beings where deliberate manipulation of human species takes shape. Yet such a consideration asks us to question how far our own sense of what counts as a norm for humankind is justified, as it is used as a way of marking out differences between humans, and also between humans and animal kinds. Further, this points to a religious sense, inasmuch as the intimated norms of beauty reflected even in imagined futures of creatures other than ourselves, points to the variegated expression of the incarnated Word, and as such is resonate with the idea of animals as our kin.

From the discussion so far it becomes clear that the consideration and interpretation of non-human animals is rather more fluid than some have cared to admit. But alongside this discussion there are debates about the moral status of animals that once more come to the surface. This issue is dealt with in the fourth section of the book. But how are such debates to be cashed out in the political sphere? In a novel chapter, Peter Scott proposes the concept of the anti-human as a way of casting in a new light any differences in capacity between the human and the non-human animal. Instead of giving theological weight to differences in capacity, he argues on the contrary that differences should be understood by reference to participation. Hence, it is possible to envisage a theological way of knowing that does not simply rest on the differences between human and animal. Scott invites us to go behind what he sees as the thoughtlessness in human treatment of animals and how they are portrayed politically. In political terms, nature, including animals, is treated as property; it is commodified and subject to the processes of production. Yet animals, some human and some non-human, share interests inasmuch as they resist exploitation. For Scott, rights are not simply aligned with citizenship, but, as natural rights, emerge as part of a common sociality and so not solely with reference to humans. Further, an anti-human stance means not always asserting human political interests, so that political scope inheres in the commonality of beings. At this point, a doctrine of ascension is theologically determinative: Jesus' human reality, as Scott puts it, functions both as an identity of God and as the ground of the participation by creatures in God. Jesus' ascended human reality provides thereby the theological rationale of the anti-human. This anti-human offers a theological place of intervention at which an alienated and artificial 'third' nature comes into view, beyond the first nature of nature as such and the second nature of convention, and so provides a stimulus towards the renewal of commonality.

But how might such political companionship between animals and humans be envisaged? Celia Deane-Drummond takes up an area that has been the subject of debate for some time in philosophical circles, namely the question of the morality of non-human animals. This asks not simply how should humans treat animals, but are animals in any sense sharing in the moral community that humans have constructed, and, more importantly, can they be considered moral within their own social worlds? In particular, she asks how far considerations of specific vices and virtues might be applicable to animals, drawing especially on the work of Frans de Waal and Marc Bekoff. Her discussion relates these studies to theological accounts of virtues such as justice, compassion and prudence. Deane-Drummond argues that Christopher Bohm's account of the evolution of conscience is valid, but doubts its comparability with theological meanings of conscience, and critiques the tendency to read into hunter-gatherer societies meanings about our human origins. Such discourse raises questions about how far animals might be considered as sharing in the image-bearing that has traditionally been assigned to human beings alone.

Neil Messer takes up the moral status of non-human animals in a more traditional way in his concern for the practical implications of animal ethics. Focusing on the two particular examples of meat-eating and bio-medical research on animals, he argues that an answer to such practical questions requires an account of the proper ends or purposes of human and animal life. He challenges too close a reliance on an evolutionary account of animal ends, since this would miss out the important theological tradition that locates human and animal purpose within the narrative of God's creative, redeeming and reconciling work in Christ. He draws particularly on the divine command ethics of Karl Barth, which he believes can engage in conversation with the natural sciences and critically appropriate insights from them. Drawing on this approach, and on Dietrich Bonhoeffer's account of ultimate and penultimate things, he suggests specific diagnostic questions as a way of interrogating whether an action is ethically justifiable. In particular, he suggests that there may be incorrect reasons for refusing to eat meat or rejecting medical research on animals, related, for example, to an anti-materialism or pseudo-asceticism. He expresses reservations about Linzey's call to 'approximate' the life of God's promised peaceable kingdom (Isaiah 11.6–9) in the present age and his critique of animal experimentation, on the grounds that human attempts to establish aspects of the peaceable kingdom run the risk of a dangerous utopianism. Rather, we need to admit to the entanglement in sin that is the lot of all human beings. In such a situation the limited use of animals is permitted, with the caveat that this is not an expression of the ultimate future hope. Messer provisionally concludes that, in contemporary Western contexts, this argues for vegetarianism, but not for the rejection of all animal experimentation.

The final section deals with wider ecological issues in their relationship with all animals, and asks us to consider more carefully the environmental issues at stake. Michael Northcott's chapter begins by squarely facing up to the central problems that come to the surface in the animal liberation and animal rights literature represented by Peter Singer and Tom Regan. In particular, he addresses the political violence against other humans associated with these movements. He then asks us to look more carefully at the roots of violence, taking cues from the Genesis text, including the story of rescue as represented in the Noah's ark account. Further, he probes the sacred nature of blood in the Jewish tradition and compares the relative constraint expressed here with modern industrialized practices. He identifies many of the problems that we now face with Kantian attempts to separate humans from other animals by elevating the reasoning powers of humans, and, in particular, sheering moral consideration from the instrumental techniques of scientists. Northcott believes that in as much as Kant failed to take into account the social nature of all animals this finds echoes in contemporary philosophical approaches such as that of Singer. He is also drawn to the ethological account of non-human animals, including not just primates, but other species as well. His final section addresses practical issues of vegetarian choice, inasmuch as it represents the ethical ideal of non-violence and the peaceable kingdom spoken of in Isaiah. Yet, rather than naming total abstinence, he argues for a pattern that takes its cues from the ascetic saints of old, limiting greed not just by a reduction in animal-keeping, but a new way of living with animals that allows for limited consumption.

Finally, Christopher Southgate's chapter considers practical aspects of human interventions in non-human species extinction exacerbated through the impact of climate change. The theological basis for conservation of species is the goodness of creation, and Southgate's ethical approach is informed both by a belief in the necessity of human stewardship of creation and by a sense of humanity's calling to be co-creator and co-redeemer. He challenges the common ecological perspective that human action should be directed at preserving the 'wild', noting that we are beyond the point where any significant part of the earth is unaffected by human activities. Southgate draws on a discussion of Pauline texts to argue that Christian engagement with the preservation of species should be other-regarding, attentive to the needs of the weak and voiceless and attentive to the community of God's creation. He argues that this may point to costly interventions to preserve non-human species, giving the assisted migration of polar bears to Antarctica as an example.

While the essays gathered together in this volume are diverse, and we discovered through conversations that we represent different positions in terms of both our focus and ethical standpoints, a number of common threads are in evidence which cross between different essays in a fruitful way. Such common threads highlight what Gross has termed the *structural rigour* present in animal discourse, namely, that there are many layers of meaning that come to the surface during the discourse. Some layers are more prominent in some chapters than others. For example, some attention to philosophical issues are addressed in virtually all chapters, and authors such as Alasdair MacIntyre are discussed in Berkman, Deane-Drummond and Northcott's contributions. The significance of Mary Midgley's work to this field is also obvious throughout the essays. The interweaving of political and philosophical issues is clearest in Scott, but it also surfaces in Northcott. Attention to the importance of scriptural text is clearest in Muers, but it is also important in Clough, Cunningham, Reed and Southgate. Again, the interweaving with feminist concerns about animals comes to view in both Muers' and Reed's chapters in particular. Attention to the virtues and the Thomist tradition is most fully elaborated in Berkman, but is also important in Deane-Drummond and to a lesser extent in Northcott. Attention to *pragmatic rigour* is also significant in many chapters, including attention to both the ethological studies represented by Frans de Waal and others in Berkman, Deane-

Drummond and Northcott, alongside consideration of evolutionary issues in Clark, Messer and Deane-Drummond. Indeed, it is the belief of the editors that dialogue with science needs to be woven into the discussion inasmuch as it is taken into account, rather than simply setting the agenda for theological discourse. In this sense, this book is offering a new way of engaging in discussion with science, for it is appreciating its claims, while at the same time appropriating other discourses as well. In addition, we can also find here due attention to what Gross terms *ontological rigour*, that is, attention to symbolic meanings of non-human animals and the utilization of these symbolically invested animals to draw the borders of human being(s). The work of Reed and Muers gives special attention to animals as symbols while the chapters by Clark, Cunningham, and Scott attend especially to the definition of human in relation to discourses on animals. The book does not cover *historical trends* in human relationships with animals, but this is admirably dealt with in other volumes.[22] Nor does it delve into details of ethical questions; rather, ethical issues form the context in which theological reflection is situated. While ethical areas such as, for example, vegetarianism and animal experimentation come up in some of these chapters, they do not form a focal point around which authors gather.[23] In addition, the areas covered are representative, rather than comprehensive, and in this sense the volume can only achieve somewhat limited engagement with different aspects of theological reflection. Furthermore, the wider cultural discussion on animals forms a backdrop to the present discourse, rather than a comprehensive interdisciplinary focus.

This volume finds a context in the burgeoning field of non-human animal studies. Recent examples of this kind of literature[24] include due attention to animals in geography, sociology, anthropology, literature, as well as philosophy and critical theory, historical and classical studies, religious studies and interdisciplinary texts. Why, one might say, given this ever-growing literature, is the work undertaken by theologians relatively thin on the ground compared with other disciplines? Theologians seem to have been left behind amidst a cultural wave of interest in this field.

---

22 For a representative list, see the select bibliography.

23 A publication that is orientated with this in mind is one edited by Rachel Muers and David Grumett, *Eating and Believing: Interdisciplinary Perspectives on Vegetarianism and Theology*, London: T & T Clark, 2008. This book does not, however, deal with animals per se, but the practices around human attitudes to animals.

24 We are grateful to Aaron Gross for drawing attention to the importance of referencing this literature and for his assistance in compiling the works listed in the Select bibliography at the end of this Introduction.

Perhaps there is a residue of guilt left towards animals that theologians do not want to face – yet they make it their business to discuss issues of guilt and reconciliation. Perhaps some judge concern for human beings should take priority over that for other creatures – yet it is not at all clear that attending to non-human creatures will have deleterious consequences for human beings. Perhaps those who are already locked into attention to anthropocentric issues do not want to move outside the established field – yet, as we have shown here, new insights into theological anthropology are one of the benefits of this kind of research. In any event, this book is an attempt to start the process of mapping out a new approach to animals in such a way that the conversation can continue. We consider that a creaturely approach to theology – doing theology with attention to one's creatureliness – will bear fruit in generating new and persuasive theological insights about relationships between human beings and others of God's creatures. There are plenty of areas left for development, but, as a start in this direction, we hope that others will be encouraged to join in the discussion. If this volume succeeds in this respect, and if it encourages students and others to think rather more carefully about different dimensions of a theology of God's creatures, then we will have achieved our goal.

Select subject bibliography on animal studies

Geography

Chris Philo and Chris Wilbert, *Animal Spaces, Beastly Places: New Geographies of Human-Animal Relations*, vol. *Critical Geographies*, London: Routledge, 2000.
Jennifer Wolch and Jody Enmel, *Animal Geographies: Place Politics and Identity in the Nature–Culture Borderlands*, London and New York: Verso, 1998.

Sociology

Arnold Arluke, *Regarding Animals*, Philadelphia: Temple University Press, 1996.
Eileen Crist, *Images of Animals: Anthropomorphism and Animal Mind*, Philadelphia: Temple University Press, 2000.
Adrian Franklin, *Animals and Modern Cultures: A Sociology of Human–Animal Relations in Modernity*, London: Sage, 1999.
Leslie Irvine, *If You Tame Me: Understanding Our Connection with Animals*, Philadelphia: Temple University Press, 2004.

Anthropology

Rebecca Cassidy and Molly Mullin (eds), *Where the Wild Things Are: Domestication Reconsidered*, Oxford and New York: Berg, 2007.

Claudine Fabre-Vassas, *The Singular Beast: Jews, Christians and the Pig*, vol. *European Perspectives*, trans. Carol Volk, New York: Columbia University Press, 1997.

Tim Ingold, *Perception of the Environment: Essays on Livelihood, Dwelling and Skill*, London and New York: Routledge, 2005.

Steve Striffler, *Chicken: The Dangerous Transformations of America's Favourite Food*, New Haven and London: Yale, 2005.

Literature

Erica Fudge, *Perceiving Animals: Humans and Beasts in Early Modern English Culture*, Basingstoke: Macmillan, 1999.

Alice A. Kuzniar, *Melancholia's Dog: Reflections on Our Animal Kinship*, Chicago and London: University of Chicago, 2006.

Akira Mizuta Lippit, *The Electric Animal: Toward a Rhetoric of Wildlife*, Minneapolis: University of Minneapolis, 2000.

Randy Malamud, *Poetic Animals and Animal Souls*, New York: Palgrave Macmillan, 2003.

Philosophy and critical theory

In addition to the Anglo-American philosophy that has already been discussed, we note:

Giorgio Agamben, *The Open: Man and Animal*, trans. K. Attell, Stanford CA: Stanford University Press, 2004.

Steve Baker, *The Postmodern Animal*, London: Reaktion, 2000.

Matthew Calarco, *Zoographies: The Question of the Animal from Heidegger to Derrida*, New York: Columbia University Press, 2008.

Matthew Calarco and Peter Atterton (eds), *Animal Philosophy: Essential Readings in Continental Thought*, London: Continuum, 2004.

Stanley Cavell, Cora Diamond, Ian Hacking, John McDowell and Cary Wolfe, *Philosophy and Animal Life*, New York: Columbia University Press, 2008.

Elisabeth De Fontenay, *Le Silence des Bêtes: La Philosophie à L'épreuve*, Paris: Favard, 1998.

Jacques Derrida, *The Animal that Therefore I Am*, trans. David Willis, New York: Fordham University Press, 2008.

Marc R. Fellenz, *The Moral Menagerie: Philosophy and Animal Rights*, Urbana and Chicago: University of Chicago Press, 2007.

Donna Haraway, *The Companion Species Manifesto: Dogs, People, and Significant Otherness*, Chicago: Prickly Paradigm Press, 2003.

Leonard Lawlor, *This Is Not Sufficient: An Essay on Animality and Human*

Nature in Derrida, New York: Columbia University Press, 2007.

M. L. Mallet (ed.), *L'animal Autobiographique: Autour de Jacques Derrida*, Paris: Galilée, 1999.

H. Peter Steeves (ed.), *Animal Others: On Ethics, Ontology, and Animal Life*, Albany NY: State University of New York Press, 1999.

Gary Steiner, *Anthropocentrism and Its Discontents: The Moral Status of Animals in the History of Western Philosophy*, Pittsburgh: University of Pittsburg Press, 2005.

Cary Wolfe, *Animal Rites: American Culture, the Discourse of Species and Posthumanist Theory*, Chicago and London: University of Chicago Press, 2003.

Cary Wolfe (ed.), *Zoontologies: The Question of the Animal*, Minneapolis: University of Minnesota Press, 2003.

Historical and classical studies

Virginia DeJohn Anderson, *Creatures of Empire: How Domestic Animals Transformed Early America*, Urbana and Chicago: University of Illinois Press, 2005.

Diane L. Beers, *For the Prevention of Cruelty: The History and Legacy of Animal Rights Activism in the United States*, Athens: Ohio University Press, 2006.

Claudine Fabre-Vassas, *The Singular Beast: Jews, Christians and the Pig*, vol. *European Perspectives*, trans. Carol Volk, New York: Columbia University Press, 1997.

Erica Fudge, *Perceiving Animals: Humans and Beasts in Early Modern English Culture*, Basingstoke: Macmillan, 1999.

Erica Fudge (ed.), *Renaissance Beasts: Of Animals, Humans, and Other Wonderful Creatures*, Urbana IL: University of Illinois Press, 2004.

Ingvild Sælid Gilhus, *Animals, Gods, and Humans: Changing Attitudes to Animals in Greek, Roman, and Early Christian Ideas*, London and New York: Routledge, 2006.

Katherine C. Grier, *Pets in America: A History*, Chapel Hill NC: University of North Carolina Press, 2006.

Kathleen Kete, *The Beast in the Boudoir: Pet-Keeping in Nineteenth-Century Paris*, Berkeley and Los Angeles CA: University of California Press, 1994.

Mark S. Roberts, *The Mark of the Beast: Animality and Human Oppression*, Indiana: Purdue University Press, 2008.

Richard Sorabji, *Animal Minds and Human Morals: The Origins of the Western Debate*, Ithaca NY: Cornell University Press, 1993.

Gary Steiner, *Anthropocentrism and Its Discontents: The Moral Status of Animals in the History of Western Philosophy*, Pittsburgh: University of Pittsburg Press, 2005.

Tristram Stuart, *The Bloodless Revolution: A Cultural History of Vegetarianism from 1600 to Modern Times*, New York: London: W. W. Norton and Co., 2006.

Religious studies

A large volume that deals with different areas of religious belief and practice is Paul Waldau and Kimberley Patten (eds), *A Communion of Subjects: Animals in Religion, Science and Ethics*, New York: Columbia University Press, 2006. The essays under the subheading Christianity dealt with Bestiaries in heretical medieval writing, a philosophically orientated essay on Descartes, and one highlighting Christian spirituality and animals by Jay McDaniel, who is heavily influenced by process theology, but also absorbs what he claims is a 'Franciscan alternative'. McDaniel largely follows Linzey in his critique of Aquinas, even while engaging with Elisabeth Johnson's neo-Thomist approach. His essay is important inasmuch as he weaves in ecological concerns through the notion of eco-justice. See, 'Practicing the Presence of Animals: A Christian Approach to Animals', pp. 132–45.

Interdisciplinary texts

Animal Studies Group (ed.), *Killing Animals*, Urbana and Chicago: University of Illinois Press, 2006.

J. M. Coetzee (ed.), *The Lives of Animals*, Princeton: Princeton University Press, 1999.

Lorraine Daston and Gregg Mitman (eds), *Thinking Animals: New Perspectives on Anthropomorphism*, New York: Columbia University Press, 2005.

Ingvild Sælid Gilhus, *Animals, Gods, and Humans: Changing Attitudes to Animals in Greek, Roman, and Early Christian Ideas*, London and New York: Routledge, 2006.

Jennifer Ham and Matthew Senior, *Animal Acts: Configuring the Human in Western History*, London: Routledge, 1997.

Aubrey Manning and James Serpell (eds), *Animals and Human Society: Changing Perspectives*, London: Routledge, 1994.

Nigel Rothfels, *Representing Animals*, Bloomington: Indiana University Press, 2002.

Part One

HISTORICAL APPROACHES

I

Towards a Thomistic
Theology of Animality

JOHN BERKMAN

This chapter examines Aquinas' understanding of both the similarities
and differences between human and non-human animals. In order to do
so, I will examine what Aquinas has to say about (a) the telos (overall purpose or end) of humans and other animals; (b) human and animal souls,
which is Aquinas' way of speaking of the kinds of living beings that
humans and other animals are, in the light of their capabilities as creatures; and (c) the kinds of appetites possessed by humans and non-human
animals. In each of these three areas Aquinas claims both a continuity
between humans and other 'perfect' (Aquinas' term for higher) animals,
and also a unique capacity or status for human animals.

From this overview of Aquinas' work, I shall then contrast arguments
of two contemporary Thomists on the continuities and discontinuities
between humans and non-human animals. While one emphasizes forms
of theoretical rationality as a means of 'drawing the line', the other
focuses on shared elements of practical rationality. I shall conclude that
the latter is a much more fruitful direction for developing a Thomistic
theology of animality.

Why Aquinas on animals?

A few prefatory and background comments are in order. First, why
bother with Aquinas on this question? According to many commentators
on Aquinas, he would seem to have little of assistance to guide us towards
a theology of animality, that is, one that thinks systematically and rigor-
ously about the nature of both human and non-human animals. Aquinas'
views are often summarized as comprising (a) a simple and perhaps naive
distinction between humans as having rational souls and non-human

animals as merely sensible souls; and (b) the view that human beings have no inherent responsibilities towards non-human animals, and in fact are not able to wrong individual non-human animals.

These criticisms, while not accurate, are not entirely without merit. Aquinas certainly has a much greater interest in the human animal than in the non-human animal, and even that is an understatement. Despite his wide-ranging interests, Aquinas never takes up the question of the nature of various non-human animals in any sustained fashion. His references to non-human animals typically arise either in the context of a discussion of human animals, to which non-human animals are unfavorably compared, or as part of a broader discussion of creation in which non-human animals are but one element. A much better resource for this task would seem to be Thomas' teacher Albertus Magnus, who was a fine theologian and arguably the greatest zoologist of the medieval period.[1]

However, Aquinas is a more felicitous choice than might at first be thought. First of all, Aquinas' account of human nature and morality are of great importance for contemporary discussion. Second, although as noted above Aquinas does not devote any sustained treatise to the nature of non-human animals, and while Aquinas at times makes overly simplistic dichotomies between human and non-human animals, if one is willing to dig and piece together his references, Aquinas in fact presents a rather sophisticated – even if arguably inadequate and incomplete – view of non-human animals, one worthy of extended review. For example, despite assumptions to the contrary, Aquinas spills a good deal of ink discussing the various forms of continuity between human and some non-human animals. Also, despite often lumping all non-human animals together, at other places Aquinas differentiates kinds of animals. For example, in his *Commentary on the Metaphysics of Aristotle*, Aquinas distinguishes between three levels of animal life.

> The first level is that had by animals having neither hearing nor memory, and which are therefore neither capable of being taught nor of being prudent . . . The second level is that of animals which have memory but are unable to hear, and which are therefore prudent but incapable of being taught. The third level is that of animals which have both of these faculties, which are both prudent and capable of being taught.[2]

---

1 See Albertus Magnus, *On Animals: A Medieval Summa Zoologica*, trans. and annotated K. F. Kitchell and I. M. Resnick, Baltimore: The Johns Hopkins University Press, 1999.

2 Thomas Aquinas, *Commentary on the Metaphysics of Aristotle*, trans. John P. Rowan, Notre Dame IN: Dumb Ox Books, 1995, Lectio 1, n. 13.

In this chapter I will be focusing on this third level of animal, also called the 'higher animals'.

Furthermore, for Aquinas human beings do not have a particularly high 'slot' in the order of creation, being ranked the lowest of creatures with intellectual natures. Thus, when human and non-human animals are seen within the grand scheme of God's creation, their differences – however significant in their own right – seem not so great.

Having shown that Aquinas is concerned with animality, even if primarily to understand human animality, it is also worth placing Aquinas' treatment of non-human animals in its historical and cultural context. Aquinas, like most medievals, was almost certainly in direct contact with a much larger number of species of animals than is true of the typical citizen of the modern West.[3] However, the medieval world was also entranced by fabulous stories of animals, as shown in medieval art and architecture, and as compiled in medieval bestiaries.

Happily, Aquinas' approach to animals is influenced, not by the bestiaries, but by the Aristotelian approach to the natural world. Aquinas was in the forefront of efforts to integrate Aristotelian modes of enquiry into the medieval curriculum. This is evidenced not only by Aquinas' integration of Aristotle's work into his systematic study of theology (e.g. the Aristotelian architectonic of the *Summa*), but also by his superlative commentaries on Aristotle's *De Anima* and parts of the *Parvi Naturalia*, among others.

Aristotle influences Aquinas' anthropology in at least two ways. First, Aquinas' anthropology builds on (though also goes considerably beyond) a set of Aristotelian theses.[4] Second, and perhaps more importantly, Aquinas takes up the epistemology and scientific methodology found in Aristotle's *Posterior Analytics* in a way that allows him to go beyond the confines of Platonic dualism and take more seriously the nature of human and animal bodies.[5]

With this understanding in place, we turn to Aquinas' understanding of animality.

---

3 C. S. Lewis, *The Discarded Image: An Introduction to Medieval and Renaissance Literature*, Cambridge: Cambridge University Press, 1964, pp. 146ff.

4 Maria L. Lukac de Stier, 'Aristotle's *De Anima* as Source of Aquinas' Anthropological Doctrine', 2000, available at <http://maritain.nd.edu/jmc/tioo/stier.htm>.

5 Benedict M. Ashley OP, 'Aristotle's *De Sensu et Sensato* and *De Memoria et Reminiscentia* as Thomistic Sources', 2000, available at <http://maritain.nd.edu/jmc/tioo/ashley.htm>.

Aquinas on animals

Aquinas on the end for animals

According to Aquinas, why does God create living creatures? What is their purpose? Readers of Aquinas will be most familiar with his discussion of the end for a human animal, which is beatitude, found in the vision of God or in friendship with God.[6] Combining this perspective with Aquinas' view that humans may freely use other animals for human benefit, one might easily conclude that God creates non-human animals for the sake of human animals. Aquinas does indeed say this, but this does not represent Aquinas' most considered view of the *telos* of non-human creatures.

If we look at Aquinas' larger picture, we see that for Aquinas the entire physical universe (for example plants, birds, non-human and human animals) is ordered towards 'ultimate perfection', which is in turn ordered to God, and by its perfection gives glory to the goodness of God.[7] Each creature manifests the goodness of God by living according to its own *telos*. Furthermore, all species by existing according to their own degree of goodness make a necessary contribution to the perfection of the universe, 'since the universe would not be perfect if only one grade of goodness were found in things'.[8] In other words, Aquinas' view is that '[t]he perfection of the universe is marked essentially by the diversity of natures, by which the diverse grades of goodness are filled up'.[9] Thus, for Aquinas, God's plan in creation, while hierarchical, is by no means anthropocentric.

The nature of animals

Having very briefly considered the end of animals, we now turn to Aquinas' account of their nature. For Aquinas, all living creatures are

---

6 Thomas Aquinas, *Summa Theologiae*, Chicago: Benziger Bros., 1947, I-II 1–5 and II-II 23. (Henceforth *ST*.)

7 Aquinas has a fourfold hierarchy of ends for creatures. First, 'each creature exists for the sake of its own act and perfection. Second, the less noble creatures exist for the sake of the more noble creatures; for instance, the creatures below man exist for the sake of man. Further, each creature exists for the sake of the whole universe. Further, the universe as a whole, with all its individual parts, is ordered to God as its end' (*ST* I 65.2).

8 *ST* I 47.2.

9 From Thomas Aquinas' *Commentary on the Sentences* (I Sent 44.1.2 ad 6), quoted in Robert Pasnau, *Thomas Aquinas on Human Nature*, Cambridge: Cambridge University Press, 2002, p. 399.

beings with souls. By soul, Aquinas is referring to the Aristotelian notion of *anima*, that immaterial element which animates a living being or makes it alive. It is the *anima* that most fundamentally distinguishes a rock from a tree (or a rock from a goat). Thus Aquinas' notion of the soul as 'the first principle of life'.[10]

Aquinas understands living creatures to be hylomorphic unions of body and soul.[11] Aquinas' view is neither the dualism of Plato or Descartes, which sees the body and soul as two different essences, nor modern materialism or physicalism, which reduces the soul to brain processes. Aquinas speaks of the relationship between soul and body as that between form and matter. He follows Aristotle in thinking it makes no more sense to try to separate soul and body in terms of what makes up a human being than it does to try to separate wax from its shape given by a seal.[12] For Aquinas, living creatures are embodied souls.

Sensible souls and animal sensation

For Aquinas, different kinds of beings have different kinds of souls. Whereas plant souls are vegetative, animal souls are vegetative and sensitive, and human souls are vegetative, sensitive and rational. The vegetative soul has three powers: the power to reproduce itself; the power to make use of food; and the power to grow. The sensitive soul has five exterior senses – sight, hearing, smell, taste and touch[13] – and four interior senses.[14] The interior senses are: the common sensory power (*sensus communis*: the ability to perceive that it is, for example, seeing or hearing); the imagination (*vis imaginativa*: for the retention of the forms taken in by the common sensory power); the estimative sense (*vis aestimativa*: to apprehend intentions not taken in through the senses); and the memorative sense (*vis memorativa*: to retain the forms apprehended by the estimative sense).

The common sensory power is, along with the five external senses, a presentative sense, in that it presents and co-ordinates forms received through the senses to the animal. Whereas the exterior senses receive sensory forms, the common sensory power co-ordinates and distinguishes these forms.

---

10 *ST* 75.1.

11 *ST* intro to I 75.

12 Aristotle, 'De Anima', in Jonathon Barnes (ed.), *The Complete Works of Aristotle: The Revised Oxford Translation*, Oxford: Oxford University Press, 1984, 412b6.

13 *ST* I 78.3.

14 *ST* I 78.4.

The other three interior senses, the imagination, the estimative sense and the memory, are re-presentative senses, in that they mediate between the presentative senses and the intellect. By the imaginative sense creatures retain forms received by the common sensory power. This allows a creature to learn from past experiences. The imaginative sense overlaps with the memory, and is the foundation of it.

Whereas the imagination retains forms received by the common sensory power, memory gives creatures particular capacities by enabling a creature to recognize certain past forms as past. It is from the memory that a creature is able to trace a received form to its point of origin, distinguish a past from a present event and have a sense of time. Memory creates experience and thus the possibility to learn from particular past events.

The estimative sense is the most complex of the senses. It is the one not directly dependent on the external senses, it is the most 'cognitive' of the senses, and as such is most significant in Aquinas' schema for thinking about the continuity between the intelligence of humans and other higher animals. The estimative sense is that which discerns the intentions of other creatures (e.g. friendship or hostility) and directs an animal in ways that further its good. Thus Aquinas' stock example of the sheep that by means of its estimative sense recognizes the wolf as a 'natural enemy' and runs away.[15]

Aquinas clearly recognizes the cognitive aspect of the estimative power. The 'intellect knows many things that the senses cannot perceive. In like manner does the estimative power, though in a less perfect manner.'[16] Similarly Aquinas explains that the estimative power is nobler than the other interior senses because in virtue of it 'animals are said to have a certain sort of prudence'.[17]

Aquinas further distinguishes two aspects of the estimative sense. The first is the apprehension of present objects, the second is apprehension of absent objects. Aquinas notes that many higher animals pursue objects not present to them because they apprehend these objects as not present. For example, dolphins or tigers hunting for prey or looking for a mate.

Although the estimative sense and the intellect would seem to act similarly in many contexts, Aquinas distinguishes the two in relation to the possibility of abstraction. According to Aquinas, whereas the estimative sense only provides an awareness of concrete relationships, the cognitive

---

15 *ST* I 78.4; 83.1.

16 *ST* I 74.4 ad 5.

17 *ST* I 74.4 ad 5; Thomas Aquinas, *Commentary on Aristotle's* De anima, trans. Robert Pasnau, New Haven: Yale University Press, 1999, Book III, Lectio 4, marietti 629.

sense allows for the possibility of abstract judgements.[18] According to Aquinas, non-human animals are only capable of the former, whereas human animals are uniquely capable of the latter. Now in many cases a non-human animal through its estimative sense may act more immediately and wisely in a concrete situation than does a human being, but nonetheless Aquinas attributes to human animals a unique capacity.

Aquinas' discussion of the estimative sense is brief and arguably weak. This could be from a lack of adequate sources for the subject, or it may betray a lack or interest in or a belief in the importance of the subject. Regarding his sources, it should be noted that Aristotle, who is Aquinas' trusted guide or point of departure for many related topics, does not discuss the estimative sense. Consequently, some commentators consider Aquinas' account to be largely drawn from Avicenna, Averroes and Alexander of Hales (see Ashley 2000), whereas others take Aquinas to be at his most creative in this discussion. Whichever may be the case, it is generally agreed that in terms of the medieval discussion of the internal senses, the estimative sense is both the most complex and least well developed. Considering that Aquinas claims that the estimative sense is able to account for the highest forms of animal functioning, his discussion of it is on its face woefully inadequate. Regarding how significant he considers the subject, Aquinas in the *Summa Theologiae* makes clear that his goal in studying the various powers of the soul is to assist him in understanding the human animal.[19] Since what non-human animals do by the estimative sense is attributed to the intellect in humans, Aquinas (and for that matter his contemporary commentators) is far more interested in understanding the human intellect, and does not appear to think it important to work out in any detailed way how the estimative sense allows non-human animals to do the things they do. In the final section of this chapter, we shall see how some contemporary Thomists seek to develop, or at least make more explicit, Aquinas' account of the estimative sense.

Sensible souls and animal desire

In addition to Aquinas' account of animal sensation, where cognition in higher animals is assigned to the estimative sense, the other main way non-human animals are on a continuum with human animals is in their

---

18 Thomas Aquinas, *Truth* [*De Veritate*], questions 21–29, trans. Robert W. Schmidt sj, Chicago: Henry Regnery Company, 1954, 24.2.

19 *ST* I 84, prologue.

desires, what Aquinas calls their appetites.[20] For Aquinas, desires are what fundamentally move animals to act. Thus one cannot understand Aquinas' discussions of human actions and dispositions (i.e., virtues and vices) apart from his conception of desire, since human dispositions are rooted in the desires that are part of human nature. The discussion of the dispositions and the seeds of such dispositions found in the desires occupy about half of the entire *Summa Theologiae*.

According to Aquinas, both human and non-human animals pursue what they pursue, desire what they desire, because in a fundamental sense they see what they desire as good. This is Aquinas' first principle of the natural law – his understanding of the fundamental intelligibility of the good – that 'good is to be done and pursued, and evil is to be avoided'.[21] Furthermore, Aquinas understands both human and non-human animals to be inclined towards certain kinds of activities as appropriate to the kind of creature that they are. Thus, Aquinas speaks of animals having 'natural inclinations' towards certain kinds of activities which are inherently good for them qua members of their particular species, such as acting to stay alive by obtaining and consuming nourishment or by fleeing from danger, propagating the species and rearing the young, and living and getting along in social groups. Acting in pursuit of these and other goods constitute reasons for acting for such creatures.

Aquinas says only creatures that can know can have appetites. Sensible (i.e., animal) desire is in itself passive, and may be incited either by apprehension of something external as good, or by internal states such as thirst, hunger, sexual desire and so forth. There are two kinds of sensible desire – the concupiscible and the irascible. Concupiscible desire is simple attraction to something (i.e., the pleasures of sense) that provokes action to attain it, or aversion to something else that provokes activity to withdraw from it. Examples of concupiscible desires are love, hatred, desire for pleasure, joy and sorrow.[22]

Irascible desires build on the foundation of concupiscible desires, as they are the powers to arduously pursue or avoid things that are not easily attained or avoided. As Aquinas puts it:

---

20 At this point we are moving, roughly speaking, from what animals know to what animals do. This is a movement in Aquinas from questions of theoretical knowledge to questions of practical knowledge, or as Aquinas puts it, 'whereas a thing is apprehended as intelligible, a thing is desired as good' (*ST* I 80.1 a2).

21 *ST* I-II 94.2.

22 *ST* I-II 26–39.

[C]oncupiscible appetite is moved by the simple pleasure of sense. But irascible appetite, leaving these pleasures behind, goes forth to do battle and seek victory, which it wins only at the price of sorrow . . . And so irascible appetite is nearer to reason and will than concupiscible appetite.[23]

The irascible desires are hope, despair, fear, daring and anger.[24]

Attributing as he does these various appetites to animals, Aquinas has no difficulty thinking of a fearful zebra, a sheep that hates, an angry monkey, or a joyful dog. These are all characteristics that Aquinas attributes to animals with sensible souls. In fact, Aquinas not only thinks non-human animals have these emotions, but that they typically have them more intensely than human animals, since humans animals (at least ideally) can moderate their desires by the directives of reason.

Because the irascible passions are not simple and/or direct responses to certain pursuits seen as good or evil but involve sustained effort, they are more complex, and would seem to be more associated with reason. Thus Aquinas draws a parallel between the estimative sense as having a greater degree of rationality associated with it than do the other senses, and the irascible desires, as possessing a greater degree of rationality than do the concupiscible appetites.

Rational animals

Up to this point we have examined Aquinas' treatment of various characteristics of animals, both human and non-human. Although most scholarly studies of Aquinas on, for example, memory or the concupiscible appetites, study them only in terms of how they function as elements of human nature, for Aquinas these are clearly elements of the nature of a variety of animals. Because Thomistic scholars focus on rationality as the defining characteristic of human beings, they tend not to discuss the multitude of things human beings do by their senses that do not involve rationality in the full or strict sense as Thomas understands it. So whether it is a child learning to walk or ride a bicycle, to hit a baseball or learn to play the piano, a student learning to regurgitate information for a test or memorize the bill of rights, or an adult knitting or making a sandwich, these are all activities that can be done without reason. Aquinas, like Aristotle, has a

23 Aquinas, *De Veritate* 24.2.
24 *ST* I-II 40–48.

narrower understanding of 'reason' than is typical in contemporary usage. This is certainly part of the reason that Aquinas' restricting of reason to human beings seems so odd. When one comes to understand adequately Aquinas' view of reason, what is perhaps most striking is not that he thinks that non-human animals are incapable of it, but how little of it he attributes to humans.

With this introduction, we are perhaps in a better position to understand what Aquinas means by rationality and why he so boldly excludes other animals from having it, even though at various points he admits that non-human animals seem to share to various degrees in different elements of rationality. Central to Aquinas' understanding of human rationality is his notion that humans can choose freely, are in control of and responsible for their actions. Thus Aquinas prefaces the *secunda pars* of the *Summa* by saying that he will discuss human beings made in the image of God 'in so far as the image implies an intelligent being endowed with free-will . . . treat[ing the human being] . . . inasmuch as he too is the principle of his actions'.[25] According to Aquinas, the human will is rational desire, that is, desire (which humans share with other animals) guided by practical reason. And what is reason? It is the ability to moderate and direct the desires in ways that allow human beings to flourish fully as human beings, to find the happiness appropriate to human beings.

Aquinas says that when humans act freely, they make a 'comparison' in the reason, also called deliberation. In other words, a human being is able to decide not to act according to a particular desire to do this, or out of training or custom to do that, but may choose to act otherwise. Such deliberation is not merely the choice to do this rather than that – the choice to order the ice cream over the apple – but also involves 'second-order' reflection on one's initial inclination to choose the ice cream over the apple. For example, after choosing the ice cream, it might occur to me that I've already eaten all the saturated fat I need for the day, or might remember it is a fast day, or that my recent bouts of lactose intolerance will keep me from sleeping well tonight if I consume the ice cream. According to Aquinas, it is this ability of humans to question and reverse their decisions, typically based on some notion of their good beyond their desires, that is indicative of reason and constitutes a distinctive quality of human beings, one that they do not share with any other animals.

In contrast to the deliberative capacity Aquinas grants humans, Aquinas thinks that while a non-human animal is capable by its estimative sense of

---

25 *ST* I-II prologue.

making a 'decision of sorts', it is a decision from 'natural instinct' rather than deliberation, precisely since it does not have the ability to evaluate critically its choice and possibly reverse its course. Thus in his stock example of the sheep seeing and fleeing from the wolf, Aquinas considers the sheep's response to be necessitated by its instinct, and not deliberating or making a deliberative choice. Aquinas continues by generalizing, 'And this is likewise true for every judgment made by brute animals.'[26]

Herbert McCabe rehearses this argument, but goes further in terms of trying to explain why it is that non-human animals are unable to make free judgements, arguing that rationality is closely tied to linguistic ability.[27] McCabe begins by comparing the actions of a hungry dog to those of himself when confronted by a tempting meal.

> A healthy and hungry dog confronted by a juicy steak interprets it as eminently edible and (unless trained in some way) cannot but try to get at it and eat it. (If it has been trained not to do so, it cannot but not do so.) Consider now me, equally healthy and hungry and confronted by the steak. I will of course share a version of the dog's sense-interpretation and desire, but I will also, as it were, talk to myself about the steak and tell myself that this steak belongs to someone else, that it is full of cholesterol, that it is the least efficient and most expensive way of acquiring protein . . . and so on indefinitely. For talking or thinking can go on indefinitely; and this Aquinas thinks, and I do, is the root of human freedom: that there are limits to the operations of the nervous system, but no limits to talk. Rational desire is desiring something under some description and I can describe it in an indefinite number of ways.[28]

Here McCabe links the possibility of choosing not to eat an otherwise appealing meal to a human being's ability to categorize their desires under different descriptions – a desire to eat this delicious steak, a desire not to eat someone else's dinner, a desire to eat only environmentally efficient sources of protein, and so on. For McCabe, reasoning, qua rational desire, consists in being able to will to fulfil desires under some descriptions and willing not to fulfil desires under other descriptions.

This seems to constitute a sufficient condition for attributing reason to an animal, but is it a necessary condition? McCabe certainly thinks so,

---

26 *ST* I 83.1. Similarly, when birds build nests or a pig squeals with delight, their actions are determined 'because they are unaware of the reason for their judgment' (Aquinas, *De Veritate* 24.2).

27 Herbert McCabe, *The Good Life*, New York: Continuum, 2001, p. 98.

28 McCabe, *Good Life*, p. 110.

since one could not choose otherwise if one does not have linguistic competency. Thus, according to McCabe:

> no non-linguistic animal can come to a decision. [The non-linguistic animal] will do this rather than that, and sometimes it will hesitate before doing this rather than that, but it is not thinking and deciding; whatever it does is what it could not but do. It is because we [human animals] have language that we can present ourselves with what is but might not be, with what is not but might be.[29]

McCabe's Thomistic comparison between the deliberation of humans versus the non-deliberation of non-human animals is rather stark, and deserves further consideration. On the one hand, the claim that we humans deliberate is certainly true to our experience. If I am confronted by a mean and aggressive dog, I may simply hold my ground, I may look for a shovel or other means to defend myself, I may hop a fence nearby, or I may simply run away. No doubt my deliberation will be done quickly, and if one response does not seem to be working well (e.g. running), I may quickly change strategies (e.g. attempt to hop a large fence).

On the other hand, let us apply this reasoning to my cat. If similarly confronted by a strange, aggressive dog, my cat may hunch her back and stand her hair up and hiss, or she might ferociously swat at the dog's face with her claws, or she might run for a tree, or she might head for the cat door of my house. And, if the first chosen strategy is not working (e.g. hissing), she may quickly change strategies (e.g. head for the tree). To this, Aquinas (and McCabe following Aquinas) would respond that if my cat initially chooses to hiss at the dog rather than run for the tree, it is not in fact a choice, since the cat could not do otherwise.[30]

---

29 McCabe, *Good Life*, p. 111.

30 Aquinas understands the cat's estimative sense to perceive not only a pattern of colours and smells to be an object, but also danger. In commenting on Aristotle's *De Anima*, Aquinas says that 'the estimative power does not apprehend an individual in terms of its being under a common nature but only in terms of its being the end point or starting point of some acting or being affected' (Aquinas, *Aristotle's De anima*, Book II, Lectio 13, marietti 398). The cat does not recognize the dog as dog, but rather as something dangerous and to be fought or fled. According to Pasnau, on Aquinas' view the cat does not put the dog into a category of dangerous animals (for that would be a universal cognition and thus the use of intellect), but simply perceives danger at the same time as perceiving this dog (Robert Pasnau, *Theories of Cognition in the Later Middle Ages*, Cambridge: Cambridge University Press, 1997, p. 53). How does the cat come to see the dog as dangerous without recognizing it as a particular kind of being (i.e. a dog)? Aquinas says that 'through the estimative power, an animal apprehends intentions that are not received through the senses – for example,

This will not likely be in keeping with the experience many people have of their cats or their dogs. Depending on the size or disposition of the dog, or the mood of my cat, I would expect her to variously choose any one of these options. And expecting that she would choose what was likely to be the most successful strategy for herself, she would have good reasons for her choice. While on the one hand my cat cannot *give* reasons for her choice (not having a developed language, she certainly can't articulate them to me), on the other hand she certainly has reasons for her choice.

If this is a conclusion with which Aquinas would agree, then it is at least clear that Aquinas' understanding of reason is indeed narrower than is our contemporary usage. It is perhaps most helpful to turn to two contemporary Thomists who try to nuance an understanding of the degree to which animals 'reason' and to better understand where exactly Aquinas sees the limits of rationality in non-human animals.

Marie George and Alasdair MacIntyre on rational vs. irrational animals

Having summarized the contours of Aquinas' account of animality, focusing both on elements of continuity and discontinuity between human and non-human animality, we now turn to work by two contemporary Thomists who look at questions of animality and present broadly Thomistic viewpoints on the nature of non-human animals. First, however, we shall recapitulate our discussion of Aquinas, contextualizing his work not only in terms of its high medieval time and place, but also in terms of the primary subject matter in which his discussions of animality occur.

The first thing of note is Aquinas' commitment to a scientific and hence empirically based understanding of animality, both human and non-human. Aquinas shows no sign of pursuing a fantastical view of animals as embodied in medieval bestiaries. Granted, at times Aquinas' distinctions between the capabilities of human and non-human animals seem stronger than what is warranted by his examples. In vigorously engaging

---

friendliness or hostility' (Aquinas, *De Veritate* 25.2). Since it cannot be a universal cognition, Pasnau concludes that Aquinas must see it as a 'nonconceptual urge' (Pasnau, *Theories*, p. 54). Similarly, Aquinas goes on to say that such a cat recognizes its kitten not as kitten but as a being to nurse, and sees a mouse not as mouse but as potential food (Aquinas in fact uses the example of a sheep, but presumably on Aquinas' account the exact same holds true for a cat).

contemporary ethological literature, Marie George and Alasdair MacIntyre recognize that an adequate Thomistic view of animality must draw on as adequate an understanding of the nature and capabilities of various non-human animals as is possible.

The second thing of note is that Aquinas, in constantly comparing the capacities of humans (e.g. human appetites, reasoning and virtues) with the capacities of non-human animals in the *Summa Theologiae*, considers it particularly apt to do so. Presumably Aquinas finds it helpful to his reader to make these comparisons and contrasts because he is profoundly aware of the similarities. At the same time, since the *Summa* focuses on God and the human response to God and since it never devotes any extended attention to non-human animals, one should not expect to find therein a comprehensive or even adequate treatment of the nature and capacities of non-human animals. In light of this, one would expect con-temporary Thomists who take up questions of animality to build on Thomas' work on this subject, rather than to follow it slavishly, drawing on modern and contemporary insights with regard, for example, to the significance of the individual (whether human or non-human) and to advances in the biological sciences (particularly with reference to evolu-tionary biology, ecology and ethology).

The two Thomists examined in the final section – Marie George and Alasdair MacIntyre – have broadly similar views on the capacities of non-human animals. And both have read widely in the relevant literature on the capacities of primates and/or cetaceans. However, despite those simi-larities, they have markedly different approaches in reflecting on non-human animals, and approach their subject with significantly different presuppositions.

In 'Thomas Aquinas Meets Nim Chimpsky', Marie George offers in three parts an account of the distinction between the human animal and all other higher animals, which evolutionary biology combined with con-temporary ethology is seeking to blur. First, she notes that Aquinas (and many Thomists) oversimplifies the distinction between sense perception and rational thought. The distinction will only be adequately understood if we (a) revise Aquinas' overly limited account of what both humans and other animals are able to accomplish by the interior senses, and (b) more clearly recognize that, by rational thought or reason, Aquinas is referring to abstract thought. Second, she argues that what various primates learn or are taught to do – which many ethologists consider reasoning – is actu-ally a form of sense perception. Third, George argues that no non-human animal has demonstrated the capacity for what is legitimately considered 'rational thought'. She goes on to offer criteria that would undermine her view, criteria that would demonstrate that a non-human animal engages in rational thought.

George's approach is to analyse various capabilities of primates and evaluate whether these capabilities are best accounted for as aspects of reason or of the interior senses. But in order so to do, George must present her account of what human and non-human animals can do by their senses – what an earlier age called one's 'wits'.[31]

According to George, the estimative sense has a kind of knowledge, which allows various higher animals to do various things, for example find mates, avoid predators, find prey, and solve various sorts of problems that in turn allow animals to do these things. So what are some examples of the way human, as well as non-human, animals learn by their senses, without the need for rationality?

George argues that there are many things that humans and animals learn to do without reasoning: for instance, a human learning to tie their shoe or ride a bicycle. Assuming one learns to do these things by being shown, and/or by trial and error, and/or by imagination, then one solves these problems, not by reason, but by one's senses.[32] George is further happy to grant that it involves no small feat to get a significant number of college philosophy students to think, that is, to support their statements with reasons.[33]

As examples of animals learning by their senses, she discusses the experiment where a population of Japanese macaques were regularly left sweet potatoes on the beach, which would be covered in sand. For a long time, all the macaques brushed the sand off the potatoes with their hands. However, at one point a macaque started washing the sand off the potato at a nearby stream. In time, a gradually increasing number of the younger macaques began to wash their potatoes. Thus, macaques clearly learn and adapt their practices. According to George, this is to be accounted for by sense rather than by intellect. Similarly, although ethologists often take 'tool-making' as a sign of rationality, George argues that chimps who use sticks to get termites out of holes or to get bananas otherwise out of reach,

---

31 C. S. Lewis, *Studies in Words*, Cambridge: Cambridge University Press, 1960.

32 Marie George, 'Thomas Aquinas Meets Nim Chimpsky: On the Debate about Human Nature and the Nature of Other Animals', *Aquinas Review* 10, 2003, p. 21. If, however, one learns how to tie a knot from studying knot theory, or learns to ride a bicycle by puzzling out gyroscopes, then George will grant that one learns these things at least in part by use of rationality.

33 'As any philosophy teacher will tell you, it is hard to get certain students beyond making simple assertions of the "I feel" sort' (George, *Chimpsky*, p. 38).

while indeed using their imagination and their memory, as well as their sight and touch, are not thinking 'in the strict sense of the term'.

George is aware that some will accuse her of making an a priori claim about animal intelligence, that no matter what ape researchers come up with to show various capabilities of chimps or bonobos, she will simply set the bar higher, in effect saying that if a chimp can do it, then it cannot be true intelligence. George is not alone in being accused of this – Aristotle and Aquinas in places seem to do the same. While seeking to be empathetic to what she acknowledges is frustration on the part of ethologists, George says that these researchers have been somewhat naive in failing to recognize the degree to which memory and experience can imitate thought.[34]

What then, according to George is intelligence 'in the strict sense'? How might we know when it would rightfully be ascribed to a chimp, a dolphin, or any other non-human animal? George gives three 'tests', all of which presuppose linguistic ability. The first is to show the ability to grasp universal concepts – such as 'banananess' as opposed to this or that banana, for to be able to do that, according to George, would show an ability to reason, to give a reason or an explanation for something, which she claims that no researcher has even been able to get an ape to show. Second, the ability to use 'insensible' terms like 'god' or 'rights' or 'integrity' in a sentence.

The third, and undoubtedly most interesting and useful, is the 'conversation' requirement. If it indeed has rationality, a chimp should be able to carry on a conversation. Now, by a 'conversation' George does not merely mean the requesting of things, or seeking the emotional approval of a human person, but actually engaging in a conversation about a topic, and being able to 'move the discussion forward' in any number of ways. She describes in some detail what is involved in a rational conversation.

The specific kind of conversation that I think provides a good test for intellect is defined by two things: (1) by the interrelated character of the statements made about one subject (broadly construed); (2) by a desire to share and acquire knowledge that is not practical or at least not of use in the near future. A typical conversation runs like this:
A: I saw this crazy woman in the supermarket today. She was stacking coffee cans in the middle of the aisle.
B: Well, how do you know that she didn't work there?

---

34 George, *Chimpsky*, p. 36, n. 75.

A: Well, she was mixing up all different brands in the stack. Besides the manager came over to ask her what she thought she was doing. This conversation could take any number of directions from here. One person might tell another crazy-person story. Or the two might speculate on the causes of the woman's craziness. Or they might start talking about the importance of sensitizing people to the problems of mental illness. Granted sometimes the ties in conversation prove to be more imaginary (stream of conscious) than rational, still people often recognize that they are moving from one topic to another, as one can see from expressions such as 'changing the subject' or 'went off on a tangent'.[35]

George does not provide a detailed account of the Thomistic distinction between activities requiring rational thought and those achievable through sense abilities, nor does she indicate whether her example of a rational conversation above constitutes a 'minimally rational' or 'high-level rational' conversation. However, she does appear to provide at least the outline of what might constitute an empirical test for the distinction. And although, as noted above, both Aristotle and Aquinas appear to make the distinction a priori, George appears committed to indicating that the distinction has an empirical basis, and that should particular species of non-human animals be found to have or be able to develop capacities to meet George's test, then she would be committed to considering such animals rational.

There are, however, a number of problems with George's account, at least to the degree it sets itself up to provide legitimate 'criteria' for thought in non-human animals. First, all the criteria presuppose rather well-developed linguistic capacity. And that is precisely what most higher animals do not have. This is also rather odd, since George herself notes that 'Aristotle . . . acknowledges that images other than words suffice for thinking certain thoughts.'[36] George fails to give an account as to why a relatively well-developed language is a precondition for rationality.

Second, she appears to come at the question of non-human rationality with an inherently sceptical bias. Throughout the article the burden of proof is on those who would attribute rationality to various higher animals, and George's approach seems to be that if we can find an account of an animal's activity that can exclude rationality, then that is to be considered the preferred account. George calls this the 'principle of

---

35 George, *Chimpsky*, p. 39.
36 George, *Chimpsky*, p. 10.

parsimony',[37] but the principle of parsimony requires that her view have equal explanatory power and be simpler, and neither seems to be the case. George's sceptical assumption is seen most clearly in the conclusion of her article. After explaining how she has shown that various linguistic and tool-making 'feats' by animals can be explained as sensory rather than rational, she further adds that 'the absence of behavior natural to intelligent beings gives reason to say that animals are not intelligent'.[38] However, since George clearly believes or presumes that 'intelligent beings' = 'human beings' and 'intelligent' = 'human-like', all that George is arguing here is that since non-human animals do not act like human beings, therefore non-human animals are not human-like. And that seems to have been the assumption at the beginning of the paper.

But what, we may ask, is problematic about George's principle of parsimony? Why should we not be sceptical of claims about the capacity of non-human animals to think, to have concepts, to understand other animals and human beings? An answer to that is offered by Alasdair MacIntyre.

In *Dependent Rational Animals*, MacIntyre seeks to show that contemporary philosophy cannot help but misunderstand the nature of human beings if it does not adequately understand their animality. And to understand human animality, it is necessary to understand more about other creatures who share animality with human animals. Thus, as one would expect in such a project, MacIntyre has much that is instructive from a Thomistic perspective to say regarding the nature and capacities of non-human animals.

MacIntyre approaches the subject of rationality in non-human animals by focusing on practical reason, reasoning about action. Like George, he notes that both Aristotle and Aquinas attribute practical reason to some non-human animals as well as human beings.[39] The basis for practical reason from an Aristotelian-Thomistic perspective is that there be a good for an individual that is good according to its species, the kind of action that contributes to an individual of that species flourishing qua member of that species. In terms of what it means to have a reason for action, an animal must recognize goods of its nature and pursue them. Here MacIntyre draws on the account of Warren Quinn, who remarks that 'a reason to act in a certain way is nothing more than something good in itself [the action]

---

37 George, *Chimpsky*, p. 28.

38 George, *Chimpsky*, p. 47.

39 MacIntyre does seem to leave open the extent to which practical reason in various non-human animals is similar and/or dissimilar to that in human animals.

realizes or serves, or, short of that, something bad in itself that it avoids'.[40] Here we bypass the issue of 'linguistic capacity'. The fact that animals pursue goods that are goods of their nature shows that such animals clearly have reasons for their action.

But that leaves open the question of whether in pursuing these goods various higher non-human animals engage in 'thinking'. As we saw with George's principle of parsimony, is not the right approach to doubt that animals can think unless we can clearly infer it from their behaviour? MacIntyre argues that this is exactly the wrong approach to take if one wants to understand animality, either human or non-human animality. Contrary to those philosophers deeply troubled by the problem of 'other minds' and those who apply the 'principle of parsimony' to what might seem to be varieties of non-human animal intelligence, MacIntyre argues that human beings come to essential understandings of themselves and other human and non-human animals *only* through pre-reflective engagement with and experience of other creatures.[41] The knowledge gained through this process he calls non-inferential knowledge.[42]

What does MacIntyre mean by non-inferential knowledge? In part, it is entering into a relationship with a human toddler or a dog or a chimpanzee not affected by 'epistemology', not bringing to the interaction a predisposition to 'figure out' the other, but by

> entering into the only kinds of relationship with dogs, or with members of certain other species, through which interpretative knowledge of their thoughts and feelings can be gained, relationships expressed in responsive activity. And what we acquire from responsive interaction, whether with small human children, or with dogs, or with chimpanzees or gorillas, or with elephants or with dolphins are grounds for approaching with suspicion a certain kind of philosophical theorizing about animals.[43]

---

40 Alasdair MacIntyre, *Dependent Rational Animals*, London: Open Court Press, 1999, p. 24.

41 Practical knowledge of humans and other intelligent animals is not by inference – but a kind of knowing how to interpret. We come to know what other animals are like by *interaction* with them. For, this kind of interactive interpretive experience of small children or other animals is such that without it 'we would be unable to ascribe thoughts and feelings to other, whether human infants or dogs or whatever' (MacIntyre, *Dependent*, p. 17).

42 Here MacIntyre would seem to be indebted to the account of non-inferential knowledge in Anscombe's *Intention*: G. E. M. Anscombe, *Intention*, Oxford: Blackwell, 1957.

43 MacIntyre, *Dependent*, p. 17.

In other words, far from beginning with an inherent suspicion of the accounts of the capabilities of various species of non-human animals, what instead must be realized is that we must at least begin with a pre-critical attempt to appreciate these accounts, even though we also must examine the various accounts in a critically reflective manner.[44]

Here MacIntyre, I believe, has provided an important insight for a renewed Thomist approach to reflection on the nature and capacities of non-human animals. MacIntyre's discussion of the possibility of pre-linguistic cognition in non-human (and human) animals raises important questions and challenges to the view that understands rationality to presuppose considerable linguistic competency. MacIntyre argues that rightly understanding the nature of pre-linguistic thought is essential for generating an adequate account of the development of practical rationality in human beings. That is certainly a central element of MacIntyre's task in *Dependent Rational Animals*.[45]

Philosophers such as MacIntyre, Gaita and Lovibond,[46] in exploring in different ways the relationship between practical reasoning in non-human and human animals, open up an important vista for a more developed Thomistic account of animality and the nature of non-human animals. Rather than forcing reflection on the 'rationality' of non-human animals through the lens of linguistic competence or of theoretical rationality, it would seem that a potentially more fruitful avenue for both philosophical and scientific analysis should be directed to practical rationality. We can look for more to come.[47]

44 For this kind of approach to philosophical reflection on the nature and status of non-human animals, see Raimond Gaita, *The Philosopher's Dog*, New York: Random House, 2002.

45 See also Sabina Lovibond, 'Practical Reason and Its Animal Precursors', *European Journal of Philosophy* 14:2, 2006, pp. 262–73.

46 And we could certainly also add the work of Cora Diamond (e.g. essays in Cora Diamond, *The Realistic Spirit*, Cambridge MA: MIT Press, 1991; Philippa Foot, *Natural Goodness*, Oxford: Oxford University Press, 2001; and Rosalind Hursthouse, *On Virtue Ethics*, Oxford: Oxford University Press, 1999).

47 Thanks to Michael Dodds OP, William Mattison and Jane Smiley for helpful comments on earlier drafts of this essay.

2

The Anxiety of the Human Animal: Martin Luther on Non-human Animals and Human Animality

DAVID CLOUGH

'But why should I speak at all of irrational animals?' Luther asks after musing on why human beings alone are tormented by death in commenting on Psalm 90.[1] The rhetorical question presupposes no adequate response, but despite this Luther speaks of animals almost everywhere in his writings. He thanks God for providing them for human use, defines what it means to be human in relation to them, illustrates theological arguments using them, finds allegorical messages in biblical texts concerning them and very frequently insults his enemies with reference to them. Notwithstanding the frequency of their appearance, references of this kind have led commentators to judge that Luther has little interest in non-human animals: Colin Gunton, for instance, concludes 'Luther is not very interested in the non-personal world for its own sake.'[2] At other points, however, Luther recognizes all that other animals have in common with human beings, proclaims the intimacy of God to them, holds them up as moral exemplars, is attentive to the detail of their lives, protests on their behalf against mistreatment and in one notable encounter takes the role of proto-hunt-saboteur in hiding a rabbit from hounds – although, to his regret, his attempt at protection is not finally successful. In this chapter, I will argue that Luther is both more various and less consistent in his consideration of animals than has previously been recognized, but that this inconsistency is a virtuous one. His vivid appreciation of the non-

---

1 Martin Luther, *Luther's Works*, ed. Jaroslav Pelikan, Saint Louis: Concordia, 1958, vol. 13, p. 112. References to this English translation of his collected works are hereafter abbreviated in the form *LW* volume number.page number (e.g. for this case *LW* 13.112).

2 Colin Gunton, *The Doctrine of Creation: Essays in Dogmatics, History and Philosophy*, London: T & T Clark, 2004, p. 72n.

human animals he encounters means that in his account they break the
fences within which he sometimes tries to restrain them and thereby indicate their need for a theological space more adequate to their place in
God's purposes.

Human superiority and dominance over other animals

For the most part, Luther is resolutely anthropocentric in his view of
God's purposes in creation. In his lectures on Genesis, he states that he
focuses on God's solicitude and benevolence towards us 'because He
provided such an attractive dwelling place for the future human being
before the human being was created'.[3] When human beings finally arrive
on the scene they find 'a ready and equipped home' and they are commanded by God to 'enjoy all the riches of so splendid a home' progres-
sively fitted out on each day of creation.[4] Creation is a lesson in God's
providence; it 'plainly teaches that God created all these things in order to
prepare a house and an inn, as it were, for the future man'.[5] When God
rests from the work of creation, it is because the home is finished and the
ruler installed.[6] Luther's doctrine of the fall also indicates the human-
centredness of creation: thorns, thistles, vermin, flies, toads and butterflies
– butterflies? – and the savagery of wild animals were part of the punishment for human sin.[7] In the flood, other animals and plants perished
because of the sin of their ruler, just as human subjects often suffer on
account of the errors of their leaders.[8]

---

3 Martin Luther, *Lectures on Genesis, Chapters 1–5*, LW 1.39.

4 *LW* 1.39. Luther follows a well-worn path at this point: Philo of Alexandria advances
a very similar view in his commentary on Genesis (Philo, *De opificio mundi* in *Philo I*, Loeb
Classical Library, trans. F. H. Colson and G. H. Whitaker, London: Heinemann, 1929, §§
25–8). This continuity is also evident at other points in Luther's doctrine of creation.

5 *LW* 1.47.

6 *LW* 1.73.

7 *LW* 1.38, 1.54, 1.73.

8 *LW* 1.183. The idea is repeated later in the Genesis commentary: the 'use and ministry
of creatures' should not be despised because 'God has created them to serve us' (*LW*
6.24–5), and also features in other parts of Luther's writings: for example, God created
everything else before human beings so as to lay up for us 'at all times a sufficient store of
food and clothing' (45.48); 'The Father gives himself to us, with heaven and earth and all the
creatures, in order that they may serve us and benefit us' (37.366); John the evangelist 'dis-
misses all brute beasts, which did not fall and sin, and concentrates his attention on human
nature, for the sake of which everything was made and created' (22.29). Luther repeatedly
interprets the creedal affirmation of God as creator to mean God makes everything to provide human comforts and necessities (Luther, 'The Large Catechism', in Theodore G.

Beyond this anthropocentric view of God's purpose in creating non-human animals, Luther also seeks to affirm the superior characteristics of humans in comparison to other animals. For him this was especially clear before the fall. While Adam still bore the image of God, which Luther believes was lost in the fall, he was 'something far more distinguished and excellent', in ways well beyond the moral and religious, surpassing all other creations in every respect:

> I am fully convinced that before Adam's sin his eyes were so sharp and clear that they surpassed those of the lynx and eagle. He was stronger than the lions and the bears, whose strength is very great; and he handled them the way we handle puppies.[9]

Adam also had 'a perfect knowledge of the nature of the animals, the herbs, the fruits, the trees, and the remaining creatures'.[10] After the fall, all is changed. Death has 'crept like leprosy into all our perceptive powers, so that with our intellect we cannot even understand that image',[11] which has been 'almost completely lost'.[12] Whereas before the fall Adam had 'a greater strength and keener senses than the rest of the living beings', now human beings are greatly 'surpassed by the boars in their sense of hearing, by the eagles in their sense of sight, and by the lion in his strength'.[13] Before the fall, the difference between humans and other animals was therefore 'far greater and more evident', but even in the post-fall state Luther argues that 'there is still a great difference between the human being and the rest of the animals'.[14] He cites Lombard's *Sentences* as authority for the view that human beings are the image of God, whereas the rest of the animals are only 'footprints' and human beings are appropriately

---

Tappert (ed.), *The Book of Concord: The Confessions of the Evangelical Lutheran Church*, Philadelphia: Fortress Press, 1959, 2.13–14. Cf. 'The Small Catechism', in Tappert, *The Book of Concord*, II.2; 'Ten Sermons on the Catechism', *LW* 51.163), although he follows this passage in the 'Large Catechism' with a protest against their misuse ('Large Catechism', 2.21). The harshness of the consequences of God's judgement for non-human animals could be seen as linked to Luther's theology of the cross requiring the annihilation of the natural, but Gregersen makes a convincing argument that this annihilation should not be understood as going beyond human sin (Niels Hendrik Gregersen, 'The Cross of Christ in an Evolutionary World', *Dialog: A Journal of Theology* 40:3, 2001, p. 197).

9 *LW* 1.62.
10 *LW* 1.63.
11 *LW* 1.62.
12 *LW* 1.67.
13 *LW* 1.62.
14 *LW* 1.67.

called a 'world in miniature'.[15] Luther also cites arguments beyond the text indicating the difference between humans and other species. In commenting on the creation of the heavenly bodies, he observes that pigs, cows and dogs cannot even measure the water they drink, whereas human beings measure the heavens using the 'divinely revealed' mathematical disciplines showing their heavenly destiny.[16] Luther also repeats the argument of classical authors that '[man's] very posture and physique strongly indicate that he belongs to the heavenly things despite his wretched and humble origin'[17] and notes that even after sin the Gentiles concluded that '[man] is a rather outstanding figure' on the basis of 'the fact that he alone walks upright and raises his eyes to heaven'.[18]

The authority human beings are given by God over the other animals is perhaps the clearest indicator of their unique position within creation. Luther comments that in the command to Adam and Eve to have dominion 'the rule is assigned to the most beautiful creature, who knows God and is the image of God, in whom the similitude of the divine nature shines forth through his enlightened reason, through his justice and his wisdom'.[19] He emphasizes that the exercise of this rule is command rather than mere permission,[20] and believes in his glorious unfallen state Adam could command lions 'as we give a command to a trained dog'.[21] If there had been no fall Adam and his family would have gathered to praise and laud God 'for the dominion over all the creatures on the earth which had been given to mankind',[22] and the restoration of God's image in humanity will bring an enhanced dominion: 'all the other creatures will be under our rule to a greater degree than they were in Adam's Paradise.'[23]

When we look at other statements Luther makes in relation to human dominion over other animals, it becomes evident that this is one area

---

15 *LW* 1.68. For a discussion of the origin of the idea of human beings as a microcosm, see Paul Santmire, *The Travail of Nature: The Ambiguous Ecological Promise of Christian Theology*, Minneapolis: Fortress Press, 1985, pp. 81–2. Elsewhere Luther notes that God only breathed a living soul into Adam (1.85–92), that only human beings will leave animal and enter spiritual life (1.65), that only human beings know their Creator (1.67), and that humans alone were created for eternal life (22.30).

16 *LW* 1.45–6.

17 *LW* 1.46.

18 *LW* 1.85. He is critical of this argument later in his Genesis commentary (*LW* 1.124–5), as discussed below.

19 *LW* 1.66.

20 *LW* 1.66.

21 *LW* 1.64.

22 *LW* 1.105.

23 *LW* 1.65.

where there are difficulties in coherence and consistency in his account. The first question concerns the purpose of dominion. Luther frankly admits that this is unclear before the fall. Adam would not have used other animals for food, did not lack clothing or money, and neither he nor his descendants would have been greedy. Therefore they would have made use of the other creatures 'only for the admiration of God and for a holy joy which is unknown to us in this corrupt state of nature'.[24] Here is an image of harmony between human and non-human animal life significantly at odds with the vivid language of authoritative rule – 'Adam and Eve knew God and all the creatures and, as it were, were completely engulfed by the goodness and justice of God'[25] – the other animals enable human worship and joy in God's creation, and the authority human beings have from God to order them about seems purposeless.

If before sin, the purpose of the dominion granted to Adam and Eve is unclear, after sin its existence is the question. Adam's extraordinary capabilities making him superior in every respect are left behind in the garden. In commentary on Genesis 1.26, Luther observes that after sin, Adam can no longer command the other animals by his word, and what we achieve in life 'is brought about not by the dominion which Adam had but through industry and skill', leaving us only with a 'bare title' of dominion almost entirely without substance.[26] In discussing Genesis 6.17, God's words 'I will bring a flood', Luther adds weight to this idea that dominion has been lost: the destruction of other animals might seem unfair to them, but it represents part of the punishment of humans to lose their dominion over other animals too.[27] In Luther's commentary on Genesis 7, however, it seems that he does not mean this punishment of loss of dominion to apply to the occupants of the ark: 'Even though the greater part of the world perishes, man nevertheless remains lord of the creatures', albeit over fewer creatures than there were previously.[28] And when he comes to treat Genesis 9.2, 'the fear of you shall be upon every beast', Luther suggests that human dominion has been increased and changed in character in comparison with that granted to Adam: 'until now the animals did not have to die in order to provide food for man, but man was a gentle master of the beasts rather than their slayer or consumer'; now 'the animals are subjected to man as to a tyrant who has absolute power over life and

---

24 *LW* 1.71.
25 *LW* 1.67.
26 *LW* 1.67.
27 *LW* 2.70.
28 *LW* 2.100.

death'.[29] Luther makes a point of noting that this was an unnecessary innovation on God's part: the permission to eat animals is given at a time when there were only a few human beings in the midst of the superabundance of the world – he does not reckon with a scarcity of vegetation after the flood. This is, then, a special indication from God of God's favourable inclination and friendliness towards humanity.[30] Luther goes further in seeing in this passage the origin and justification for the history of animal husbandry and consumption: the words 'establish the butcher shop' and 'God sets Himself up as a butcher'.[31] For Adam 'it would have been an abomination to kill a little bird for food', under this new regime 'the dominion of man is increased, and the dumb animals are made subject to man for the purpose of serving him even to the extent of dying'.[32] Luther judges that God did not lie in promising human beings dominion over the earth: 'In the Flood this is taken away, not forever but for a time; and even then it is not taken away entirely.'[33]

This vision of God's blessing of enhanced dominion over other animals is hard to square with Luther's lament over the glories that were lost in the fall and his affirmation of a future restoration of the image of God when 'all the other creatures will be under our rule to a greater degree than they were in Adam's Paradise'.[34] This promised restoration seems preempted by God's response to Noah. This is the height of Luther's anthropocentrism, and Gunton's claim about Luther's lack of interest in the 'non-personal' world for its own sake is entirely apt here.[35] Luther is struck at one point by the pedagogical value of stressing the loss of dominion as part of the plight of being heirs to Adam's sin, and at another by the value of emphasizing God's graciousness in realizing the dominion promised despite human disobedience in Eden and before the flood. In both cases, there is no recognition that God's relationship with others of God's creatures could be of significant independent concern.

---

29 *LW* 2.132. Luther does not believe, however, that there are no limits to the exercise of this new dominion: animals can only be killed for sacrifice or food so 'wanton and irreverent killing is forbidden' (*LW* 2.139). He also suggests that human beings would be better off if consumption of meat had never been introduced (*LW* 1.36).

30 *LW* 2.133.

31 *LW* 2.133.

32 *LW* 2.133.

33 *LW* 2.100.

34 *LW* 1.65.

35 Gunton, *Doctrine of Creation*, p. 72n. Scott Ickert agrees that Luther 'was not interested in animals per se as a theological topic' ('Luther and Animals: Subject to Adam's Fall?', in Andrew Linzey and Dorothy Yamamoto (eds), *Animals on the Agenda: Questions about Animals for Theology and Ethics*, London: SCM Press, 1998, p. 90).

Luther's uncertainty about the role of dominion is mirrored by instability in other parts of his account of human superiority over other animals. The role of reason and philosophy in providing either insight into human superiority or a differentiating feature between humans and other animals is a significant case in point here. While, as cited above, at times he seems impressed by the way the erect posture of human beings confirms their divinely ordained dominance,[36] elsewhere he criticizes the use philosophers make of this argument, and argues that only Scripture can show the superiority of the human.[37] Whereas philosophy defines a human being as a rational animal, 'a theologian discusses man as a sinner'.[38] A similar inconsistency pertains to his consideration of reason as a distinguishing mark between humans and other animals. He often depends on this in his discussion,[39] even construing reason as 'a kind of god' creating dominion and differentiating between humans and other animals.[40] Yet elsewhere, his critique of dependence on reason is famously strong: in his last sermon in Wittenberg in 1546 he instructs his congregation to 'hold reason in check and do not follow her beautiful cogitations. Throw dirt in her face and make her ugly. Reason is and should be drowned in baptism.'[41] Luther therefore understands the philosophers he cites as valuing reason as a unique and supremely valuable human accomplishment, reliably distinguishing between humans and other animals, but in his own scheme this identification is ambivalent, claiming too much for itself in a prideful sense and often tending to lead the faithful astray.[42] At the least, we should recognize that reason cannot function in his theological system in the same way as it does in the philosophical schemes to which he refers, thus opening up the question of the appropriate basis for distinguishing between humans and other animals in a theological framework.

---

36 *LW* 1.46, 1.85.

37 *LW* 1.124–5.

38 *LW* 12.310. Elsewhere he asks who dares argue that the philosophical definition is true in theology (*LW* 13.125).

39 E.g. 'since man has understanding' even 4-year-old boys can rule much stronger creatures (*LW* 12.209); 'a man by reason tames a wild horse and an enormous lion' (*LW* 15.125); the 'rational sacrifice' called for by Paul in Romans 12.1 means one that is human, rather than animal (*LW* 36.145).

40 *LW* 34.137.

41 *LW* 51.376–7.

42 Whether Luther is right to see in Plato or Aristotle a discontinuity between the human and non-human on the basis of reason is a different question. For an engaging exploration of this question, see Catherine Osborne, *Dumb Beasts and Dead Philosophers: Humanity and the Humane in Ancient Philosophy and Literature*, Oxford: Clarendon Press, 2007.

A further area of uncertainty in Luther concerning non-human animals is whether they have any part in the world to come. For the most part Luther seems clear that only human beings participate in eternity, judging through most of his commentary on Genesis that this is the chief difference between humans and other animals. At one point, he even pictures a rapture in which the saved are carried heavenward while everything on earth perishes in ashes.[43] On occasion, however, he seems to picture other aspects to eternal life: in his commentary on 1 Corinthians 15 he envisions playing in our spiritual bodies with the sun, moon and 'all the other creatures'[44] and looks forward to the time when a new essence comes into being 'not only in us human beings but also in all other creatures'.[45] In commentary on Psalm 8 Luther asserts that there will be 'a broad and beautiful heaven and a joyful earth, much more beautiful and joyful than Paradise was',[46] and a passage in the *Table Talk* affirms that in the future life the earth will be adorned with trees.[47] Elsewhere in the *Table Talk* Luther is reported to have answered in the affirmative when asked if his dog Tölpel would be in heaven: 'Certainly . . . Peter said that the last day would be the restitution of all things. God will create a new heaven and a new earth and new Tölpels with hide of gold and silver.'[48] Again, here, Luther is clear at points that human and non-human creatures belong in different categories in relation to eternal life, but also seems drawn to a vision of a renewed and restored earth with room for non-human creatures.

We cannot leave consideration of the aspects of Luther's thought where he stresses the superiority of the human without noting the many occasions where he uses animal characteristics as insults to his enemies. While his expostulation 'Listen now, you pig, dog, or fanatic, whatever kind of unreasonable ass you are . . . go back to your pigpen and your filth'[49] is particularly memorable, it is far from unique,[50] and in his commentary on

---

43 *LW* 28.201.
44 *LW* 28.194.
45 *LW* 28.194.
46 *LW* 12.121.
47 *LW* 54.41, no. 305.
48 D. *Martin Luthers Werke: Kritische Gesamtausgabe, Tischreden*, 6 vols, Weimar: Hermann Bölhaus Nachfolger, 1912–21, no. 1150, trans. Roland Bainton, in 'Luther on Birds, Dogs and Babies: Gleanings from the "Table Talk"', in Roland H. Bainton, Warren A. Quanbeck and E. Gordon Rupp, *Luther Today*, Martin Luther Lectures, vol. 1, Decorah IA: Luther College Press, 1957, p. 9. Bainton notes several other passages in the *Tischreden* where Luther is admiring of dogs, including nos. 869 and 2849a.
49 Luther, 'That these words of Christ, "This is my body", etc., still stand firm against the fanatics' (*LW* 37.68).
50 Of the many examples that could be chosen here, Luther claims that men become

Deuteronomy Luther refers extensively to the bestiary tradition associating particular animals with various vices.[51] These are balanced by more favourable comparisons of humans with animals, as we shall see in the next section, but show that rhetorically Luther had no compunction about belittling comparisons with non-human animals in order to make vivid characterizations of those he criticized.

Human commonality with and compassion for other animals

In Luther's commentary on Genesis, alongside the radical anthropocentrism we have seen above, it is striking to find Luther repeatedly recognizing deep similarities between human beings and other animals. Human beings share the life of land animals: they were created on the same day and had a 'common table' in the herbs and fruit of trees.[52] Adam's physical life was meant to be similar to 'that of the other beasts': 'Just as the beasts have need of food, drink, and rest to refresh their bodies, so Adam, even in his innocence, would make use of them.'[53] Human beings 'increased and multiplied in the same manner as other beasts' – Luther comments that the semen 'congeals in the womb and is given form in an identical manner' and concludes with no apparent concern for the impact of the comparison that 'Here there is no difference between a pregnant cow and a woman with child.'[54] A little later he delves further into the common physiology humans share with other animals in commentary on God's breathing life into Adam in Genesis 2.7:

> If you consider the animal life about which Moses is speaking here, there is no difference between man and the donkey. Animal life has need of food and drink; it has need of sleep and rest; their bodies are fed in like manner by food and drink, and they grow; and through hunger they become faint and perish. The stomach receives the food, and when the food has been digested, passes it on to the liver, which produces

---

'brutes and beasts' through their contempt of sound doctrine (*LW* 1.336), that antinomian opponents 'become apes' (*LW* 5.309), that Epicureans live the life of an animal (*LW*. 7.117), that some people live like sows, others like wolves (*LW* 30.181) and that some parents are 'despicable hogs and venomous beasts, devouring their own young' (*LW* 46.210).

51 *LW* 9.136.
52 *LW* 1.36.
53 *LW* 1.57.
54 *LW* 1.83.

blood, by which all the limbs are given fresh strength. In this regard there is no difference between man and beast.[55]

The beasts 'greatly resemble' human beings:

> They dwell together; they are fed together; they eat together; they receive their nourishment from the same materials; they sleep and rest among us. Therefore if you take into account their way of life, their food, and their support, the similarity is great.[56]

As regards our physical life 'we drink, we eat, we procreate, and we are born just like the rest of the animals',[57] and after the expulsion from Eden we share the place of the other animals as well as their food.[58] At the flood, there was a common sorrow between Noah and the beasts and after the flood the covenant God makes is with Noah, his family and all the other animals.[59] These texts provide strong evidence that Luther considered there to be much in common between human beings and other animals.

To say that Luther recognizes human–non-human continuity is not to say that he values it. It is striking that almost all of the passages cited above discussing this commonality do so with the rhetorical purpose of highlighting the distinctiveness of human beings despite these similarities, a distinctiveness often appreciable only through the revelation provided in Scripture. Luther's mode of reasoning is that the human experience of living alongside other creatures and comparing ourselves to them gives us a strong sense of our animality, but that this observation of what we have in common with other animals provokes the anxiety that we may be no more than cows, donkeys or other beasts. The structure of his argument depends on this negative interpretation of continuity: if intimations of our animality did not make us anxious, we would not be in need of the good news proclaimed in Genesis that we have a different status in the world from those other creatures to which we seem so similar.[60] Luther's con-

---

55 *LW* 1.85.
56 *LW* 1.56.
57 *LW* 1.121.
58 *LW* 1.230.
59 *LW* 2.106; 2.143–4.
60 Therefore Rasmussen is wrong to say that Luther's recognition of what humans have in common with other animals 'does not bother Luther one whit' (L. L. Rasmussen, 'Luther and a Gospel of Earth', *Union Seminary Quarterly Review* 51:1–2, 1997, p. 4). Luther is bothered by the thought that we might be no more than animals, and depends on his readers sharing this view in order to present them with the good news he finds in Genesis that humans have a different origin and destiny.

cern about the distinctiveness of the human in the face of observations to the contrary arising from knowledge of the natural world shows that he had wrestled with the issue more than two centuries before the work of Darwin provoked further reflection on it and shows anxiety about continuity between human and non-human animals is not dependent on a belief in an evolutionary lineage of descent connecting them.

In other writings Luther seems to be much less anxious about affirmations concerning the commonality between human beings and others of God's creatures. The most obvious place in which this different attitude is evident is in his sacramental theology, where he develops an understanding of God's presence throughout creation. This is most poetically expressed in a 1527 tract where he insists that the power of God 'must be essentially present [*Wesentlich und gegenwertig*] at all places, even in the tiniest tree leaf'.[61] Luther describes this essential presence in way that is at once lyrical and thoroughgoing:

> [God] must be present in every single creature in its innermost and outermost being, on all sides, through and through, below and above, before and behind, so that nothing can be more truly present and within all creatures than God himself with his power. For it is him that makes the skin and it is he who makes the bones; it is he who makes the hair on the skin and it is he who makes the marrow in the bones; it is he who makes every bit of the hair, it is he who makes every bit of the marrow. Indeed, he must make everything, both the parts and the whole.[62]

Luther confesses that holding together the idea that God is present everywhere in creation but not circumscribed by it is 'infinitely incomprehensible', but multiplies images of the intimacy of God's relationship to creation:

> The Divine Majesty is so small as to be present in essence in a kernel, on a kernel, above a kernel, throughout a kernel, inside and outside – and, even though it is one single Majesty, can nevertheless be completely and entirely present in every individual thing, countless in number though they be.[63]

Luther is then faced with the question of how to speak of God's unique presence in Christ. His answer is that in relation to all creatures, we can

---

61 *LW* 37.57.
62 *LW* 37.58.
63 *LW* 37.59.

say 'There is God, or God is in it', whereas only in relation to Christ can we say 'This is God himself'.[64] This fundamental contrast between Christ and creatures is reiterated in Luther's 1528 'Confession concerning Christ's supper': Christ is 'beyond and above all creatures'; 'Beyond the creatures there is only God.'[65] Elsewhere he repeats the assertion that all animals, including human beings, derive their life from God, and recognizes that the Hebrew word for soul denotes all animal life that lives and breathes.[66] He also maintains that even the mouse is a 'divine creature', beautiful in form, with 'such pretty feet and such delicate hair' that it must have been created with some plan in view.[67] It seems, then, that when Luther is preoccupied with creaturely realities, he is inclined to see a significant division between human beings and other animals, whereas at those times when he enlarges his vision to creation in the context of its Creator, it is obvious to him that the fundamental categories are Creator and creatures.[68]

The intimacy of God's relationship with all creation is also evident in God's care for non-human animals. In commenting on the Genesis flood narrative, Luther notes that God remembers not just Noah but the beasts too;[69] when preaching on the opening of John's Gospel, he notes the

64 LW 37.59. In the lectures on Genesis Luther states that 'the face of God shines forth in all His creatures' (LW 6.173) and in commentary on Psalm 78 he portrays every creature as an utterance of God (LW 11.39). The theme of all creatures having their life in God is also present in Luther's Christmas sermon on John 1.4: 'everything that lives has life of him and through him and in him' (LW 52.53). In a passage in the Table Talk Luther laments that this would have been a more common recognition before the fall: 'Oh, what thoughts man might have had about the fact that God is in all creatures, and so might have reflected on the power and the wisdom of God in even the smallest flowers!' (LW 54.327).

65 LW 37.229.

66 LW 22.30, 22.37, 28.191. This broad vision of creatureliness also seems operative when Luther is discussing Romans 8: criticizing philosophical accounts that are inattentive to the final end of creation he comments 'whoever searches into the essences and actions of creation rather than its groanings and expectations is without doubt a fool and a blind man, for he does not know that creatures are also a creation of God' (LW 25.362). Andrew Linzey comments that this text seems to indicate a 'non-humanocentric' perspective in Luther (Animal Theology, London: SCM Press, 1994, p. 189).

67 LW 1.52.

68 Rasmussen thinks Luther has gone too far in his admiration for mice (Earth Community, Earth Ethics, Geneva: WCC Publications, 1996, p. 275n). Rasmussen also seems to overstate the significance of the passage cited concerning the kernel, arguing that it shows Luther to be engaged in 'earthbound theology' that is 'boldly pan-en-theistic' (Earth Community, p. 273), and that Luther believes that 'Trying to rise above nature is, for earthbound creatures like us, the essence of sin' ('Luther and a Gospel of Earth', p. 3). It is clear even from the survey presented here that Luther often endorsed such an attempt to rise above nature on biblical grounds on terms very distant from panentheism.

69 LW 2.106.

importance of affirming that God is still working to sustain the whole of creation;[70] and when lecturing on 1 Timothy he cites Psalm 36.6, 'Man and beast Thou savest, O Lord', and affirms that God is rightly called the 'Saviour of all beasts'.[71] When he comes to consider a later passage (1 Tim. 5.18) concerning not muzzling an ox when treading grain, he first calls the text 'pure allegory', citing Paul's dismissive comment, 'Is it for oxen that God is concerned?', but he cannot quite rest with this conclusion, noting the Psalm 36 text again and insisting that God is concerned for all things.[72]

God's concern for all creatures is reflected in Luther's own views and practice. He pities the plight of oxen and flocks without pasture pictured by Joel,[73] and stories from the *Table Talk* depict him playing with his puppy Tölpel, using dogs as examples of concentration and faithfulness, remarking on the beautiful eyes of small birds, and wishing that they were aware of his good intentions towards them so that they would not fly away.[74] A few remarkable texts supplement these brief indications. The first is a jocular letter he wrote to himself in 1534 on behalf of the birds in the Wittenberg Wood complaining at the traps his servant Wolfgang Sieberger has set for them. It begins:

> To our good and kind Dr. Martin Luther, preacher in Wittenberg. We thrushes, blackbirds, linnets, goldfinches, along with other well-disposed birds who are spending their summer at Wittenberg, desire to let you know that we are told on good authority that your servant, Wolfgang Sieberger, out of the great hatred he bears to us, has brought some old rotten nets to set up a fowling-ground for finches, and not only for our dear friends and finches, but in order to deprive us of the liberty of flying in the air and picking up grains of corn, and also to make an attempt upon our lives, although we have not deserved such a punishment at his hands.[75]

---

70 *LW* 22.28–9.

71 *LW* 28.326.

72 *LW* 28.348.

73 *LW* 18.86.

74 *LW* 54.37 (no. 274); 54.175 (no. 2849b); 54.192 (no. 3223a). Luther also comments on the faithfulness of dogs in his lectures on Isaiah (*LW* 17.265). The *Table Talk* includes Luther's reported approval of rather different behaviour of dogs: one who is accused by a priest of being a Lutheran after urinating in the holy water and another who defecated into the grave of the bishop of Halle (*LW* 54.421, no. 5418).

75 Luther, *The Letters of Martin Luther*, ed. Margaret A. Currie, London: Macmillan & Co, 1908, p. 300 (letter no. 312). For information on Wolfgang Sieberger and his trapping, see *LW* 49.158n.

While the letter is tongue-in-cheek and does not represent a considered position against the trapping of birds,[76] it does show at the least attentiveness to them and empathy for their position. This attention to birds is also evident in a 1530 letter to George Spalatin, in which he is struck by the jackdaws at Coburg, and the similarity of their gathering to the diet he is on his way to attend:

> We sit here with great pleasure in [this] diet, as idle spectators and listeners. For in addition to the fact that that uniform and beautiful black color wonderfully refreshes us, seeing that these heroes are so magnificently dressed, the unanimity of all their voices, which are saturated with beautiful melodies, also delights us beyond measure . . . [Consequently] if something could be accomplished by wishing it, we would wish that they might be free of that defamatory name *monedula* [Latin for 'jackdaw'] or rather from the accusation that they are thievish, and that they might be praised with names worthy of their dignity – that is, that they all together might be called 'lancers' or 'spearmen'.[77]

Luther was involved in a more immediate encounter with non-human animals when he tried hunting for two days in Wartburg in 1521. In another letter to Spalatin, he describes his ambivalence about his participation: 'However great the pleasure may be from these things, the mystery, of pity and pain mixed into it is equally great.' He allegorizes the experience in seeing hunting as the work of the devil, 'who hunts innocent little creatures with his ambushes and his dogs'. Yet this allegorizing does not make him disregard the actuality of the event:

> By my efforts we had saved a little live rabbit. I had rolled it up into the sleeve of my cloak and left it alone for a little while. In the meantime the dogs found the poor rabbit and, biting through the cloak, broke its right hind leg and killed it by choking it.[78]

---

76 See, for example, an equally jovial letter to Justas Jonas asking him to buy 'whatever in that airy kingdom of our feathered friends is subject to the dominion of man' (*LW* 50.94–5).

77 *LW* 49.292–5 (no. 207, 24 April 1530). Bainton notes that some doubt the authenticity of this letter because the original has been lost and there is a problem with the date, but judges that 'the style is certainly *echt*' ('Luther on Birds', p. 5). This attentiveness to animals is also evident in correspondence about his translation of the Old Testament: in 1522 he wrote to Spalatin for descriptions and classifications by species for various birds of prey, game animals and reptiles (*LW* 49.19).

78 *LW* 48.295.

In the letter Luther goes on to reflect on this as an illustration of the way 'pope and Satan rage to destroy even the souls that have been saved', but also confesses 'I am sick of this kind of hunting', stating a preference for hunting creatures that could be allegorized as 'wicked teachers', such as bears, wolves, boars and foxes.[79] Again, this text does not represent a considered judgement against hunting, but the allegorizing, as well as his sabotage of the hunt in attempting to save the rabbit, show his innate sympathy for the plight of the creatures being pursued and his inclination to protect them.

It is notable that even at the end of the hunting letter, Luther describes his comments as joking, making this a common thread in each of these letters in which he identifies and empathizes with the situation of non-human animals. The obvious way of reading this self-confessed lack of seriousness when attending to birds and animals is that Luther was not seriously interested or concerned for them, instead using them as merely occasions for humour, or as sources for theological allegory. Against this interpretation, however, we must count the real sympathy evident in Luther's concern for the other innocent creatures hunted, and the attentiveness with which he observes and empathizes with them.[80] This points to another explanation of his dismissal of his writings on animals as jovial: that he is aware that this is an eccentric interest which may not be well understood by Spalatin or other friends with whom he corresponds. If so, it may not be overstating the case to suggest that the humour in these letters serves as a signal of a tension Luther experiences between his sympathy for the animals he observes and general societal attitudes to them, or even that the humour is an indicator of an unresolved tension between his own relationships with animals and his theological positioning of them. Given that he is elsewhere committed to the view that animals are provided by God merely for human use, it must seem odd to him to care that Wittenberg birds are being trapped in nets, or

---

79 Luther's ambivalence about hunting is reflected in other writings: in his lectures on Genesis he is critical of the damage done by princes during hunts (*LW* 4.382), insists that the sole legitimate purpose for hunting is to provide food (*LW* 7.267) and uses the image of a hunted hind or stag for the tribe of Naphtali, escaping the hunters through the protection of God. The editors of Luther's *Works* note that his commentary on Psalm 147 was a present for Hans Löser in gratitude for his hospitality during a hunting trip in which Luther expounded the psalm in preference to hunting.

80 This is further supported by Bainton's observation that in his struggles with depression, Luther found it helpful to watch birds and babies who took life blithely ('Luther's Struggle for Faith', *Church History* 17:3, 1948, p. 201).

majestic jackdaws are disrespected as thieves, or that a rabbit is caught by hounds.[81]

One final indication of Luther's good opinion of animals is the many other instances in his writing where he holds them up as good examples to be emulated by people. In commentary on Luke 1.49 – where there is no obvious animal referent – Luther is moved to comment:

> A bird pipes its lay and is happy in the gifts it has; nor does it murmur because it lacks the gift of speech. A dog frisks gayly about and is content, even though he is without the gift of reason. All animals live in contentment and serve God, loving and praising Him. Only the evil, villainous eye of man is never satisfied.[82]

This theme of animals praising God is repeated in signing off one of his letters from Coburg: 'In the land of the birds that sing sweetly in the branches and praise God with all their power night and day.'[83] Elsewhere he compares the sexual restraint of non-human animals favourably with human traits,[84] considers it shameful that some parents do not care adequately for their children when animals do this by nature,[85] and – in his earliest sermon – observes that animals keep the law of loving their neighbour while human beings do not.[86] In 'The Bondage of the Will' he cites Psalm 73.22, 'I am become a beast before thee', as a positive image of the human will living in faithfulness to God, in contrast with being ridden by Satan.[87]

---

81 Paul Santmire and John Cobb argue that a key problematic in Luther's theology of nature is the need he saw to shut his eyes to the world around in order to listen to God (H. Paul Santmire and John B. Cobb Jr., 'The World of Nature According to the Protestant Tradition', in Roger S. Gottlieb (ed.), *The Oxford Handbook of Religion and Ecology*, Oxford: Oxford University Press, 2006, pp. 116–18). The attention to animals detailed here shows clearly that Luther was not consistent in this methodology, which perhaps is another reason for his lack of ease with the affection for nature he reports.

82 *LW* 21.320.

83 *LW* 48.236.

84 *LW* 1.116, 5.289.

85 *LW* 6.17, 45.353.

86 *LW* 51.10–11.

87 *LW* 33.65–6. For further discussion of this image, see Marjorie O'Rourke Boyle, 'Luther's Rider-Gods: From the Steppe to the Tower', *Journal of Religious History* 13:3, 1985, pp. 260–82. Luther also pictures small flowers, leaves or birds as preaching God's forgiveness, but this tends towards reading creation as a message from God for human beings, rather than seeing creation in its own right (*LW* 21.126). Bainton notes that, unlike Melanchthon, Luther 'restricted himself to the animals before his eyes' for such illustrations ('Luther on Birds', p. 4).

The most striking positive image of a non-human animal in Luther's writings, however, is a christological one. In a sermon on Jesus' lament over Jerusalem (Matt. 23.34–39), he explores in detail the comparison with a hen:

> Let us observe how a natural mother-hen acts. There is hardly an animal that takes care of its offspring so meticulously. It changes its natural voice turning it into a lamenting, mourning one; it searches, scratches for food and lures the chick to eat. When the mother-hen finds something, she does not eat it, but leaves it for the chicks; she fights seriously and calls her chicks away from the hawk; she spreads out her wings willingly and lets the chicks climb under her and all over her, for she is truly fond of them – it is, indeed, an excellent, lovely symbol. Similarly, Christ has taken unto himself a pitiful voice, has lamented for us and has preached repentance, has indicated from his heart to everyone his sin and misery. He scratches in the Scripture, lures us into it, and permits us to eat; he spreads his wings with his righteousness, merit, and grace over us and takes us under himself in a friendly manner, warms us with his natural heat, i.e., with his Holy Ghost who comes solely through him, and in the air fights for us against the devil.[88]

This comparison is more than allegorical: the passage speaks of careful observation of hens with their chicks, and Luther sees in their attentive maternal care nothing short of an image of Christ, rooted in Christ's self-identification with a mother hen.[89]

Fences under strain: tensions in Luther's account of animals

In the survey I have provided of Luther's discussion of animals, I have pointed to several points at which his discussion seems under strain. In his commentary on Genesis, he repeatedly emphasizes that observation of the world shows us how much humans are like other animals, but that Scripture reveals that humans have a different origin and destiny. This is not consistently rendered, however, with occasional references to natural

---

88 *LW* 52.97–8.

89 We should also note in this context Luther's reported appreciation of Aesop: two comments in his *Table Talk*, recorded by different visitors to his table, note his appreciation of Aesop's Fables as superior to Jerome (*LW* 54.72) and alongside Cato second only to the Bible (*LW* 54.210).

signs of the superiority of humans despite critique elsewhere of philo-sophical affirmations of human dignity. Luther's discussion of reason is particularly fraught: he sometimes accepts the philosophical definition of human beings as rational animals, but his emphasis on sinfulness as the fundamental element in a theological anthropology challenges this, and his tirades against reason make him an unlikely advocate for rationality as a marker of unique human superiority. Dominion seems a more straight-forward category for Luther to distinguish human and non-human theo-logically, but he is unclear about its purpose before the fall, and about whether to emphasize the loss of dominion as punishment for sin or God's graceful extension of it after the flood. Luther makes clear and uncompro-mising anthropocentric statements affirming that God made creation to provide for human beings, but his attentiveness and concern for the ani-mals with which he came into contact speak of a concern for them for their own sake, in line with the affirmation in his sacramental theology of the intimacy of God's presence in all creatures. Luther is self-contradictory about the role of non-human creatures in eternal life, and I have suggested that his identification of reports of his observation and care of animals as humorous may in itself indicate his own difficulty in seeing how to fit his obvious empathy with non-human animals with his broader theological commitments.[90]

At one key point the tension implicit in Luther's thinking about the relationship between humans and other animals becomes explicit. In com-mentary on Genesis 2.7, he delivers his judgement that to say that human beings are both the image of God and have a life in common with the ani-mals is nonsensical: 'The statement that though man is created according to the similitude of God, he does not differ from cattle in his animal life is clearly contradictory, or, as they call it in the schools, "a contradiction in the predicate".'[91] Luther is not clear about the nature of the contradiction here, but presumably his concern is that if we believe that human beings are both like God and like cattle, this suggests the unacceptable conclusion that God is like cattle. As we have seen, in the passage discussed at the end

---

90 The lack of fit between different elements has been noted by Santmire, who contrasts the 'anthropocentric-soteriological' centre to Luther and Calvin's thought with a 'theocen-tric-ecological' circumference and maintains that the tension between the two was never resolved (*Travail of Nature*, pp. 131–2). Rasmussen cites Santmire's view in his critique of Luther ('Luther and a Gospel of Earth', pp. 22–5). My account here develops this tension and adds the further complexity of Luther's interest and self-conscious affection for the birds and animals with whom he found himself in relationship, as well as proposing a resolution based on a hermeneutical method Luther himself employs.

91 *LW* 1.87.

of the previous section, Luther had no reservation in accepting the conclusion that Jesus is like a mother hen, but here he is not prepared to countenance a divine–animal resemblance. Nor, unsurprisingly, is he content to rest with the judgement that Scripture is contradictory. Instead, he sees this apparent contradiction between human as both animal and imaging God as pointing beyond itself: 'By a very beautiful allegory, or rather by an anagoge, Moses wanted to intimate dimly that God was to become incarnate.'[92] Luther is saying that the text here is anagogical – containing a spiritual truth anticipating the future revelation of Christ. Within the interpretative frame of the Genesis text, it does not make sense to say both that humans are animals and that they are images of God: the assertions are contradictory. The tension caused by the contradiction can only be resolved by recognizing it to be an intimation of something beyond itself, signifying the need for resolution in a different context, in this case the context of the entire Christian canon.

My proposal for what we should make of Luther's discussion of non-animals takes his recommendation here as a model. As I have noted, when we survey the whole of Luther's thinking about animals, we encounter a broad range of perspectives, from those that are straightforwardly anthropocentric, in continuity with the mainstream of the tradition he inherited, to those that verge on pantheistic as he meditates on God's intimate presence in creation. This may be in part because non-human animals are rarely the focus of his discussion, and when they are, he apparently feels the need to excuse his idiosyncrasy as a joke. To resolve the tension created by taking stock of the multiplicity of Luther's perspectives on animals that I have collected in this chapter, we could consider arguments to accept one trajectory or another from it as normative: we could judge that his anthropocentric statements should be used to interpret all other aspects of his thought, or that it is appropriate to begin with his minute exploration of God's presence in a tiny seed and to interpret all else taking this as the norm.[93] To proceed in this way would be, in terms of the contradiction we have just considered, to opt for the view either that human beings are the image of God, or that they are animals, and reject the alternative. This would no doubt have the virtue of clarity and simplicity, but it would miss half of what the text was telling us about the relationships between God, humanity and other animals, which – apart from fidelity to Scripture – was

---

92 LW 1.87.

93 Ickert seems close to this latter track in concluding that for Luther God-given dominion means 'human beings are given an unequivocal responsibility to care for and protect the non-human creation' ('Luther and Animals', p. 98).

presumably what held Luther back from doing so. I suggest that we will be better interpreters of Luther in relation to animals if we resist the desire to resolve the tensions evident in the many ways in which he talks about animals, and instead interpret these tensions anagogically: as pointing beyond themselves, as intimating the need for resolution in a different context than the one in which he was working, and as showing that the animals who appear so frequently in his writing cannot be contained behind the fences he sometimes held them behind.

What then would be the context in which Luther's insights could find a resolution beyond themselves? My favourite illustration of the change of perspective required is from a parable from the Jewish philosopher and theologian Moses Maimonides. He pictures an individual in a city who believes that the final end of the ruler of the city is to keep the individual's house safe from robbers. Maimonides comments that this is true from a certain point of view, since the house is kept safe because of the ruler's action.[94] Whenever Luther speaks of God's provision of other creatures for the benefit of human beings, he is always seeking to assure his audience of God's grace towards humanity: to set out the good news that, despite appearances at times, in God's ongoing activity of creation God is concerned to establish a place for human beings to live and thrive.[95] Within the terms of Maimonides' parable, Luther is providing assurance that the ruler is indeed ensuring the safety of the house. If we accept the insight of the parable that this may not be a complete account of the purposes of the ruler – that the ruler might also be concerned with the safety of the other houses in the city – we can ask whether, within the generous economy of God's creative grace, God might be concerned in a similar way for parts of creation other than the human. Within this broader context, we could do justice both to Luther's bold pronouncements of God's graciousness towards humanity and to his intimations that other forms of creaturely life, such as birds and rabbits and dogs, might also have their own place in God's purposes. Just as Luther interprets Genesis anagogically, as containing a tension that points beyond itself to the incarnation, this is a proposal to interpret Luther's thought on animals as an anagoge, intimating the need for a wider perspective on God's dealings with human and non-human animals.

---

94 Moses Maimonides, *The Guide of the Perplexed*, trans. Shlomo Pines, Chicago: University of Chicago Press, 1963, 3:13.

95 Walter Brueggemann argues that the dating of Genesis to the exilic period means that the creation narratives themselves were attempting a similar task of reassuring the Israelites that despite appearances they had place in God's purposes. Walter Brueggemann, *Genesis*, Louisville KY: John Knox Press, 1982, p. 14.

3

Animals in Orthodox Iconography

ESTHER D. REED

Christianity's cardinal error, writes the philosopher John Gray, is the sup-position that humans are different from all other animals.[1] The peculiarly Christian content of this myth is now in tatters but its bastard offspring, secular humanism, continues to fuel the conceit that humans are unlike all other animals in their ability to understand the world, act morally and direct its destiny. Secular humanism perpetuates a perverted version of Christianity's error, namely, that humans are different from all other animals and will enjoy a destiny different from that of non-human animals.[2] There is some grandiose ludicrousness in his complaint that whatever atrocities have been committed against non-human animals in modern, Western, humanist societies have their origin in Christianity. Gray assumes that the course from Christian teaching about the relation between humans and non-human animals to our current precarious state with respect to climate change, the prospect of mass human mortality, massive loss of biodiversity, etc., is rectilinear. Yet his anti-theology keeps us close to questions about the kind of coexistence between human and non-human animals that Christian faith engenders; and it seems pointless to bicker over statements that are difficult to prove and even more difficult to refute.

Gray's charge that Christianity's 'meaningless babble' has morphed into an attitude toward non-human animals that seems fated to wreck the bal-ance of life on earth is overly simplistic. His claim that promises of tech-nological salvation are the mistaken heirs of Christianity and the Enlightenment – that 'eschatology and technology belong together' – is open to challenge.[3] But there is no denying that he represents a now

---

1 John Gray, *Straw Dogs: Thoughts on Humans and Other Animals*, London: Granta Books, 2002, p. 4.
2 Gray, *Straw Dogs*, p. 4.
3 Gray, *Straw Dogs*, p. 139.

familiar indictment of Christianity. And his castigation of the conceit that scientific progress will ensure that humanity will not destroy its planetary host or kill its own life on earth 'hits home'; the human species currently has little option but to realize that we can no more be masters of our destiny than any other animal because collapsing ecosystems will not be redeemed by the promise of technological advancement. Mindful of these realities, this chapter seeks a constructive response to Gray's challenges by attending afresh to Orthodox iconography. The aim is to consider how non-human animals are perceived in Christian thought and the implications for particular practices.

Amid a surge of recent interest in Orthodoxy that has opened the way for a reappreciation of icons as visible representations of Orthodox faith, this chapter is about whether and/or how Orthodox iconography can provoke Christian people to the acts of confession and asceticism needed to avert the crises that environmentalists predict. The thesis is that Orthodox iconography can assist believers in acknowledging the sacramentality of all creation and the inclusion of non-human as well as human animals in Christ's renewal of all creation (Rev. 21.1). It is not demonstrated easily. Icons do not always give easy access to their wisdom. Moreover, what for Gray is a stumbling block – namely, the difference between human and non-human animals because of the former's creation *imago Dei* – remains at issue.

Icons and the reading of biblical texts

Western believers are unaccustomed to the contemplation of icons for a range of historical and ecumenical reasons. The moderate iconoclasm adopted by the Frankfurt council (AD 794) and subsequent tendency in Western spiritual art to depart from the many conventions of Orthodox iconography, not least by mixing secular and ecclesial art, contributed historically to a loss in the West of a theological understanding of icons. Tensions between the principle of *sola scriptura* in Protestantism and that more akin to *prima scriptura* in Eastern Orthodoxy contributed also to the reticence of Western believers to pray with icons as visual representations of what the words of a biblical narrative offer the ear. 'For what writing presents to readers, this a picture presents to the unlearned who behold, since in it even the ignorant see what they ought to follow; in it the illiterate read.'[4]

---

4 St Gregory the Dialogist, Epistle to Bishop Serenus of Marseilles, in Philip Schaff (ed.), *Nicene and Post-Nicene Fathers*, series 2, vol. XIII, p. 53.

So Gregory I (590–604) spoke of icons as being Scripture to the illiterate.[5] Today, when visual communication and graphic design are important aspects of commercial and corporate communication, when logos and subliminal messages in advertisements proliferate, and when the perception of a product can be vastly different from its actuality, Orthodox iconography is no longer 'the poor man's Bible' but one of the languages of theology to which we rarely attend.

With this in mind, I offer a note about icons and their relation to the Bible. The working assumption in this chapter is that icons of canonical subjects are depictions of biblical texts in theological form. Icons are not holy Scripture but their inner logic invites believers to make connections across and within the entire corpus of the Bible. Moreover, we can approach icons as exercises in *theoria* analogous to the methods of reading holy Scripture developed by Gregory of Nyssa and other of our forebears in the early Church. This thesis cannot be demonstrated here as fully as might be desired. Suffice it to point briefly to the techniques developed by Gregory and other patristic writers.

Briefly, Gregory of Nyssa distinguishes relatively clearly between *historia* and *theoria*, between the distinction between attempted historical reconstruction (*historia*) and the employment of typological and allegorical reading strategies. Gregory often takes liberties with details of the biblical text (*historia*) in order to maximize the rhetorical impact on readers. His account in *The Life of Moses* of Moses' life puts together bits and pieces of historical information gleaned from various books of the Bible to construct a coherent story from his birth and placement in a basket daubed with pitch and slime in order to escape the dire consequences of Pharoah's law to his final words of prophecy and death on a high mountain overlooking the promised land. As John J. O'Keefe and R. R. Reno comment: 'Gregory makes no effort to probe the veracity of the events or to reconstruct the true nature of Moses' encounter with Pharaoh'; his concerns are more with narrative sequence and spiritual truth than with historical accuracy.[6] His approach to *historia*, however, supports later typological and allegorical readings. Of interest to us is how his juxtaposition of biblical text against biblical text, allegory adjacent to rhetorical allegory, invites readers into a dynamic interplay of possible interpretation. As Gregory juxtaposes different passages of

---

5 Also known as Gregory I or St Gregory the Great.

6 John J. O'Keefe and R. R. Reno, *Sanctified Vision: An Introduction to Early Christian Interpretation of the Bible*, Baltimore and London: The Johns Hopkins University Press, 2005, pp. 14–15.

Scripture to dramatic effect, so too the complex composition of these icons are depictions of biblical texts in dramatically theological form.

Like Gregory of Nyssa's reading strategy, Orthodox iconography starts from the relation of diverse aspects of the canon rather than from solitary or isolated passages. The result is a theologically rich series of juxtapositions that make connections between different events in the story of salvation. So, for instance, the faces of Christ and of the first Adam are identical at the time of creation in the twelfth-century Byzantine mosaics in the basilica of Monreale, Sicily.[7] The *Old Testament Trinity*, *c.*1420, continues the early Christian and Byzantine tradition of seeing the three pilgrims who appear to Abraham at Mamre as an image of the holy Trinity, but this icon also contains items that represent Christ's passion and the Divine Liturgy. The bread on the table represents the Lamb, the knife is the lance that pierced his side, bread is cut into triangles according to the Russian practice at the Eucharist.[8] Icons of the nativity often portray the vigilant Mary watching over the Christ-child wrapped like a corpse and lying in a grave-like cave that symbolizes hell.[9] Like the reading strategy in Book II of Gregory of Nyssa's *Life of Moses*, many icons not only recount *historia* but provide the conditions for successions of visual echoes to be set in process by viewers. Diverse reading strategies, notably lexical, dialectical and associative strategies, are employed by Gregory within a framework that sees Christ Jesus as fulfilling the meaning of the Scriptures and which invites their interpretation as an interlocking whole.[10] So too, icons of the last judgement are complex, interlocking wholes that synthesize material from diverse books of the Bible in order to construct a continuous narrative.

---

7 This is observed by Michel Quenot, *The Resurrection and the Icon*, trans. Michael Breck, Crestwood NY: St Vladimir's Seminary Press, 1997, pp. 23–4. Some of these mosaics are reproduced at The Joy of Shards available at <http://www.thejoyofshards.co.uk/visits/sicily/monreale/> (accessed 19 October 2007).

8 *Old Testament Trinity c.*1420. Saint Petersburg, Russian Museum. Reproduced in Alfredo Tradigo, *Icons and Saints of the Eastern Orthodox Church*, trans. Stephen Sartarelli, Los Angeles CA: The J. Paul Getty Museum, 2006, p. 69.

9 E.g. *The Nativity*, *c.*1475 The Novgorod School, Vicenza (Italy), Gallerie di Palazzo Leoni Montanari, Banca Intesa Collection. Reproduced in Tradigo, *Icons and Saints*, p. 105.

10 Lexical reading strategies assigned reliable meanings to key words and elements in biblical texts. Dialectical readings studied contradictions and difficulties in the text in order to probe their deeper truths. Associative readings looked for points of connection between particular words and images. See O'Keefe and Reno, *Sanctified Vision*, ch. 1.

Animals at the last judgement?

Orthodox icons of the last judgement typically foretell the recreation of the natural order when human and non-human animals are no longer in submission one to the other but united with the heavenly and invisible. Typically complex in composition and involving many scenes and figures, they permit a larger degree of individuality in the artists' treatment of their subject than is common elsewhere – the result being that some subjects and scenes are treated in more or less detail; different groups of figures are placed closest to Christ. Characteristically, both the composition and subject matter centre upon a visual embodiment of the majesty of Christ, ruler of the universe. The symbolism is derived mainly from the visions of the prophet Ezekiel (Ezek. 1.3–28), the visions of Daniel (Dan. 7.2–8), and the Apocalyse (Rev. 4.1–3). Animals feature frequently in these dramatic compositions and summon to mind the final acts of all human history. Christ, the righteous judge, is often represented as enthroned and surrounded not only by Mary, John the Baptist, apostles, saints and angelic ranks, but also elephants, cheetahs, lions, and more besides.

Christ himself is typically portrayed as seated on a throne with his right hand raised in blessing, holding an open Gospel, and surrounded not only by seraphim but symbols of the evangelists (an angel, an eagle, a lion and a calf) who brought his word to the four corners of the earth. John the Baptist and the Virgin often pose in prayer on behalf of humankind. At Christ's feet, typically, are Adam and Eve. The apostles stand either side of Christ holding open books as, at the end of the world, God's final judgement of humankind is underway. Men and women approach for judgement; the righteous are elevated to the right of Christ and sinners descend to his left. Above, the sky is being rolled up by the angels. Below, a great lake of fire disgorges the serpent who tries to bite Adam's heel but fails because Adam is safe with Eve under the throne of Christ.

Two sixteenth-century icons of the last judgement are especially interesting because of the ways in which they represent non-human animals. The first, now at the Solvychegodsk Museum of History and Art, is remarkable for its lower left corner which portrays the paradise into which the righteous may enter. Its white background, trees and birds suggest a lush garden that contrasts sharply with the lake of fire fed by incandescent lava flowing straight from God's throne.[11] The second icon, *The Last Judgment* in the Hermitage Museum, is divided into two parts,

---

11 Painted between 1580 and 1590. Reproduced in Tradigo, *Icons and Saints*, p. 161.

with paradise to the left and hell to the right.[12] A great lake of fire in the bottom right-hand corner shows Satan with the soul of Judas in his arms. Below Christ's throne is a set of scales on which human souls are to be weighed. Ten rectangles along the bottom edge list the mortal sins and the respective punishments of the damned. Starkly drawn contrasts of heaven and hell tend to be unconvincing to modern readers because of their perceived severity. For our purposes, however, the issue is not a punishment model of heaven and hell but how these icons might bear upon a theologically informed ethics of the relation between human and non-human animals. I want neither to downplay the imagery of the 'dreadfulness' of beasts in a theological world-view within which the human is often conceived as suspended between a celestial and terrestrial nature nor create an impression that icon painters wanted to speak to precisely this point.[13] The question is whether, despite these qualifications, icons of the last judgement yet image relations between human and non-human animals that break apart overly anthropocentric construals and help us to envisage afresh biblical witness to how the flourishing of each requires the flourishing of all.

Initial answers are not promising for those of us seeking a spirituality of cautious harmony with non-human animals and not arrogant supremacy over them. While non-human animals are present in the icons, they are not involved directly in the trials through which human souls must pass. Non-human animals do not of themselves share in the drama of the punishments of the damned and elevation of the redeemed to the holy city of Jerusalem. Instead, they perform largely symbolic functions. Witness the ochre-coloured circles that contain the four beasts that Daniel saw in his vision:

> The first was like a lion, and it had the wings of an eagle. I watched until its wings were torn off and it was lifted from the ground so that it stood on two feet like a man, and the heart of a man was given to it. And there before me was a second beast, which looked like a bear . . . one that looked like a leopard . . . and there before me was a fourth beast – terrifying and frightening and very powerful. It had large iron teeth; it crushed and devoured its victims and trampled underfoot whatever was

---

12 This icon can be seen at <http://www.hermitagemuseum.org>. Stylistic indications suggest Novgorod traditions, but the Museum believes that it was the work of a master from the Russian North.

13 Giorgio Agamben, *The Open: Man and Animal*, trans. Kevin Attell, Stanford CA: Stanford University Press, 2002, ET 2004, p. 29.

left. It was different from all the former beasts, and it had ten horns. (Dan. 7.2–8 NRSV)

None of the beasts is identified in Daniel's vision except to the extent that they represent four kings or kingdoms that shall arise out of the earth (Dan. 7.17). The icon painters have not given us images of non-human animals on earth as we know them but dreadful and terrible emperors or kings who devour flesh, defeat enemies without mercy, trample, break in pieces and speak arrogantly. The ochre-coloured circles are positioned on the right of the icon as one views it, on the left-hand side of Christ, representing the damned.

The circles in which the animals are painted are also of interest. Enclosed circles are a common means of representing a sphere of life or order of existence. So, for instance, in the seventeenth-century Russian icon known as *Saint Sophia the Wisdom of God*, the Virgin Mary is enthroned with the Christ-child inside a circle that represents the new seat of Wisdom.[14] In the mid-sixteenth-century Russian icon known as *Blessed Be the Host of the Celestial King*, the high-walled city of Jerusalem is placed in a tricolour circle that repeats the colours of the tent of blessing under which the city is placed, and through which issues a river of grace along the edges of which grow vigorous saplings and other plants.[15] This contrasts with the city of Babylon which is completely encircled in a ring of flames and smoke. Sinuous wavy lines are sometimes substituted for circles, for example, the line that encloses scenes of the first homicide and funeral lament for Abel in a detail of the mid-sixteenth-century *Quadripartite Icon* by the Pskov masters. Enclosed circles or other spaces represent realms of existence – whether of blessing, wisdom or cursedness. In the icons selected for special study, the dreadfulness of the beasts is curtailed and closed off from other activity in the icon. These beasts are excluded from the benefits of salvation; the spheres that they inhabit are not open to the future transformation when the energies of God will permeate the whole world.

Yet more significant is the narrative direction of the icons toward the heavenly city of the New Jerusalem. Cities are rarely as conducive to animal life as gardens or open countryside. The New Jerusalem appears to be no exception. While some icons image the river of the water of life and the tree of life with its twelve kinds of fruit (Rev. 22.2), few if any represent

---

14 Reproduced in Tradigo, *Icons and Saints*, p. 45.

15 Reproduced in Engelina Smirnova, *Moscow Icons: 14th–17th Centuries*, trans. Arthur Shkarovsky-Raffé, Oxford: Phaidon, 1989, p. 175.

the New Jerusalem as a city in which non-human animals thrive. Like Basil the Great's homily to the effect that humans are the only animal to be deified, icons of the last judgement appear not to assist readily theological attempts to envision an indissoluble bond between human and non-human animals before God, a sense of how humans share with other animals the immediacy of praise to their Creator, or a sequence of events in which both are made new together.[16]

Westerners might be forgiven at this point for recalling the teaching of Thomas Aquinas as problematic. If Jerusalem is a place for the perfection of contemplative life and not natural life, will non-human animals be excluded from the heavenly city?[17] Animality is condemned to corruption.[18] The resurrection pertains to a dispensation in which eating, drinking, sleeping and reproduction have no place (Matt. 22.30) and, because non-human animal life is characterized by these activities, it is excluded from paradise. In Giorgio Agamben's words: 'All flesh will not be saved, and in the physiology of the blessed, the divine *oikonomia* of salvation leaves an unredeemable remnant.'[19] We must be clear, however, that the anthropology of the patristics is different to that of Aquinas – at least, if we adopt a reading of his work based on these texts and without reference to other aspects of his teaching how humanity's imaging of God is by virtue of its being part of wider creation.[20] While patristic authors emphasize the uniqueness afforded to humanity and the kingly responsibility this entails, this does not equate to the supposition that non-human animals are excluded from the divine economy of salvation. To interpret it as such would be a glaring example of misinterpretation and corruption of Orthodox tradition. Aquinas' writings might be capable of reclamation. But this is not our purpose here. Rather, our concern is to establish that, while the fathers speak of the intelligible soul that humanity has received for free communion with God, this need not be understood to mean that non-animals are unredeemable.

---

16 Basil the Great, *Hexaemeron*, Homily IX.

17 Thomas Aquinas, *The Summa Theologica of St. Thomas Aquinas* (*ST*) III *Supplement*, q. 81, c. second and revised edition, trans. Fathers of the English Dominican Province, 1920. Online Edition Copyright © 2006 by Kevin Knight. Available at <http://www.newadvent.org/summa>.

18 Aquinas, *ST* III *Supplement*, q. 91, a. 5, c. ad 3.

19 Agamben, *The Open*, p. 19. Agamben wonders if concentration and extermination camps distinguish the human from the in-human along similar lines to that suggested by Aquinas.

20 On this, see M. Wynn, 'Aquinas's Appropriation of the Dominion Tradition', in D. Horrell et al. (eds), *Towards an Ecological Hermeneutic: Biblical, Historical, and Theological Perspectives* (forthcoming).

Again, the task is not always easy. Witness Gregory of Nazianzus' observation about how humans are different from all other animals: 'For akin to Deity are those natures which are intellectual, and only to be comprehended by mind; but all of which sense can take cognisance are utterly alien to it.'[21] The spiritual nature of the second stage of creation, the material and visible world which succeeds the incorporeal cosmos of the angelic beings and precedes the third stage of creation which is humanity, is elsewhere described by Gregory as that alien (*xenos*) to God in the sense that it is not akin (*oikeois*) to his incorporeality and invisibility, and is not inbreathed by his Spirit.[22] Such teaching calls attention to the central and decisive role that humanity plays in the history of the world. Arguably, however, it should not be misconstrued as teaching the unredeemability of non-human animals but, rather, the prophetic, kingly and priestly offices of humanity in the 'churching' of the world, that is, in employing rational faculties to celebrate how the entirety of material creation participates in the glory of God.

While there can be no denying that creation in the image of God reflects trinitarian and christological doctrine with respect to the Persons of the Trinity, the communion of persons in the Church, and says something about the entirety of the human psychosomatic being, the Church today does not need a new account of the doctrine of the *imago Dei*. It needs to reclaim the witness of the ancient Church to why and how this teaching unites humanity with the whole universe. To this end, the imagery of the New Jerusalem in icons of the last judgement need not be read as excluding non-human animals but as representing the participation of all material creation in the glory of God.[23] Anestis G. Keselopoulos summarizes the teaching of Maximus the Confessor to this effect:

> The churching of the world is to be understood as a gathering of all things that exist into one unity, so that none of them is in opposition or conflict or at enmity with any other, and so as to secure the one nature of sensible things and the 'one nature of things created.'[24]

---

21 Gregory of Nazianzus, *Oration* 38.x.

22 See Donald F. Winslow, *The Dynamics of Salvation: A Study of Gregory of Nazianzus*, Cambridge MA: The Philadelphia Patristic Foundation, 1979, pp. 45–53.

23 Space did not permit consideration of mosaics of biblical accounts of the creation.

24 Anestis G. Keselopoulos, *Man and the Environment: A Study of St Symeon the New Theologian*, trans. Elizabeth Theokritoff, Crestwood NY: St Vladimir's Seminary Press, 2001, p. 154. Citing Maximus the Confessor, *To Thalassius*, Question 48 (PG 90.436B).

Orthodox theology continues to speak of humanity as created in the image of God both before the fall and as 'flesh', that is, in our fallen state. The gifts and powers associated with human creation *imago Dei*, including the functions and faculties of reason, are naturally oriented towards the consummation and perfection of all creation and this sometimes creates the impression that liberation from corruption and death are liberation from animality and physicality. Arguably, however, the dynamic of icons of the last judgement towards the New Jerusalem is about the dynamic progress of *all* creation towards transfiguration in Christ. Icons of the last judgement portray humanity's relationship with the world as an essentially ecclesial reality. Humanity's creation in the image and our relationship to the rest of creation is eucharistic.

Animals included in the resurrection?

Those of us who want less ambiguous answers might recall the half-dream recounted by St Sophronius, a seventh-century Patriarch of Jerusalem, in which saints entered a temple with many icons inside. St Cyrus and St John stood together with a youth suffering from gout before a 'great and amazing image' of God with the Virgin on the left and John the Baptist on the right, as well as a host of apostles and prophets. Together with the suffering youth, 'they stood before the icon, they beseeched God bending their knees, and striking their heads on the ground, and begging for healing'.[25] The healing that we seek is not as immediately forthcoming as might be wished! These icons sometimes make us work hard before they yield their spiritual riches. With this in mind, we turn to icons of the resurrection with our same questions about how non-human animals are perceived in Christian thought.

It might seem odd to turn to icons in which non-human animals do not appear. But icons of the resurrection express the essence of Orthodox faith and require believers to confront the anthropocentrism that characterizes much of its teaching. Orthodoxy has only two icons of the resurrection: the myrrh-bearing women at the tomb and Christ's descent into Hades. Traditional iconography of the latter represents the events of Holy Saturday when Christ himself went to the farthest depths of the fall; that 'place' where evil crouches in its ultimate despair and from where he

---

25 Recounted from Presbyter Ioann Damaskin's account by Kira V. Cekanskaja, 'Traditional Veneration of Icons in the Russian Orthodox Church', *Acta Ethnographica Hungarica* 51:3–4, 2006, pp. 265–80, here p. 266.

delivers the great mass of the dead from its darkness. Adam had been held captive deeper down than all the rest and his release from the very bowels of hell means that nowhere in creation, no place to which God's calling might take human beings, is beyond the Saviour's reach. Christ hauls Adam up from the abyss (Eph. 4.8), and with him all humanity.

Few, if any, animals or instances of plant life feature explicitly in icons of Christ's descent into hell or limbo.[26] Indeed, iconography of the resurrection typically assumes that the real significance of creation as a whole resides in the human destiny of theosis and that this vocation distinguishes humans from the rest of creation. Gregory of Nazianzus is representative of much patristic teaching in this respect when he writes:

> Let us become like Christ, since Christ became like us. Let us become God's for His sake, since He for ours became Man. He assumed the worse that He might give us the better; He became poor that we through His poverty might be rich (2 Cor. 8.9).[27]

In the garden of Eden, only humans had the potential to grow into the likeness of God; to go 'up' or 'down'. Adam and Eve chose to disobey God's word and 'fell', taking all creation with them. All non-human animals and plant life are sustained by the Word of God and have what Maximus the Confessor called spiritual meanings of *logoi* within them; all of creation, including human and non-human animals, participate in the uncreated energies or light of God by virtue of their creation. Nevertheless, Christ is the new Adam who redeems the world that now experiences the effects of sin because of human choices and activities. The whole of creation suffered when humankind fell and, when humankind is made anew in Christ, the whole of creation is also renewed. These icons teach that non-human animal life participates in the transfiguration of humanity because the *imago Dei* is that whereby creation enjoys a special kinship (*syggenes*) with God. Significantly, however, there are no icons of non-human animals apart from humans. The peculiar vocation of humankind in its ecclesial calling is union with Christ (Rev. 21.9).

Orthodoxy's reply to the question of missing animals is that they are not missing but included within the noble colour of the mountains and the resonant quality of the mountains that is a reflection of the beauty of the

---

26 E.g. *The Descent into Hell*, a late fifteenth-century icon from the iconostasis of the Church of the Dormition of Volotovo, near Novgorod. Reproduced in Quenot, *The Resurrection and the Icon*, p. 85.

27 Gregory of Nazianzus, *Oration* 1.v.

kingdom of heaven.[28] Non-human animals are present implicitly by means of iconographic convention. Icons of Christ's descent into hell or limbo include non-human animal life in the light-bearing rocks and mountains that symbolize all creation. Rocks and mountains reflect the light which has its source in the resurrected Christ and represent the participation that all creation has in divine life. The action that takes place in the very depths of the earth presupposes that the goal of theosis marks humans off from the rest of creation as the potential glory of the created cosmos. Yet the dynamic of salvation to which the icon bears witness reaches every part of the cosmos. Light from Christ's robes extends even to the borders of the icon. The destiny of the entire created order is transfiguration in Christ. Anthropology and cosmology are presented together within a christological framework. Light from Christ's robes reaches every part of the cosmos which, in turn, reflects the glory of the resurrected Christ. In other words, the mountains reflect the uncreated divine energy, or Hesychasm, that shone from the body of Christ at his transfiguration and resurrection. Non-human animals are included within this cosmic vision.

Is this answer adequate to our present-day spiritual and practical needs in the face of the ecological crisis that besets our planet? Is it a partial or sufficient 'solution' to the problem of humanity's reaching and deluded arrogance? Traditionally, there has been no compromise with respect to the theandric character of the *imago Dei* relation. The economy of salvation is primarily (in the sense of 'in the first instance' or 'originally') an interplay between the human and the divine. It is not exclusively this and Christian tradition has too often omitted to reflect upon how all created beings participate in the meaning (*logos*), highest attributes or generative energies (*logoi*) of the divine life. Our question is whether this part of Orthodoxy's answer to the problem of missing animals has the power to sustain believers struggling to stay focused on a biblical vision of human and non-human animals reconciled, and to make their actions more caring and ecologically sustainable.

Viewed sympathetically, the cosmic vision of these icons entails a symbolic depth that we need desperately today. They speak of the impossibility of respecting non-human animals without due respect for the environment they inhabit. These mountains can be understood not as a denial of plant, animal and bird life but as a plea for their preservation.

---

28 This point is made by Irina Yazykova, 'The Theological Principles of Icon and Iconography', in Lilia Evseyeva et al., *A History of Icon Painting*, trans. Kate Cook, Moscow: Grand-Holding Publishers, 2007, p. 16.

The radiance of the mountains protests against the tragic propensity of humans to relate to the earth and each other through technology, that is, by reducing the other to the status of 'tool'.[29] Every beauty matters, including that of the rocks and soil. There is no sharp line of demarcation between the physical or material and the spiritual. The silence and tranquillity of the mountains speaks of an interconnectedness of all things (Col. 1.17; Eph. 1.10) and of the divine presence throughout the entirety of this world. Orthodoxy is familiar with apophatic ways of thinking that strip images down in order to see behind and through them. Indeed, apophatic ways of doing theology are often preferred to cataphatic ways because humans cannot grasp the spiritual realities of the divine energies by conceptual and rational means. The risk, of course, is that those who do not share this attitude miss the witness of the icons to the entirety of creation and recreation in the light of Christ and see only irrelevance and obfuscation. And the fact remains that non-human animals, birds, fish, etc. are not represented explicitly. The literal presence of these creatures is, at best, concealed. But it is also true that the earth which we share in common with all living creatures is our only homeland. Let us attend!

That animals are included in the resurrection also finds testimony in hagiographical icons and folktales pertaining to them. So, for instance, the Orthodox of a small island called Caphalonia in the Ionian Sea recount that, on 15 August every year, snakes that have a cross on their heads and are known to be harmless crawl over the countryside to the local church along with the human worshippers. Believers often pick them up and carry them into the church. The snakes crawl up to the main icon of the Virgin Mary and rest upon it until the service is finished. The people approach and kiss the icon, while the snakes are resting upon it, after which the snakes leave the church and cannot be caught. This annual miracle commemorates an event long ago when pirates landed and attempted to rob and kill the nuns of the monastery on the hill. The Abbess prayed fervently to the Virgin Mary, Mother of God, and, when the pirates reached the top of the hill, they found the monastery filled with snakes, and no nuns to be found. 'Thus we see', says Joanne Stefanatos who recounts the miracle, 'that people and animals share the same *mystery*.'[30]

Such tales resonate with occasional emphases found in ancient Orthodox theology. St Symeon the New Theologian writes:

---

29 Agamben, *The Open*, p. 22.

30 Joanne Stefanatos DVM, *Animals Sanctified: A Spiritual Journey*, Minneapolis MN: Light and Life Publishing Company, 2001, p. 92.

Just as a bronze vessel that has become old and useless, becomes new again when a metal-worker melts it in the fire and recasts it, in the same way also the creation, having become old and useless because of our sins, will be as it were melted in the fire by God the Creator and recast, and will appear new, incomparably brighter than it is now. Do you see how all creatures are to be renewed by fire?[31]

The triune God gave all these creatures to Adam and Eve and fore-ordained before the creation of the world that they should not remain in corruption but might be renewed together with humankind.

Just as in the beginning, first the whole creation was created incorrupt, and then from it man was taken and made, so also it is fitting that again first of all the creation should become incorrupt, and then the corrupt-ible bodies of men should be renewed and become incorrupt.[32]

All created beings are bearers of the divine logoi and revelatory of his meaning.

Animals and the cosmological role of the Virgin Mary

So far, our study of Orthodox iconography has challenged Gray's sum-mary of how Western metaphysics has understood what it is to be human by means of an oppositional distinction with animals. We have also refuted Agamben's charge that (Orthodox) Christian eschatology leaves non-human animal life as an unredeemed and unredeemable remnant. The work has not been easy and we are struggling still with the incon-gruity in the divine economy between human and non-human animals. So far, however, we have seen that these icons speak in symbols that signify the interconnectedness of all things in God and of the hope of the transfiguration of humanity towards reconciliation with the sacredness of the non-human, non-technological world. They do not yield as directly as we might wish truths that help us to envisage how the transfiguration of the world in Christ entails the renewal of material creation, including ani-mal and plant life. This concluding section asks if Orthodox iconography

---

31 St Symeon the New Theologian, *The First-Created Man: Seven Homilies by St Symeon the New Theologian*, trans. Fr Seraphim Rose, from the Russian edition of St Theophan the Recluse, Platina CA: St Herman of Alaska Brotherhood, ET 2001, p. 101.

32 St Symeon the New Theologian, *The First-Created Man*, p. 100.

yields more to assist our spiritual struggles at a time of ecological crisis. Mindful of Gregory of Nyssa's synthesis of material from diverse books of the Bible in order to construct a continuous narrative, we return to icons of the last judgement to probe related intellectual, spiritual and moral concerns (*theoria*).

This time our eyes are drawn to the symmetry of the entire form of these icons and again to the imagery of the circles. We look in particular at the circles of white and gold set over against those enclosing the grey, sin-weary earth and the beasts in Daniel's vision. These circles represent paradise and surround the Virgin enthroned and attended by angels, oftentimes with the patriarchs Abraham, Isaac and Jacob to her left and the Good Thief to her right. The Virgin's throne represents a cosmological role exercised from the garden. In Orthodox churches from the late fourth century where the Virgin Mary is depicted in the apse immediately above the altar, somewhere, as Chryssavgis observes, between heaven and earth, 'She constitutes the bridge and the link between the One who creates and *contains all things* (Christ the *Pantokrator*) and the world.'[33] In these icons, by virtue of her God-given role in the economy of salvation, she also sits as a bridge uniting celibacy and motherhood, spiritual and material, celestial and terrestial, temporal and eternal. In the fifteenth-century icon of the last judgement in the Cathedral of the Dormition, Moscow Kremlin Museums, groups of the righteous, including the apostles Peter and Paul, approach the gates of paradise by which she sits.[34] The righteous are headed not only towards the city of Jerusalem but towards the garden of Eden from which non-human animals were never expelled. In other words, the apparently simple dynamic of the icon as a movement upward toward the New Jerusalem is disrupted internally by the tension between differently articulated hopes. These gold- or white-coloured circles recall that paradise awaits Adam and Eve's return.

Cutting across the hope of the New Jerusalem for those akin (*oikeois*) to the divine incorporeality and invisibility is the hope of return to the garden that non-human animals never left. As the Virgin Mother, Mary brings opposites into unity by reminding us that everything material is created by the Spirit of God, and that the immanence of God in creation is the basis of its intelligibility and hope. Her eternal fecundity represents

---

33 John Chryssavgis, *Beyond the Shattered Image*, Minneapolis MN: Light and Life Publishing Company, 1999, p. 145.

34 E.g., in the fifteenth-century icon of the last judgement in the Cathedral of the Dormition, Moscow Kremlin Museums, inv. no. 3225, reproduced in Smirnova, *Moscow Icons*, p. 113.

the earth as a manifold, material reality that bears the seed of God. As the 'Mater' who gave birth to the Christ-child, she here represents the entirety of the created order in which the divine Logos eternally takes flesh.[35] In the dynamic narrative of this part of the icon, the direction of change is not toward non-human animals becoming more 'knowing' like humans, or left unredeemed because they lack rationality, but toward humans becoming truly animal again. The non-human animal zone of knowledge does not mean in these circles that non-human animals are unsavable, an unredeemable remnant of the flesh of creation. Rather, the Virgin Mary's encompassing of duality suggests that Adam and Eve might once again be reconciled with their animal nature. As *Theotochos* (God-receiver) and *Christotokos* (bearer of the Word as human), she encompassed the ultimate duality. As the queen of heaven enthroned in a garden, she signifies the integrity of human life not in its elevation to the perfection of its rationality but in its return to the true animality of its creation *imago Dei*.

Seated in the garden of paradise without the Christ-child, at the same level as the circles enclosing the grey earth and the beasts in Daniel's vision – in the zone of created beings and not at the level of the cosmic Christ in glory – the Virgin Mother's material reality is witness to the immanence of God in all creation. In her, the material and physical concelebrates with heaven. She waits with non-human animals to receive Adam and Eve as they return to union with their animality that does *not* 'know good and evil' like the gods (Gen. 3.5 NRSV, alternative reading) and is therefore not condemned to corruption. Feminist theologians, especially Protestants, often hesitate before speaking about Mary because of the impossible ideal of virgin-mother that she is thought to represent for women, and because this impossible ideal is mapped with reference to Eve's (woman's) supposed responsibility for the entry of sin into the world. In these icons, it is through the cosmological role of the Virgin Mother that we learn something about the hope of heaven – less in terms of human release from the animality of life than of reconciliation with it.

Again, this mariological emphasis might not be the answer expected or sought. At the least, however, Orthodox icons require us to ask questions about the relation between human and non-human animals in ways that, to borrow a phrase from Agamben, recognize that 'the caesura between the human and the animal passes first of all within man'.[36] Whatever else

---

35 I draw here on Chryssavgis' words, in turn derived from Philip Sherrard, *Human Image, World Image: The Death and Resurrection of Sacred Cosmology*, Cambridge: Golgonooza Press, 1992, pp. 176ff.

36 Agamben, *The Open*, p. 16.

might be said, human creation *imago Dei* includes our materiality, physicality and animality. Furthermore, the uncertainty of what separates us is increasingly the place to relearn ways of living without setting 'the anthropological machine into action'; the 'Shabbat of both animal and man'.[37] In the meantime, Gray is not alone in tracing the core of the environmental problem to the hearts and minds of human persons. 'Technical progress', he writes, 'leaves only one problem unsolved: the frailty of human nature. Unfortunately that problem is insoluble.'[38] It remains to be seen whether he is correct.

---

37 Agamben, *The Open*, p. 92.
38 Gray, *Straw Dogs*, p. 15.

Part Two

SYSTEMATIC APPROACHES

4

The Redemption of Animals in an Incarnational Theology

DENIS EDWARDS

How does the Christ-event, the life, death and resurrection of Jesus relate to the world of animals? In Revelation there is a remarkable vision of all the creatures of Earth united in a great song of praise of the Lamb, the symbol of the crucified and risen Christ:

> Then I heard every creature in heaven and on earth and under the earth and in the sea, and all that is in them, singing, 'To the one seated on the throne and to the Lamb be blessing and honor and glory and might for ever and ever!' And the four living creatures said, 'Amen!' And the elders fell down and worshiped. (Rev. 5.13–14)

The animals, insects and fish of our planet are imagined as sharing in the resurrection of the Lamb and joining in the great cosmic liturgy. That there is a real connection between Christ's life, death and resurrection and the whole creation is made clear in the range of New Testament texts, many influenced by Wisdom motifs, which speak of the creation and reconciliation of *all things* in Christ (1 Cor. 8.6; Rom. 8.18–25; Col. 1.15–20; Eph. 1.9–10, 20–23; Heb. 1.2–3; 2 Peter 3.13; John 1.1–14; Rev. 21.1–5; 22.13). Today the challenge is to think more explicitly about animals and their participation in salvation in Christ.

In exploring this issue, I will use the word redemption, like the word salvation, in the wide sense of transformation in Christ, rather than in the limited sense of forgiveness of human sin. For humans, liberation from sin is a central dimension of what constitutes redemption, but it is not all of redemption. As well as forgiveness, redemption/salvation involves healing, reconciliation, fulfilment, liberation from death, resurrection life, transformation in Christ, and communion in the life of the trinitarian God with all God's creation.

In what follows, I will begin by proposing the need today for a more universal theory of redemption. Then, as the central part of this work, I will attempt a re-reading of what I take to be the classical statement of redemption through incarnation, in the work of Athanasius. Finally, I will suggest that this kind of incarnational theology provides the basis for seeing kangaroos and chimpanzees, kookaburras and dolphins as participating in redemption in Christ.

Rethinking redemption

For many today, the theology of redemption is something of a scandal. On the basis, perhaps, of half-remembered sermons, or a general impression of what Christians believe, they associate it with a vengeful and violent God who demands appeasement. In this context theologians have found the need to rethink the theology of redemption and it seems that we are at the beginning of a much-needed renewal in this fundamental area of Christian theology.

The New Testament uses a variety of images for what God does for us in Christ. Paul, for example, uses ten different images – justification, salvation, reconciliation, expiation, redemption, freedom, sanctification, transformation, new creation and glorification.[1] Each has its value and limitations. In a recent book, Peter Schmiechen makes a helpful distinction between images and theories of redemption.[2] Images can exist alongside each other, with each providing a partial insight into the Christ-event, without necessarily forming a coherent whole. In a theory, an image or concept becomes the cornerstone for a coherent interpretation of Jesus' life, death and resurrection that carries meaning for us and for our world today.

I am convinced that twenty-first-century Christians are in need of a theory of redemption that can offer a viable alternative to theories such as those built around sacrifice, satisfaction and substitutionary atonement. An appropriate theology of redemption for today will be one that communicates the meaning of the Christ-event in a way that is faithful to the central Christian tradition and that is coherent and life-giving for believers in the twenty-first century. It will be one that refuses to locate

1 See Joseph A. Fitzmyer, 'Pauline Theology', in Raymond E. Brown, Joseph A. Fitzmyer and Roland E. Murphy (eds), *The New Jerome Biblical Commentary*, London: Geoffrey Chapman, 1990, pp. 1397–401.
2 Peter Schmeichen, *Saving Power: Theories of Atonement and Forms of the Church*, Grand Rapids MI: Eerdmans, 2005, p. 5.

violence in God, but reveals redemption as the act of the God proclaimed in the words and deeds of Jesus. It will be a theory that includes the biological world as well as the world of matter. I will work towards such a theology in two steps. First, I will propose a theory of redemption through incarnation, based on a re-reading of Athanasius. Then I will begin to sketch how this kind of incarnational theology might be extended to include kangaroos and chimpanzees, kookaburras and dolphins.

Redemption and deification through incarnation in Athanasius

Athanasius (*c.*296–373) faced issues far different from those which confront twenty-first-century ecological theology. As bishop of the great city of Alexandria, his life was dominated by commitment to what he saw as the integrity of Christian faith, in the midst of the politics of the empire, a schism in his local church with the Melitians, and his fierce controversy with the Arians. He spent 17 years of his 46 as bishop in exile. Because of the Arian conflict, he was constantly defending Nicaea's teaching that the Word is not a creature, insisting over and over again that it is truly God who embraces creation in the Word made flesh. I will highlight three aspects of Athanasius' incarnational theology, the God–creation relationship, the centrality of Christ's death and resurrection in his view of the incarnation and his theology of deification.

The God–creation relationship

Athanasius sees the created world as 'both very fragile and most wonderful'.[3] It has a goodness, beauty and harmony that come from the continual presence and creative action of divine Wisdom. Athanasius uses 'Wisdom' and 'Image' as alternative ways of speaking of the eternal 'Word'. Athanasius' approach to creation is sacramental: we are called to treat creation with love and to venerate it as bearing the imprint of God's own Wisdom.[4] He sees Wisdom as revealed to us in a number of ways, in creation, in the depths of our own souls and above all in Christ:

> [God] placed in each and every creature and in the totality of creation a certain imprint (*typon*) and reflection of the Image of Wisdom . . . We become recipients of the Creator-Wisdom, and through her we are

---

3 Alvyn Pettersen, *Athanasius*, London: Geoffrey Chapman, 1995, p. 25.
4 Pettersen, *Athanasius*, pp. 35, 46.

enabled to know her Father . . . God has made the true Wisdom herself take flesh and become a mortal human being and endure the death of the cross, so that henceforth all those that put their faith in him may be saved.[5]

Because God desires to make God's self known in an unambiguous way, the Wisdom we encounter in the creation and in our souls is made flesh in Jesus. In Athanasius' work more generally there is a fourfold structure of revelation: Wisdom comes to us in creation, in one's soul, in the Bible, and finally in the bodily humanity of Jesus. There is always an inner link between creation and incarnation in this theology:

Athanasius's stress upon Christ as the Wisdom of God and upon creatures as witnessing to the Agent of their creation encourages one to see a strong continuity and not discontinuity between God's work as Creator and Redeemer . . . It invokes in one the memory that salvation is to include this world.[6]

Athanasius' view of the relationship between God and creation finds expression in his double foundational work, *Against the Greeks* and *On the Incarnation*. Early in this work he tells us that God is 'beyond all being' and beyond all conception, and is the generous source of all created being.[7] Creatures, on the other hand, exist *ex nihilo*, not only in terms of their origin, but at every moment of their existence. They derive from non-being and tend towards disintegration and nothingness. In the divine generosity, God continually enables creatures to exist by the Word:

So seeing that all created nature according to its own definition is in a state of flux and dissolution . . . after making everything by his eternal Word and bringing creation into existence, he did not abandon it to be carried away and to suffer through its own nature, lest it run the risk of returning to nothing. But being good, he governs and establishes the whole world through his Word who is himself God, in order that creation, illuminated by the leadership, providence, and ordering of the Word, may be able to remain firm.[8]

5 *Orations against the Arians*, 2.78. The translation is from Khaled Anatolios, *Athanasius*, London and New York: Routledge, 2004, pp. 171–4.

6 Pettersen, *Athanasius*, pp. 51–2.

7 Athanasius, *Against the Greeks*, 2 translated in Robert Thompson (ed. and trans.), *Athanasius: Contra Gentes and De Incarnatione*, London: Oxford University Press, 1971.

8 *Against the Greeks*, 41 (Thompson, p. 115).

Every creature in the universe is held in being by the Word of God. The Word is the agent of what we would call today continuous creation. In this universal context, Athanasius focuses his attention on human beings. The God who is good and generous, 'who envies nothing its existence' and 'makes everything through his Word, our Lord Jesus Christ', does something unique for human creatures:

> And among these creatures, of all those on earth he has special pity for the human race, and seeing that by the definition of its own existence it would be unable to persist forever, he gave it an added grace, not simply creating the human like all irrational animals on the Earth, but making them in his own image and giving them also a share in the power of his own Word, so that having as it were shadows of the Word and being made rational, they might be able to remain in felicity and live the true life in paradise, which is truly that of the saints.[9]

In creating human beings, God gives them a special grace, a participation in the image of the Word, which means that unlike other creatures they will not die but live in God. For Athanasius, nature and grace both refer to God's creation of the human. While nature refers to our orientation to nothingness, grace constitutes us in the image of the Word and gives us eternal life.[10] Human sin destroys this structure of creation, and God responds with a new creation. Both creation and new creation are the work of the same eternal Word.[11] While sin is a fall and a descent, the incarnation that culminates in Christ's death and resurrection is a divine descent that 'accompanies, supplants, and reverses human fallenness, even while reasserting the divine glory that was manifest in the act of creation'.[12]

There is a structural relationship between Athanasius' view of the God–creation relationship and his theology of incarnation. At the centre of the debate with Arians is the question: Does the Word belong to the world of creatures, or to God? While the Arians appeared to locate the Word on the side of creation, Athanasius defends the divinity of the Word and locates the Word in God. Because the Word who becomes incarnate is truly God, God and creation meet in Christ so that creation is trans-

---

9 Athanasius, *On the Incarnation*, 3 (Thompson, p. 141, modified).
10 Anatolios, *Athanasius*, 42.
11 Athanasius, *On the Incarnation*, 1 (Thompson, p. 137).
12 Anatolios, *Athanasius*, p. 51.

formed and taken into the life of God. *The saving act of incarnation is precisely about the union of God and creation in Jesus Christ.* As Anatolios puts it, the relation between God and creation is 'the architectonic centre of Athanasius's theological vision'.[13] For Athanasius, the understanding of God and creation is directly christological. His account of the relation between God and creation is thus ultimately 'a Christology conceived in the most universal terms'.[14]

Death and resurrection in Athanasius' view of the incarnation

The incarnation, for Athanasius, is not centred on the beginning of Jesus' life. It involves the whole event of the Word made flesh. Death is central to his view of creaturely existence, and his incarnational theology is particularly focused on the way God enters into death in Christ and transforms it in the resurrection. The defeat of death and corruption is at the centre of the saving work of the incarnation. The Word takes bodily humanity, the body damaged by sin and doomed to death, in order to renew in humanity the image of the Word and to bring resurrection life:

> So the Word of God came in his own person, in order that, as he is the image of the Father, he might be able to restore the human who is the image. In any other way it could not have been done, without the destruction of death and corruption. So he was justified in taking a mortal body, in order that in it death could be destroyed and human beings might be again renewed in the image. For this, then, none other than the image of the Father was required.[15]

While God might have saved us from sin by an external decree, this would have returned us to an original state where we might fall again. In Christ something radically new occurs: the divine goodness transforms our humanity from within, securing our future in God.[16] We are saved by the Word entering into bodiliness, deformed by sin and become subject to death, so that death is defeated from within and we are bound securely to the life of God.

---

13 Anatolios, *Athanasius*, p. 39.
14 Anatolios, *Athanasius*, p. 40.
15 Athanasius, *On the Incarnation*, 13 (Thompson, p. 167, modified).
16 Athanasius, *Orations against the Arians*, 2.68.

In Athanasius' view, while God's goodness wants our salvation and life, God's truthfulness cannot simply ignore the decree that stated that 'death and corruption' would be the consequences of sin.[17] Sin and death need to be transformed. This transformation occurs in the incarnation, above all in the death and resurrection of Jesus. Athanasius uses sacrificial language for the death of Christ, influenced by the New Testament, and also, it seems, by the Eucharist. Jesus, the Word of God, 'intercedes' for us, 'offering' his own body as a 'sacrifice' and a 'ransom' for human sin, thus liberating humanity from its descent into death.[18] In the death and resurrection of the Word made flesh, humanity attains ultimate security and stability in communion with God.

The radically ontological nature of this transformation is made clear by the way Athanasius speaks of creatures being made 'proper' to God or 'appropriated to God' in Christ. In his trinitarian theology, he uses the word *idios*, meaning 'belonging to' or 'proper to', in order to show that the Son belongs to the very being of the Father. He uses the same kind of language to speak of the ontological transformation of humanity that occurs in Christ. Through the enfleshed Word, we are made proper to God or appropriated to God, so that we belong to God in the most radical way.[19] We are adopted into God's life and are changed at the deepest level of our being.

Deification through incarnation

Particularly in his later writings, Athanasius uses the word deification to speak of this ontological transformation. The first time this word appears in his work in a Christian sense is the well-known exchange formula in *On the Incarnation* 54: 'For he became human that we might become divine.'[20] Athanasius is clearly building on Irenaeus: 'He became what we are in order to make us what he is in himself.'[21] Athanasius goes on to use the language of deification freely in his *Discourses against the Arians*. In a recent, thorough monograph on deification in the Greek patristic tradition, Norman Russell points out that in all of the 30 instances where

---

17 Athanasius, *On the Incarnation*, 3.
18 Athanasius, *On the Incarnation*, 10 (Anatolios, *Athanasius*, p. 59).
19 See Anatolios, *Athanasius*, pp. 66–74.
20 Thompson (trans.), *Against the Greeks*, pp. 268–9 (modified).
21 Irenaeus, *Adversus Haereses* 5, Praef. See Norman Russell, *The Doctrine of Deification in the Greek Patristic Tradition*, Oxford: Oxford University Press, 2004, p. 169.

Athanasius speaks of Christian deification, he uses only the verb *theopoieō* and the noun he coins, *theopoiēsis*.[22]

Athanasius gives priority to an ontological rather than to an ethical notion of deification. In an ethical approach, closeness to God is thought of as occurring through living a Christian life, and deification is seen more in terms of a process. But what Athanasius emphasizes is the radical change that occurs when the Word is made flesh. This brings about a change in the very *being* (the ontology) of creation. For Athanasius, there is a transformation already at work in the world in the event of the incarnation itself. Through the flesh assumed by the Logos, God communicates divine life to all flesh *in principle*. I will propose that this event has practical meaning for the whole creation.

It is clear that Athanasius sees deification for human beings as transmitted *in practice* in the life of the Spirit, and as working through faith and the sacraments of the Church. It is important to insist that for him, and for the whole patristic tradition, deification never means that we become divine in the sense of possessing the divine nature. It means that, by God's grace, the Spirit of God dwells in us and we become adopted children of God (Rom. 8.14–17). Through this indwelling Spirit we participate in divine life, so that the Scripture can speak of us as 'participants of the divine nature' (2 Peter 1.4). We are taken into the life of the Trinity. This is understood as a real transformation in God, a real participation in God by grace.

In the once-for-all ontological transformation that occurs in the incarnation, the body of Jesus is the instrument (*organon*) for the salvation of all. The flesh is the *organon* of salvation, although *sarx* in Athanasius stands for the whole human nature, soul as well as body.[23] Athanasius has little to say about the soul of Christ, but as Russell notes, his physical emphasis is a helpful antidote to the intellectualism of Origen, even if it needs the completion that would come with Cyril of Alexandria.[24] It is precisely Athanasius' emphasis on the flesh that can, I believe, find new meaning today in a theology of the redemption of all flesh in the incarnation of divine Wisdom.

Athanasius opposes the Arian view that the Word of God is deified. He insists that the Word is the source of deification and is not subject to deification. He points out that even in the past, long before the birth of the Saviour, the Word of God was the source of deification. It is through the

22 Russell, *Doctrine of Deification*, p. 168.
23 Russell, *Doctrine of Deification*, p. 186.
24 Russell, *Doctrine of Deification*, 188.

eternal Word that Moses and others were long ago adopted and deified as children of God.[25] Athanasius, however, does see a very important deification at work in the incarnation. It is a deification, not of the Word, but of the bodily humanity of Jesus. This deification of the created flesh of Christ is fundamental to our salvation: 'The Word was not diminished in receiving a body, that he should seek to receive a grace, but rather he deified that which he put on, and moreover bestowed it freely on the human race.'[26] The Word of God takes on fallen flesh and as a result we share in his deified flesh. The body of Christ was prepared 'that in him we might be capable of being renewed and deified'.[27]

For Athanasius, there is a solidarity in the flesh: what is deified is both the body of Christ and our fleshly humanity. The Logos assumes a created human body 'that having renewed it as its creator, he might deify it in himself, and thus bring us all into the kingdom of heaven in his likeness'.[28] Later Athanasius writes:

> For if the works of the Word's divinity had not taken place through the body, humanity would not have been deified; and again, if the properties of the flesh had not been ascribed to the Word, humans would not have delivered completely from them.[29]

Anatolios comments: 'Our whole salvation and deification are rooted in our human condition's being "ascribed" to the Word, for that is what essentially constitutes our being "Worded"'.[30]

In his *First Letter to Serapion*, Athanasius focuses his attention on the Holy Spirit. Having argued vigorously for the divinity of the Word, he now argues in a similar way for the divinity of the Spirit. Since it is by the Spirit that we become 'partakers of the divine nature' (2 Peter 1.4), the Spirit who divinizes us must be divine.[31] In the context of articulating his theology of the Spirit, Athanasius speaks of *creation* being deified in the Spirit through the Logos. He writes of the Holy Spirit:

---

25 Athanasius, *Orations against the Arians*, 1.39.
26 Athanasius, *Orations against the Arians*, 1. 42 (Russell, p. 171).
27 Athanasius, *Orations against the Arians*, 2.47 (Russell, p. 171).
28 Athanasius, *Orations against the Arians*, 2.70 (Russell, p. 172).
29 Athanasius, *Orations against the Arians*, 3.33 (Russell, p. 173).
30 Khaled Anatolios, *Athanasius: The Coherence of His Thought*, London and New York: Routledge, 1998, p. 143.
31 Athanasius, *First Letter to Serapion*, 1.25.

In him (the Holy Spirit), then, the Logos glorifies creation, and deifying it and adopting it brings it to the Father. That which unites creation to the Logos cannot itself belong to the created order. And that which adopts creation cannot be foreign to the Son . . . the Spirit does not belong to the created order, but is proper to the Godhead of the Father, in whom the Logos also deifies created things. And he in whom creation is deified cannot himself be outside the divinity of the Father.[32]

This text is remarkable not only because it is an early defence of the full divinity of the Holy Spirit, but also because it speaks of the creation being deified and adopted. The Holy Spirit unites creation to the Word. The adoption and deification of creation is the work of the Word and the Spirit together and both are equally divine. It may be when Athanasius speaks of creation in this text, humanity is still at the forefront of his mind. But there is an openness here to a more universal development of thought, to the idea that in some way the whole creation is adopted and deified in Christ.

This is confirmed in a text where we find Athanasius insisting that Christ will be 'the firstborn of *all* creation' in reference to Colossians 1.15, and that 'creation *itself*' will be delivered from the bondage of corruption into the glorious freedom of the children of God in reference to Romans 8.19–20.[33] Although Athanasius does not focus much attention on the redemption of non-human creation, not only is his system of thought, redemption through incarnation, open to this development, but occasionally he makes it clear that he assumes, with Colossians 1.15–20 and Romans 8.18–23, that the whole creation will in some way share with human beings in final redemption. In what follows I will build on his broad and inclusive theology of redemptive incarnation towards a more explicit theology of the redemption of animals.

Elements for a twenty-first-century theology of the redemption of animals

While Athanasius' focus was the defence of the divinity of the Word against his Arian opponents, a twenty-first-century theology finds itself confronted by a human-induced crisis of the community of life on Earth, and the need to develop an ecological theology that is also a theology of

32 Athanasius, *First Letter to Serapion*, 1.25 (Russell, p. 175).
33 *Orations against the Arians*, 2.63. See Anatolios, *Athanasius*, pp. 156–7.

animals. There are differences not only in context, but also in theological assumptions, particularly with regard to the cause of human death. Athanasius assumed a reading of Genesis in which human beings were originally preserved from death by the grace of God and then lost this gift by wilfully turning from God in sin. Along with other theologians, I see the narrative of the fall as offering an account of the sin that confronts us, from our origin, in the violence of our history, in our social structures, and in the depth of our own beings, but differ from Athanasius in seeing biological death not as the result of sin but as part of human participation in the evolutionary community of life. But there is no doubt that sin distorts our approach to death and inflicts death on a massive scale to human beings and to other creatures.

While differences in context and in assumptions need to be taken into account, I believe that a theory of redemption through incarnation in the tradition of Athanasius can provide meaning today, in a theology of salvation that includes humans and other animals. The following eight elements might contribute to the beginning of such a theology:

1 Salvation through incarnation is a coherent theory of redemption, one that can communicate the meaning of the Christ-event in a new time. As a theory, it offers a viable alternative to theories of redemption based on satisfaction, substitutionary atonement and sacrifice. It has the great advantage of bringing into focus the overwhelming and unthinkable generosity of God. It presents redemption as a divine act of self-bestowal rather than as something that changes God. God gives God's self to us in the Word made flesh and in the Spirit poured out in grace. The Word enters into the world of flesh, that in the Spirit the community of fleshly life might be forgiven, healed, freed from violence, reconciled, and find its fulfilment in the life of God.

2 Redemption through incarnation is a theory of redemption cast in the most universal terms, those of creation and God. As a theory, it is not limited to a focus on human sin, although it certainly embraces liberation from sin. In a theory based on Athanasius' theology of incarnation, the relationship between God and God's creation is the *architectonic centre* of the theology of salvation in Christ. In this theology, creation and incarnation are united in a theology of Wisdom/Word: it is through the Wisdom of God that living creatures flourish on Earth in all their diverse forms, from bacteria to whales and human beings; it is this same divine Wisdom who becomes flesh, with a limited, specific body and the particular face of

Jesus, embracing bodily existence and death in love, and transforming death into life.

In Jesus of Nazareth, anointed by the Spirit and led by the Spirit, Wisdom dwells in the finitude of illness, pain and bodily limits, as a presence of boundless, personal, self-giving, compassionate and radically forgiving love. Jesus the Wisdom of God announces salvation, the coming reign of God, a realm of non-violence, of justice and of peace. He is rejected and resisted with all the violence available to the Roman state, yet freely pours out love in death itself, and God transforms this violent death into the beginning of life for the whole creation.

3 'All things', including every wallaby, dog and dolphin, are created through the eternal Wisdom of God, and redeemed and reconciled through Wisdom made flesh in Christ. The structure of Athanasius' theology can be extended today in a more explicit theology of the redemption of animals. As I suggested earlier, a foundation for this claim can be found in a number of texts, including Romans 8.18–25 and Colossians 1.15–20. In the theological approach proposed here, the solidarity of the flesh in the doctrine of the incarnation is not limited to the human community. Flesh is understood as involving the whole 3.8 billion-year evolutionary history of life on our planet, with all its predation, death and extinctions, as well as its diversity, co-operation, interdependence and abundance. Flesh involves all the interconnected ecological relationships that make up life on our planet. The proposal being made is that the Christ-event is saving not only for human beings, but also in some real way for other creatures, including dogs and horses and eagles. We 'wait for a new heaven and new earth, where righteousness is at home' (2 Peter 3.13) and where all God's creation finds its fulfilment. But the question remains: what does it mean to speak of Christ bringing salvation to other creatures? How does it take effect? A first but only partial answer is that it changes human beings in their relationships to other creatures.

4 In Christ's death and resurrection, human competition, exclusion and violence are transformed by redemptive non-violent love. In this section I am proposing that the theory of redemptive incarnation can be brought into creative dialogue with Raymund Schwager's very different evolutionary theology of original sin and salvation.[34] Schwager sees early

---

34 Raymund Schwager, *Banished from Eden: Original Sin and Evolutionary Theory in the Drama of Salvation*, Leominster: Gracewing, 2006. Schwager builds on insights of René

human beings as surviving and flourishing in a competitive environment by building social relations, and in the process diverting the aggressive potential of their group outwards against a victim or a common enemy (the scapegoat mechanism).[35] Sin takes the form of violence and exclusion. Not only co-operation and community, but also exclusion and aggression, are selected for in human biological history. A tendency to sin and violence has become part of human genetic inheritance.

In such a world Jesus appears, sent by God and empowered by the Spirit to bring healing and liberation. He proclaims a realm in which violence and sin are overcome through non-violence and love of the enemies. What is required is a faith in God's grace that can move mountains. Conversion is the proper response to Jesus' proclamation of the reign of God. It represents God's way of salvation and grace. But the call to conversion is rejected and Jesus himself is cast out and killed with extreme violence. Jesus does not strike back, but allows himself to be hit by the collective violence of his enemies, giving his life in fidelity to God and in non-violent love for others, including those who persecute him.

God does not directly will the violent and evil act of crucifixion, but takes it up, transforming it in the power of the Spirit to be the means of salvation. Jesus gives himself in love, in a profound yes to God and is raised up by God as the principle of resurrection life for all. In Jesus' death and resurrection, 'God uncovers and overcomes the whole subliminal, violent and repressed past of humanity.'[36] Through the sending of the Holy Spirit Jesus' disciples are formed and sent as a community of salvation. As sin is built into communal life, so non-violent liberating love is to be lived out in community. This is a task not only for the Church, but ultimately for the whole of humanity.[37]

Schwager notes that there are parallels between the behaviour practised by humans and some other animals: both share the double morality of altruism towards one's own group and aggression towards those outside.[38] This theology of original sin and redemption offers a way of seeing the Christ-event as radically liberating not only in the context of our experience of personal sin but also in the context of evolutionary history. The competition of natural selection does not have the last word. The

---

Girard. See Schwager, *Jesus in the Drama of Salvation: Towards a Biblical Doctrine of Redemption*, New York: Crossroad, 1999.

35 Schwager, *Banished from Eden*, p. 53.
36 Schwager, *Banished from Eden*, pp. 70–1.
37 Schwager, *Banished from Eden*, p. 107.
38 Schwager, *Banished from Eden*, p. 97.

truth of God, the ultimate truth about creation, is revealed in Christ as non-violent self-bestowing love.

In so far as the human community lives in the redemptive way of non-violent love, this will radically change human interaction with all other animals, and with the whole planetary community of life. The human community is called to a truly redemptive interaction with its fellow creatures. In so far as human beings respond to this call, this becomes one way in which the Christ-event can be understood as bringing redemption to animals, among other important ways taken up below.

5 In the light shed by the cross, God can be understood as redemptively involved with the evolutionary history of life on Earth, and as the faithful companion of the lives and deaths of individual creatures. In this and the next section, I will propose extending Athanasius' theory of redemptive incarnation so that it explicitly includes God's response to the suffering of animals. Pain and suffering have become an integral part of evolutionary history with the emergence of creatures with neurons. As Holmes Royston says, suffering is 'the shadow side of sentience, felt experience, consciousness, pleasure, intention, all the excitement of subjectivity waking up so inexplicably from mere objectivity'.[39] The only way to consciousness, as far as we know, is through flesh 'that can feel its way through that world'.[40] In this process, pain is eminently useful in survival and it will be naturally selected on average. Pain that is not useful for survival will tend to be eliminated by natural selection. Pain and struggle can be seen as the other side of prolific creativity in the story of life.

In Jesus, in his life and death, God embraces the pain of the world, suffering with suffering creation. In the resurrection, death is in principle transformed into life. The Christ-event reveals a God who not only feels *with* suffering creation, but who is already at work transforming suffering of every creature into life. It points to something that is not obvious from a reflection on creation in all its beauty and ambiguity – that God is a God of boundless and overwhelming love and compassion, a compassion that reaches out to every human being and to every sparrow that falls to the ground (Matt. 10.29; Luke 12.6). The compassion that we humans sometimes feel for this or that creature can be but a pale reflection of the intensity of the divine feeling for individual creatures.

---

39 Holmes Rolston III, *Genesis, Genes and God: Values and Their Origins in Natural and Human History*, Cambridge: Cambridge University Press, 1999, p. 303.

40 Rolston, *Genesis, Genes and God*, p. 304.

The presence of God in the Spirit to each creature is the presence of boundless love. Each entity in the universe exists only because it is embraced by the Creator in the relationship of ongoing creation. This divine act of creation is an act of love (Wisd. 11.24—12.1). In the Spirit, God is present to every creature in the universe, accompanying each with love. God really does know every sparrow that falls to the ground (Matt. 10.29; Luke 12.6). God is with every sparrow, every beetle, every Great White shark, every creature hunting another for food and every creature that is the prey of another.

Paul tells us that creation waits with 'eager longing' for its liberation from 'bondage to decay' and for 'the freedom associated with the glory of the children of God' (Rom. 8.19–23). In the light of Christ, the pain of creation can be seen as the pain of giving birth to the new: 'For we know that the entire creation has been groaning together in the pangs of childbirth up till now' (Rom. 8.22). The Creator Spirit is not only the companion of creation in its travail but the midwife to the birth of the new, groaning with creation in its labour and rejoicing with creation the new.[41]

In the light of the cross, Paul sees the whole world of living things as the place of God's redemptive action, and the pain of creation as the pain of creation giving birth. In this light, the struggle and creativity of creation and the lives of individual creatures can be seen as paschal, as being taken up in Christ. Resurrection is revealed as the meaning of the whole creation. The completely unpredictable and unthinkable event of the incarnation reveals that Christ crucified is the 'power and the wisdom of God' (1 Cor. 1.24), but that this is the power and wisdom at work in creation. Because the Wisdom of the cross is the Wisdom at work in creation, the cross can illuminate God's action in creation. It reveals a God who acts not by overpowering but by working in and through the processes of the natural world, suffering with suffering creation and promising the fullness of life.

In the Word made flesh, God embraces the whole labour of life on Earth, with all its evolutionary processes, including death, predation and extinction, in an event that is both a radical identification in love and an unbreakable promise. What does this mean for individual creatures? I think it means two fundamental things: the first, discussed in this section, is that God is with them in love, as loving companion in their struggle and travail; the second, discussed in the next section, is that they will be brought to fulfilment and life.

---

41 I have discussed this in more detail in Edwards, *Breath of Life: A Theology of the Creator Spirit*, Maryknoll NY: Orbis Books, 2004.

6 Animals will reach their redemptive fulfilment in being taken up into the eternal life of the Trinity. In Luke's version of the saying about the sparrow, Jesus says that not one sparrow is 'forgotten before God' (Luke 12.6). I take this as suggesting that every single sparrow can be thought of as inscribed in the divine memory. It is called forth and exists because God loves and remembers it.

In the liturgy of the Church, we remember the wonderful things God has done. Above all, when we celebrate the Eucharist in memory (*anamnēsis*) of Jesus, we are dealing with a remembrance that not only brings to mind the past, but acts powerfully in the present and anticipates an eschatological future. For the Bible, while our memory of God is a fundamental requirement, it is God's remembrance that is primary. God remembers God's covenant with us for ever (Ps. 105.8). We pray that God will hold us in memory (Job 7.7; 10.9; 14.13; Ps. 78.39). We exist because God remembers us and holds us in God's provident care (Ps. 8.4). Alexander Schmemann writes of the biblical concept of divine memory:

> Memory refers to the attentiveness of God to his creation, the power of divine providential love through which God 'holds' the world and *gives it life*, so that life itself can be termed abiding in the memory of God, and death the falling out of this memory. In other words, memory, like everything else in God, is *real*, it is that life that he grants, that God '*remembers*'; it *is* the eternal overcoming of the 'nothing' out of which God called us into 'his wonderful light.'[42]

I think it can be said that God does not forget any creature that God loves and creates, but inscribes it eternally in the divine life. The sparrow that falls to the ground is not abandoned, but is gathered and brought to redemptive new life in Christ, in whom 'creation itself will be set free from its bondage to decay' (Rom. 8.21). The sparrow that falls to the ground is among the 'all things' that are reconciled (Col. 1.20), recapitulated (Eph. 1.10) and made new (Rev. 21.5) in the risen Christ.

We know very little about the *how* of our risen life in Christ, let alone that of other creatures. We hope for what is beyond our capacity to imagine because our hope is in the God who remains always incomprehensible mystery. We hope for what we do not see (Rom. 8.24) and cannot imagine, the transformation of the whole creation in Christ. What we know is

---

42 Alexander Schmemann, *The Eucharist: Sacrament of the Kingdom*, Crestwood NY: St Vladimir's Seminary Press, 1988, p. 125.

the promise of God given in the resurrection of the Word made flesh. We can hope that, in our participation in the communion of saints, we will also participate in God's delight in other animals within the abundance of creation that reaches its fulfilment in God.

In particular we may hope that the relationship we have with particular creatures, such as a beloved dog, does not end with death, but is taken into eternal life. In the incarnational theology being suggested here, each sparrow is known and loved by God, is enabled to exist because of the indwelling Creator Spirit, is eternally inscribed in God, participates in redemption in Christ, and is eternally held and treasured in the life of the Trinity. The creatures that spring from the abundance of divine communion find redemption in being taken up eternally into this communion in a way that we cannot fully articulate.

7 Animals can be thought of as participating, at least in part, in the redemptive way of life revealed in Christ. For the biblical tradition, animals are part of God's good creation. They are thought of as nourished and cared for by the Creator (Ps. 104) and as praising God by their unique existence: 'Praise the Lord from the earth, you sea monsters and all deeps . . . wild animals and all cattle, creeping things and flying birds!' (Ps. 148.7–101). As Athanasius tells us, their goodness and ordered interrelationships exist because of the eternal Wisdom of God. They bear the imprint in their beings of divine Wisdom.

And, as Athanasius also insists, this same Wisdom takes flesh in Jesus. A new way of life is revealed, that of following Jesus who gave his life for others (Phil. 2.5). Michael Northcott points out how the cross determines the moral life of Christians in a particular way: there is a moral priority for the weak that finds expression, however inadequately, in Christian practices in relation to those who are poor, widows, orphans, sick, aged and children.[43] The narrative of Christ's life, death and resurrection gives a particular meaning to the world of bodies, with their fragile and mortal flesh. It makes clear that redemptive life involves community, sharing and priority for the poor and weak.

While this is commonly thought to be the opposite of what occurs in the natural world, particularly in the processes of natural selection, Northcott points to some instances of animals participating in something of this redemptive pattern. Ethologists report, for example, on dolphins living

---

43 Michael S. Northcott, 'Do Dolphins Carry the Cross? Biological Moral Realism and Theological Ethics', *New Blackfriars* 84, 2003, pp. 547–8.

interdependent, nurturing and communal lives. Northcott allows that dolphins can also be violent and self-destructive, but notes that they are perhaps less so than humans. He finds good reasons for humans to love dolphins:

> They are in their exuberant playfulness, and richly communicative and intelligent lives, exemplars of a generous God who shared godlike qualities of community and intelligence well beyond those whom the Christian community has traditionally said were exclusively made in the image of God.[44]

An incarnational theology, then, would not only agree with Athanasius that we can see in animals and their behaviours a reflection of God and a participation in God through the creative presence of God's Wisdom and life-giving Spirit. It could also find, with Northcott, that there are instances, such as in a dolphin's care for the vulnerable, of what we know, although only through Jesus' preaching and practice, death and resurrection, to be a truly redemptive way of living and acting. The Wisdom reflected in dolphins and in their care for one another is the same Wisdom made far more explicit in the flesh in Jesus, and in his cross.

8 Human beings who would live redemptively are called to participate in the healing of the world, through commitment to the flourishing of animals and to ethical relationships with them. A redemptive incarnation that involves all flesh has implications for human practice with regard to other animals. As Christopher Southgate has said, a theology of salvation for today will need to involve the idea that 'humans have a calling, stemming from the transformative power of Christ's action on the Cross, to participate in the healing of the world'.[45] He rightly insists that we human beings have an important role in the redemption of creation. We are responsible to do what we can to heal the harm we have done and to ensure the flourishing of the biodiversity of our planet. Southgate sees the future of humans and the rest of creation as radically interrelated. He suggests that it is only by being humbly involved in the healing of nature that we human beings can become fully alive.

The theological vision of God made flesh clearly involves an ethics based on respect for other animals and on right relations with them. One

---

44 Northcott, 'Do Dolphins Carry the Cross?', pp. 551–2.

45 Christopher Southgate, 'God and Evolutionary Evil: Theodicy in the Light of Darwinism', *Zygon* 37, 2002, p. 817.

of the things that the preaching and practices of Jesus make clear is that his followers are called to be participants and collaborators in the healing, liberation and peace of the coming reign of God. While redemption is always the work of the Word and Spirit, it also always involves our participation. To participate in redemption in the Word made flesh includes an ethical commitment to the well-being of our fellow animals. It will involve us in the search for ethical farming, buying, eating, conservation and political practices.

At a deeper level still it commits us to a spirituality in which other animals have their places as fellow sentient creatures before God. To participate in the life of God is to seek to participate in God's feeling for individual creatures. It involves remembering that every sparrow that falls to the ground is loved and held in the living memory of God.

5

The Way of All Flesh: Rethinking the *Imago Dei*

DAVID S. CUNNINGHAM

What can be rightly said, *theologically*, about the differences between human beings and the other animals? While a wide variety of academic disciplines and discourses may investigate these differences in other ways (biologically, behaviourally or ethically), it is the special province of theology to explore this question with respect to a particular tradition's understanding of God and God's relationship with the created order. Within the Christian tradition (from which I write), as in many other theological traditions, such explorations must always proceed with a certain degree of apophatic reserve; our best understanding of God and God's relationship with the world is extremely limited, and is dependent on God's acts of divine revelation. But with such caveats in mind, we can (and must) continually seek to develop a clearer and fuller theological account of the relationship between humans and other animals.

In this chapter, I wish to raise some critical questions about the traditional interpretation of the Christian doctrine of the *imago Dei* as describing human beings, and human beings alone, as created in the image and likeness of God. I want to suggest that, for a variety of reasons, the *imago Dei* can also describe other elements of the created order – and that, in fact, the entire creation bears the 'mark of the Maker' to at least some degree. This is not to deny, of course, that a wide variety of differing senses of this term might well be attributed to various elements within the created order; but these differences, I believe, will always be matters of degree rather than a simple opposition of inclusion and exclusion from the attribution 'created in the image of God'.

The goal of this chapter, therefore, is to gesture towards a form of theological language that can account for real distinctions within the created order, while avoiding a dichotomous characterization of one (or more) species as created in the image of God, while all others are not. I am convinced that the doctrine of the *imago Dei* has too frequently, and too facilely, been used to postulate that the most important distinction within creation is to be located between human beings and everything else. Such a distinction is artificially imposed; the biblical and theological warrants for this claim are tenuous at best. As an alternative, I will suggest that a more theologically appropriate way of distinguishing among creatures may be discovered through an investigation into the word *flesh*.

My argument therefore will proceed under three headings, each consisting of a single word: *distinction*, *image* and *flesh*. The first section is primarily descriptive, examining and questioning the tendency to construct the most significant distinctions within the created order between human beings and all other creatures. The second section is primarily critical, arguing that the Christian doctrine of the *imago Dei* should not be used to support such a distinction. The third section is constructive (though perhaps, due to its brevity, it would be better to label it 'suggestive'). I want to postulate the word 'flesh' as a more theologically and biblically warranted category for drawing distinctions within the created order. Precisely because the word flesh aligns human beings with a great many other living creatures, it helpfully blurs the boundaries between human beings and other animals. It thereby has the potential of providing us with a considerably stronger foundation for ethical and theological arguments about the relationship between human beings and the rest of the created order.

Distinction

In the first stage of my argument, I want to raise some questions about the definitive distinction between human beings and other animals that seems to be presumed within many theological accounts of the created order. As several chapters in this collection have noted,[1] such distinctions are commonplace in the history of Christian theology; in fact, so obvious does this distinction seem to many theological commentators that they simply never bother to argue the case. We might hypothesize that, in this line of inquiry as in so many others, the theological imagination is often easily overwhelmed by empirical data and by the cultural assumptions under which it operates. In short, human beings are assumed to be radically

---

1 See, in particular, the chapters in Part 1 of this volume.

different from other animals because they look different, they act differently, and they are treated differently. These same indicators are among those that have been used, over the centuries, to render poor theological judgements about the differences between men and women, the distinctions among various races and ethnicities, and the divide between gay and straight people.[2] In all these cases, empirical and cultural judgements were used to bolster, falsely, a claim that a significant *theological* distinction existed between, for example, men and women.[3] Needless to say, this historical tendency does not prove that theologians have overstated the distinction between human beings and other animals; nor (I hasten to add) am I suggesting that the latter distinction is theologically inappropriate to the same degree as those that have sometimes been used, within the human species, to divide people along the lines of sex, race or sexuality. I am simply suggesting that history should make us cautious about too quickly assuming that empirical and cultural distinctions are theologically warranted.

It will therefore behove us to consider whether the hard-and-fast distinction between human beings and other animals has typically been justified along specifically *theological* lines, or whether theologians have tended to rely on other kinds of assumptions. In an essay entitled 'All God's Creatures: Reading Genesis on Human and Non-human Animals',[4] David Clough has suggested that the latter has often seemed to be the case. He suggests that the ease with which this distinction is sometimes proffered is due primarily to theology's traditional reliance on assumptions (typically made within the tradition following Aristotle) about the natural order. The rationale among Aristotelians for placing human beings in a separate category from all other natural beings was based on

---

2 On the connection between the human–animal distinction and racial divisions, see Peter Singer, *Animal Liberation: A New Ethic for Our Treatment of Animals*, London: Jonathan Cape, 1990; for the connection between the human–animal distinction and the construction of gender, see Carol J. Adams, *The Sexual Politics of Meat: A Feminist-Vegetarian Critical Theory*, New York: Continuum, 1990.

3 Thomas Aquinas' well-known assessment of women as 'defective men' is a classic example of this tendency: the assumptions of his day concerning biology, education and culture were granted more weight than was, for example, the New Testament witness concerning the important role of women in the earliest Christian communities, or (for that matter) St Paul's claim that 'there is no longer male and female; for all of you are one in Christ Jesus' (Gal. 3.28) – though clearly, at other points in the canon, St Paul (and/or those who wrote in his name) were just as willing to allow themselves to be influenced by contemporary cultural attitudes towards women.

4 Forthcoming in Stephen Barton and David Wilkinson (eds), *Reading Genesis After Darwin*, Oxford and New York: Oxford University Press, 2008.

his assumption that rational thought and language-use are exclusively human faculties. Even though Aristotle himself may have allowed for other categories of creatures that fell 'between' human and non-human species,[5] the tradition which followed him granted a fairly significant role to rational thought and linguistic competence.

But even if we accept the Aristotelian classification scheme as definitive, a great deal of recent scientific evidence has brought our assumptions about rationality and language-use into question, particularly with respect to other animals. In particular, Clough argues, the work of Charles Darwin raised serious questions about whether the special status of human animals can be constructed as firmly as the Aristotelian tradition had assumed. (Darwin was obviously not the first thinker to raise these questions, but he certainly brought them into much sharper focus than had previously been the case.) Clough argues quite persuasively that, if Christian theology continues to maintain this distinction, it must do so with specifically *theological* arguments – rather than relying on a scientific distinction that has long since fallen out of favour. The point is not that we must believe Darwin rather than Aristotle; the point, rather, is that Darwin has reminded us that we had placed a great deal of faith in Aristotle; that we had done so for so long that we were often not even aware of how thoroughly we relied upon his categories; and that there are certainly many other ways of making an argument about the divisions within the created order.

We might suggest the following analogy: relying on Aristotle's arguments about the special place of humanity within creation would be similar to claiming that the reason that we know that God cares more for the earth than for the other planets is because everything revolves around the earth, just as Ptolemy told us. The alternative proposed by Copernicus does not require us to become Copernicans, but it does provide us an opportunity to ask whether we must necessarily remain Ptolemaists. Moreover, the very introduction of the Copernican alternative can lead us to raise serious questions about how we had hitherto constructed our theological argument. (For example, do we really want to base an argument about God's special care for the earth on the current state of scientific knowledge about the physical position of the earth with respect to the rest of the universe?)

We can generalize the point to some degree, and make the following claim: a shift in scientific thinking need not require us to create a new

_____

5 As noted by Stephen Clark in his chapter in this volume.

argument based on the new science; but it may well behove us to stop basing our arguments on the old science. And this may lead us to observe that we had perhaps been relying rather too heavily upon manifestly a-theological or anti-theological accounts to buttress our (supposedly) theological arguments. The history of ideas provides copious instances of this tendency; theology has, from time to time, placed excessive faith in, for example, the biology of Thomas Aquinas, the politics of John Locke and the economics of Thomas Hobbes.[6] The service provided to Christian theology by the likes of William Harvey, Karl Marx and Wendell Berry is not so much to replace our reliance on the older forms with the newer ones; it is, rather, to force us to ask why we had been so captivated by the older forms in the first place.

Clough's essay explores a number of possible theological justifications for what he calls the 'human-separatist' view, that is, the claim that the most important distinction to be drawn within the created order is the distinction between human beings and everything else. I will not rehearse all his arguments here, but merely commend his essay and summarize its conclusion as follows: that none of the traditionally invoked theological categories for this sharp separation – neither creation, nor election, nor even incarnation – really holds up under close scrutiny.

To Clough's conclusions, we may add another factor: that throughout the narrative of Genesis 1—11, human beings are grouped or categorized with a widely varying range of constellations of the other elements of creation. Certainly, human beings are not always described as being in a category of their own; and, when mentioned in conjunction with other creatures, the groupings are not consistent with one another. This would seem to imply – theologically speaking, at least – that any attempt neatly to divide human beings from other creatures is not nearly so straightforward as some have assumed it to be.

In Genesis 1, for example, the various elements of creation would seem to be divided from one another by their having been created on separate days: first the separation of light from darkness, then of water from dry land, then the creation of the sun and the moon; then fish and fowl. But notice that human beings are not even considered sufficiently distinct to

---

6 On Locke, see William T. Cavanaugh, 'The City: Beyond Secular Parodies', in John Milbank, Catherine Pickstock and Graham Ward (eds), *Radical Orthodoxy: A New Theology*, London and New York: Routledge, 1999; on Hobbes, see M. Douglas Meeks, *God the Economist: The Doctrine of God and Political Economy*, Minneapolis: Fortress Press, 1989; on biology, see Eugene F. Rogers Jr., *Sexuality and the Christian Body: Their Way into the Triune God*, Oxford: Blackwell, 1999, and David S. Cunningham, *These Three Are One: The Practice of Trinitarian Theology*, Oxford: Blackwell, 1998.

merit their own day of creation; rather, they are created on the same day as the other land animals. Similarly, at the time of the flood, other creatures are saved in the ark alongside Noah and his family, while those animals who perish in the flood do so alongside human beings. Here, however, the distinctions are different to those during the days of the creation. The birds of the air, created on the fifth day with the fish of the sea, are now grouped not with sea creatures (who are not mentioned in the narrative of the flood at all, and who would presumably survive it), but rather with the land animals. In fact, in the flood narrative, the chief distinction is not between human beings and animals, nor between any specific categorization of species or order; it is, rather, a *theological* distinction between the remnant that is saved and the remainder who perish. Note also that after the flood, and in spite of the Noachic covenant that allows human beings to eat animals, God nevertheless enters into a covenant not merely with human beings but with all living creatures (Gen. 9.8–10).

The very fluidity of the distinctions and groupings among various categories of created beings, as narrated by the book of Genesis, might best be interpreted as a reminder that the sharp distinction that we have drawn between human beings and the other animals represents only one of many possible ways of accounting for the diversity of creation. Any such categorization, whether put forth in the biblical text, by theologians over the centuries, or by other observers of the created order, must ultimately come to terms with the fact that they operate from a particular perspective. The very decision to construct such distinctions, and thereby to posit some ultimate categorical difference between human beings and other animals, is a human choice not a divinely ordered reality.[7]

Image

It is true, of course, that the biblical text very clearly attributes to human beings at least one description that it does not employ as an attribute of any other element of creation. This is the claim that human beings are created in the image and likeness of God. Along with this unique

---

7 Useful in this regard are some of the essays in Norman C. Habel and Shirley Wurst (eds), *The Earth Story in Genesis*, vol. 2 of *The Earth Bible*, Sheffield: Sheffield Academic Press; Cleveland: Pilgrim Press, 2000, which offer a much more nuanced reading of the relationship between human beings and other animals – including the accounts of that distinction in the biblical texts.

attribution, human begins are also endowed with dominion over all other living things:

> Then God said, 'Let us make humankind in our image, according to our likeness; and let them have dominion over the fish of the sea, and over the birds of the air, and over the cattle, and over all the wild animals of the earth, and over every creeping thing that creeps upon the earth.' So God created humankind in his image, in the image of God he created them; male and female he created them. God blessed them, and God said to them, 'Be fruitful and multiply, and fill the earth and subdue it; and have dominion over the fish of the sea and over the birds of the air and over every living thing that moves upon the earth' (Gen. 1.26–28).

The claim that human beings are created in the image and likeness of God, and that they are endowed with dominion over other living creatures, is probably the most significant *theological* justification for claiming a significant distinction between human beings and other creatures.

At the outset, however, it should be noted that the biblical text never denies the attribution of 'image of God' to any other element of creation. One can certainly infer that its absence with respect to other creatures is significant; nevertheless, anyone who attempts to make the theological claim that some (or all) other creatures are not created in God's image in any sense of the term must depend upon an *argumentum e silentio* – an approach that has proved somewhat hazardous, particularly with reference to the Bible. We can easily hypothesize a number of other reasons why the biblical authors might have mentioned the language of 'the image of God' only in reference to human beings; we will return to some of these possible reasons below. In the meantime, we can simply acknowledge that the Bible's silence with respect to the attribution of the *imago Dei* to non-human elements of the created order cannot, by itself, serve as an argument for a strong distinction between human and non-human creation in this regard.

In fact, as many commentators have noticed, the relative rarity of the language of 'image of God' in the Hebrew Bible (and therefore in the Christian Old Testament) raises some immediate concerns about the heavy theological freight that this distinction is asked to bear.[8] The term is somewhat more common in the New Testament; but there, its centre of

---

8 In addition to Genesis 1.26–27, the attribution occurs only at Genesis 5.1 and Genesis 9.6.

gravity is not on human beings in general but on Christ as 'the image of the invisible God' (Col. 1.15; see also John 1.18, 14.8–9; 2 Cor. 4.4; Heb. 1.3). In this sense, we might well argue that the real distinction implied by the *imago Dei* is between Christ (as the true image of God) and the rest of humanity, or perhaps the rest of creation, in which that image is secondary at best. This is the line taken by Bruce Marshall, in his explication of theological truth as a form of correspondence to the first Person of the Trinity:

> Everything corresponds to the Father in some fashion, however distant and remote. He is the unoriginate source of all things, and even the humblest creature is like him in some respect. In contrast with the perfect likeness of himself [viz., Christ, the Word] whom the Father eternally generates, those things the Father freely creates by way of the Son resemble him (whether individually or collectively) in more or less partial and incomplete ways . . . Not only human beings, but all creatures, are ordered toward a share in the risen Christ's correspondence to the Father, if not precisely to being personal bearers of his image.[9]

I find this to be a quite convincing point, and it suggests that any casual effort to base the distinction between human beings and other animals on the doctrine of the *imago Dei* is insufficiently attentive to the christological centrality of this doctrine.

But even if we were to grant that the language of the *imago Dei* could be applied, at least in a limited sense, to all human beings and to them alone, we are unlikely to settle on any clear understanding of what this actually means. As is well known, the precise meaning of the term has been one of the more contested sites of theological reflection throughout the centuries.[10] Interestingly, many of the interpretations of its meaning are based on some hypothesized distinction between human beings and other animals. In other words, theologians have tended, first, to assume that human beings are created in the image of God and that animals are not (relying on an 'argument from silence', concerning which we have already raised serious objections). Then, they have used the distinctions

---

9 Bruce Marshall, *Trinity and Truth*, Cambridge Studies in Christian Doctrine, ed. Colin Gunton and Daniel W. Hardy, Cambridge: Cambridge University Pres, 2000, pp. 272–3.

10 An excellent account of the contested nature of this concept can be found in J. Richard Middleton, *The Liberating Image: The* Imago Dei *of Genesis 1*, Grand Rapids MI: Brazos Press, 2005. See also Ruth Page, 'The Human Genome and the Image of God', in Celia Deane-Drummond (ed.), *Brave New World? Theology, Ethics, and the Human Genome*, London and New York: T & T Clark, 2003.

that they have observed (or that their cultural milieu assumes must exist) between human beings and other animals as a way of defining the *imago Dei*. But if (as in this chapter, and in fact throughout this book) the very distinction between human beings and animals is being called into question, this will in turn raise serious questions about the use of this supposedly 'given' distinction as a basis for defining what it means to be created in God's image. Using the *imago Dei* to 'prove' the unique status of human beings depends on both an argument from silence and a willingness to turn a blind eye to the highly contested nature of this terminology.

Of course, the mere fact that many theologians have based their ruminations on a commonly held conviction about the distinctions between human beings and other animals certainly has not resulted in any unanimity of opinion on the matter. Admittedly, one can map a certain degree of common analysis through the patristic and early medieval period, such that David Cairns can conclude: 'In all the Christian writers up to Aquinas we find the image of God conceived of as man's power of reason.'[11] However, Cairns goes on to note that precisely what constituted 'reason' varied considerably among these early authors; we might raise the further complication that, in the light of recent scientific analysis of reasoning behaviour among certain non-human animals (some of which is described elsewhere in this volume[12]), these differing definitions of reason and rationality become particularly important. But even if we consider theological reflection up through the medieval period to have been relatively uniform, the same cannot be said about notions that develop in the Reformation and beyond. In Luther, the image of God is a much more relational and dynamic notion, describing humanity's original justified nature before God (which would be lost in the fall). Calvin attempted to merge Luther's relational perspective with the older, more substantive focus on reason, pointing to the whole human being as the seat of the *imago Dei*:

> Therefore by this word the perfection of our whole nature is designated, as it appeared when Adam was endued with a right judgment, had affections in harmony with reason, had all his senses sound and well-regulated, and truly excelled in everything good. Thus the chief seat of the divine image was in his mind and heart, where it was eminent: yet

---

11 David Cairns, *The Image of God in Man*, London: SCM Press, 1953, p. 110.
12 See, for example, the chapter by Celia Deane-Drummond.

was there no part of him in which some scintillations of it did not shine forth.[13]

Later commentators, including Herder, Hegel and Troeltsch, would describe the language of the *imago Dei* in broad and sometimes rather florid terms, such that it came very close to equating humanity with divinity.[14]

Karl Barth found this variety of interpretations troubling; he argued that most of them were nothing more than the commentator's anthropological predilections writ large.[15] Barth proposed a relational interpretation of the doctrine, in which human beings most clearly resemble God in their ability to relate to God, and to one another in community (which he believed to be strongly implied by the plural and multiform nature of the human creature, designated in Genesis 1.27 as 'male and female'). But as many commentators have observed, Barth's interpretation can appear (particularly when viewed from our current cultural setting) to be as beholden to the anthropological assumptions of his own age as his predecessors' interpretation was to theirs. As Richard Middleton observes, 'Whatever his disclaimers, Barth thus shares with previous interpreters of the image an evident dependence on theological paradigms and agendas derived from outside the biblical text.'[16] Middleton goes on to identify a 'functional' interpretation of the *imago Dei* language, particularly advocated by scholars of the Old Testament, which suggests that human beings are like God in their calling 'as God's representatives and agents in the world, granted authorized power to share in God's rule or administration of the earth's resources and creatures'.[17] Other writers have offered 'existentialist' and 'eschatological' interpretations of the doctrine.[18] Perhaps we can give Calvin the last word on the matter, who, in his commentary on Genesis, begins his entry on 'in our image' with the following claim: 'Interpreters do not agree concerning the meaning of these words'.[19]

---

13 John Calvin, *Commentaries on the First Book of Moses Called Genesis*, ed. and trans. John King, Grand Rapids MI: Baker Books, 1999, pp. 94–5.

14 See, for example, the comments in Karl Barth, *Church Dogmatics*, trans. J. W. Edwards, O. Bussey and Harold Knight, vol. III/1, Edinburgh: T & T Clark, 1958, p. 193; further comments may be found in Middleton, *The Liberating Image*, ch. 1.

15 Barth, *Church Dogmatics*, vol. III/1, p. 193.

16 Middleton, *The Liberating Image*, p. 24.

17 Middleton, *The Liberating Image*, p. 27.

18 See, for example, J. Wentzel van Huyssteen, 'Human Uniqueness and the Image of God', in *Alone in the World? Human Uniqueness in Science and Theology*, Grand Rapids MI: Eerdmans, 2006.

19 Calvin, *Genesis*, p. 93.

Thus far, we have taken two steps away from the comfortable use of the *imago Dei* as a differentiation between human beings and other animals. First, we have noted that the text of Genesis does not deny this attribution to other animals, and that there are good reasons for recognizing that all creatures resemble their Creator to at least a small degree. Second, we have noted that, even if the language is primarily predicated of human beings, its theological significance has been so variably interpreted that we are unable to determine its meaning. We now need to take a third step: namely, that even if we were to agree on both the unique applicability of the *imago Dei* to human beings and the specification of its theological meaning, we would still not be able to agree on how much theological distance between human beings and other animals would be specified by such claims. Providing a justification for this claim will require us to investigate the grammar of the word 'image'.

A careful examination of this word and its usage will pose a significant challenge to anyone who wishes to draw a sharp line between those elements of natural order that are and are not created in God's image. This is because the word 'image' does not lend itself to a simple either/or test. Imagine a painting that you know well; it might be Van Gogh's *Vase with Fifteen Sunflowers* or Caravaggio's *Calling of St Matthew* or Mary Cassatt's *The Child's Bath*. Now imagine a very fine reproduction of that painting, of the same size and shape, with every detail precisely in place, right down to the texture of the paint and the irregularly faded colours of the pigments. This reproduction – so accurate it borders on forgery – would certainly be an image of the original. Now imagine a slightly less accurate reproduction – smaller, perhaps, or without texture. It would seem odd to deny such a work the label of 'image', when a momentary glance would immediately identify it as a reproduction of the famous painting. Now make the image a bit less detailed – a very small reproduction, perhaps, printed from a home computer on a printer with fairly low resolution. Still an image? How about one of those modern digital mosaics, in which the various colours of the whole are duplicated by individual blocks that are themselves images of something else altogether? When we get up close, this will look very different from the original; but from a distance it is clearly recognizable as a reproduction. Now imagine a child's watercolour drawing of the painting, unrecognizable as such to anyone but the fondest parent. At what point (in this journey of increasing distance from the original) does the attempted copy cease to be appropriately described as an image?

The point, I hope, will be clear: the word 'image', as it is used in our

language, is a designation of degree. We describe a reproduction of a painting as a better or a worse image of the original; we allow for a certain
degree of invention and innovation (as with the mosaic created with tiny
pictures); we even continue to use the word in spite of variations in genre –
an image of a painting could be another painting, a print, a photograph, a
digitized image, a line drawing, or even simply an act of the imagination
working in concert with the memory and the will. All these examples serve
to remind us that it can be very difficult to assess a range of possible images
of a particular archetype and to say, straightforwardly and with conviction, that certain ones are images while others are not. The grammar of the
word is based on degree, not on a simple distinction between attribution
and non-attribution. The word 'image' is not a Boolean operator (like
true-or-false); we use it more like we ordinarily use words for a certain
colour (say, 'yellow'). Such a word does not specify only one colour of a
certain hue and saturation but rather an entire range of colours (in which
the transition into other colours is often difficult to discern).

The foregoing analysis might give the impression that the degree to
which something is an image of something else can be charted along a
spectrum, with the most exact reproductions at one end and those that
bore the least likeness to the original at the other. (One imagines an
analogy to a 'great chain of Being', in which the range of images consist of
'an infinite number of links ranging in hierarchical order from the
meagerest kind of existents, which barely escape non-existence, through
"every possible" grade up to the ens perfectissimum'.[20]) My description in
the foregoing paragraphs of a series of decreasingly accurate reproductions of a painting would certainly lend itself to such an interpretation, as
would my use of the analogy of colour.[21] Unfortunately, however, the
construction of such a spectrum would be impossible, because of another
feature of the word 'image': namely, that something can be the image of
something else in a variety of different ways.

Consider, for example, the degree to which various artistic endeavours
might be said to offer an image of a particular human being. Imagine a
series of such efforts, in various media: a painting, a sculpture, a literary

20 Arthur O. Lovejoy, The Great Chain of Being: A Study of the History of an Idea,
Cambridge: Harvard University Press, 1942, p. 59.
21 Bruce Marshall's account of resemblance and correspondence (in his Trinity and
Truth) can also give rise to this notion, particularly given his reference to resemblance occurring 'in more or less partial and incomplete ways' (p. 272) and to certain traces being 'more
remote' than others (p. 273). But he tends to avoid any direct implication of a sliding scale
of resemblance, partly (presumably) for the reasons mentioned in this paragraph, and partly because he wants to emphasize the christological focus of the imago Dei.

description, a photograph, a dramatic enactment on the theatre stage, a motion picture, a dance, a hologram. A good argument could be made for each of these as an image of a human being, and it would be difficult to rank them in order. While a photograph might offer an excellent visual image, it fails to provide the depth and dimensionality of the sculpture. The hologram appears incredibly lifelike, with movement and depth, but its see-through character makes it a rather ghostlike image. An actor on the stage seems the best image, until we remember that her lines are scripted and memorized.

Now complicate the picture further: the sculptures might range from Rodin's *The Kiss* to Joan Miró's *Woman*; the paintings would include both Rembrandt and Picasso; the performers might be doing Chekhov or *The Vagina Monologues*; the photograph might be Richard Avedon for the *New Yorker* or a passerby with a cell phone. Which of these are images? Which are the 'best' images? How would one arrange them along a spectrum, from greatest degree of likeness to least? Merely asking the question would seem to answer it.

And yet, the problem that we face is even more complex than these examples would suggest; for the cases that we have been examining, we have clear and relatively unobstructed knowledge of the archetype that is being compared to the images that we are evaluating. We can travel to Rome, enter the church of San Luigi dei Francesi, and scrutinize Caravaggio's *Calling of St Matthew* in detail, then attempt to pronounce on various reproductions of it. We have direct experience of living, breathing human beings with whom we can compare the images offered by various artists. In the case of the *imago Dei*, however, we have no direct access to the archetype. Certainly, God has been revealed to us in various ways, but as Gregory of Nazianzus remarks, even those who have been privileged to approach the presence of God have really only seen the back parts of God, as Moses did when he was placed in the cleft of the rock.[22] God remains sufficiently a mystery to us that we cannot easily point to specific features of the human being and say, *that* detail in our makeup is what makes us most like God. Is it that we have a certain degree of free will? That we have rational intellectual powers? That we are capable of loving others, beyond the ties of blood and clan? That we have dominion over other creatures? That we are related to others in a com-

22 St Gregory of Nazianzus, 'Oration 28: On the Doctrine of God', in Frederick W. Norris (ed.), *Faith Gives Fullness to Reasoning: The Five Theological Orations of Gregory Nazianzen*, trans. Lionel Wickham and Frederick Williams, Supplements to Vigiliae Christianae, vol. 13, Leiden: E. J. Brill, 1991, p. 225.

munion of persons? Each of these has arguments in its favour, and yet the degree to which any of them identifies us as 'created in the image of God' depends first and foremost on our theology of God and our theology of revelation.[23] It is not a matter of simply having a look at God and at human beings and finding them similar.

Because the language of image names neither an absolute condition nor a linear spectrum of degrees, it makes little sense to think of the language of the *imago Dei* in these ways. It is neither an absolute condition (in which human beings are created in the image of God and everything else is not), nor a series of receding approximations of likeness to the divine, as though human beings were 97 per cent like God, whereas gorillas were 84 per cent godlike, rabbits 63 per cent, kingfishers 44 per cent, mosquitoes 21 per cent, flobberworms 9 per cent and blast-ended skrewts only 2 per cent (and that only on a good day). Although some such sliding scale of likeness to the divine has significant psychological appeal, any attempt to fill out the details would quickly run aground. The birds are like God in their ease of movement; the bees are like God in their simultaneous unity and multiplicity; the penguins in their constancy; the rocks in their steadfastness; and the cats, as T. S. Eliot reminds us, in their mystery (possessed, as each one is, of a 'Deep and inscrutable singular Name'[24]).

My conclusions thus far might seem, at first glance, to suggest a grand levelling of the creation, in which no species or element can be distinguished from any other element. If everything is created in God's image, how can we account for the fact that God would appear (at least according to the biblical text) to be in a more active relationship with human beings, and to a lesser extent with animals, than with inanimate objects and with distant stars? In order to point towards a possible answer to this question, I turn to my final term.

Flesh

In the biblical narrative, and in the theological tradition that builds upon it, the most important distinguishing term within the created order is not 'humanity' (as opposed to all non-human creation), nor 'image' (in spite

---

23 On this point, see Middleton, 'The Challenge of Interpreting the *imago Dei*' in *The Liberating Image*.

24 'The Naming of Cats' in *Old Possum's Book of Practical Cats*, in T. S. Eliot, *Complete Poems and Plays*, London: Faber and Faber; New York: Harcourt Brace and World, 1969, p. 209.

of the traditional tendency to rely on this term), but rather 'flesh'. The primary focus of God's relational life *ad extra* is not only with human beings; it extends to all flesh, all living creatures. This suggests that many common accounts of the Christian doctrine of creation may need to be rethought – moving away from a central focus on humanity as the image of God, and developing a broader field of vision in which human beings take their place within the larger context of all flesh.

Admittedly, we cannot provide an exact definition of the word 'flesh' such that it becomes perfectly clear just exactly which species are included and which are not. But this fact, far from providing an objection to the significance of the term, is actually one of the warrants in its favour. By blurring the distinctions among species, the word 'flesh' brings us into greater conformity with the rather fluid boundaries that are sometimes present in the biblical narrative – not to mention those that consistently arise in our contemporary scientific investigation of the similarities and differences among species.

Clearly, in the small space remaining to me here, I cannot develop a fully articulated account of how a focus on the category of flesh would reshape the Christian doctrine of creation. I cannot even provide a thorough account of the rationale for such a reshaping. What I can do, however, is to provide a brief but suggestive list of reasons why theologians ought to take the category more seriously in constructing their accounts of the created order and God's relationship to it. These indicators, particularly when placed alongside the rather more ambiguous interpretive history of the *imago Dei*, provide us with a fairly strong argument for re-imagining the overall shape and primary focus of the doctrine of creation. I offer five such elements here.

1 *Abundance of biblical reference.* The word 'flesh' appears 321 times in the NRSV, including the Apocrypha. (This fact alone should suggest to us that it might be worthy of at least as much attention as the relatively rare 'image of God'.) The word typically translates the Hebrew *basar* and the Greek *sarx*. Many of the references are to the physical stuff that makes up the body of an animal; notably, whether the flesh is that of a human being or another animal, the same word is used. Some instances of the word refer to the idea of kinship ('this is flesh of my flesh'). In the Old Testament, a number of instances refer to 'eating the flesh' of a person as a means of punishment; in the New Testament, Paul uses the word as a euphemism for sin. Frequently, though, the word is used to describe all living creatures, often with the addition of the word 'all'. The phrase 'all

flesh' is common, occurring 36 times in the NRSV, approximately pro-
portionally across the Old and New Testaments and the Apocrypha; its
meaning appears to be relatively stable, referring to all living creatures.

2 *The relationship between God and all flesh.* Some of the most significant language in the biblical text concerning God's continuing relationship to the world refers not just to human beings, but to 'all flesh'. When
God decides to flood the earth, the focus is not just on humanity but on all
flesh (Gen. 6.13, 17, 19; 7.15, 16, 21; 8.17). As already noted, the
covenant that God makes after the flood is not with human beings alone,
but with all flesh:

> Then God said to Noah and to his sons with him, 'As for me, I am
> establishing my covenant with you and your descendants after you, and
> with every living creature that is with you, the birds, the domestic
> animals, and every animal of the earth with you, as many as came out
> of the ark. I establish my covenant with you, that never again shall all
> flesh be cut off by the waters of a flood, and never again shall there be a
> flood to destroy the earth' (Gen. 9.8–11; cf. Gen. 9.15–17).

Similarly, the dependence of the whole creation on God is accented by the
claim that 'if he should take back his spirit to himself . . . all flesh would
perish together' (Job 34.14–15). God supplies sustenance to all flesh (Ps.
136.25), for which all flesh unites in blessing and praise of God (Ps.
145.21).

3 *Commonality and differentiation.* Unlike the language of the *imago
Dei*, which (as already noted) suggests something of an either/or character, the language of 'flesh' allows us to see both what unites human beings
with other living creatures and what differentiates them. All living
creatures share flesh, and they also share a relationship with God; but the
category of flesh has certain distinguishing marks within it, such that (for
example) cold-blooded and warm-blooded animals are both understood
to have flesh, but different kinds of flesh. 'Not all flesh is alike, but there
is one flesh for human beings, another for animals, another for birds, and
another for fish' (1 Cor. 15.39). This closely mirrors our own empirical
observations, allowing us both to identify those aspects of life that human
beings share with other species, and to differentiate ourselves as well.[25]

---

25 See the related discussion of the Hebrew conception of 'blood' and its relevance to
non-human animals in Michael Northcott's chapter in this volume.

4 Linking Christology and creation. In contrast to the language of the 'image of God' (which, as noted above, is actually something that separates Christ – the one true image – from the rest of creation), the 'flesh' is precisely that element of creation that Jesus shares most fully. The flesh is, of course, central to the doctrine of the incarnation. In its Latin form (derived from *caro/carnis*) and in its Greek form (derived from *sarx*, both in the Nicene Creed – *sarkothenta* – and in John 1.14, *kai ho logos sarx egeneto*), the roots of the incarnation are located first and foremost in the language of fleshliness, and only secondarily in that of humanity (see also Eph. 2.14; 1 Tim. 3.16; 1 John 4.2). God's incarnation is defined not so much by the accidental properties of this flesh (Jewish, male, human) as it is by its essential fleshly character, which human beings share with many other creatures.[26] As Andrew Linzey has observed, Christianity has had a long tradition of recognizing the impact of the incarnation on the entire cosmos – not just on human beings: 'By becoming flesh, the Logos identifies, according to this paradigm, not only with humanity but with all creatures of flesh and blood.'[27]

5 The need for redemption throughout the entire cosmos. As is well known, St Paul has some rather negative things to say about the flesh; as noted above, the word often serves as a euphemism for sexual sin (or at least the potential thereof). Although his use of the word 'flesh' (and the related, but very different, word 'body') are much more complex and nuanced than is sometimes imagined,[28] Paul's usage might lead us to develop a clearer account of how the physical nature of human (and other animal) flesh is related to sin and the fall. Most theologians have recognized that regardless of how one might account for the matter of moral culpability, the fall affects all creatures in some way. While we might want to leave aside the question of the degree to which other animals participate in the fall, and whether they are 'fallen' in the same sense as humanity, one might at least observe that the fall puts them under divine

26 This notion is hinted at, but not developed in any detail, through the language of 'deep incarnation' in the work of Niels Henrik Gregersen. See, for example, 'The Cross of Christ in an Evolutionary World', *dialog: A Journal of Theology* 40:3, Fall 2001, pp. 192–207. See also Marshall, *Trinity and Truth*, and Clough, 'All God's Creatures'.

27 Andrew Linzey, 'Introduction: Is Christianity Irredeemably Speciesist?', in Andrew Linzey and Dorothy Yamamoto (eds), *Animals on the Agenda: Questions about Animals for Theology and Ethics*, London: SCM Press, 1998, p. xvi.

28 Here I would simply recommend the careful, nuanced account of these and related terms in Dale Martin, *The Corinthian Body*, New Haven and London: Yale University Press, 1995.

judgement – as suggested by the narrative of the flood, and by a wide range of other biblical references to God's judgement of 'all flesh'.[29] In addition, the writers of the early Church often pointed to the broad cosmological significance of the fall, such that 'all is not well' in the created order. All flesh is in need of healing; and this, in turn, further emphasizes the preceding point – that the incarnation needs to be understood as a divine assumption of flesh, not just of humanity.

As I suggested earlier in this chapter, the abbreviated nature of this final section makes it more suggestive than constructive. Nevertheless, I hope that it can still function in the constructive mode, in the sense that it might help to open up certain avenues for further theological investigation. I believe that if we were to give as much attention to the central biblical concept of flesh as we have to that of the *imago Dei*, we would be able to develop a theology that could better account for the complex and nuanced relationship between human beings and other animals. And this in turn would have significant implications for ethics, worship and the Christian practice of everyday life.

But even if we must leave these larger implications for future reflection, we can still make several conclusions on this basis of our explorations here. We have raised serious questions about the widespread tendency to construct a great theological divide between reflection on human beings and reflection on other creatures. We have noted that this tendency – based (as it often is) on a fairly simplistic reading of the doctrine of the *imago Dei* – does not seem wholly warranted. When claims about creation 'in the image of God' are subjected to more careful linguistic and theological analysis, they prove to be less supportive of a strong separation between human beings and other animals than might have been surmised. As an alternative, an account of the theological significance of flesh provides a better starting-point for reflection on the relationships among elements of the created order, precisely because it blurs the boundaries among various species and thereby emphasizes their interdependence. Such an account appropriately mirrors the ambivalence that we often feel – and that is so ably explored in essays on 'creaturely theology' in this volume and elsewhere – concerning the relationship between human beings and other animals.

---

29 For further reflections on this important issue, see the work of Celia Deane-Drummond, including her chapter in this volume.

Part Three

HERMENEUTICAL APPROACHES

6

The Question of the Creature: Animals, Theology and Levinas' Dog

AARON S. GROSS

To bring together theology and animals today is to do so following an ongoing critical turn towards animals that has led to the establishment of a new subfield, 'animal studies' or, alternatively, 'human-animal studies'. It is now taken for granted *that* 'animals matter'; various discourses have now begun to explore *how* they matter.[1] Reflecting broadly out of this turn towards animals, I propose three hermeneutical tasks, or rigours, that theology may undertake to critically address and bring its robust resources to bear upon animals: pragmatic, ontological and structural rigours.

The pragmatic rigour, which deserves a certain priority, calls us to attend to the day-to-day, 'local' interactions with animals – animals we learn about from common sense and science, and who suffer or thrive at our hands. The ontological rigour allows us to see that these biological animals are always both intertwined with symbolic ones and with an imagination of 'the animal' that delimits 'the human'. Finally, the structural rigour reminds us that an encounter with animals never takes place on one plane – animals and 'the animal' interact to radiate meaning in multiple registers such that to refuse meat can be to lack virility or to eat a pig can be to betray one's community. In offering this systematic reflection on the interpretive demands of creaturely theology, I will be in dialogue with Emmanuel Levinas' essay, 'The Name of a Dog; or, Natural

---

1 I refer here to the often-overlooked classic on animal ethics, philosopher Mary Midgley's *Animals and Why They Matter*, Athens: University of Georgia Press, 1983. Among the small handful of fine philosophers that have engaged animal ethics in a sustained manner for 25 years or more, I especially recommend to theologians the work of Stephen Clark, Mary Midgley and Bernard Rollin for their unusually penetrating, accessible and pragmatic engagements with the broader arc of Western thought.

Rights'. I will turn to his essay after a brief overview of the challenges facing creaturely theology.

The starting point for this chapter is the unique manner in which animals – and words about them – present a problem for critical thought and theology. The problem begins with the word and category 'animal' itself. Perhaps surprisingly, it is far from easy to agree on just what an animal is or what creatures should be included in any discussion of animals. Are we talking about animals the biological individuals (animals we might eat or sacrifice or protect), animals as symbols (for example, the Lamb of God), or animal parts of ourselves (our animal passions)?[2] Are we concerned with all three at once? Can we even avoid speaking of all three at once? Is the general category 'animal' even coherent?

Just what is an animal? The noted anthropologist Timothy Ingold explored this question in a revealing manner by posing it to a diverse group of scholars representing social and cultural anthropology, archaeology, biology, psychology, philosophy and semiotics. There was little agreement among the scholars except for two points: 'first, that there is a strong emotional undercurrent to our ideas about animality; and, secondly, that to subject these ideas to critical scrutiny is to expose highly sensitive and largely unexplored aspects of the understanding of our own humanity.'[3] I imagine the diverse contributors to this volume could only agree with these points.

Consider just how fraught the category animal becomes outside of its most common-sense usage where we understand 'animal' as a natural category. What challenges are posed to our understanding, for example, by our knowledge of communities who say that they are or become what we call animals – like the Bororos of Brazil who are somewhat (in)famously reported to assert that they are red parrots?[4] What are we to make of the fact that the category animal (let alone creature) is simply absent in many cultures? For example, the Cree and other northern

---

2 The myriad ways in which diverse human communities understand their own nature through the detour of animals is the focus of my own forthcoming edited volume with Anne Vallely, *Animal Others and the Human Imagination*.

3 Tim Ingold (ed.), *What Is an Animal?*, London: Unwin Hyman, 1988, p. 2.

4 As admirably documented by Jonathan Z. Smith, the exemplum of the Bororos can be traced back to an 1894 ethnographic study by Karl von den Steinem. Especially under the influence of Lucien Lévy-Bruhl, von den Steinem's report became the exemplary illustration of just how far 'primitive mentality' differs from modern. The notion of a 'primitive mentality' has, of course, been discredited, but the fact that views of animals were seized upon to articulate this difference remains telling. J. Z. Smith, 'I am a Parrot (Red)', in *Map Is Not Territory*, Chicago: University of Chicago Press, 1978, pp. 266–7.

hunters, explains Ingold, reject 'an absolute division between the contrary conditions of humanity and animality. . . . Personhood for them is open equally to humans and non-human animals (and even non-animal) kinds.'[5] And what are we to learn about the category animal from our own history of insisting that some of the beings we now consider human are in fact animals? It was not long ago that debates were heard on whether Jews or Blacks or women were fully human.

It is often observed that before we oppress or kill others, we 'animalize' them and indeed the habit in our languages of describing oppression in general as treating a human like an animal shows the basic plausibility of this idea. Theory and theology would do well to take this observation seriously, but also to push beyond it. What, exactly, is animalization? When we talk of the animalization of Jews or Blacks, for example, we mean a particular kind of animalization whose contours and genealogy merit serious attention. Léon Poliakov, in his pioneering studies of the history of Western anti-Semitism and racism, is noteworthy for his efforts towards understanding the specific character of various 'animalizations'. His work brings us the important insights that in Western history Blacks were more likely to be animalized while Jews were more likely to be demonized.[6] This observation calls for deeper inquiry. The scandalous links between our everyday construction of the category animal and the most shameful depths of our racism make the question of the animal more proximate to issues of race, racism and anti-Semitism than is comfortable to admit.

And all these complications, of course, primarily raise the question of what an animal is; the related question of how we ought to regard and treat animals takes us into ever-deeper waters. Significantly, ambiguities and disagreements around what animals are and how we ought to regard them constantly blend together. Consider, for example, that the only US federal legislation mandating humane animal slaughter, the 1958 Humane Slaughter Act (HSA), does not apply to most animals slaughtered in the USA because chickens and turkeys are not considered animals for purposes of this law. In this case, it is impossible to discern if there was disagreement on what constitutes an animal or disagreement on how animals should be treated or both.[7]

---

5 Tim Ingold, 'Hunting and Gathering as Ways of Perceiving the Environment', in Roy Ellen and Katsuyoshi Fukui (eds), *Redefining Nature*, Oxford: Berg, 1996, p. 131.

6 Léon Poliakov, 'Humanity, Nationality, Bestiality', in Elisabeth Weber (ed.), *Questioning Judaism*, Stanford: Stanford University Press, 2004, p. 94.

7 The complex story of the HSA, of course, is not reducible to the single sentence I have given above without distortion.

The question of what counts as an animal in the first place haunts all words about animals – and it haunts Jewish and Christian theologies in a particularly striking manner. The charge of animals is so high in Christian and Jewish traditions in part because questions about animals unfold, perhaps unexpectedly, to resonate with questions about fundamental ontology – the very being of humanity and divinity – questions about the nature of religion itself. There is, so to speak, a direct line connecting core theological concerns and animals. In decisive ways, 'the question of the animal' – or, as this chapter puts it, the question of the creature – proceeds and determines the very space of both Jewish and Christian theologies. Theology can never become simply a tool to think about animals without first entering a kind of self-inquiry.[8]

Christian and Jewish theologies also hold the promise of adding clarity, depth and alternative perspectives to contemporary discussions of and relations with animals. Theology is exceptionally well suited to address precisely the ambiguities and complications I have quickly run through above. Theology is optimally poised to address the fact that our relations with animals are, in the words of comparative historian of religions Kimberly Patton, 'something charged, something holy, something that social construction can only partially interpret, but to which the religious imagination, with its unflinching reach into the depths of the human heart, must instead respond'.[9]

The name of a dog

In Emmanuel Levinas' 'The Name of a Dog; or, Natural Rights' we encounter three dense pages about a singular human–animal encounter and a single biblical verse, Exodus 22.31, 'You shall be men consecrated to me; therefore you shall not eat any flesh that is torn by beasts in the field; you shall cast it to the dogs.'[10] In the manner of a postmodern

---

8 The phrase 'the question of the animal' is most closely associated with the work of Jacques Derrida, especially in regard to his critique of Martin Heidegger's writings on animals (for example, in *Of Spirit: Heidegger and the Question*, Chicago: University of Chicago Press, 1989). By titling the present chapter 'the question of the creature' I mean to signal my own debt to and sympathy with Derrida's writings on animals.

9 Kimberley Patton, '"Caught with Ourselves in the Net of Life and Time": Traditional Views of Animals in Religion', in Paul Waldau and Kimberley Patton (eds), *A Communion of Subjects: Animals in Religion, Science, and Ethics*, New York: Columbia University Press, 2006, pp. 36–7.

10 Emmanuel Levinas, 'The Name of a Dog; or, Natural Rights', in *Difficult Freedom*, trans. Seán Hand, Baltimore: John Hopkins, 1997, p. 151. As this is the main text under

midrash and indeed engaged with early rabbinic midrashim, Levinas spins from this verse a set of diverse reflections that interrogates the multiplicities of meaning that radiate from the 'nom d'un chien', 'the name of a dog'.[11] Indeed, the title itself is suggestive of the herd of meanings that Levinas will ultimately wrangle; the French of the title 'nom d'un chien' is well known as a polite alternative to the explicative 'nom de Dieu'.[12] Why does Levinas choose this title that invites us to move between *chien* and *dieu*, dog and God? What is the invisible thread that connects canine and divine?

In the opening paragraph of the essay Levinas imagines that the 'spectacle' of the torn flesh spoken of in Exodus may have suggested 'the horrors of war', and then, unexpectedly, the reader is no longer in the space of the Bible. The 'horrors of war', Levinas tells us,

> can also come to you at the family table, as you plunge your fork into your roast. There is enough there to make you a vegetarian again. If we are to believe Genesis, Adam, the father of us all, was one! There is, at least, enough there to make us want to limit, through various interdictions, the butchery that every day claims our 'consecrated' mouths! (151)

This is a remarkably provocative statement. What is the connection Levinas sees between the horrors of war and unrestrained carnivory? Has Levinas, himself a survivor, just suggested that these same horrors are invoked by the practical, day-to-day phenomenon of a roast? He has. But as soon as these potentially destabilizing words are spoken (words worth pausing over) we are rushed along. 'But enough of this theology!', Levinas exclaims, 'I am thinking of Bobby' (151). Bobby, we learn at the end of the essay, is the name of a dog – the name Levinas and his fellow prisoners give to a dog while interred 'in a forestry commando unit for Jewish

---

consideration and to eliminate clutter, hereafter references to this essay will be cited parenthetically by number only.

11 Past scholarship has suggested that the Bible *always* portrays the Israelite view of dogs as negative. This view has been effectively challenged by Geoffrey David Miller who recently reviewed both negative and positive Israelite views towards dogs recorded in the Bible (thanks to David Clough for bringing his essay to my attention). Interestingly, Miller, presumably unaware of Levinas' essay, cites the very verse Levinas examines, Exodus 22.31, as a paradigmatic example of a verse where it is impossible to tell if the view towards dogs is positive or negative. Geoffrey David Miller, 'Attitudes Toward Dogs in Ancient Israel: A Reassessment', *Journal for the Study of the Old Testament* 32:4, 2008, pp. 487–500.

12 This is noted by Seán Hand, the English translator of Levinas' essay (299).

prisoners of war in Nazi Germany' (152). The people around them, Levinas explains, 'stripped us of our human skin. We were subhuman, a gang of apes' (153). Bobby, however, 'would appear at morning assembly and was waiting for us as we returned . . . For him, there was no doubt that we were men' (153).

There is much we might consider here. What does it suggest about the nature of animals that a dog recognized – and conveyed (!) – an appreciation of Levinas' humanity that other humans disavowed? Can an animal 'with neither ethics nor *logos*' (152) give us to ourselves – give a human humanity?

Can the face of an animal confront us '*as if* God spoke through the face'?[13] That is the final question given to us by Levinas and Bobby.

The pragmatic rigour

For our present aim of offering a typology of the rigours necessary for theology to approach animals critically, consider the direction of the first gestures Levinas makes in his essay: first he moves from biblical, mythical space (Exodus) to the dinner table (a roast); he then moves from a theology of how another creature may constitute one's sense of being human to an individual dog named Bobby (152). These movements towards the everyday and the individual begin the first and most important rigour of creaturely theology, the pragmatic.

Levinas himself calls our attention to this concretizing direction of his thought. Sometimes he does this directly: 'But enough of allegories! We have read too many fables and we are still taking the name of a dog in the figurative sense.' More profoundly, however, he signals his interest in moving towards the concreteness of the individual animal by emphasizing that the dog is given a proper name. This naming is best understood in relation to the importance given the proper name by the German Jewish thinker Franz Rosenzweig in his classic *The Star of Redemption*, which Levinas claims as the major inspiration for much of his thought. Rosenzweig defines the 'proper name' in a manner somewhat analogous to Levinas' definition of the 'face', a concept that we will encounter shortly. For Rosenzweig,

---

13 The phrase is Levinas' own. Tamara Wright, Peter Hughes and Alison Ainley, 'The Paradox of Morality: An Interview with Emmanuel Levinas', in Robert Bernasconi and David Wood (eds), *The Provocation of Levinas*, London: Routledge, 1988, p. 169 (emphasis added).

in the proper name, a breach is opened in the fixed wall of thingliness. That which has its own name can no longer be a thing or everyone's thing; it is incapable of being entirely dissolved in the genus, for there is no genus to which it could belong; it is its own genus unto itself.[14]

Just as Bobby helped establish Levinas' humanity when human gazes denied it, so Levinas' naming of Bobby is an attempt to lift this dog over the 'wall' of animality and confront him as an individual. This act of reaching towards the individual animal, of recognizing animals as creatures that 'can no longer be a thing or everyone's thing', is the basis of the pragmatic rigour.

The pragmatic rigour asks simply that we attend and respond to the local, day-to-day interactions that occur between humans and animals in their radical, 'genus-less' individuality. This rigour asks us to respond not only to the groans of creation, but the groans and sorrows of particular creatures. This implies attending not just to animals today, but reflecting on the practical context out of which previous reflection on animals has occurred, for example querying the relationship between ancient Israelite husbandry and the sacrificial systems described in the Bible. In the memorable phrasing of religious studies scholar Paul Waldau, the pragmatic rigour asks us to think about 'the nearby biological individuals outside human communities'.[15]

Much of this pragmatic thinking about animals will come to us through science, an institution that heavily shapes the context in which theological reflection on animals now arises. I will not pursue this vibrant area of inquiry here, but direct the reader to the able explorations of these issues in the chapters by Stephen Clark, Celia Deane-Drummond and Neil Messer later in this volume.

Turning from the institutions of science to the institutions of agriculture, it is easy to see that the pragmatic arrangements of farming have played a significant role in theological reflection in both Jewish and Christian traditions long before the rise of science. To cite one example that will be known to all, we can note the frequent use by biblical, early rabbinic and patristic authors of language and imagery that likens divinity to the good shepherd – a common ground for both Jews and Christians.

---

14 Franz Rosenzweig, *The Star of Redemption*, trans. Barbara E. Galli, Madison: University of Wisconsin Press, 2005, p. 201.

15 Paul Waldau, 'Seeing the Terrain We Walk: Features of the Contemporary Landscape of "Religion and Animals"', in Paul Waldau and Kimberly Patton (eds), *A Communion of Subjects: Animals in Religion, Science, and Ethics*, New York: Columbia University Press, 2006, p. 40.

Few would argue with either the centrality of such imagery or its obvious debt to a pragmatic relationship between humans and animals, namely traditional livestock husbandry. The more controversial step to take – the one that I am urging here – is to also recognize the *ongoing* centrality of pragmatic relationships with animals for present and future theology. That is to say that while it may appear that our relationship with animals – with creatures – has little to do with our religious lives, the many and constant influences of our relations with animals could not be more profound or pervasive.

It seems astonishing, for example, that it could be a matter of indifference to Jewish and Christian thought that not merely the shepherd but the entire tradition of husbandry to which the shepherd belonged has been largely replaced in the last century by corporately owned factory farms and assembly-line slaughter and processing facilities. These new and global reconfigurations in animal agriculture are potentially as theologically significant as the notion of shepherding, but they remain largely unthought.

What would it mean, theologically, if our ranches were places where animals thrived and our slaughterhouses brought quick, peaceful deaths? What if there were no slaughterhouses? Both are human possibilities and both are far from reality.

More importantly, what does it mean, for example, that today 50 billion (!) chickens live their entire lives confined and drugged in the stinking, filthy buildings of factory farms – rows upon rows of the special sorrow of birds? Is this a matter only for animal ethicists? Of course there is an injustice here, but only injustice? Is there not also something even more disturbing? Are the groans of 50 billion not an event? As pursued by Jacques Derrida:

> However one interprets it, whatever practical, technical, scientific, juridical, ethical, or political consequences one draws from it, no one can deny this event any more, no one can deny the *unprecedented* proportions of this subjection of the animal [in the factory farm] . . . Neither can one deny seriously any more the disavowal that this involves. No one can deny seriously, or for very long, that men do all they can in order to dissimulate this cruelty or to hide it from themselves in order to organize on a global scale the forgetting or misunderstanding of this violence.[16]

---

16 Jacques Derrida, *The Animal That Therefore I Am*, trans. David Willis, ed. Marie-Louise Mallet, New York: Fordham University Press, 2008, p. 394.

Attention to the pragmatic level is not as straightforward as is often thought, and calls for changes in our daily relationships with animals are unlikely to be heard without engaging in other forms of theological attention to animals. Indeed, crucial to the position I am staking out with this ultimately arbitrary formula of a threefold rigour is the need to *combine* attention to animals at a pragmatic level with other forms of attention.

It is worth highlighting that I emphasize that attentiveness to pragmatic concerns (say Derrida's objections to factory farming) be combined with the ontological and structural rigours I discuss below because of challenges internal to pragmatic concerns. In my own experience it is precisely the challenges of pragmatic-political efforts on behalf of animal protection (say, directing people away from factory farmed animals in their eating choices) that most illuminate the need to recognize the complex, multivalent and often counter-intuitive ways that animals proliferate meanings. The profound investment of food with layers of familial, cultural, ethical and religious meaning, for example, make it difficult to talk about the pragmatic implications theology may draw about eating animals without engaging a host of other questions that ultimately cut to basic understanding of the ethical and religious status of the human. The pragmatic rigour leads to the ontological and structural rigours as it unfolds. To put it another way, I make a point of the need for more than pragmatic conclusions in creaturely theology not to go 'beyond' pragmatic concerns, which I argue retain a certain priority for theology, but to *fulfil* them.

The ontological rigour

Beyond Levinas' opening reflection on the horrors of war seen in the torn flesh of animals and his closing reflection on the power of the living presence of animals to make one human, he moves through layers of possible meanings of the dog referenced in his biblical verse. He wonders if the dog might be some kind of stand-in for society or other allegory (151), if the dog is 'Literally a dog!' (152), or if the dog is what we might call a mythic dog – a dog descended from Egypt that, as one Rabbinic interpretation of Exodus has it, did not bark and thereby allowed the ancient Israelites to escape from bondage.[17] Levinas has particular enthusiasm for this last possibility:

---

17 See, for example, *Exodus Rabbah* 31:9.

At the supreme hour of his institution [the Exodus], with neither ethics nor *logos*, the dog will attest to the dignity of its person. This is what the friend of man means. There is transcendence in the animal! And the clear verse with which we began is given a new meaning. It reminds us of the debt that is always open. (152)

In these words, as with a few other small portions of his corpus, one senses Levinas flirting with an idea he never commits to or entirely denies: that the animal too might participate in the existential structure that is definitive of the human, a 'face'. In other words, that an animal might primordially call one to a 'debt that is always open' – to ethical obligations that exceed our abilities and comprehension.[18]

Part of Levinas' importance in contemporary ethics is his radical suggestion that ethics is not 'self-given', not something an autonomous self adopts like a pledge or promise. Rather, ethics, through the existential structure that Levinas describes as the 'face', precedes our births, constituting our subjectivity in fundamental *relationships* before we achieve a *consciousness* that could make a promise. Do these ethical relationships that constitute our own being occur only with human 'others' or do animals – do creatures – also constitute our being even before we consciously consider them? This is the question Levinas raises in his essay.

For Levinas, the encounter with another's face is the very production of the space of religion, so the question of whether an animal has a face is also the question of whether animals too participate in the relation Levinas designates religion. In *Totality and Infinity*, Levinas defines religion as 'the bond that is established between the same and the other without constituting a totality'.[19] Interpreting far too quickly, religion is a relation with the other that does not demand the other's assimilation; it is an encounter with the overwhelming command of the other's face looking down upon us.

---

18 That is, using the helpful language of Jean-Luc Marion, the animal may be a 'saturated phenomenon' – a phenomenon that we can endlessly interpret and yet still not exhaust in meaning. Of course, for Marion, it is the human – and precisely in the human's break with animality – that is the exemplary example of a saturated phenomenon. As a saturated phenomenon, the human is 'radically separated from every other being in the world by an insurmountable and definitive difference that is no longer ontological, but holy'. Jean-Luc Marion, 'Mihi magna quaestio factus sum: The Privilege of Unknowing', *Journal of Religion* 85:1, 2005, pp. 16, 23.

19 Emmanuel Levinas, *Totality and Infinity: An Essay on Exteriority*, trans. A. Lingis, Pittsburgh: Duquesne, 1990, p. 40.

So, we must ask, did Levinas encounter a face in Bobby's 'friendly growling, his animal faith . . . born from the silence of his forefathers on the banks of the Nile' (153)? The thrust of Levinas' corpus, especially his masterwork *Totality and Infinity*, would suggest the answer should be no.[20] The face, for Levinas, is the structure of encounter with the *human* other and it calls forth discourse and language, which are also imagined as uniquely human.

However, despite the subtle dependence of *Totality and Infinity* on the notion of a 'break' between the human and animal, Levinas does not provide any robust sense of what he has in mind when he talks about animals. Indeed, it is not clear to me that Levinas so much intends to speak of animals at all as much as he is simply caught in an almost reflexive stance of philosophy that asserts in advance of any examination that whatever is most fundamental to the human being should be articulated as a break with the animal.

So, yes, Levinas as we know him in his major works does seem to deny or, better, forget the animal face.[21] This disavowal, however, is more passive than active – accomplished more by saying very little about animals than by any careful exclusion of them. Levinas seems simply not to have worked through – or even asked – the question of the creature. The creature is the unthought remnant of Levinas' philosophy – an unassimilable agitator that, in brief moments, surfaces to trouble his ruminations.

This perhaps unsatisfying reading tells us less than we might want about Levinas' views on animals, but it tells us a great deal about how easy it has been for religious and philosophical thought to forget animals – at least until recently. The intellectual winds have shifted and today the question of the animal is not quite so easy to avoid. Levinas' thought comes to a conclusion just as these winds have picked up speed. Consider that Levinas' most direct discussion of animals is not in his major works at all but, tellingly, in the response Levinas gives to a group of three

---

20 Derrida presents a forceful case for the failure of Levinas to consider the animal in his classic essay '"Eating Well" or the Calculation of the Subject', in Elisabeth Weber and Peggy Kamuf (eds), *Points, Interviews, 1974–1994*, Stanford: Stanford University Press, 1995. Matthew Calarco critically considers Derrida's arguments in his fine essay 'Deconstruction Is Not Vegetarianism: Humanism, Subjectivity, and Animal Ethics', concluding that though Derrida's reading of Levinas is problematic, Derrida is correct that Levinas' thought remains marked by a 'profound humanism' that denies the animal its own face (*Continental Philosophy Review* 37, 2004, p. 182).

21 Walter Benjamin theorizes animals as 'receptacles of the forgotten' in a manner that, had we more time, would be helpful here. For discussion, see Beatrice Hanssen, *Walter Benjamin's Other History*, Berkeley: University of California Press, 2000, p. 146.

graduate students from the University of Warwick who pressed him on this issue in a 1986 interview. (Curiously, this story is told in the literature I surveyed without mentioning the then students' names: Tamara Wright, Peter Hughes and Alison Ainley; they are referred to simply as graduate students.)

This interview, as I imagine it, is almost a symbol of the intellectual moment: three students, two of them women, are in dialogue with the distinguished thinker of the previous generation and press him to greater clarity on the question of the animal. The voices do not come from his equals; these are voices from the margins, nameless, that press from the ground up. A substantial quotation is in order,

> *But is there something distinctive about the human face which, for example, sets it apart from that of an animal?*
> [Levinas:] One cannot entirely refuse the face of an animal. It is via the face that one understands, for example, a dog. Yet the priority here is not found in the animal, but in the human face . . . In the dog, in the animal, there are other phenomena. . . . But it also has a face.
> There are these two strange things in the face: its extreme frailty – the fact of being without means and, on the other hand, there is authority. *It is as if God spoke through the face.*[22]

The ambiguities generated here are multiple and unresolved. First, it is not clear whether Levinas means to talk about all animals or just dogs or dogs as representative of a class of animals; 'in the dog, in the animal' he writes as if to talk of one is talk of the other. And just what does it mean that we cannot '*entirely* refuse the face of an animal'? Especially since Levinas also says here simply that the dog 'has a face'. Is Levinas both giving and not giving the animal – the dog or Bobby – a face? That may be the best reading. If we insist, however, on a unitary reading of the interview and of Levinas, his final articulation appears to be that the ethical does extend to animals, but does so in a derivative manner – the animal lacks 'priority'.[23] So the animal has a face, but this face is borrowed from the human – an echo or shadow of 'man'.

In the end, I am not persuaded that Levinas' various statements on animals can be so neatly stitched together. His thoughts are essentially unresolved. The Levinas who encounters Bobby cannot be assimilated

---

22 Wright, Hughes and Ainley, 'Paradox', p. 169 (emphasis added).

23 Matthew Calarco ably and incisively evaluates Levinas' thought on animals in this interview in his essay 'Deconstruction Is Not Vegetarianism' (see n. 20).

with the Levinas who theorizes the face as uniquely human. Given the tone of the interview, I am not satisfied that the (ad hoc?) idea that the animal has a derivative, low-priority face satisfied even Levinas.

This lack of resolution is in fact suggested in the subjunctive tense that Levinas employs throughout 'The Name of a Dog; or, Natural Rights'. As we have seen, in this essay Levinas suggests that a dog *might* impose upon us a 'debt that is always open'. That is, an encounter with an animal *may* hold us 'hostage' to the unexpected and unlimited demands of the other. Perhaps, as Levinas also suggests in another of his major works, 'Man is responsible for the universe, the hostage of the creature . . . pressed from his front and rear . . . asked to account for things which he did not will . . .'[24]

The ontological rigour asks that we take as a foundation something like what Levinas has raised here only as a possibility – that animals call us with something like a 'debt that is always open' and thus can be said to call us into and constitute our very being. We might choose to ignore these responsibilities, but to do so is not to abandon an ethic, but to disavow a part of ourselves as religious and ethical beings. The challenge of the ontological rigour is the recognition that there is no simple – and perhaps no satisfactory – way to exclude animals from this decisive role in the constitution of our selves. Put simply, the ontological rigour asks us to take seriously the role the animal other plays in the constitution of human being(s).

At the very least the ontological rigour asks that we attend to the crucial role of the animal in *imagining* the 'chain of being' – that is, recognizing the manner in which fundamental Christian and Jewish understandings of both humanity and divinity are intelligible only against the shadowy background of animality.

This hidden insinuation of the animal at the heart of theology has been illustrated in a masterful fashion by Giorgio Agamben. In *The Open*, drawing broadly on a range of Western theologians and philosophers, Agamben presents an intricate argument for the centrality of the human–animal border to the broad trajectory of Western thought about humanity. Again and again he shows how theological stances about humanity unexpectedly hinge on the meaning of animality. *The Open*'s fifth chapter, for example, offers a penetrating reading of how the 'physiology of the blessed', articulated by John Scotus Erigena, Augustine of Hippo and

---

24 Emmanuel Levinas, *Nine Talmudic Readings*, trans. A. Aronowicz, Bloomington: Indiana University Press, 1990, p. 170.

Thomas Aquinas, is ultimately dependent on, and may even be driven by, divisions between human and animal that have roots in Aristotle.[25] And if the animal, as Agamben argues, is implicated in deep and motley ways in the production and space of the human, how could it not participate in forming the space of religion and theology? The ontological rigour asks that we attend to this circle in which the very fabric of religion and theology – the humanity of the human but also the divinity of the divine – is imagined already with and through animals.

The structural rigour

Our analysis of the first two rigours allows us to consider the final, structural rigour relatively quickly. Let us summarize the pragmatic rigour as marked by an attention to 'animals', the biological individuals, while the ontological rigour is marked by an attention to 'the animal' as a principle construct in the constitution (or imagination) of humanity and divinity. The structural rigour can then be understood as a form of interpretation that gives attention to the links between the 'animals' (of the pragmatic rigour), 'the animal' (of the ontological rigour) and still other registers of meaning. When we acknowledge the significance of animals found in the pragmatic and ontological rigours, it is a small step to realize that the immense freight of the human–animal border does not float in a vacuum, but is sustained in relationships with other structures and oppositions.

The structural rigour proceeds from the observation that animals, in one way or the other, often become decisive levels of classification in larger structures of meaning and serve as links connecting and shoring up these different orders. Despite other difficulties with his thought, Claude Lévi-Strauss is lucid on this point:

> What is significant is not so much the presence – or absence – of this or that level of classification as the existence of a classification with, as it were, an adjustable thread which gives the group adopting it the means of 'focusing' on all planes, from the most abstract to the most concrete . . . without changing its intellectual instrument.[26]

---

25 Giorgio Agamben, *The Open: Man and Animal*, trans. K. Attell, Stanford: Stanford University Press, 2004, p. 16.

26 Claude Lévi-Strauss, *The Savage Mind*, Chicago: University of Chicago Press, 1973, p. 136.

Animals, as Lévi-Strauss among others has observed, are exceptionally well suited to function as just such 'an adjustable thread', allowing the condensation of meanings 'from the most abstract', like the idea of natural rights, 'to the most concrete', like the name of a dog.

The animal, the dog and even Bobby function as adjustable threads for Levinas. His reflection on Bobby does bring our attention to the question of ethical obligations to animals, but it equally – and simultaneously – sharpens our thinking about the nature of humanity and considers allegorical valences of the dog. Simultaneously at stake are pragmatic issues (the question of diet) and ontological concerns (the responsibilities that constitute our subjectivity).

The structural rigour invites us to investigate the linkages between different pragmatic, ontological and related registers of meaning. Consider, for example, that Levinas' statement 'We were subhuman, a gang of apes' has implications both for the ontological status of the human and the pragmatic status of the animal. The statement implies both an ontological order in which humans are superior to animals and an ethical order in which the confinement Levinas suffers would be acceptable if done to apes.

Often the structural rigour will bring to our attention links between pairs of binary oppositions. In Jewish and Christian contexts the human–animal binary is frequently connected with such binaries as male–female, eternal–mortal, spirit–letter, rational–irrational, and so on. Thus to speak of humans reduced to apes is instantly also to speak of a victory of the irrational over the rational and of chaos over order, and to call a text mere animal scratches is also to say it is all letter and no spirit. These linkages are often stated explicitly, as in this striking example from the influential eleventh-century Rabbi Shlomo Yitzhaqui, Rashi. Rashi glosses 'master it' in Genesis 1.28, which is generally taken to refer to human mastery of the earth and its animals, as 'master her'. Rashi explains, 'to teach you that the male masters (כובש) the female.'[27] And, as a Jewish contributor to a volume focused on Christian theology, it seems especially worth noting that the animal–human binary has been used historically by both Christian communities to construct the otherness of Jews and by Jewish communities to construct the otherness of Christians.[28]

---

27 Rashi translations are my own.

28 Two recent works of particular note in this regard are Elliot Wolfson's *Venturing Beyond: Law and Morality in Kabbalistic Mysticism*, Oxford: Oxford University Press, 2006, which examines the medieval Jewish mystical construction of gentiles as inhuman and beastly (see especially pp. 42–6), and Claudine Fabre-Vassas' *The Singular Pig: Jews,*

Taken together, these rigours ask us to attend to the ways in which reflection on animals is never '*just* reflection on animals'. All the more is this true when we theologize the 'creature' – a word whose unique connotations have only been gestured at in this chapter. Creaturely theology, in the end, is simply theology entered into by way of creatures and creatureliness.

Conclusion

To summarize, animals – creatures – are vulnerable others in our everyday lives familiar to everyone. At the same time they are root others who help us imagine ourselves and who call us to, and constitute, our being. Even further, particular creatures serve as 'adjustable threads', linking, condensing and embodying different structures of meaning. Imagined at the cusp of the sacred and the profane, the creature casts light in both directions. Creatures proliferate meanings of dizzying complexity: the meanings of their own subjectivities and meanings created in the webs of our own and our Scriptures' discourses. Most simply and significantly, in creatures we encounter fellow subjectivities that demand our concern.

All this is to say that our relationships with animals are stranger, deeper and more disturbed than we generally allow – even those of us working in animal studies or animal rights. Consider the factory farm. Industrial agriculture's creation of unprecedented violence in our relations with animals is not only an ethical or political concern, but a religious one. As this article went to press, the *New York Times* became the first American newspaper to editorialize against the factory farm as such and endorse specific steps to alter the direction of animal agriculture.[29] No American religious community has (yet) done anything similar, and that is a loss for us all. The popular media, advocates and a long list of disciplines in the humanities and social sciences are now helping us interpret and respond to this event, but their resources are ultimately insufficient to comprehend, for example, the groans of 50 billion. It is perhaps not the kind of exemplum Patton had in mind, but the factory farm itself is a relation to animals, 'that social construction can only partially interpret . . . [something that] the religious imagination, with its unflinching reach into the depths of the human heart, must instead respond'. The parts of the human

---

Christians, and the Pig, New York: Columbia University Press, 1997, which traces the strange, anti-Semitic linkages between pig and Jew in European Christian culture.

29 *New York Times*, 'The Worst Way to Farm', 31 May 2008.

heart that the question of the creature calls us to consider should not be romanticized.

To reduce it to a phrase, the rigours of creaturely theology, however they are numbered, are simply a means of critically attending to animals while also facing the possibility that we are held hostage by these others too, that God might speak through them also. We and our theologies are, as Levinas had it, 'hostage of the universe. Extraordinary dignity. Unlimited Responsibility.'

7

The Animals We Write On: Encountering
Animals in Texts[1]

RACHEL MUERS

Introduction: animals in the margins

Carol Adams, in *Neither Man Nor Beast*, suggests that non-human animals in Christian history do not even get as far as being 'marginalized'. They are, literally and figuratively, what we write both our central texts and our marginalia onto.[2] When we look at the Dead Sea Scrolls, to use Adams' example, we focus on the text and not on the animal skin. We do not see a dead animal; we see a writing surface. The very act of writing the text reduces the animal not only to voicelessness, but to invisibility as anything other than a resource for human use. Writing on animals is, for Adams, metonymic for a set of cultural practices that render animals invisible as agents and sufferers, and that prepare the way for ontologies of the animal that deny the significance of animal action and suffering. In Adams' accounts, practices (here, writing on animal skins) ground an epistemology (animals cannot be seen or known as agents or patients), which gives rise to an ontology (animals are 'completely other than us' or 'made for our use'), which in turn provides a basis for the practices. I have written elsewhere about the usefulness for Christian theology and ethics

1 This chapter draws on work from the research project 'Vegetarianism as Spiritual Choice in Historical and Contemporary Theology', funded by the Arts and Humanities Research Council, which support I gratefully acknowledge. David Grumett, as the post-doctoral research associate on this project, has contributed to the background research for this chapter and helped to shape my thinking on the issues. Discussions at the colloquium for this collection helped me to think through several questions, and I particularly thank David Clough and Aaron Gross for their help and advice as I prepared and revised the chapter. I also thank Susannah Ticciati for valuable discussions of Job.
2 Carol J. Adams, *Neither Man Nor Beast: Feminism and the Defence of Animals*, New York: Continuum, 1994, p. 203.

of Adams' basic account of how attitudes to animals are formed.[3] In this chapter I wish to focus more on the arresting image of 'writing on animals', and to explore whether and how this is the way Christian texts work. I shall suggest that the question of how to read non-human animals in texts has much to do with the question of how to treat the 'literal sense'.[4]

When I saw a fragment of a Dead Sea Scroll at a recent exhibition of Jewish, Christian and Muslim sacred texts I did not – as Adams predicted I would not – think much about the animal on whom it was written. There were, however, at the same exhibition, innumerable animals on whom one could not but focus. These were the animals that had made it into the margins, and often beyond the margins, of the sacred texts, chiefly of Christianity but also to some extent of Judaism. Initial capitals were illuminated with or as animals; marginal notes were written in micrographia in the forms of real or imaginary animals; animals crept around the pages and worked their way into the texts. They arrested the eye immediately, whether or not the text was in a language or a script one could decipher; they held up the reading. I wondered what these animals, taken together, meant; and why it seemed to make no sense to ask what any one, taken individually, 'meant' – and whether the answers to either of these questions would help to clarify my doubts about Adams' presentation of the animals we write on.

The marginal animals in the illustrated manuscripts are not, it seems to me, being instrumentalized in the service of a larger project of meaning-making. If the *text* stands at this point for the larger project of meaning-making, the marginal animals if anything detract from it. Quite often, they make the text considerably harder to read. (I could not imagine trying to follow the micrographia around the twists and turns of a serpent in order to make out the marginal note.) In their very gratuity, their oddness, their apparent irrelevance, they seem to invite a pause before reading.[5] They make the text more opaque; they invite attention to the materiality of the book, the inks, even the writing surfaces. Viewed in an exhibition behind a glass case, by people who are not trained in the interpretation of the scripts they surround, they reinforce the sense of the text itself, before

---

3 See my article in the collection, Rachel Muers and David Grumett (eds), *Eating and Believing: Interdisciplinary Perspectives on Vegetarianism and Theology*, London: T & T Clark, 2008.

4 This develops an argument advanced in my article, 'Setting Free the Mother Bird: On Reading a Strange Text', *Modern Theology* 22:4, October 2006.

5 I am indebted to Ben Quash, Mike Higton and others for comments in, and on, a conversation in the Scriptural Reasoning Theory Group that suggested this idea to me.

any reading, interpretation or application, as sheer given, as object over against its readers. One thinks – it is remarkable *that this is*. One is invited to wonder. The marginal animals reinforce a sense of the text's resistance to, and capacity to exceed, any particular use to which it is put by its interpreters.

Of course, these marginal animals are not flesh and blood, and they are fashioned according to a particular scribe's or artist's intention. They are being used to say something – even if what they are there to say is 'pause, look, do not read too quickly, do not consume too quickly'. So it is important not to jump from the marginal animals to an assertion that the deepest instinct of the Christian tradition is, not to write on animals but to wonder at them. Nonetheless, it is worth asking: is it coincidental that it is so often animals – rather than anything else – that appear to interrupt reading? We know that people enjoy drawing animals; there is a playful exuberance about these marginal beasts that would be hard to attain with inanimate objects. There may also, however, be an aspect of the texts themselves that invites us to let the animals appear not only in the margins but on the capitals and in the headings – and that might make us think twice about writing on them in such a way as to write them out.

In beginning to explore this idea, I want first to consider an earlier and influential account of 'writing on animals', and an intriguing absence within it.

Beast and 'man' in the Hebrew Bible

Mary Midgley presents, in *Beast and Man* (and elsewhere), an extensive, lucid and damning indictment of various ways in which Western culture, and in particular its anthropology, has been written on animals.[6] The 'Beast', generally and by species, has been used for centuries, Midgley demonstrates, as the negative or positive foil for humanity. From the commonest proverbs (the 'greedy pig', the 'sly dog') to the seminal texts of modern ethics (Midgley has much to say about the 'Kantian beast'), animals have been used as building-blocks for models of humanity as it should, or should not, be. Animals have not – this is Midgley's key point – been permitted to appear as themselves; so the more complex lessons that might thereby have been learned, about humanity and the world we inhabit, have been lost. The actual behaviour of wolves in the wild, with

---

6 Mary Midgley, *Beast and Man: The Roots of Human Nature*, Ithaca: Cornell University Press, 1978, especially ch. 2.

its numerous intriguing analogies to aspects of human social behaviour, is of no concern in the claim that 'man is a wolf'. Animals are made to carry moral weight, positive or negative, as it suits our larger projects of self-interpretation. The use of animals to symbolize negative moral character-istics (as is most common) does not, Midgley recognizes, *inevitably* result in the ill-treatment of the animals themselves. Nonetheless, she is clear that both we and the other animals lose something by our propensity to write ourselves on animals; we lose *inter alia* the ability to recognize our-selves as animals, and they do often suffer ill-treatment as a result of our failure to recognize them as kin.

The evidence Midgley marshals for the historical aspect of her argu-ment is extensive and persuasive. For the theologically minded reader there is, however, one very noticeable gap. She adduces no examples from the Bible. The story she tells begins in classical philosophy; the 'Christian-ity' that appears in her pages is a Christianity that traces its intellectual lines of descent through Platonism and Stoicism.[7] Her only biblical exam-ple, as I shall discuss below, is used to support her own position over against the myth of the 'Beast'.

Why is this? One possibility is that Midgley adduces no examples, from the Bible, of animals being used as negative or even positive images of human traits because there are rather few such examples to use. The biblical writers do not often or consistently use animals in this way. This is a surprising hypothesis to be able to advance.[8] The picture Midgley paints is readily recognizable, and the temptation, especially having read her discussion, is to assume that this happens everywhere. Indeed, in investigating my hypothesis I found several initially promising pieces of counter-evidence, which on investigation proved not to be so (or not obvi-ously to be so). For example, Ecclesiastes 3.21 ('Who knows whether the human spirit goes upwards and the spirit of animals goes downwards to the earth?'[9]) has been read as emphasizing the difference between human-

---

7 See Midgley, *Beast and Man*, p. 47.
8 Boria Sax locates the Nazi symbology of animals in Germany's pre-Christian and clas-sical (particularly Greek) inheritances, and contrasts this with the attitude evinced in the Hebrew Bible. Boria Sax, *Animals in the Third Reich: Pets, Scapegoats and the Holocaust*, London: Continuum, 2000, p. 19. Stephen Webb, while very anxious to assert that the Hebrew Bible teaches human *superiority* over animals (something I would dispute), nonetheless emphasizes the extent to which animals in this text are permitted to 'be them-selves', rather than representing aspects of human behaviour or acting as negative foils for humanity. Stephen H. Webb, *Good Eating: The Bible, Diet and the Proper Love of Animals*, Grand Rapids: Brazos, 2001, pp. 36–9.
9 All scriptural quotations are from the NRSV.

ity and the 'beasts that perish'.[10] In context, however, it makes more sense as a reminder of how questionable the dividing line is between us and the 'beasts'. Is there an anxiety about becoming too closely identified with the animal, evident in some (Christian) commentaries but rather less evident – or at least, subjected to critique – in Ecclesiastes?

There are, of course, several examples in the Hebrew Bible of the comparison of people with specific animals, often to the implied detriment of the animals and of any people who are 'like' them.[11] It is perhaps noteworthy that many of these occur within dialogue, and are often in the mouths of characters whose perspective the reader is not expected to share. Besides the example discussed below, we might recall the negative uses of 'dog' in 1 Samuel 17.43 (Goliath) and 24.14 (David describing himself), 2 Samuel 9.8 (Mephibosheth), 16.9 (Abishai – in a comment immediately contradicted by David). Wild dogs and lions also appear in more threatening guise as images of human enemies – notably in Psalm 22, where the point appears to be less to denigrate the enemies than to emphasize the danger faced by the psalmist. (Note also the comparisons with snakes in Ps. 58.4; 140.3.) The blessing of Jacob (Gen. 49.1–27) has perhaps the densest concentration of animal comparisons – used of tribes rather than individuals. The condemnation of Israel's rulers in Zephaniah 3.3f. and the parallel in Ezekiel 22.25–27 probably comes closest to the sort of negative comparison that Midgley finds pervasive in Western thought. Commentaries on these texts tend to take for granted the appropriateness of comparing rulers to 'lions' and 'wolves' – pausing only to note that the lion, as the more 'noble' animal, is a suitable image for the princes.[12]

The book of Proverbs is perhaps the main place where those seeking to undermine the hypothesis advanced here might look for evidence. Here, certainly, there are repeated appeals to non-human animals as sources of wisdom for human life. Animals are frequently teachers of wisdom and of virtue by positive example (as, famously, Prov. 6.6ff. – 'Go to the ant, you

---

10 Thus Matthew Henry's commentary: 'The soul of a beast is, at death, like a candle blown out – there is an end of it; whereas the soul of a man is then like a candle taken out of a dark lantern, which leaves the lantern useless indeed, but does itself shine brighter. This great difference there is between the spirits of men and beasts.'

11 The major exception seems to be the lion, which is often the object of positive comparison – though not, as others have noted, nearly as frequently or consistently as in other bodies of ancient literature that helped to shape Western Christianity.

12 See, for example, Walther Zimmerli, *Ezekiel 1: A Commentary on the Book of the Prophet Ezekiel, Chapters 1–24*, trans. Ronald E. Clements, Philadelphia: Fortress Press, 1979.

lazybones; consider its ways, and be wise . . .'; see also 28.1; 30.24ff.), but they also function as exemplars of folly (7.22ff.; 26.3; 26.11). Particularly in this second group of examples, there does seem to be an attempt to associate folly – being less than a human being should be – with being animal-like. It is particularly noteworthy that the first two – with the ox led to the slaughter and the wild animals trapped (7.22ff.), the horse whipped and the donkey bridled (26.3) – refer explicitly to human domination of non-human animals. The fool by his folly relegates himself to the status of 'animal' and receives similar treatment. It would be foolish of *me* to deny that there are some signs here of the tendency of which Midgley speaks, to use the animals as the negative foil for 'good' human behaviour, and some material here that could be taken up by those who developed the full-scale 'moralization' of animals in (for example) the bestiary tradition. Even here, however – and perhaps also in some of the texts Midgley does discuss – there seems to be rather more demand for attention to the animals themselves than would be compatible with obscuring their real characteristics in the way Midgley describes. The 'lazybones' is invited to *go to* and *consider* the ant.

This can be linked to calls elsewhere in the Hebrew Bible to 'consider' non-human animals, which are not obviously linked to any particular 'lesson' about human moral behaviour. The marginal animals that surround biblical texts, interrupting the reading process and drawing attention to their own and the texts' materiality, are, I suggest, in keeping with at least some of the appearances of non-human animals within the texts. I turn to the source of Midgley's biblical quotation – the book of Job – in order to explore this more closely.

Behemoth and the beasts

Two passages in the book of Job illustrate neatly the potential critique of 'writing on animals' that emerges from the Hebrew Bible. One of the few biblical examples outside Proverbs of the use of a negative characterization of animals to (implicitly) exalt human beings is in Job – and, significantly, it is put in the mouth of one of the unreliable witnesses, the friends who are declared at the end not to have spoken what is right. 'Why are we counted as beasts [*behemah*] and stupid [*tamah*, vile] in your sight?' asks Bildad (Job 18.3). The last thing the friends want to be is *behemah*. Job insults them by treating them as *behemah*. *Behemah* are not-human and not-us. Perhaps there is a direct reference here to Job's call to the friends to learn from the beasts (12.7); something in the situation has apparently triggered an anxiety about getting too close to beastliness.

In the whirlwind speeches – the section of the book quoted by Midgley – the voice of God, at the climax of a series of instructions to Job to contemplate the non-human creation, calls on Job to look at Behemoth (Job 40.15).[13] As several commentators note, Behemoth, grammatically the plural of *behemah*, can be plausibly translated 'The Beast'. Even if Behemoth is (as has often been argued) a hippopotamus, he looms larger than do the various other named animals that precede him; and this effect he has within the text cannot altogether be accounted for through the suggestion that he is the mythical cosmic ox. Rather, it can be argued that Behemoth is 'all the beasts', summed up (or whatever the animal equivalent of 'personified' would be) in a single larger-than-life beastie.

What happens when Job's attention, and the reader's attention, is directed to Behemoth? Behemoth is viewed first as something *close* to Job. Thus Norman Habel: 'Behemoth and Job have a common origin, and their destinies are bound up together in some way.' Behemoth is not, Habel notes, introduced with a rhetorical challenge to Job, as something over which he is called to display his (in fact non-existent) power; 'Job is not called on to do anything except look, listen and learn.'[14] Behemoth is not something wholly other than Job, or by implication than anyone else. Perhaps there is in fact not so much difference between Job's friends and the *behemah*. Perhaps part of their problem is that they are not prepared either to look at *behemah* or to see themselves 'as *behemah*'; they are not prepared to have the distinction between themselves and the *behemah* called into question or denaturalized.

But then the description of Behemoth (as, even more so, the description of Leviathan that follows it) invites contemplation of its otherness, its givenness, its non-negotiability, its persistence over against any attempts to assimilate it for human use. *Behemah*, or at least some of them, may be there for the taking; but Behemoth is not. Like all the other animals in this second whirlwind speech, Behemoth first appears in all its fascinating detail at the margins of Job's complaint and then, by divine invitation, starts to take over.[15] It holds up the search for meaning in the reading of

---

13 For what follows I am much indebted to Susannah Ticciati, whose *Job and the Disruption of Identity*, London: T & T Clark, 2005, has shaped the reading of Job presented here – although it includes little explicit discussion of Behemoth.

14 Norman C. Habel, *The Book of Job*, London: SCM Press, 1985, p. 558.

15 Ticciati discusses the extent to which the whirlwind speeches repeat the vocabulary of Job's own initial complaint, but make non-human nature the central focus rather than the marginal illustration of Job's story. Ticciati, *Job*, pp. 102–9.

the book. By this stage, after all, we have 'got the point', have the feeling Job has got the point, and want to skip to the end; but we are being told to take a look at Behemoth, apparently for no particular reason. Rather few potted summaries of the 'meaning of Job' have much to say about Behemoth save as a rather elaborate illustration.

I have suggested, however, that Job is invited to look at Behemoth because he has something in common with him/it – namely, that they are both creatures (or, if the Greek text is to be followed, that Behemoth is 'with' Job). This has two functions. First, once Job or the reader has been freed from the need to define himself primarily by or as non-beastliness, Job or the reader might be able to rethink the ways in which he understands himself and the 'beasts'. He may not be the same as Behemoth, but, when he does not need to base his identity on the exclusion of Behemoth, he might be able to see his own 'beastly' characteristics more clearly. Second, both Job and Behemoth (and all the other 'beasts') have a relation to God that renders them properly ungraspable. They are not there simply to be ciphers in, or parchments for, other people's texts. In wondering at Behemoth, Job can wonder at himself – but he does not have to ground that wonder in any particular mark of his superiority over the beasts.[16] He is freed to be 'man' without being 'not-beast' – and thereby freed to look at Behemoth as something other than a threat requiring material or symbolic subjugation.[17]

This invites a further reflection about the place of Behemoth within the text as a whole, and on what happens when people read about Behemoth. Behemoth does not, I have suggested, add to the 'point' of the text and does not help anyone draw a better or clearer moral from Job. Behemoth seems, like the marginal animals, to hold up the search for meaning. As such, Behemoth recalls for the reader the text's own 'ungraspability' – its resistance to, and persistence over against, attempts to reduce it to its interpretations. The elaborate description with no apparent point forces the reader to focus, to use more standard terminology, on the text in its literal sense. Both Behemoth in the world and Behemoth in the text resist being turned, through interpretation, into something other than their particular and puzzling selves.

---

16 See for a further discussion of this point in terms of the centrality of *election* for Job's identity, Ticciati, *Job*, pp. 109–15. I owe to David Clough the idea of using the doctrine of election to reconstrue the relationship between humanity and the other animals.

17 As several commentators note, Behemoth, as described, is a non-threatening creature (to humans or other animals – his vegetarian diet is the first detail mentioned, Job 40.15).

Consuming the pig

This, the suspicious reader might say, is all very well, but Christian tradition clearly does go in for the symbolic consumption of animals. Indeed, Ingvild Gilhus has recently argued that the symbolic consumption of animals is characteristic of Christianity in late antiquity, marking it off from the Graeco-Roman context within which 'real' animals were accorded more religious significance. Christianity from the New Testament onwards, Gilhus claims, allegorizes animals[18] and thereby 'points away from their inherent value as animals and locks them forever into human hermeneutical processes'. Like Midgley, whom she quotes with approval, Gilhus traces Christianity's lineage (as regards attitudes to animals) primarily through Stoicism and Platonism, although she assumes that the 'Judaeo-Christian' tradition has an inherent tendency towards the symbolic consumption of animals. Christianity, in Gilhus' account, is responsible for significant innovations and developments in the late antique symbolization of animals and in the binary polarization of the human and the animal – for example in the 'systematic use of animals to describe religious dissenters'.[19]

The Christian propensity to turn animals into symbols is perhaps most obvious of all where there is a desire to render insignificant the literal consumption of animals, that is, in reading the Hebrew Bible's food laws in the context of (imagined or real) disputes with Judaism. Many of the more shameful aspects of this history are well known – such as the symbolic association of Jews with 'carnal' interpretations of animal texts, and hence with carnality and 'bestiality' (in multiple senses, all of them negative). Animals and Jews, the animals Jews do not eat and the animals they symbolically 'become' – to name names, pigs[20] – have frequently been put

---

18 Ingvild Gilhus, *Animals, Gods, and Humans: Changing Attitudes to Animals in Greek, Roman and Early Christian Thought*, London: Routledge, 2006, pp. 167–72. Many aspects of Gilhus' reading of the New Testament texts could be queried, not least her labelling of many of them as 'allegorical'. There are relatively clear instances of the symbolic use of animals for human self-definition in the New Testament – consider the 'ravening wolves' preying on the sheep in Matthew 7.15 and Acts 20.29 (an example for which I am indebted to David Clough) – but, as with the Hebrew Bible, it would be harder to argue that this is the sole or primary function of animals.

19 Gilhus, *Animals, Gods, and Humans*, p. 264; and see her discussion of Epiphanius, pp. 238–42. She does admit that this was picking up and developing an older Graeco-Roman tradition of comparing one's enemies with beasts.

20 See Claudine Fabre-Vassas, *The Singular Beast: Jews, Christians and the Pig*, trans. Carol Volk, New York: Columbia University Press, 1997, for a fascinating analysis of the history of the pig as focal symbol of Christian identity over against Judaism in medieval Europe.

to use in definitions of Christian identity. Biblical interpretation, with the food laws relating to animals as a key set of texts, has of course been crucial in the various historical shifts in Christian attitudes towards Jews and Judaism.[21] Are animals (and especially pigs) in this context simply something on which Christians write their arguments, their polemics or their caricatures? It would certainly seem that, in their disputes with Jews over the food laws and their interpretation, Christians have had a particular interest in not allowing pigs to appear *as pigs*. Nonetheless, I would suggest that there is scope even within the tradition of Christian reinterpretation of the food laws for the animals themselves to reappear, to attract attention and perhaps to claim their kinship with us.

Augustine's *Against Faustus the Manichaean* provides an intriguing example of, and source for, the tradition of reinterpreting animals in the food laws.[22] Recall that in this text Augustine is fighting, as it were, on two fronts – directly against the Manichaean who rejects the Old Testament and its God altogether, indirectly against rabbinic Judaism, or against the charge that the acceptance of the Old Testament necessarily implies the acceptance of 'Jewish' interpretations. A theology of creation, and a theory of signs and their interpretation, are implicitly put to work in reading, or writing on, the pig.

One of Augustine's striking moves is to compare the pig – and its positive/permitted counterpart, the lamb – to a word.

> For instance, a pig and a lamb are both clean in their nature, for every creature of God is good; but symbolically, a lamb is clean, and a pig unclean. So the words wise and fool are both clean in their nature, as words composed of letters, but fool may be called symbolically unclean, because it means an unclean thing.

---

21 David Grumett's work for the 'Vegetarianism as Spiritual Choice' project draws attention to the numerous contexts in which Hebrew Bible food laws had continuing 'literal' force for Christians, for many centuries. It has been proposed by Abigail Firey (see 'The Letter of the Law: Carolingian Exegetes and the Old Testament', in Jane Dammen McAuliffe, Barry D. Walfish and Joseph W. Goering (eds), *With Reverence for the Word: Medieval Scriptural Exegesis in Judaism, Christianity, and Islam*, New York: Oxford University Press, 2003, pp. 204–24) that the Carolingian interpreters effected a major shift both in attitudes to Judaism and in attitudes to the food laws by developing extended 'spiritual' interpretations of these texts. Grumett's research suggests that the picture is somewhat more complicated. The relationship between readings of the Old Testament and Christian dietary restrictions was never a straightforward 'reading off' of laws taken to be directly binding on all Christians, although the Old Testament (and not merely Acts 15) did exert significant influence on decisions on dietary questions during the conversion of northern Europe.

22 Augustine of Hippo, *Against Faustus the Manichaean*, 6.7.

We might assume that at this point, by being turned into something 'symbolically unclean', the pig has been (as it were) written all over, such that it cannot appear as anything other than a determinate unit of meaning; its pigness has been consumed by what it signifies. This is not, however, the full force of Augustine's comparison. Rather, confronted with the Manichaean who wants to deny the goodness of creation, he goes to some length to emphasize the goodness of words *as things*, and the goodness of 'wordness' itself, of the capacity to signify. He encourages people to pause where they usually do not pause – in contemplating the words themselves. 'Fool' is, he says, as good a word as 'wise'; the things signified are vastly different, but the words are equally good as sounds, and equally good at being words. Likewise, the pig and the lamb are both included within the creation that God declares to be good. They are (in a derived but real way) good in and as themselves, good at being the particular creatures they are; and they are also good at being signifiers of divine meaning.

Augustine notes that the pig, in the context of biblical revelation, comes to signify folly rather than wisdom; but that casts no aspersions on the pig itself. It turns out that the avoidance of pork, in obedience to the law, is for Augustine an absolutely indispensable stage in the 'reading' of the pig. Without it, the pig means nothing in particular.[23] Furthermore, even once the pig has acquired its symbolic meaning in Christian interpretation, the real unconsumed pigs (and for that matter the real consumed lambs) remain as 'things', as good parts of the good creation, whose significance exceeds human attempts to exhaust or control it. God gives the pig its meanings through the history of revelation, and as a creature and sign of God it retains its surplus of potential and future meaning – a surplus that can be glimpsed as people contemplate its created pigness.

It seems to me that Augustine in this text makes the pig less into a blank writing surface than into a decorated letter. He does, of course, proceed fairly swiftly to describe his opponents as pigs, which is precisely the sort of move identified by Gilhus as characteristic of Christians' symbolic consumption of animals.[24] What Augustine (unlike Epiphanius, the focus of Gilhus' discussion) does not do, however, is to make his opponents

---

23 Jeremy Cohen is among the scholars to draw attention to the *relatively* positive interpretation of Judaism – at least when compared to that of late medieval writers – implied by Augustine's biblical hermeneutics. See his *Living Letters of the Law: Ideas of the Jew in Medieval Christianity*, Berkeley: University of California Press, 1999, esp. ch. 1.

24 Gilhus also describes the Manichaean avoidance of animal flesh as evidence of 'a more compassionate ethic towards the animal world than [that of] Christians' (*Animals, Gods, and Humans*, p. 260), while noting that this abstinence had 'little to do with concern for the well-being of animals' (p. 261)!

'bestial' and only himself human. The texts from which he is working simply do not allow him to make so much of the dividing line between human and non-human animals. He has to assign animal characters to everyone – the pigs to the Manichaeans, the lambs to the orthodox. 'Animalness' as such is not used to define the 'bad', the 'other-than-human' or the 'other-than-us'. Even the use of animal-based insults, it becomes apparent as we consider this passage, has a range of different possible implications and underlying logics. The Christian 'bestialization' of Jews in the later Middle Ages – and for that matter the Jewish 'bestialization' of the nations[25] – was linked to a binary construction of humanity and the 'beasts' that does not appear in Augustine's text.

That is all very well, Adams (or somebody arguing her line) might say, again, but would it not have been better for the pigs – and especially for the lambs, who had the misfortune to be categorized as 'clean' – if they had not been written on at all? They are, after all, still being treated as 'words' and as 'meat';[26] they are symbolically consumed to form the social bodies of religious communities, and they are literally consumed by the people who make this symbolic use of them. Could the texts not simply leave them alone? Once the non-human animals have appeared and have been allotted meanings within a theological system, there is always the possibility that they will be reduced to just these meanings, that it will come to be thought that they matter only in so far as they serve to hold up these systems – to feed us meat or to teach us a lesson.

This is a fair point, and one against which there is no easy defence. We have already seen that even within the Hebrew Bible – which I have held up as a source for Christian resistance to the symbolic consumption of animals – examples can be found of 'writing on animals'. Christians are bound not only to read and reread these scriptural texts, but to read and reread a tradition of interpretation that does frequently mandate the symbolic consumption of animals. It is no doubt true, as Midgley, Adams and many others argue, that Christian thought has tended to work – in the West at least – for the instrumentalization of non-human animals and for the drawing of sharp dividing lines between 'man and beast'. My discussion should not be taken as a defence of 'Christianity' in general against this accusation. Nonetheless, I do want to highlight the fact that the

---

25 I am indebted to Aaron Gross for this point.
26 Adams, with other animal ethicists, has discussed extensively the processes (material and cultural) by which many individual 'animals' become the mass noun 'meat'; see, for example, *Neither Man Nor Beast*, ch. 6. See also Noélie Vialles, *Animal to Edible*, Cambridge: Cambridge University Press, 1994.

Christian inheritance of 'the West' includes not only the animals we write on but also the animals we *draw in*.

We live with the other animals; ignoring them altogether in our texts is not an option (and even if it were, it would not necessarily mean that we related to them better). We also, in one way or another, live off the other animals, materially and symbolically; we interpret them and learn from them, and even if we do not eat or wear them we need them to maintain liveable environments for us. One way and another, we depend on other creaturely life, and this dependence is seen in our symbolic as well as our material existence. We cannot pretend that we do not need the non-human animals. So non-human animals are drawn into our lives and our texts, and once they have been drawn in they are in some way at risk. The question is whether we can draw them in to our spheres of interest and concern without consuming them completely.

As I have attempted to indicate in this chapter, this is linked to further questions about how Christians negotiate the relationships between literal and non-literal or more-than-literal interpretations of the biblical texts themselves – and about how they negotiate their relationships to Jewish communities and Jewish readings of the texts. Negative assessments of 'the animal', 'the literal' and 'the Jew' have often gone together in Christian history, with results ranging from the faintly problematic to the disastrous. For multiple reasons, therefore, including the rethinking of relationships between and within human communities, it may be time to look again at the animals in the margins.

8

Elves, Hobbits, Trolls and Talking Beasts[1]

STEPHEN R. L. CLARK

Oral and archaeological prehistory

Once upon a time, the story goes, we humans could encounter elves, dwarves, goblins, giants and maybe hobbits. We could also, sometimes, talk to non-hominids, and expect a reasoned answer. Giants, typically, are rather stupid; dwarves are great craftsmen, but avaricious; elves and goblins depend on glamour and delusion; mermaids are forlorn, and also – like elves – dangerous. Even now there may be occasional sightings of wild men, Bigfoots and mysterious aliens with peculiar habits.[2] These particular stereotypes are those of northern Europe,[3] but very similar stories are told across the world. We may choose to explain them as animistic fantasies, natural to a species that sees mood and intention everywhere. Perhaps they embody doctrines about the dead, and our own destinies.[4] Or maybe they are relics of real encounters with other human tribes, whose ways seem 'elvish' and unnatural. Maybe the stories are extrapolated from the evidence of long-extinct life forms or geological epochs: stone arrowheads are named 'elf-shot', as readily as the rocks of the Giants' Causeway are reckoned, exactly, as the work of giants, or

---

1 Earlier versions were considered by all contributors to this volume, by those attending a Lancaster University conference on animals, especially Stephen Bostock, by Prof. Simon Conway Morris, and by Liverpool graduate students. My thanks to all.

2 See Patrick Harpur, *Daimonic Reality*, London: Arkana, 1994, for an interesting study of connections between present-day 'alien abduction' narratives and the like and the older 'fairy tales'.

3 See Katherine Briggs, *The Fairies in Tradition and Literature*, London: Routledge & Kegan Paul, 1966.

4 W. Y. Evans-Wentz, *The Fairy Faith in Celtic Countries*, London and New York: H. Frowde, 1911. See also Stephen R. L. Clark, 'How to Believe in Fairies', *Inquiry* 30, 1988, pp. 337–55.

dinosaur bones are dragons.[5] Or maybe the stories are just fictions, play-ful exaggerations of ordinary human characters and concerns.

One other possibility is that they are folk memories, not of encounters with other human tribes but of the millennia during which there were indeed, the newer story goes, a great many hominid species.[6] It is not a new thought, and has – obviously – served more than scientific ends:

> Aided by the new science of archaeology, euhemerism (the belief that myths and folk beliefs arise from actual historical persons or events) became a major explanation of fairy origins, raising issues related to Victorian ideas of race and empire. Were the originals of the fairies a lowly, perhaps aboriginal British tribe or were they a superior group who brought magical knowledge to those they invaded? The new euhemerism climaxed in the 1890s in David MacRitchie's once famous, now discredited 'pygmy theory' of fairy origins. By the turn of the century, however, Darwin reinterpreted (or misinterpreted) gave rise to the idea of fairies as invisible life-forms, not yet understood, that had developed on a separate branch of the evolutionary tree, but that would soon be classified and verified by scientific means.[7]

This last thought, of course, appealed to occultists more than to respect-able scientists (though the classes are not quite distinct). The more con-ventional story was simply that those other kinds died out, and we have remembered tales about them. The stories would have had to last a long time: in Europe, the last Neanderthals seem to have died about 24,000 years ago; in Indonesia, if the newly identified remains are truly of a separate hominid species, now nicknamed 'hobbits', they died out 12,000 years ago.[8] If folk tales record still earlier species, *Giganthropus* or *Homo habilis*, they have lasted longer than the oldest oral epic. Of course, that is

---

5 See Adrienne Mayor and Michael Heaney, 'Griffins and Arimaspeans', *Folklore* vol. 104, no. 1/2, 1993, pp. 40–66.

6 See Bernard Wood, 'Hominid Revelations from Chad', *Nature* 418, 11 July, pp. 133–5, though this discussion relates to an even earlier period, 5 or 6 million years ago (and well beyond any plausible folk memory).

7 Carole G. Silver, *Strange and Secret Peoples: Fairies and Victorian Consciousness*, New York: Oxford University Press, 2000, p. 7.

8 See Mike Morwood and Penny van Oosertzee, *A New Human*, New York: Smithsonian Books, 2007. Their particular oddity is that their brains are considerably small-er than those hitherto expected for hominids, but 'restructured in a way that meant [they were] probably smart, had language and could plan ahead' (p. 177). Recent studies seem to show that their wrist structure is closer to australopithecine than hominid, which would confirm that they were indeed a different species.

likely enough: if the earliest human experience was of a world with many communicative, hand-crafty and symbolizing species, then stories about those encounters might be a central theme of any human narrative. And it is not surprising that the stories often carry a sense that those times are not now: fairyland is always long ago 'and who of late for cleanliness found sixpence in her shoe?'[9] I acknowledge at once that this may also reflect our memory of childhood, when everything was 'elvish' because nothing much made sense. As Paul Veyne has pointed out, we all remember a time when there were giants[10] (and it is no surprise that those remembered giants are typically quite stupid!).

The folk tales, European or otherwise, are not strong evidence that there is folk memory of times so many thousands of years ago, nor do they tell us anything secure about the characters of those other species. Any ethnographical analysis will probably find more evidence, in them, of the characters of our own species, or of particular tribes. Whatever the stories meant in their beginnings, there have been many thousand years of human invention in which their style, substance, morals and metaphysics have been altered. But there is nonetheless good reason to believe that there were indeed encounters between 'us', our ancestors, and 'them', our distant cousins, and no surprise that even earnest palaeoanthropologists can rarely resist the temptation to describe them. The commonest assumption is that 'we' somehow destroyed 'them', whether by direct assault (as, after all, we often have destroyed such weaker human tribes as we encountered[11]), or by contagious diseases, or by out-breeding them, or altering their habitats. Even if Neanderthals were not the brutes of popular mythology, they were at any rate 'uncreative' (or so we are told), content with the same sort of axes for millenia, and maybe not even able to speak grammatically. Why else would they have died out? To which one answer may be that this is what species do: there may be no one reason why a

---

9 'Farewell, Rewards and Fairies': Richard Corbet (1582–1635) lamenting the vanishing of fairyland with the Reformation. But the fairies had already gone in Chaucer's day (see 'The Wife of Bath's Tale'), and even in Homer's Phaeacia.

10 See Paul Veyne, *Did the Greeks Believe in Their Myths? Essay on the Constitutive Imagination*, Chicago: University of Chicago Press, 1988.

11 This is the running theme of Esteban Sarmiento, G. J. Sawyer and Richard Milner, *The Last Human: A Guide to Twenty-two Species of Extinct Humans*, New Haven and London: Yale University Press, 2007. Nicholas Ward, *Before the Dawn: Recovering the Lost History of our Ancestors*, New York: Penguin, 2005, is also confident that *Homo sapiens* exterminated both *Homo neanderthalensis* and *Homo erectus*, once one ancestral band managed to break out from Africa. Perhaps so, but we have no actual archaeological evidence of the imagined butchery.

species fades away, nor any need to invoke the possibility of deliberate or unthinking genocide. The very stories we tell about such matters reveal *our* preconceptions and concerns just as much as Corbet's did. That so many theorists are content to think that our ancestors were genocidal apes is intriguing: does this suggest that we are rather ashamed of more recent episodes, or that we are covertly pleased to think ourselves survivors?

What Indonesian 'hobbits' were like (if they were real), we cannot guess. What Neanderthals were like, we guess too often! Were they 'cavemen' and therefore obviously brutish? Or in a swift reversal of popular prejudice were they the gentle woodsmen of William Golding's imagination?[12] Perhaps they sang before they thought to talk, as Steve Mithen has suggested.[13] Perhaps they resembled the fairies of Victorian (and later) fantasy, in lacking any empathy or concern for 'us'.[14] Perhaps they were the Elder Folk described by Michael Scott Rohan, survivors of an earlier Ice Age, masters of a high technology that seemed magical to our less cultured ancestors, and also – except in their last decay – exceptionally 'moral'?[15] Maybe they were even predatory magicians, who never needed our stone-age technology, as in Jack Williamson's spooky story *Darker than You Think* (though I doubt it).[16]

But first consider why some people don't want these stories to be true, even in outline. Why Desmond Morris supposes that 'the existence of Mini-Man [or of any other hominid species] should destroy religion'[17] I have no idea, unless – absurdly – he identifies 'religion' with 'creationism' (itself a misnomer for a largely American, largely Protestant sect infected by a naively literal interpretation of the Bible). But it is true that there have been reasons to suspect the motives of those who think too readily that there are many human species. The biblical narrative insists that there is but one humanity, created in Adam and redeemed in Christ, although some apocryphal writings suggest that we have cousins, born of Lilith or

12 William Golding, *The Inheritors*, London: Faber, 1955.

13 Steven Mithen, *The Singing Neanderthals: The Origins of Music, Language, Mind and Body*, London: Weidenfeld & Nicolson, 2005.

14 Silver, *Strange and Secret Peoples*, p. 12.

15 Michael Scott Rohan, *The Winter of the World*, London: Macdonald, 1986–89.

16 Jack Williamson, *Darker than You Think*, London: Gollancz, 2003 [1948]: this story, involving a conspiracy to breed back to those ancient predators, speaks to the paranoia of Cold War America, but also to a more general paranoia, evident in worldwide beliefs about changelings and witches.

17 http://news.bbc.co.uk/2/hi/uk_news/magazine/3964579.stm (accessed 8 December 2007), quoted by Morwood, *New Human*, p. 187.

begotten by Cain.[18] This monophyletic conception of humanity may well have been something to maintain, in the face of anthropologists who proposed that there were many distinct races, that we could not be of one blood with Bushmen, Hottentots or Aboriginals,[19] that Hottentots or pygmies (for example) were pre-Adamite in origin, and our inferiors.

For those using the rhetoric of the three Cs, commerce, culture, and Christianity, to justify imperial claims, it was often convenient to describe the colonized as less or other than human. In one striking manifestation of this view, Ota Benga, an African Pygmy, perceived as alien even among other racial specimens (he was from a tribe different from that of his fellow Pygmies, spoke a distinctive language, and had teeth filed into points), was consigned for several weeks to the Monkey House of the Bronx Zoo. The floor of his cage was artificially strewn with bones to intimate that he was a cannibal, while he was billed as a 'missing link' and exhibited with an orangutan.[20]

Personally, I would rather that even orangutans were not treated so disrespectfully, but it may still be a good idea, politically, to insist that pygmies are really human, and that this matters! Even modern geneticists, who typically suggest that a genome is more like a loose-leaf folder than a tight-bound volume, and that species are no more than sets of interbreeding populations, still prefer to believe that there is a firm distinction

---

18 There were also 'giants (*nephilim*) in the world in those days' when 'the sons of God' bred with 'the daughters of men' (Genesis 6.4): all these lines were presumably extinguished at the flood (as is suggested in the *Book of Jubilees* 7.21–25; cf. Numbers 13.33).

19 See Philip Almond, 'Adam, Pre-Adamites, and Extra-Terrestrial Beings in Early Modern Europe', *Journal of Religious History* 30, issue 2, 2006, pp. 163–74, pp. 168f: 'Thus, for example, in 1625, the philosopher Nathanael Carpenter in his Geography maintained that Moses' motivation, in writing his genealogical lists was so that all people would understand themselves to be descended from the same original "then which there is no greater meanes to conciliate and ioyne mens affections for mutuall amitie and conversation" (Nathanael Carpenter, *Geography Delineated Forth in Two Books* (Oxford, 1625), 2:207). Similarly, in 1656, the year of La Peyrère's *Men before Adam*, John White remarked in his commentary on Genesis that the reason for God's having created only one couple was to unite all men in love to one another so that "we cannot shut up our bowels of compassion from any man, of what Nation or Kindred soever he be" (John White, *A Commentary Upon the Three First Chapters of Genesis* (London, 1656), 1:111). Some forty years later, Richard Kidder, Bishop of Bath and Wells, suggested that the origin of all people was from one man to ensure that claims of racial superiority could not arise, that "men might not boast and vaunt of their extraction and original . . . and that they might think themselves under an obligation to love and assist each other as proceeding from the same original and common parent" (Richard Kidder, *A Commentary on the Five Books of Moses* (London, 1694), 1:6.).'

20 Silver, *Strange and Secret Peoples*, p. 134.

between humans and all other animals (since they want to go on using 'animals' in their experiments). The real possibility that there were or might be *other* human or hominid species introduces the sort of betwixt-and-betweens that make such moral distinctions vain.

The fact, if it is one, that we are one species now does not imply that we always were, or always shall be. Darwin's insight, after all, exactly was that the many interbreeding varieties of a given species might diverge enough to be species by themselves, that blocks against inter-breeding might be geographical or cultural or physiological, and that it was this isolation of one population from another that permitted them to diverge in other ways. That was why there were many different sorts of finch on the Galapagos Islands: particular changes, whether effects merely of the 'founder principle' or actually offering an intelligible advantage in particular contexts, were not swamped by other changes. Speciation may also occur even within a given region when different lines adopt entirely different modes of life. Maybe there has not been sufficient time for isolated human populations to diverge (or else no populations, not even the Australians, have really been entirely isolated): members of our species are more like each other genetically than West African chimpanzees are like East African, despite overt dissimilarities. But back in the old days any hominid population was probably much smaller than our tribes, and easier to isolate. Some palaeoanthropolo-gists have in the past supposed that we could construct a simple linear progression through the fossil forms, but it is just as likely that most of them are only rather remote cousins. That 'Lucy' (the type-specimen of *Australopithicus afarensis*, found in Ethiopia) was our ancestress, or even the sister of our ancestors, is too much serendipity to quite believe.[21] We cannot even be entirely sure that the theoretically identified common ancestor and ancestress of all of us (Y-chromosome Adam and mitochondrial Eve[22]) were both clearly of 'our own species', since the very notion of a 'species' is only applied palaeologically by inference.[23]

---

21 See Ann Gibbons, *The First Human: The Race to Discover our Earliest Ancestors*, New York: Doubleday, 2006.

22 We shall never dig up their bones: they are imagined on the basis of present-day descriptions of what characters are shared on the Y-chromosome and in maternal mitochon-dria, respectively: assuming that the rate of change in these genes is steady, 'mitochondrial Eve' lived about 140,000 years ago in Africa, 'Y-chromosome Adam' between 60,000 and 90,000 years.

23 That is, the moment when *habilis* changes to *erectus* (if that is the historical progres-sion) is determined only by palaeontological guesswork, not by the blunt criterion that one does not breed true with the other.

The common ancestors of elves, dwarves and men, of course, were certainly not of the same species as ourselves!

So even if our folk tales don't record any actual memory, even a distorted memory, of the elder days, those days, most probably, were real. There really was a time when our own ancestors could have encountered other hominid species, peoples who could talk, use tools and decorate themselves – and their graves. There was much less difference for them between 'the human' and 'the non-human' because there were many sorts of, as it were, 'para-human'. Darwin expected that there would one day be an even greater gap between human and non-human, 'for it will intervene between man in a more civilized state, as we may hope, than the Caucasian, and some ape as low as a baboon, instead of as at present between the Negro or Australian and the gorilla'.[24] Correspondingly, there was once much less of a gap – and probably even less excuse for judgements about relative 'inferiority'.

The assumption, mentioned before, that our ancestors probably killed off the others, gets its strength from historical acts of genocide. But not all migrations have been bloody, and it is not always true that people have been repelled by creatures a little too like themselves. On the contrary, xenophilia is also an abiding motive: we are attracted, often, by the exotic. Maybe dwarves, trolls and goblins are ugly, in our terms, but elves, mermaids, dryads and the rest can cast a glamour – even if we later regret this (for elves and the rest are certainly dangerous, in part because their emotions are not quite ours). Our present species is one species because we find each other attractive, and often more attractive for being unlike ourselves. When our ancestors encountered the other hominids they were already fully speciated: it does not follow that they were all unattractive. But it is also likely that our natural responses, facial expressions, tastes and inhibitions were subtly or not-so-subtly different. Meeting other humans, we can usually recognize smiles and frowns at least, even if particular gestures are culturally determined. The expressions of chimpanzees don't necessarily mean the same as ours. The other hominid and australopithecine species, obviously, were more closely related to us than pongids, but we might easily find ourselves at odds. We can guess that all hominids will be charmed by the young of any hominid species (since we're charmed by the young of most mammalian species!), but we may not respond as easily to differing gestures of appeasement, nor understand

---

24 Charles Darwin, *The Descent of Man*, New Jersey: Princeton University Press, 1981 (a facsimile of the 1871 edition), vol. 1, p. 201.

when actions are 'in play' and when they are really serious. Each species will be peculiar or grotesque to others, whether we are entranced by this or not. They may be as different in their manners as bonobos from chimpanzees, or rhesus monkeys from stump-tailed macaques. Among the easiest fancies about our differences might be that other hominid species had distinct breeding seasons, and that the sexes mostly kept apart,[25] or that some were as sexually dimorphic as gorillas.[26] Perhaps some were obligate carnivores, or far more solitary than the primate norm. Perhaps some were very much kinder. Perhaps their specialist adaptations to differing environments (whether they differed geographically or functionally) would have made much of their behaviour quite opaque to us, entirely other than we can fit into. Maybe they relied much more on smell and taste than we do, or responded to a wider electromagnetic spectrum. Maybe their sense of time was very different. One of our most enduring self-conceptions is that human beings can imitate any social form, that we are supremely generalists – but maybe this is a delusion, and all human variations are within a biologically determined space which other hominid species did not share. This too need not require us to suppose that we were always hostile: on the contrary, the very differences between us might have helped us coexist (as our ancestors and Neanderthals coexisted for millennia). After all, we coexist with, and co-operate with, dogs, most of whose pleasures and innate expressions we don't share! Our chief rivals are our conspecifics.[27] It is easier for creatures of many different species to inhabit the same objective space than the same number of conspecific individuals.[28] Mostly they ignore each other – but they can also co-operate.

25 As in Sawyer's imagined history, where it was Neanderthals who survived: see Robert Sawyer, *Hominids*, New York: Tom Doherty Associates, 2002, and its sequels.

26 This seems to have been true for some robust australopithecines: see Ann Gibbons, 'Hominid Harems: Big Males Competed for Small Australopithecine Females', *Science* 1363, 07/11/30, 2007, p. 1443.

27 It has even been suggested recently that chimpanzees and gorillas grew *less* like our common, bipedal ancestor, so they did not need to compete with hominids: see Aaron G. Filler, *The Upright Ape: A New Origin of the Species*, Franklin Lakes NJ: New Page Books, 2007.

28 Witness the cichlids of the East African lakes: Melanie L. J. Stiassny and Axel Meyer, 'Cichlids of the Rift Lakes', *Scientific American* February 1999, pp. 44–9: see Stephen R. L. Clark, *Biology and Christian Ethics*, Cambridge: Cambridge University Press, 2000, p. 56.

The coming races

What's past is prologue. Once upon a time there were many hominid species. Just at the moment there is only one – though many human varieties might have been different species if things had gone only a little otherwise, and Darwin thought that 'the Negro and the European are so distinct that, if specimens had been brought to a naturalist without any further information, they would undoubtedly have been considered by him as good and true species'.[29] The thought, of course, should lead to the suspicion that it is not so easy to say that fossil specimens are of different species, and that we should beware of prejudice. But we might also wonder why their 'being of different species' might matter (except to a taxonomist). Different species have different liabilities and responses (so that knowing exactly which species a particular plant or bug may be will sometimes matter when we want to kill or cultivate it). But it seems likely that the underlying thought is that different species can't matter to each other, since they can never share viable offspring. Even this is not entirely clear: now that we understand that bars against interbreeding are of differing strengths we can also suspect that species sometimes separate and merge again – as hominids and pongids maybe did.[30] Whether 'modern man' and Neanderthal also interbred is a matter still undecided. But suppose that 'good and true species' really don't interbreed. Suppose even that it does turn out that some existing 'human' population is already a distinct species. What follows from this, except – perhaps – that we may discover that members of that population are differently susceptible to this drug or that, or that they are largely immune to certain common diseases, or have a different digestive system? We might even find that some human populations produce better (or worse) mathematicians, athletes or musicians. Is that sufficient reason even to imagine that they have fewer or different 'rights' than 'mainstream humans'? After all, it is already true

---

29 Darwin, *Descent*, vol. 2, p. 388.

30 See http://news.bbc.co.uk/2/hi/science/nature/4991470.stm reporting N. Patterson, D. J. Richter, S. Gnerre, E. S. Lander, D. Reich, 'Genetic Evidence for Complex Speciation of Humans and Chimpanzees', *Nature* 441, 2006, pp. 1103–1108 (29 June: published online 17 May 2006): 'Our analysis also shows that human–chimpanzee speciation occurred less than 6.3 million years ago and probably more recently, conflicting with some interpretations of ancient fossils. Most strikingly, chromosome X shows an extremely young genetic divergence time, close to the genome minimum along nearly its entire length. These unexpected features would be explained if the human and chimpanzee lineages initially diverged, then later exchanged genes before separating permanently.' <http://www.nature.com/nature/journal/v441/n7097/abs/nature04789.html> (accessed 20 September 2007)

that adult Europeans are unusual in being able to stomach cow's milk, that Tibetans can cope in thinner air, that some human lineages carry damaging recessives, that we smell differently to each other (though mostly from different diets), and both Chinese and Ashkenazi Jews generally do score higher than Europeans on standard IQ tests! Any of these distinctions might have made us different species. As it is, the human lineage has passed through at least one genetic bottleneck, and we are *all* more closely related, more alike, than most other well-travelled species. But this need not have been, and may soon change. It has even been suggested that

> Human races are evolving away from each other. Genes are evolving fast in Europe, Asia and Africa, but almost all of these are unique to their continent of origin. We are getting less alike, not merging into a single, mixed humanity.[31]

But while there are indeed different evolutionary pressures in these different areas, there are probably enough overlapping populations to make speciation, under the present circumstances, somewhat unlikely – unless some characteristic strongly selected in one region accidentally makes fertile matings between that population and another just a little less likely: that is how species begin.

There are at least three futures in which this is more probable.[32] First, in the aftermath of nuclear war, and the following nuclear winter, or some equivalent catastrophe, such tribes as survive will be isolated (and probably also subject to an increase in random mutation). After a few tens of thousand years their descendants may meet up again and find they are now quite different. It's a likely enough story, but not an enlightening one. Second, we may suppose that we actually succeed in spreading from this one planetary system to a wider world, but without the sort of (imaginary) Faster Than Light transport that would keep our scattered clans in touch. Multi-generational starships, or automata carrying embryos or frozen volunteers, might colonize the neighbouring stars in only a few tens of thousand years (and one of the standing puzzles, the Fermi Paradox, is

---

31 Henry Harpending's suggestion at <http://www.physorg.com/news116529402.html> (accessed 20 December 2007).

32 This is not to say that these are the only possible futures. On the contrary, there are at least two others: one in which our various varieties are unified (most probably black-haired, brown-skinned and rather skinny); and another in which, like almost every species, we die out.

that this does not seem to have happened already – with some other species as the colonizers[33]). This future too is possible, though maybe less likely than the first,[34] but is also not very enlightening – except as a reminder on the one hand that such diversity will give our lineage a better hope of survival and on the other that we would be well advised to create some long-lasting tradition of mutual help and admiration while we have the chance! Both scenarios allow us to imagine other possibilities more distant from the mainstream human than mere cultural variation. But there is a third scenario that makes these imaginings more immediately relevant.

> The sub-conscious popular instinct against Darwinism was . . . that when once one begins to think of man as a shifting and alterable thing, it is always easy for the strong and crafty to twist him into new shapes for all kinds of unnatural purposes. The popular instinct sees in such developments the possibility of backs bowed and hunch-backed for their burden, or limbs twisted for their task. It has a very well-grounded guess that whatever is done swiftly and systematically will mostly be done by a successful class and almost solely in their interests. It has therefore a vision of unhuman hybrids and half-human experiments much in the style of Mr. Wells's Island of Dr Moreau . . . The rich man may come to be breeding a tribe of dwarfs to be his jockeys, and a tribe of giants to be his hall-porters.[35]

In other words we may deliberately breed different human species: that is, the powerful may breed them (and perhaps maintain a small class of scholars or innovative engineers to do the actual work[36]). Maybe this need not be overt oppression: after all, it would pay the powerful to ensure that each of their new specimens preferred the life they lead, and it is doubtful

---

33 See Stephen Webb, *If the Universe Is Teeming with Aliens . . . Where Is Everybody? Fifty Solutions to Fermi's Paradox and the Problem of Extraterrestrial Life*, New York: Copernicus Books, 2002.

34 All such predictions have to reckon with another puzzle, 'the Doomsday Argument', which seems to show that we here-now are very much more likely to be born in the largest (and perhaps the last) of human generations: see John Leslie, *The End of the World: Science and Ethics of Human Extinction*, London: Routledge, 1996.

35 G. K. Chesterton, *What's Wrong with the World*, London: Cassell & Co., 1910, p. 259.

36 On which, see Stephen R. L. Clark, 'Posthumanism: Engineering in the Place of Ethics', in Barry Smith and Berit Brogaard (eds), *Rationality and Irrationality: Proceedings of the 23rd International Wittgenstein Symposium*, Vienna: ÖbvetHpt, 2001, pp. 62–76.

that any of these could sue for having been made the way they are. Nor need they suppose that the new kinds are 'inferior': on the contrary, a 'good dwarf' would be valued as much as a good horse, however strange he or she looked by mainstream standards. Might it not be a very good thing to think of there being different species, just because there will then be different norms? It is difficult, now, not to see – say – a Down's syndrome child as 'odd', but if he or she were conceived not as a mainstream human but as a fine example of another, kindlier kind, we should be no more squeamish than about any other non-conspecific. In other words, we retain, at least at an emotional level, some notion of species as norm-driven, and are affected by those who stray too far from ours. Recognizing them as judged and guided by a different norm we may see their actual excellence. As Adam Sedgwick remarked, in complaint against what he and Richard Owen took to be the implications of Darwinian theory, 'the reptilian fauna of the Mesozoic period is the grandest and highest that ever lived':[37] dinosaurs were not defective, and later generations of animal organism were no 'fitter' (in the easy sense of 'better')!

As he so often did, Chesterton asked the appropriate question in a work of fiction:

Suppose he [that is, a particular 'backward' child] did remain more like a child than the rest of us. Is there anything particularly horrible about a child? Do you shudder when you think of your dog, merely because he's happy and fond of you and yet can't do the forty-eighth proposition of Euclid? Being a dog is not a disease. Being a child is not a disease. Even remaining a child is not a disease.[38]

The older biological synthesis, it is true, might also think of idiots (and women) as 'defective', or judge all creatures by their closeness to the 'human' (which is to say, the adult, rational, male) form. But it was also open to believers to acknowledge every real existent, and specifically every human child, as equally a child of God, not to be judged 'defective' in comparison with Us. Chesterton again:

When your parliaments grow more corrupt and your wars more cruel, do not dream that you can breed a Houyhnhnm like a race-horse, or

---

37 As reported by Richard Owen in 'Objections to Mr Darwin's Theory of the Origin of Species', *Edinburgh Review* 11, 1860, pp. 487–532, reprinted in David L. Hull (ed.), *Darwin and His Critics*, Chicago: University of Chicago Press, 1983, p. 163.
38 G. K. Chesterton, *Four Faultless Felons*, London: Cassell, 1930, p. 39.

summon monsters from the moon, or cry out in your madness for something beyond the stature of man. Do you in that day of disillusion still have the strength to say: these are no Yahoos; these are men; these are fallen men; these are they for whom their Omnipotent Creator did not disdain to die.[39]

I shall return to this question. But first I want to modify the scenario, in the light of current theories and techniques. After all, once we have accepted the possibility of breeding people, recreating Neanderthals, manufacturing mermaids or giving lions the power of speech, why should we bother with distinct species? It may be that some particular types will be of general value, and therefore become a staple of the industry, but each organism can be designed for a specific purpose, and its genome be available for any further use, without preserving the biological species. We could draw on non-human, non-hominid genomes just as well as human. As above, a genome is more like a loose-leaf folder than a bound volume. As Freeman Dyson has proposed, 'We are moving rapidly into the post-Darwinian era, when species will no longer exist, and the evolution of life will again be communal.'[40] Genes will be shared around as easily among us as they are among bacteria (for which species distinctions have always been moot). Once we have identified the genes that enable human language we could even scatter them through the biosphere by retroviral infection (and so realize the animistic dream).

Dyson, it seems to me, is a great deal too optimistic in his description of the early years:

In the post-Darwinian era, biotechnology will be domesticated. There will be do-it-yourself kits for gardeners, who will use gene transfer to breed new varieties of roses and orchids. Also, biotech games for children, played with real eggs and seeds rather than with images on a screen. Genetic engineering, once it gets into the hands of the general public, will give us an explosion of biodiversity. Designing genomes will be a new art form, as creative as painting or sculpture. Few of the

---

39 G. K. Chesterton, *The Judgement of Dr. Johnson* (1927), in D. J. Conlon (ed.), *Collected Works*, vol. 11, San Francisco: Ignatius Press, 1989, p. 294.

40 Freeman Dyson, 'The Darwinian Interlude', *Technology Review*, March 2005: <http://www.technologyreview.com/read_article.aspx?id=14236&ch=biotech> (accessed 3 September 2006). Dyson takes his cue from Carl Woese, 'A New Biology for a New Century', *Microbiology and Molecular Biology Reviews*, vol. 68, no. 2, June 2004, pp. 173–86 <http://mmbr.asm.org/cgi/content/abstract/68/2/173> (accessed 3 September 2006).

new creations will be masterpieces, but all will bring joy to their creators and diversity to our fauna and flora.

Even ordinary dog-breeders have managed to create varieties of dog with innate deformities. What 'the general public' will do if licensed to perform such vivisections I cannot quite imagine, nor endure. Will we be able to resist the fashion? Will anyone desire to keep 'the human lineage' clear? How long will there be 'a general public' in the sense that Dyson imagines?

The divine image

Is this a future to be resisted from the start? Not all its variants are necessarily inhumane, though most will be, as it were, inhuman. The creation of talking lions, as in John Crowley's *Beasts*,[41] might be a genuine advance – if only to rebut Wittgenstein! The ancient dreams of mermen and winged humans could be realized.[42] Not all imagined chimeras could be created: it is difficult to see how centaurs could work, but something enough like them might be possible. And though it seems uncomfortably realistic to expect that many creatures would be made precisely to be oppressed, the alternative moral might perhaps be drawn, that all of us are equals, all endowed by our creators with equal rights, to life, liberty and the pursuit of happiness. Our creators, after all, would have no reason to think one artefact more deserving than any other. Which they prefer would be an aesthetic judgement (and fantasists have usually preferred cat-people: they are tidier, prettier and stronger than us naked apes). The creators too would probably themselves be artefacts. Maybe they would keep a 'normal' population somewhere safe, in case of accidents, but *they* would not be 'normal'. Most likely they would equip themselves and their immediate heirs with the sort of 'animal' equipment that has always served to signify imperial power.

But it is clear that many people may also find fault with the very idea of merging 'animal' and 'human' characters. Even the combination of cow egg and human DNA, for the purposes of stem-cell research, is allowed only on condition that the zygote is never even an embryo, let alone a neonate. And even quite hard-headed scientists express some disapproval of such hybrid forms as we can already create, like geeps (goat-sheep

---

41 John Crowley, *Beasts*, London: Futura, 1978.

42 Not by adding wings to the present hominid frame, but by adding language and associated talents to appropriate birds or bats or pterosaurs.

hybrids), not only because their creation may involve physical and mental suffering. Some opposition to Darwinian theory (indeed to almost any evolutionary theory) has always turned on disapproval of the suggestion that we are 'animals'. This is, from my own point of view, extremely strange, but I must acknowledge that it is deeply felt, and therefore, somehow, still 'an image of the truth'.[43]

The intuition that 'humanity', just as such, is worth our worship struggled into life during the so-called Axial Era all across the world:[44] humanity is both a moral norm and a constitutive reality. Every one of our conspecifics stands in for all: to kill one human being is to kill anyone.[45] Even animal liberationists are more affected by a human corpse than by a cat's, and not just because it's bigger. However ridiculous it may be, on almost any moral theory, to suggest that a hybrid of ape and human would have or should have fewer rights than us, such a fantasm does, somehow, excite quite different attitudes. On the one hand, she has a claim to be human; on the other, it is but an ape, and even people who care for apes don't usually see them as 'divine'. Seeing 'animals' as divine (that is, as worthy of reverence) was the crime attributed to Egypt in Virgil's *Aeneid*: Octavian is victorious over Cleopatra and the 'monstrous gods of Egypt'. Humanism, in order to safeguard the interests of other human tribes, requires us to despise the non-human. Only humanity is supposed to be 'in the image of God'.[46]

It is not difficult to see why animals have often struck us as divine, and why rulers have often sought to seize their mystique for themselves, choosing lion or eagle or horse or wild boar as their emblems. We recognize their beauty and their power – and much of the outrage felt at factory farming, and bad zoos, has more to do with the sense that they should not be thus diminished than with the mere judgement (true as it often is) that they are, as individuals, miserable or in pain. Chimps, perhaps, are too

---

43 William Blake, *Marriage of Heaven and Hell* (1790–93), in G. Keynes (ed.), *Complete Writings*, London: Oxford University Press, 1966, p. 151. It is an *image* only, of course, and merely intimates or suggests the truth that makes it partly credible.

44 See Karl Jaspers, *The Origin and Goal of History*, trans Michael Bullock, London: Routledge & Kegan Paul, 1953 (first published in German, 1949).

45 As stated in the Qur'an 5.32: 'whosoever killeth a human being for other than manslaughter or corruption in the earth, it shall be as if he had killed all mankind, and whoso save the life of one, it shall be as if he had saved the life of all mankind.'

46 This is a larger topic than can be tackled here. I note only that the Stoic interpretation of this claim identifies 'the wise' as having 'the mind of God' (with the proviso that only human beings ever become wise). The Hebraic claim is very different: the point of the story in Genesis is that Adam is to look after the world God made, not that only human beings deserve respect.

undignified to get much worship, but gorillas inspire awe (even or especially in the sad shape of Guy). These emotions, of course, don't necessarily result in our treating individual animals fairly: being an incarnate god has always been a mixed blessing. The individual is only an instance of that god, and can, with proper ritual, be killed. Even while alive it is likely to be coerced into behaving as a proper emblem rather than as its own recalcitrant self (that is why kings have so often kept royal menageries, uncaring that the 'symbolic beasts' are, as individuals, wretched). And it is all too often the case that romantics turn from praising the beauty of animals to gobbling their factory-farmed flesh.

If animals are seen as worshipful we may hope to embody something of their characters, and thereby lose a little of our own humanity – or so the suspicion runs. We may reasonably not much care for rulers who self-identify as lions or eagles, however gloriously they posture. We may reasonably be worried by anyone who seeks to copy what he thinks is 'animal behaviour' (by which he will usually and mistakenly intend 'amoral' or 'uninhibited' or 'natural' behaviour). The effort to see human beings as worshipful is a moral victory. A human being's value does not lie, as the simpler utilitarians must suppose, in her contribution to total happiness, and she is no less to be 'worshipped' for being sick or silly, miserable or miserly. Nor is it simply a product, a projection, of some notional agreement not to hurt each other. She must be sacred to us because she stands for all humanity. Even her leavings (her corpse and its organs) must be sacred to us, and such use of them as degrades or trivializes them must be foresworn. Once again, such worship may not always be humane: whenever we demand that others act out a role, even or especially the role of suffering humanity, we make them suffer, quite as much as the animals we 'worshipped'. And what we worship we also imitate. If 'animals' are seen as unmerciful then it may be best not to worship them – but it is a strange argument that thence infers that it is somehow right to oppress them, for not being merciful.

William Blake's poem 'The Divine Image'[47] portrays 'the human form divine' as 'Mercy Pity Peace and Love', the object of all prayer and the reason for us to love it 'in heathen, turk or jew'. But it is worth recalling that Blake himself, as a good Christian Platonist, supposed that

---

47 William Blake, *Songs of Innocence* (1789), in Keynes, *Complete Writings*, p. 117. He was of course aware that there was another side to humankind. In 'A Divine Image', etched in 1794, he adds that 'Cruelty has a Human Heart,/And Jealousy a Human Face;/ Terror the Human Form Divine,/ and Secrecy the Human Dress' (p. 222).

Each grain of sand,
Every stone on the land,
Each rock and each hill,
Each fountain and rill,
Each herb and each tree,
Mountain, hill, earth, and sea,
Cloud, meteor, and star,
Are men seen afar.[48]

Humanity, for Blake, does not only reside within our species: on the contrary, it – that is 'Mercy, Pity, Peace and Love' or what evokes them – is manifested everywhere. Recognizing a 'divine humanity' at work in everything is also to recognize something profoundly 'other' than ourselves, a demanding presence that summons us also to be 'human' in an extended sense. So in very brief conclusion, I suggest that the divine image may still be visible even in Freeman Dyson's World, in which there are no longer any species at all. One version of that world would indeed be unutterably vile – a world in which there is nothing sacred.

Don't you see that that dreadful dry light shed on things must at last wither up the moral mysteries as illusions, respect for age, respect for property, and that the sanctity of life will be a superstition? The men in the street are only organisms, with their organs more or less displayed.[49]

But there is an alternative reading. 'Even of a fish it is blasphemy to say it is *only* a fish',[50] and Christians above all need not be alarmed to say that even fishes can represent the divine, and even that there is something divine in them. Biological species are only sets of populations, but they have intimated norms of beauty, each of which should excite our awe, and also our compassion. Elves, hobbits, trolls – and even stranger future creatures – aren't 'failed humans', any more than women are 'defective males': they are other forms of beauty, other syllables of the Divine Word being spoken in creation. And all the creatures in whom it is being spoken will be (as they already are) our kin.

---

48 Letter to Thomas Butts (2 October 1800), in Keynes, *Complete Writings*, p. 805.
49 G. K. Chesterton, *The Poet and the Lunatics*, London: Darwen Finlayson, 1962 [1929], p. 70.
50 Chesterton, *The Poet and the Lunatics*, p. 70.

Part Four

THE MORAL STATUS OF ANIMALS

9

Slouching Towards Jerusalem?
An Anti-human Theology of
Rough Beasts and Other Animals[1]

PETER MANLEY SCOTT

> *And what rough beast, its hour come round at last,*
> *Slouches towards Bethlehem to be born?*
> W. B. Yeats[2]

> *Spider and Bee all mimicking at will*
> *Displaying powers that fools the proudly wise*
> John Clare[3]

> *Clare broke under the strain, for he had one significant disadvantage;*
> *he couldn't both live on the process and escape its products, as some of*
> *the others were doing and indeed as became a way of life – this is a very*
> *bitter irony – for some of the most successful exploiters.*
> Raymond Williams[4]

In this chapter, I develop the theological resources of God's constitution of a shared realm to propose a concept of *anti-human* sovereignty or animal rule – of the human in coalition with the animal. The argument consists of four steps. First, I note that the presence of animals raises the issue of the nature of the human, and note how the human has often been contrasted with the animal. The concept of the anti-human is introduced

---

1 I would like to thank the participants in the colloquium, 'Towards a Theology of the Animal', 2–4 November 2007, and Michael Hoelzl and Stefan Skrimshire, for their responses to an earlier version of this chapter.
2 W. B. Yeats, *Selected Poetry*, London: Pan, 1974, 'The Second Coming', p. 100.
3 John Clare, *Selected Poems*, London: Penguin, 2000, 'The Crab Tree', p. 82.
4 Raymond Williams, *Problems in Materialism and Culture*, London: Verso, 1980, p. 80.

at this point. Second, I argue that under the present and extreme conditions of the commodification of animals – human and non-human – the best way to describe this situation is in terms of class analysis. We are in the middle of a class agitation, in which some animals – human and non-human – are exposed and exploited. Third, the concept of the anti-human is elaborated upon in order to rediscover the life-in-common of animals, human and non-human. Fourth and last, an account of 'animal rule', framed and resourced by the notion of the anti-human, is presented, together with a commentary on the theological basis of such rule as found in the doctrine of the ascension.

Ape epistemology?

Given animals, what is the human? At the end of the novel *The Woman and the Ape* by Peter Høeg, the reader is presented with a reversal as an answer to this question.[5] It is revealed that apes have already infiltrated human civilization (the novel is set in London!) and are presented as intellectually superior to humans. Whereas readers' prejudices invite a reading that it is the woman who is acting beneath her station by consorting with the ape, suddenly we are presented with the opposite view. Instead, the ape is playing his part in a *noblesse oblige* drama in support of humans. The novelist needs us actively to deploy our prejudices in order for the ending to have its effect. The difficulty with this narrative is that the straightforward reversal, although surprising, leaves everything else in place. For this revolution is simple: the wheel turns and now the inferior is revealed as the superior.

Nevertheless, this exercise in fictional imagination does enable the following thought. Notwithstanding efforts to the contrary, we are accustomed to appreciating the human as primary in creation, which in turn leaves the non-human animal as secondary in creation. I must confess at this point that originally I had written 'we are accustomed to appreciating the human as the culmination and pinnacle of creation'. However, it seems to me that my first attempt prejudges the issue. That is to say, there are two ways of exploring the difference between the primary and the secondary: the first is the difference of capacity and the second is the difference of participation. Later in this chapter I shall be developing an account of difference based on participation. There can be no escaping

---

5 Peter Høeg, *The Woman and the Ape*, London: The Harvill Press, 1997.

that such participation is asymmetrical; the qualities of participation are not identical across all animals and the *qualities* of participation cannot simply supplant the differing *quantities* of capacity. Nonetheless, to stress participation is to foreground the active constitution of a common realm of animals by God.

Yet, I consider that most ways of exploring the duality of primary/secondary are based in the difference of capacity. We can grasp this more fully if, of the contemporary effort to rethink the status of animals, we note two tendencies of special significance: (1) a re-consideration of the moral status or considerability of animals; and (2) a sustained attempt to close the gap between the human and some animals. These two tendencies are of course linked. Both resist the placing of animals as property and refuse the assertion of a fixed order in which the human and the animal are placed. Both are vested in the difference of capacity. Following Val Plumwood, I consider that the anthropocentric reading based in difference of capacity has dominated the western imaginary.[6]

Theology makes its own contribution to this anthropocentric imaginary. This imaginary is based upon what John Gray, with his customary tact, calls 'Christianity's cardinal error – the belief that humans are radically different from all other animals'.[7] Although Gray offers little detail on this alleged error, how might Gray's charge be amplified? What is theology's contribution? First, the doctrine of creation proposes the human as *imago Dei*. Although the content of this imaging is debated (freedom, reason and language are candidates), it is restricted to the human. Even before we consider the matter of what makes the human distinctive in contrast to the other animals, we may also note that agency – of the sort that the human is considered to enjoy – requires a concept of will. This has far-reaching consequences. As Gordon Kaufman notes, the difference between God and humans is renegotiated by reference to the claim that both have a will. Such willing alienates the human from the rest of nature: 'Nature is not conceived primarily as man's [*sic*] proper home and the source and sustenance of his being but rather as the context of and material for teleological activity by the (nonnatural) wills working upon and in it.'[8]

---

6 Val Plumwood, *Feminism and the Mastery of Nature*, London: Routledge, 1993.

7 John Gray, *Straw Dogs: Thought on Humans and Other Animals*, London: Granta, 2003 [2002], p. 37. Cf. p. 4.

8 Gordon D. Kaufman, 'A Problem for Theology: The Concept of Nature', *Harvard Theological Review* 65, 1972, pp. 337–66, here p. 353.

Second, the affirmation of the human in the incarnation reinforces the view that the human somehow represents the creaturely. Moreover, although the universal claim that inheres in the incarnation must be respected for this representative role to be convincing and efficacious, such universality does not exceed the human. Indeed, such universality identifies the human as the site of the incarnation of the Logos. Once more, and because it lacks universality, the animal is considered to be excluded. Even those, like Andrew Linzey, who wish to broaden incarnation to affirm flesh other than the human must find some way of showing how it is that non-human animals participate in Jesus' human flesh.[9] In a more heterodox interpretation, Sallie McFague extends the reference of incarnation by de-privileging the particular person, Jesus of Nazareth, and recommending that we speak of the incarnation of God in a more 'comprehensive' fashion.[10] Such a view of course undoes traditional notions of the soteriological finality of Christ and calls into question Christ's status as, in Karl Rahner's phrase, 'ultimately significant for salvation'. In this essay, I am holding to a more traditional interpretation, and accept the strains that follow.

Third, we find a similar pattern in redemption: fulfilment is associated with judgement, and only the human can be judged. When Dietrich Bonhoeffer writes that in redemption nature is not reconciled from sin but set free from its curse, he intends to be generous: redemption addresses non-human nature, albeit in a different way from the human. Thus Bonhoeffer writes: 'Nature stands under the curse which God laid upon Adam's ground . . . Nature, unlike man and history, will not be reconciled, but it will be set free for a new freedom.'[11] Yet looking past the generosity, we may note that once more the difference between the non-human and the human is being presented.

Theology is therefore concerned in multiple ways – as I have tried to show – with the identification and re-inscription of the difference between the human and the non-human by asserting the primacy of the human in creation, liberation and redemption. Or, at least, one way of reading the theological traditions of the Latin West is as the assertion of this primacy.

---

9 As it turns out, Linzey ducks the challenge of developing an intermediate, bridging metaphysics and instead proposes the notions of rights to award moral considerability to animals. According to his argument, you do not need incarnation to offer theological support for 'theos-rights'; a doctrine of creation is adequate to this purpose. See Andrew Linzey, *Christianity and the Rights of Animals*, London: SCM Press, 1987, especially chs 3 and 5.

10 Sallie McFague, *Models of God: Theology for an Ecological, Nuclear Age*, London: SCM Press, 1987; *The Body of God: An Ecological Theology*, London: SCM Press, 1993.

11 Dietrich Bonhoeffer, *Christology*, London: Fount, 1978, p. 64.

And we can appreciate the logic of this position. Once you've granted the non-natural willing of God *and* humans in creation, as Kaufman notes, you cannot withdraw it in liberation and redemption. In such fashion, a distinction between the human and the animal introduced in the doctrine of creation insinuates itself through the theological themes of liberation and redemption.

What would happen if we retained the theological architecture but denied that the difference of capacity between the human and the animal has theological backing? In other words, that there are differences – including differences of capacity – between the human and the animal is not to be denied. What I am suggesting, however, is that these differences be granted no theological weight, warrant or validation. The inscribing of these differences does not reside in the soteriological workings of the Spirit of God either in creation or redemption. This refusal would leave the way open for a reconsideration later in this chapter of the construal of difference between human and animal based in participation.

If its first weakness resides in the technique of a simple reversal, a second weakness of *The Woman and the Ape* is its lack of conflict. The true status of the apes is based in the relation between appearance and reality. In other words: while it appears that the ape is intellectually inferior to the human, the reality is the opposite. The matter is one of true perception. Of course, once the true situation becomes clear to the humans, conflict follows. Yet this is not the conflict required to secure change. It is the conflict that follows from a realization that the situation is different from what was previously believed. It is the conflict of reception rather than the conflict of praxis.

I mention this because in my view any extended and sustained change in our view of animals and our treatment of them will require a wider social and political dislocation. The present settlement that turns upon the difference of the human and the animal will need to be unsettled. I say this because of my sense of the depth and stability of this difference, as both the newspaper and radio appear to bear witness. In front of me I have a newspaper article that discusses the retailing of a chicken for the price of £2 by British supermarket Asda – the cheapest in Europe for decades, it reports.[12] According to the article, Asda concedes these chickens are 'not free-range, corn-fed or organic but were all grown in Britain to EU standards'. So the article speculates that these chickens must be raised in battery cages. According to the article, the chickens get so little exercise

---

12 Untitled article by John Vidal, *The Guardian*, 4 August 2007, pp. 29–30.

that when they are eaten most of the calories from their flesh comes from fat rather than protein.

The radio news reports that fisher folk in Northern Ireland are removing both claws from crabs they have caught and then returning the crabs to the sea.[13] The claws are sold subsequently for their crabmeat. This practice is based on the – apparently correct – view that crab claws regrow. The crabs can thereby be harvested for their claws over and over again. The only flaw in the practice – according to the expert interviewed for this news item – is that crabs need their claws to feed. With both claws removed, the crabs die. There followed some discussion as to whether it might be a better farming practice to remove only one claw. The crab would then be able to feed, and the removed claw could regrow. The expert pointed out that there was some evidence that crabs suffered shock from having even only one claw removed, although no one was quite able to say the word 'cruel'. (In that there is some debate as to whether crustaceans feel pain, cruel here refers to depriving an animal of its ability to feed itself and thereby denying its interest in life/flourishing.) Finally, we were informed that the manner of claw removal was very important: inducing a crab to shed a claw is very different from cutting it off.

It is hard to know how to respond to news stories such as these. Perhaps the pertinent question here is: what are the practical sources of the treatment of animals as evidenced in these news reports? In Latourian terms, how do we move from treating animals as matters of fact to be roughly handled to treating animals as matters of concern and as actors in a wider sociality?[14] That is, how do we move to considering non-human animals as *public* entities or things?

What is perhaps most troubling in these stories is the thoughtlessness evidenced by the actions of producers, collectors and consumers. What is the source of such thoughtlessness? Stephen R. L. Clark argues that 'It is admitted that dogs, cows and chickens may suffer, or lose enjoyments, in our service, but such costs do not weigh with us, because dogs, cows and chickens do not weigh with us.'[15] These news stories I have reported offer little evidence of the sympathy and friendship that Clark grounds in our evolutionary development: ' . . . our recognition that here is another creature with whom there are more profitable modes of relationship. We

---

13 News report on BBC Radio 4's *Today* programme, 5 October 2007.

14 Bruno Latour, 'Is There a Cosmopolitically Correct Design?', lecture given at the University of Manchester, 5 October 2007.

15 Stephen R. L. Clark, *The Political Animal: Biology, Ethics and Politics*, London: Routledge, 1999, p. 24.

are equipped to share another creature's viewpoint, to find that creature significant, to be friends or at least be friendly.'[16] We do not need to accept the biological grounding of Clark's argument to grasp its profundity: foundational to human living is sociability across many spheres. Differently from Clark, I would ground such an orientation in a doctrine of revelation that discloses and apprehends the reconciling action of God slouching towards Jerusalem.[17] In such sociability the human participates and thereby learns further of such sociability. Of course, such sociability is not given; it has to be learned and relearned; and it can be, and is, distorted.

Although I have much sympathy for Clark's anti-statist argument that declines to invest in the state-as-saviour and thereby implicitly stresses the social action of groups in civil society, I shall be suggesting that the roots of thoughtlessness towards animals are to be found in a class division. Some non-human animals and some human animals are placed in a class agitation and it is deeply vested in a class interest for this agitation to be obscured and minimized. In this section of my argument, liberation is here directed to freeing the human and the animal: emancipation does not mean freeing humans from their attaching animals but rather freeing the human into and beyond animals, and freeing animals into and beyond the human.

The concept of the anti-human is proposed as an agitator in this context: as the source of conflict, and as the promoter of sympathy and the discourager of thoughtlessness. The anti-human is not misanthropic although it is steadfastly opposed to thoughtlessness and disregard. The anti-human is directed towards 'us'. (More on this 'us' below.) It seeks the reworking of theology on lines that do not privilege the human in a comparative sense. 'Some differences are playful,' writes Donna Haraway, whereas 'some are poles of world historical systems of domination.'[18] The anti-human resources and commends differences in reconciliation and not the difference of domination between the human and the animal. In a way, the arrival of the concept of the anti-human is made smoother if we acknowledge the intensive, varied and variable modes of interaction

---

16 Clark, *The Political Animal*, p. 26.

17 See Peter Scott, *A Political Theology of Nature*, Cambridge: Cambridge University Press, 2003, which argues for God's self-disclosure by way of the peregrinations of Israel and the resurrection of Jesus Christ as the simultaneous disclosure of a common realm of God, nature and humanity.

18 Donna Haraway, *Simians, Cyborgs and Women: The Reinvention of Nature*, London: FAB Books, 1991, p. 161.

between the human and the non-human. 'If we talk only of singular Man and singular Nature we can compose a general history,' writes Raymond Williams, 'but at the cost of excluding the real and alternative social relations.'[19] In other words, we must pay attention, as Kate Soper argues, to the 'different historical modes of "human" interaction with [nature]'.[20]

Where are animals?

My argument inches forward. In this chapter, I am attempting a political and theological interpretation of the status of animals. By a political interpretation, I intend to identify the power relations in which animals are held and by which what it means to be an animal today is constituted. In order to identify the power relations in which animals are held, we need to answer the question: where are they? To answer this question comprehensively, the circumstance of animals today requires a wider enquiry into the circumstances of non-human nature. That is, animals are part of the commodification of nature.

If human relations with the non-human are varied and have a specific form, how shall we understand today's form? Two tendencies are worth noting at this point. The first I shall call the hyper-capitalization of nature: the rendering of animals as dis-placed property. The second tendency I shall call affirmations of relationships that operate helpfully in support of closing the gap between humans and animals.

Consider the first tendency: animals are both brought into the human economy and rendered alien. That is, they are commodified and subjected to production processes. Of course, nature is unruly and sometimes animals escape our control (as in BSE, Avian flu). Such periodic – in richer countries always temporary – escapes simply provoke from us more furious efforts at control.[21] The commodification of animals – this we all recognize; my news items presented above suggest as much. Nonetheless, has the commodification of non-human nature recently developed in intensity, even to the point of substitution?

To get a sense of what I mean by substitution, consider the following example offered by Neil Smith: 'In Georgia, International Paper is breeding the endangered red-cockaded woodpecker on land it owns; wood-

---

19 Williams, *Problems in Materialism and Culture*, 'Ideas of Nature', p. 84.

20 Kate Soper, *What Is Nature?*, Oxford: Blackwell, 1995, p. 19.

21 It would be interesting to explore whether this applies equally, although in different modalities of course, to livestock, pets and wild animals.

pecker credits have already traded at $100,000 and International Paper hopes in the future to earn as much as $250,000 per credit for these.'[22] We are already familiar with the phenomenon of 'nature credits'; carbon and wetland credits are perhaps the most well-known examples. Now we are presented with the generalization of this trading: a developer 'offsets' the loss of the red-cockaded woodpecker's habitat – and presumably the woodpecker itself! – by means of the 'substitutionability' of nature. As long as there is no net loss of habitat and woodpeckers, the development may proceed.

Although this work of 'substitutionability' may seem at first glance an example of how, as Clark points out, animals do not count with us, it is difficult to discern quite what is wrong with this approach. Those that argue that such alteration in nature is wrong do appear to be trading, as Kate Soper points out, on an argument that implicitly criticizes human alteration of nature by suggesting that nature is reduced in value through human activity.[23] Yet this renders alien the human from nature and identifies all human activity as anti-natural: if the human must alter nature in order to survive, then the life of the human is thereby rendered anti-natural. A different set of background beliefs is required to maintain that animals do count with us, and that specific animals count with us.

At this point, we may consider the second tendency: affirmations of relationships that operate helpfully in support of closing the gap between humans and animals. In *Nature Cure*, Richard Mabey recounts an encounter with a deer:

> Once in my wood I had a face-to-face meeting with a female muntjac deer. It wasn't a sudden encounter, a collision round a bush and a moment of mutual fluster. We'd sidled up to each other, both with a slight tilt of the head that universally signals curiosity, caution, an uncertainty about what may happen next, and an unwillingness to be either provocative or provoked. We got to about 10 feet from each other and then just stared. I looked into her large eyes and at her humped back and down-pointed tail, which signified she wasn't alarmed. I thought about what race-memory she might have of her species' Chinese homeland, about what she made of an English beech-wood and whether she's looked at a human's face before. She looked at

22 Neil Smith, 'Nature as Accumulation Strategy', in Leo Panitch and Colin Leys (eds), *Coming to Terms with Nature*, London: Merlin Press, 2006, pp. 16–36, here p. 19.
23 Soper, *What Is Nature?*, p. 18.

my eyes and passed her tongue repeatedly over her face, wondering if I was dangerous or musty. I thought she was pretty and plucky. She thought I was odorous and interesting and curiously shaped and things I could never know. We conversed in this way, two curious and diffident strangers, then went our separate ways.[24]

It is easy to be a little sceptical about such a report: there is anthropomorphism here as well as a claim that such feelings of empathy with animals are innate. Yet, perhaps theologians should be less suspicious of anthropomorphism, except in connection with discussions of God: as Lorraine Daston has argued, perhaps anthropomorphism is both unavoidable and unsuccessful.[25] Furthermore, we may be cautious about the sensibility that assigns redemptive powers to nature. Yet, Mabey associates this sensibility with the refusal of substitutionalism: 'I've never been able to fit my feelings about nature into this kind of value system, weighing its usefulness and scarcity value like some kind of commodity dealer.' 'I like common things,' Mabey concludes, 'and the idea of commonality – "a Council of all Beings".'[26]

How, we might ask, is the distance between a muntjac deer and a declawed crab to be negotiated? What is the relationship between a concept of common nature and the plight of animals in factory farming (Asda's £2 chicken)? How does the notion of a council of beings criticize the commodification of a red-cockaded woodpecker? To answer these questions, I plan to investigate the commodifying processes a little further. This will lead to the view that there is class agitation taking place, in which some animals and some humans together present a common interest towards the affirmation and construction of a human–animal coalition, a joint sovereignty.

All animals are equal . . .

In exploring the capitalist production of nature, Neil Smith argues that this process of production invites us to regard nature as external and as rendered productive through the capacities of social labour. These capac-

---

24 Richard Mabey, *Nature Cure*, London: Pimlico, 2006 [2005], pp. 21–2.
25 Lorraine Daston, 'Intelligences: Angelic, Human, Animal', in L. Daston and G. Mitman (eds), *Thinking with Animals: New Perspectives on Anthropomorphism*, New York: Columbia Press, 2005, pp. 37–58, here p. 41.
26 Mabey, *Nature Cure*, p. 15.

ities have been deepened, he argues, to the extent that in some ways we are moving away from a conventional model of production in which exchange value is created by the interaction of external nature and social labour. Instead, Smith argues that the production of nature is being transferred to social labour itself.[27] A GM seed is perhaps a good example here: nature is not only improved, it is improved in the laboratory, and this improvement can then be repeated at little cost to the producer.

Of course, what also happens is that human workers are co-opted into such processes. From the cloning of a sheep to collecting cockles on a beach to working on a production line for chicken, workers are subjected to the imperatives of production. These three examples are rather different of course and indicate different degrees of the production of nature; that is, different degrees of the penetration of nature by social labour. (In the case of cloning, arguably we have the transfer of nature into social labour whereas in the example of cockle collection we have the harvesting of the results of nature's own fecund processes by human labour.) Nevertheless, none of this could be achieved without social co-operation. And yet this co-operation, and its productive outcomes, are achieved by the subsumption of nature by capital, of the integration of nature into the financial circuits of capital towards the maximization of relative exchange value.

For Smith, it is important to note the depth of this process. With regard to genetically modified organisms (GMOs), for example, it now becomes part of a strategy for the supply of food that food staples are made in part from genetically modified material. And these commodities – the product of nature out of social labour – circulate through financial markets in a different sense: for example, the red-cockaded woodpecker is available for purchase as an ecological credit.

If for reasons not easy to define – substitutionality? poor environmental protection? irreversible changes? death of individual animals? – we find these processes a little uncomfortable, we may pose the question: what would a better production of nature consist of? In turn, what sort of co-operation seems appropriate in a better production of nature? Which means that we are obliged to confront the political interests in the various types of the production of nature and the democratic arrangements in which judgements about political interests might be made. In terms of political interests, do some humans have more in common with some animals than they do with other humans? For example, do the technicians

---

27 Smith, 'Nature as Accumulation Strategy', pp. 26–7.

working on GM maize have interests in common with those animals whose habitat is damaged by the introduction of GM maize? Both groups are concerned with contamination and perhaps with the difficulty of, once released, recalling all GM 'contaminants'. And perhaps there is a connection to be made between the exploitation of organisms and the expropriation of the labour power of technicians.

To say this is not to deny, of course, that Monsanto's technicians also have interests in the financial profitability of their company and in the long-term sustainability of their pension plans. Yet it does seem that there is a partial alignment of some interests between rough beasts and other animals: in not being exploited, in having control over their environment, in having conditions for flourishing – an anti-human event, a coalition of animals.

The anti-human

The anti-human proposes that the human cannot be considered without its attachments.[28] The anti-human opposes the human by seeking always to overcome the occlusion of these attachments. My opening question can now be reformulated thus: given attaching animals, what is the human? According to the consideration above, some humans share an interest with some animals against exploitation. What is enforced upon them is their objectivity and what is denied to them is their subjectivity. In this sharing of an interest, what the human is cannot be disentangled from what the animal is, and vice versa. Given such entanglement and class division, one way of answering this question is to identify the political circumstance of animals.

What is this circumstance? Politically, the anti-human is the recollection of natural life. If Giorgio Agamben is correct, politics is today constituted by a distinction between the citizen and the non-citizen.[29] An earlier distinction of belonging to 'bare life' and belonging to the monarch has ended. Rights no longer inhere in bare life but have reappeared as the subjective human rights of citizenship. Without citizenship, you have no rights. Or, as Leo Strauss puts it, in a rather different context: '[A]ll citizens are, in fact, "made" and not "born".'[30] If this analysis seems unduly

28 Cf. Latour, 'Is There a Cosmopolitically Correct Design?'
29 Giorgio Agamben, *Homo Sacer: Sovereign Power and Bare Life*, Stanford: Stanford University Press, 1998.
30 Leo Strauss, *Natural Right and History*, Chicago: University of Chicago Press, 1965 [1953], p. 104.

'mythic', there is some evidence that supports Agamben's analysis. Consider Chloé Bregnard Ecoffey's analysis of the rules governing immigrants in Switzerland. She argues that the Swiss federal government's response to immigration has been to deny rights to immigrants and asylum-seekers. Part of this process has involved making it a criminal offence for Swiss citizens to provide food and shelter for these foreigners.[31] They end up begging, sleeping in public toilets, etc. – and of course are arrested. What is this apart from living in bare life under state power?[32] And given a tradition of hospitality, what is the duty of Swiss churches in response to this enforcement of bare life?

The concept of the anti-human that I am developing refuses this fusing of citizenship and rights. Why this refusal? Because as a result of the fusing of rights and citizenship, animals are placed outside the polity; they are not citizens, and the political interests that they may share with humans find no political place. This refusal links to the theme of the commodification of non-human nature. Animals are either agriculture/ medical commodities or pets or wild. As the first, they are commercial property; as the second, they are domestic companions, to be abused or fussed over and well treated; as the third, they are beyond human society. None of these approaches citizenship. Through the processes of commodification the animal is rendered as commercial, as private. Where does this leave human political relations with animals except as an aspect of citizenship? And yet as citizenship is a state for humans only, governance must proceed without animals.

What then are the marks of anti-human citizenship? Political status can only be granted to animals if we go back behind the fusing of rights and citizenship. That is, 'right' – but not rights – inheres in all as pre-citizens, as alive, as bodies. This would be a way of recovering a natural history of animals in, for and without human society. Although such a natural history is a concept, it points to a pre-conceptual actuality of living; a living and communicative realm that can be identified but not fully described. A polity is not a narrow people but a wide-ranging community of animals, human and non-human. All efforts at governance – a *parlement of foulys* and other animals – are derived from this actuality of right. This state is

---

31 Chloé Bregnard Ecoffey, *Asylum in Switzerland: A Challenge for the Church*, unpublished MA dissertation, University of Manchester, 2007.

32 Of course, these immigrants are not 'disappeared' or murdered in the street by the state. Yet it remains unclear whether this respect of bare life resides in residual sentiment regarding human life or is vested in legal protection. Once more, we are presented with the curiously ambivalent legal status of those living in a zone of exception.

anti-human in that such right is shared by and distributed among that which is living.

Moreover, theology is not troubled by this affirmation of right because it knows that true humanity – that is also true animality? – is already pre-served by God through the ascension of Christ. The anti-human is grounded in the ascension: in that true humanity as performed by Christ is rescued and preserved by God, there is no requirement for other rough beasts to try to identify their own humanity nor be distracted by anthropocentric construals of their humanity.[33] Because for God the human cannot disappear, there is no compulsion to identify the difference of the human from the animal because there is no requirement to identify the human *simpliciter*. And, a second time, because for God the human cannot disappear, theologically speaking there is no need to govern as if the overriding priority of human governance is ensuring that the human does not disappear.

In this theology of exaltation, it is the *ascended* Christ who is important. In the perspective I am developing here, a theology of animals is possible, and legitimated, because Jesus Christ is an animal and God. The particu-larity of this rough beast's slouching towards Jerusalem is secured by his ascension: it is Jesus of Nazareth and none other who 'takes "the same full share" in God's being and work in creation'. And Douglas Farrow continues:

> As God's self-disposition in time, the man Jesus lives a history which belongs to God and is backed by God's own indissoluble temporality. For all its creaturely particularity it cannot be confined by, but rules over, its own spatio-temporal boundaries. It [Jesus' history] becomes constitutional for every creaturely history, and for history as a whole, since (by divine election) it is constitutional for the creator himself.[34]

Jesus' humanity thereby participates in the shared life of God and is the 'place' from where he participates in God's redeeming work in the world as God. Moreover, by way of this humanity, which is constitutional for

---

33 Cf. Haddon Willmer, 'Images of the City', in Anthony Harvey (ed.), *Theology in the City*, London: SPCK, 1989, pp. 32–46, here p. 46: '[W]e may look to God with deeper faith, hope and love, because there humanity is faithfully kept for us . . .'

34 Douglas Farrow, *Ascension and Ecclesia: On the Significance of the Doctrine of the Ascension for Ecclesiology and Christian Cosmology*, Edinburgh: T & T Clark, 1999, pp. 287–8.

God, this Jesus is constitutive of the history of all creatures, human and non-human.

It remains vital to stress that the incarnation of this Christ is not a divine episode, and that the humanity of Jesus is active eschatologically, so to speak. Jesus' resurrected life is a human reality (just as his pre-existence is a human reality), and his resurrected human reality is consti-tutive of creatures and constitutional for God. The central insight here is not the affirmation of matter in the light of the resurrection, and then the development of an argument to show how non-human creatures are also matter in the required, soteriological, sense. (Such an argument, despite its protestations, is always anthropocentric, for it must work from a resurrected human body; and it is, despite its protestations, always anthropomorphic, as it must seek out other creatures.) Instead, the central insight I am offering is that the human reality of Jesus is secure both as an identity of God and as the constitutive ground of the participation of creatures in God's creating and redeeming. Creatures thereby are already placed in the humanity of this Christ and are directed towards the escha-tological renewal of creaturely participation. Paradoxically, the securing of Jesus' human reality by reference to his ascension is the ground of undercutting the duality of human/animal for the reason that all creatures participate in this flesh – by which, out of God's unity, God is and does.

On these grounds, theology may refuse the following gibe by Gray:

If humanists are to be believed, the Earth – with its vast wealth of ecosystems and life forms – had no value until humans came onto the scene. Value is only a shadow cast by humans desiring or choosing. Only *persons* have any kind of intrinsic worth. Among Christians the cult of personhood may be forgiven. For them, everything of value in the world emanates from a divine person, in whose image humans are made. But once we have relinquished Christianity the very idea of the person becomes suspect.[35]

Contra Gray, an anti-human theology accepts that the earth has value without the human; there are five days of creation before God's creating of the human on the sixth. Additionally, as this brief exploration in a theology of exaltation has shown, not only persons have value. Indeed, if reference to the ascension is persuasive, an anti-human theology need not

---

35 Gray, *Straw Dogs*, p. 58.

concern itself with establishing abstracted hierarchies of value based in the superiority of the human over the non-human animal.

In that there is no need to claim superiority and do everything to insure against the disappearance of the human, the human is thereby enabled to live sacrificially. Humans may act in support of the diversity of life. The anti-human is therefore the 'true humanism'. To be truly human is for the human to sacrifice themselves for others, and included among these others are animals.[36] Being 'human' then becomes the assertion of the human against other life forms; being anti-human means not always asserting our interests. Indeed, it may become problematic to identify what our political interests are. (Do we finally have to face the dismal thought that it may be too late for humans to secure the sustainable conditions for human living but that it is not too late to secure the conditions for other life? And that our properly hopeful efforts should be expressed in a pro-animals praxis? And if we do not undertake such pro-animals praxis, then we are re-inscribing an anthropocentrism.)

To summarize: the anti-human is the attempt to overcome the occlusion of animals as attachments of the human. Rather than decentre the human – as if the only problem was anthropocentrism – the anti-human calls into question the separation of natural right and citizenship. This separation leaves the animal outside the *polis*. The anti-human reasserts the importance of the right that inheres in the commonality of beings, the latter disclosed in the exaltation of Jesus of Nazareth. The anti-human is thereby a political concept: it seeks to identify the source of citizenship in animal – human and non-human – right. It refuses the displacement of animals entirely into the worlds, both private, of the *oikos* and the economy, and thereby seeks to re-establish the comprehensive scope of sociality. It seeks to push the human out of human citizenship in order to re-establish citizenship emerging out of the shared realm of animals.

If I am right that the anti-human re-relates the human with the animal, then anti-human work marks the movement into 'third nature'. That is, the anti-human troubles the distinction between first and second nature in which the second nature of cultured and technological humanity dominates non-human nature.[37] (And is not this second nature often understood in deterministic ways – for example, the 'logic' of the market, the

---

36 Douglas John Hall seeks to develop this approach in *Imaging God: Dominion as Stewardship*, Grand Rapids: Eerdmans; New York: Friendship Press, 1986.

37 Sven Lütticken, 'Unnatural History', *New Left Review* 45, 2007, pp. 115–31, here p. 129.

uncheckability of global processes – and thereby as in some way 'natural', an independent force?) Instead, third nature tries to capture the class diversity of social relations between the human and the non-human in third nature: the class relations of the production of nature, featuring both the biomedical, transhuman efforts to overcome our mortality and the possibility of an overheated, less habitable earth in the conditions of increasing poverty.[38]

Animal rule?

This right, this realm of life, is not, as in some 'state of nature' arguments, fictional or counterfactual. Rather, it asserts that any rule or sovereignty is not vested in citizenship but in the commonality of human–animal right. This is not, I appreciate, how natural right has traditionally been understood. Although natural right has stressed the distinction between nature and convention, the focus of natural right has been the naturalness of human nature, so to speak.

What is involved in extending natural right in this way towards what I shall call postnatural right? It means that human sociality is anti-human; human sociality is always already animal sociality. It means that the transition into society is not only a movement granted, or secured, by the human – but by creatures, human and non-human. What are the political implications of this? That who governs, and what is governed in the exercise of sovereignty, is not only the human. The human represents the non-human in governing, and governs over the non-human as well as the human. Governance is mixed so as to ensure that animals may contribute to and support the continued existence of the human. Postnatural right indicates that humans are placed with animals, and must secure their preservation and conservation. In short, that human rule is always rule with, as well as on behalf of, the animal. Put differently, there are agents other than humans who have a political stake in the affirmation of the sustainability of living conditions.

---

38 According to Lütticken (see n. 37) what we understand third nature to be depends on the meanings of first and second nature and their interaction. Commonly, second nature refers to human convention, a realm of freedom separate from natural necessity. In this chapter, the production of nature out of social labour structured by class suggests an 'alienated' third nature. Such third nature now includes the medical fantasies of transhumanism, a disembodied future of the post-human, and the difficulties being caused by global warming. In other words, third nature refers to the production by social agents of a new nature – or visions of that nature – out of the interaction between first and second natures.

To be sure, there are considerable difficulties in developing a theory of postnatural right. According to Leo Strauss, natural right requires common knowledge – knowledge arrived at by the human qua human, and not by some group or individual – and the distinction between the natural and the conventional. Neither of these conditions is easy to meet. The first condition relates uneasily to my stress on class divisions in the production of knowledge. So a concept of third nature will be required such that knowledge that transcends particular interests can be generated out of a particular interest; that particularity transcends itself towards a liberative universalism. The second condition seems to be called into question by my elaboration of a third nature in which the natural and the artificial are confused. So a concept of third nature will be required that refuses the division between freedom and nature and founds sociality in the coincidence of freedom and necessity and yet does not collapse everything into convention, into artifice.

Finally, a political order oriented towards animals will require obedience and discipline and the relocation of religious communities – including churches – within civil society. For postnatural right presents us with political matters 'from the way in which they present themselves in political life, in action, when they are our business, when we have to make decisions'.[39] Animals may be understood as part of civil society in the manner of obedience and discipline. Obedience, because we must acknowledge the stake that animals have in human decisions; discipline, because we must be attentive to the ways in which decisions taken emerge out of class divisions that affect the future of animals. Yet, this will involve – to follow a distinction made by José Casanova – religious communities relocating themselves to 'political society', that is, to a newly created part of society that surrounds and is attentive to the state, legislature and judiciary.[40]

With regards to discipline, the churches are among a penumbra of institutions and associations that will provoke and raise the question: given animals, how are we to live? Given that animals are attached to humans in a diversity of ways, varied by class, how are we to live? Given that animals have an extra-human interest in life, how are we to live in ways that acknowledge this animal concern? With regard to obedience, the Church will wish to enact its obligations by postnatural right. There are two ways that it might do this: by association and by performance. That the Church

---

39 Strauss, *Natural Right and History*, p. 81.

40 José Casanova, 'Rethinking Secularization: A Global Comparative Perspective', *The Hedgehog Review*, vol. 8, nos. 1 and 2, 2006, pp. 7–22.

associates and performs are not mutually exclusive ways of exercising political will. That is, it joins with those groups that also wish to serve animals and it also performs its own acts of hospitality.

In this fashion, Bruno Latour's proposal for a 'Parliament of Things' is radicalized. Latour argues that in this parliament both nature and the citizen are represented.[41] Yet, for Latour, the representation of nature is secured through the participation of scientists. In the nascent proposal offered here, animals are represented but this time additionally through the mediations of political society. Developing governance in this way – based on postnatural right, in obedience and with discipline – may offer a different future for rough beasts and other animals.

---

41 Bruno Latour, *We Have Never Been Modern*, New York: Harvester Wheatsheaf, 1993, p. 144.

10

Are Animals Moral? Taking Soundings through Vice, Virtue, Conscience and *Imago Dei*

CELIA DEANE-DRUMMOND

What does morality mean?

An association of morality and animals raises questions about the moral status of non-human animals, that is, how far and to what extent do they really matter to humans? While this is an important question, and one that has been the basis for much of the discussion on animal rights, this chapter sets out to put the question in a different way and explores whether morality is confined to the human species or not. Most definitions of morality exclude the possibility that animals might be moral, or view human morality as somehow reacting to curb tendencies present in 'lower' nature. But if we define morality in a much more general way as 'to judge right and wrong, good and bad, and to behave accordingly',[1] then there is a possibility that animals might have this capacity. Of course, the more complex our definition of morality, the less likely we are to find such capacities in non-humans. However, from a biologist's point of view, what matters is the extent to which *underlying capabilities* are present, regardless of how far this might then come to be expressed in different shapes and forms in social and cultural terms. In other words, it is the capacity to make these kinds of judgements that is relevant, not whether there is a sophisticated system of ethics that is the prerogative of the human animal. No one is suggesting, for example, that a chimpanzee could come up with a sophisticated system like Kantian ethics or a sonnet in Shakespeare if only it were given enough time. But the establishment of

---

1 S. Planalp, *Communicating Emotion: Social, Moral and Cultural Processes*, Cambridge: Cambridge University Press, 1999, p. 161.

a system of rules in order to promote some behaviour and not others is quite a reasonable possibility. It is here that much confusion seems to lie, for philosophers regularly object to the idea of morality in animals on the basis that morality requires sophisticated mental abstraction that is not available to animals. Even an animal lover like the philosopher Stephen Clark resists the idea of morality in animals for the following reasons:

> Beasts, so far as we can tell, do not draw out from their own actions any principles of action on which they can comment, from which they can gradually dissent . . . If I cannot bear to generalise my principles, do I have principles at all? . . . All these perplexities are our affair. Beasts may sometimes feel them too, but if they do, we do not know it, and it seems more likely, in general, that they do not. Beasts, let us say, are ethical; that is they respond to aspects of a situation and to features of their kindred that a good man would also respect. But they are not moral: for they do not, as far as we can see it, have any occasion to moralise about themselves or to construct intellectual systems to accommodate their immediate responses.[2]

He goes on further to suggest that rationalists, 'emphasising the moral, are likely to find beasts wholly other than human; empiricists, like David Hume, recognise beasts as our cousins, moved by ethical concerns that move us also'.[3]

It is interesting to note what Clark is doing here. First, he is suggesting that the kind of abstractions that are found in human rational thinking makes human morality what it is. Once we do this, then humans and animals seem to be radically 'other'. On the other hand, he associates ethics with particular emotional responses that may also be found in animals. Hence, whether we think of non-human animals as potentially moral or not will depend on our assumptions about the extent and degree of abstraction needed for something to be counted as 'moral'. Holmes Rolston aligns morality and ethics, and morality with complexity in describing primate behaviour as 'pre-ethical', and 'Ethics is distinctively a product of human genius'.[4] But what might animals be capable of according to the work of current animal behaviourists?

---

2 Stephen Clark, *The Nature of the Beast: Are Animals Moral?*, Oxford: Oxford University Press, 1982, p. 107.

3 Clark, *Nature of the Beast*, p. 107.

4 Holmes Rolston, *Genes, Genesis and God: Values and Their Origins in Natural and Human History*, Cambridge: Cambridge University Press, 1999, pp. 212–13.

Animal emotions and complex behaviour

Frans de Waal is, arguably, one of the leading international experts in primatology and has researched extensively on the behaviours of primates. He argues that the social nature of the behaviour of animals is crucial in thinking about morality.[5] He suggests that the choice we have is to view morality as a cultural innovation achieved *only* by the human species, or see it as an outgrowth of social instincts that we share with non-human animals, that is, a product of social evolution. According to him, the problem with the first theory is that morality seems more like a veneer hiding an otherwise brutish nature. Richard Dawkins, among others, takes this stance in that he views ethics as a reaction to inbuilt tendencies towards immoral and self-seeking behaviour.[6] Any altruistic behaviour is seen as self-deception. De Waal believes that this was the dominant theory among biologists until quite recently. This leaves the second option as the only reasonable one, namely that morality is an outgrowth of social instincts that form the 'building blocks'. But are these alternatives too stark? Veneer theory would seem mistaken in as much as it implies a dualistic approach to behaviour, though engineering parallels between cultural and biological evolution through, for example, Dawkins' meme theory is also artificial. Yet the level and degree of sophistication of cultural activities found in human societies is distinct from animal social activity in a way that de Waal does not fully appreciate, that is, there is rather more room for innovation in human societies than his model implies. In other words, in de Waal's schema ambiguities do not come sufficiently to the surface. With Leonard Katz,

> We may wonder with Darwin how exactly to divide the credit for morality between natural selection, culture and learning, but suspect like him that, especially in the later stages of the evolution of morality, culture and learning, both individual and social, had the larger roles.[7]

---

5 F. de Waal, 'Primate Social Instincts, Human Morality and the Rise and Fall of Veneer Theory', in Stephen Macedo and Josiah Ober (eds), *Primates and Philosophers: How Morality Evolved*, Princeton: Princeton University Press, 2006, pp. 6–7.

6 Dawkins, for example, claims that 'We, alone on earth, can rebel against the tyranny of the selfish replicators'. Richard Dawkins, *The Selfish Gene*, 30th anniversary edition, Oxford: Oxford University Press, 2006, p. 201. His dual inheritance theory envisages memes being passed on in an analogous way to genes. There are considerable problems with memetic theory, not least because it fails to conform to biological models of natural selection, while, at the same time, forcing cultural traits into a pseudo-biological model.

7 Leonard D. Katz, 'Towards Good and Evil: Evolutionary Approaches to Aspects of

Leaving debates about different theories of social evolution to one side for the moment, it is worth considering de Waal's insistence on the evolution of co-operative and sympathetic tendencies in non-human animals. Charles Darwin also speculated in this vein, and he suggested:

> Any animal whatever, endowed with well marked social instincts, the parental and filial affections being here included, would inevitably acquire a moral sense or conscience, as soon as its intellectual powers had become as well developed, or nearly as well developed, as in man . . . Many animals sympathize with each other's distress or danger.[8]

De Waal argues that those tendencies for sympathy have evolved in social species, like elephants, wolves, dolphins, primates and, of course, humans. He suggests that such an impulse has survival value, so that:

> The impulse to help was therefore never truly without survival value to the ones showing the impulse. But, as so often, the impulse became divorced from the consequences that shaped its evolution. This permitted expression even when payoffs were unlikely, such as when strangers were beneficiaries.[9]

Such a view allows de Waal to claim that helping behaviours were beneficial initially in evolutionary terms, but also explains puzzles like helping strangers, without going down the route of self-deception. In other words, genuinely co-operative behaviours have evolved.[10]

Empathy is also a capability that exists in non-human animals that is there even before the influence of language and culture. There is a high selection pressure in its favour, because non-human primates rely on emotional mediation for their communication with one another. *Emotional*

Human Morality', in Leonard D. Katz (ed.), *Evolutionary Origins of Morality: Cross-Disciplinary Perspectives*, Thorverton: Imprint Academic, 2000, p. ix.

8 Charles Darwin, *The Descent of Man*, Princeton: Princeton University Press, 1981 [1871], pp. 71–2, 77.

9 De Waal, 'Primate Social Instincts', p. 15.

10 The alternative evolutionary theories about how such behaviour might have evolved include reciprocal altruism and kin selection, or even group selection, but all view altruism as an *evolved capacity*. The issue under discussion here is not so much whether such a capacity has evolved, but what we mean when we use the language of altruism in relation to non-human behaviour. Of course, as Holmes Rolston points out, fully mature moral reasoning is somewhat removed from simple altruism, as altruism implies self-sacrificing behaviour, whereas the Golden moral rule speaks about helping others and self equally, that is, it is about justice. Rolston, *Genes*, pp. 215–22.

contagion is perhaps the first stage of empathy, which allows the animal to feel the distress of another. True helping motivations will go beyond this. In order to illustrate that apes are capable of the latter, and not just emotional contagion, the following story about a female bonobo named Kuni, recounted by Frans de Waal, shows a somewhat remarkable exchange between two unrelated species:

> One day Kuni captured a starling. Out of fear that she might molest the stunned bird, which appeared undamaged, the helper urged the ape to let the bird go. Kuni picked up the starling with one hand and climbed to the highest point of the highest tree where she wrapped her legs around the trunk so that she had both hands free to hold the bird. She then carefully unfolded its wings and spread them wide open, one wing in each hand, before throwing the bird as hard as she could towards the barrier of the enclosure.[11]

De Waal, using experimental evidence based on numerous observations, believes that monkeys are only capable of emotional contagion, with genuine helping and consolation behaviour confined to apes. Such capabilities also seem to be related to the degree of self-awareness as shown by mirror self-recognition. In addition, social animals show a degree of acceptance towards those in their group that are injured or born with difficulties, as shown by examples of tolerance of, for example, a mentally retarded monkey in a group of rhesus macaques. In this instance, and many others, the popular idea of individual survival of the fittest does not make sense.[12]

Yet we should be wary of painting too glowing a picture of primate behaviour. Characteristics that would in human beings be called 'sin' are also present in ape behaviour as well through their tendencies towards violence to one another.[13] Reconciling strategies, which have a particular protocol depending on the species concerned, may also follow violent eruptions. These behaviours seem to be learned, rather than arriving

---

11 De Waal, *Primates*, p. 31.

12 De Waal, *Our Inner Ape: The Best and Worst of Human Nature*, London: Grant Books, 2006, p. 217.

13 I am aware that 'sin' is often defined as specific breakdown in relationship with God, in which case such a category would be inappropriate. But if sin is considered in social terms, then animals could be said to share in 'sin'. This, of course, raises other theological issues; see C. Deane-Drummond, 'Shadow Sophia in Christological Perspective: The Evolution of Sin and the Redemption of Nature', *Theology and Science* 6:1, 2008, pp. 13–32.

simply out of some sort of supposed 'blind' instinct. Where conflicts of interests arise within groups, many non-human primates seem to show similar strategies to humans for resolving, managing and preventing these conflicts of interest. The behaviour expressed is, for example, reciprocity and food-sharing, reconciliation, consolation, conflict intervention and mediation, which are 'the very building blocks of moral systems in that they are based on and facilitate cohesion among individuals and reflect a concerted effort by community members to find shared solutions to social conflict'.[14] Putting together rhesus and stumptail juvenile monkeys, where normally only the rhesus exhibits quarrelsome behaviour, showed that over time the rhesus monkey learned to be more tolerant.[15] This, and other experimental work, shows that primates are able to *learn* traits such as tolerance, rather than it simply arising out of inbuilt instincts.

Are other animals capable of consolation behaviours? In some fascinating work, Marc Bekoff has observed play behaviour among canids. Dogs, coyotes and wolves all learn quickly to play in a way that is fair according to the rules set up by the particular species. Those that fail to engage in fair play become more isolated and drift away from the group, where their chance of survival falls drastically.[16] Fair play seems to foster group stability and overall survival rates of those in the group. Particular 'rules' for fair play include play invitation signals, variations in sequence of actions, self-handicapping and role reversing. He suggests that co-operation is more common than we might think, and 'When animals cooperate, they're doing what comes naturally, and cooperation relies on established, well maintained social standards of behaviour – that is moral codes.'[17] Bekoff suggests the following:

> It's clear that morality and virtue didn't suddenly appear at the evolutionary epic beginning with humans. The origins of virtue, egalitarianism and morality are more ancient than our own species. While fair play in animals may be a rudimentary form of social morality, it still could be a forerunner of more complex and more sophisticated human moral systems.[18]

---

14 Jessica C. Flack and Frans B. M. de Waal, 'Any Animal Whatever: Darwinian Building Blocks of Morality in Monkeys and Apes', in Katz (ed.), *Evolution of Moral Systems*, p. 1.

15 De Waal, *Our Inner Ape*, pp. 147–8.

16 Marc Bekoff, *The Emotional Lives of Animals*, Novato: New World Library, 2007, p. 102.

17 Bekoff, *Emotional Lives*, p. 107.

18 Bekoff, *Emotional Lives*, p. 109.

In addition to the sense of fairness outlined above, many non-human animals are also capable of feeling love, where love is defined as preferring the company of another and protecting their interests. Animals also show signs of grief when loved ones die.[19] Animals also seem capable of showing care, even where there seems to be no advantage to them. Companionships between blind animals (including humans) and other animals abound, including some unusual liaisons such as that between a 1-year-old hippopotamus and a century-old tortoise. Joy is also in evidence in social play, with the same neurochemicals released in the brain of animals as in humans.[20]

Bekoff also suggests that 'if we try to learn more about forgiveness, fairness, trust and cooperation in animals, maybe we'll also learn to live more compassionately and cooperatively with one another'.[21] This comes close to naturalistic ethics, that is, what we learn of non-human animal behaviour gives us a model for human acting and behaving. But before we dismiss this too readily, it is appropriate to consider the extent to which virtue ethics is grounded in biological realism.

Of course, there are always sceptics who object to the categorization of non-human animals in terms of their similarity to human behaviour, such as found in the writing of de Waal or Bekoff for that matter, with the claim that just because behaviours look like, for example, peace-keeping or justice-making or empathy, they do not necessarily equate with similar underlying psychological motivation to that found in humans.[22] There is also the difficulty of the anecdotal nature of much of the early evidence for complex traits.[23] Ethologists respond by pointing to the frequency of observations and the heuristic advantage of taking an anthropomorphic

---

19 Bekoff, *Emotional Lives*, pp. 62–70.
20 Bekoff, *Emotional Lives*, p. 56.
21 Bekoff, *Emotional Lives*, p. 109.
22 I. S. Bernstein, 'The Law of Parsimony Prevails: Missing Premises Allow Any Conclusion', in Katz (ed.), *Evolutionary Origins of Morality*, pp. 31–8. John Dupré also raises similar questions. J. Dupré, *Humans and Other Animals*, Oxford: Clarendon Press, 2002, pp. 217–35.
23 Dupré, for example, strongly objects to conclusions arrived at through such methods involving anecdotal evidence, though he recognizes the difficulty of designing experimental methods that would not interfere with outcomes. Dupré, *Humans*, p. 220. However, rather more extensive experimental evidence in support of such traits, as shown by learned behaviour, for example, is available since he published this work. His more important insight, perhaps, is that we should not seek after particular mental traits in non-human animals, for example specific language skills, in an essentialist way. Dupré, *Humans*, pp. 236–56. Ethologists such as Bekoff do not seem to me to be making this mistake, in that they are trying to find what is apparent *within the worlds* occupied by the species under investigation, rather than any sort of essentialist mapping onto human experience.

stance, as discussed below. Further objections based on the supposed lack of intentions of animals revolve around the suggested impossibility of animals feeling guilt, because guilt requires that a voluntary act has both hurt another and could have been suppressed.[24] More strident still, perhaps, is the denial by authors such as Hans Kummer that what is being observed in ethological studies is anything more than objects observed by human value judgement in such a way that they are presented as 'shared solutions', rather than reflecting individual learning, a view that he prefers.[25] Flack and de Waal respond to such objections by arguing that they are making the case for the existence of *moral sentiments* in animals, rather than sophisticated moral judgement, and that the former are 'building blocks' of morality, rather than the kind of morality that is found in human societies. Moreover, such building blocks are not equated with the resultant behaviour, but show the capacity for developing something like that behaviour, much of which arises through social learning. Moreover, behaviour should not be judged good or bad according to human moral standards, but show evidence of mental and social capacities that allow the construction of societies where shared values constrain individual behaviours.[26] While it is difficult to prove that underlying psychological tendencies are similar, the fact that similar neurons are present is strongly suggestive of close parallels. To resist this possibility entirely seems to fly in the face of the evidence and be based on prejudicial attitudes towards animals.

Aquinas, MacIntyre and virtue ethics

The possibility that forms of human behaviour have analogues in non-human animal behaviour should perhaps come as no surprise to us, for such an approach is common to thinking grounded in Aristotelian and Thomistic philosophy.[27] While Aquinas' instrumental approach towards animals is well known, this parts company with his recognition of the

24 Jerome Kagan, 'Human Morality is Distinctive', in Katz (ed.), *Evolutionary Origins of Morality*, pp. 46–8. Kagan argues that the continuum that de Waal sets up between primates and humans is a mistake.

25 Hans Kummer, 'Ways Beyond Appearances', in Katz (ed.), *Evolutionary Origins of Morality*, pp. 48–52. Others doubt whether the proposed 'building blocks' of morality that de Waal claims to have found in non-human primates bear much relation to the complex characteristics associated with human morality. See John Troyer, 'Human and Other Natures', in Katz (ed.), *Evolutionary Origins of Morality*, pp. 62–5.

26 Jessica Flack and Frans B. M. de Waal, 'Being Nice Is Not a Building Block of Morality: Response to Commentary Discussion', in Katz (ed.), *Evolutionary Origins of Morality*, pp. 67–77.

27 See also J. Berkman's chapter in this volume.

extent and complexity of animal emotions and responses in a way that sounds remarkably modern. There are certainly treatments of Aquinas that associate his thinking with René Descartes, and suggest that he thought of animals as unthinking automata.[28] Such a perspective has also been exploited by Andrew Linzey, who has regularly castigated Aquinas for his attitude to animal treatment in a way that ignores other aspects of his thought.[29] The discussion of the meaning of instinct in Aquinas is crucial here. While Descartes associated instinct with unthinking behaviour, a view that has crept into popular consciousness today, Aquinas understood instinct as more closely aligned with *intellectual* activity, in particular, he associated it with the estimative sense,[30] and also prudence, or practical wisdom.[31] In other words, he viewed instinct as analogous to reasonable behaviour in humans.[32] Hence:

> In Dumb animals the sensory orexis is obviously not obedient to reason. Still it has the guidance of the estimative faculty, which is sub-

---

28 See, for example, Aquinas' comparison between an archer's arrow and the activity of non-human animals, or a clock to the human mind, the difference being that this expresses the art of God. *Summa Theologiae: Volume 17 (1a2ae. 6–17), Psychology of Human Acts*, trans. Thomas Gilby, London: Blackfriars, 1970, q. 13.2. This alignment with Descartes is common not just among animal rights campaigners, but also some more traditional Thomist scholars, who generally dismiss any concern for reasoning in non-human animals, for example James Royce, *Man and His Nature*, New York: McGraw Hill, 1961, p. 355. It is important to note that this particular passage concerns the possibility of choice in irrational animals, though his linking of the acts of bees, spiders and dogs showed perhaps a lack of discrimination. There are important differences between Aquinas and Descartes, in that Descartes insisted that there was a difference in kind, rather than just difference in degree. Aquinas does not make such a distinction as clear-cut as Descartes. In addition, Descartes is not as hostile to animals as his subsequent interpreters have implied. John Dupré incorrectly claims that 'Animals for Descartes were what many contemporary philosophers refer to as zombies, machines with no inner life'. Dupré, *Humans*, p. 12. Descartes also admitted to the possibility of feelings in animals. See J. Cottingham, 'A Brute to the Brutes? Descartes' Treatment of Animals', *Philosophy* 53, 1978, pp. 551–9.

29 Andrew Linzey, 'Animal Rights', in P. Clarke and A. Linzey (eds), *Dictionary of Ethics, Theology and Society*, London: Routledge, 1996, pp. 29–33.

30 Thomas Gilby translated estimative sense as instinct: 'Instinct translates *vis aestimativa*', *Summa Theologiae: Volume 17*, p. 13.

31 The relationship between instinct and prudence is particularly clear: 'And he allows wise judgment to "a few animals", and not exclusively to man, because even certain brute animals have a sort of prudence or wisdom, in that they instinctively form correct judgments on what they need to do.' *Commentary on Aristotle's de Anima*, trans. Kenelm Foster OP and Sylvester Humphries OP, New Haven: Yale University Press, 1951; html edition by Joseph Kenny OP at <http://www.diafrica.org/kenny/CDtexts/DeAnima.htm#34> (accessed 1 July 2008), Book III, Ch. 3, Lectio 4, n. 629.

32 Aquinas, *Summa Theologiae: Volume 21 (1a2ae. 40–48), Fear and Anger*, trans. John Patrick Reid, London: Blackfriars, 1965, q. 46.4.

ject to higher reason, namely God's; and to that extent their emotions bear some resemblance to moral goodness.[33]

He also acknowledged the presence of hope and despair in non-human animals, but he believed that animals appear to act as if they saw into the future, and that instinct is 'bestowed by the divine intellect which does see into the future'.[34] In other words, those capacities of animals that seem to us to resemble that found in humans do so because as creatures under the divine law they share in divine reason. Indeed, it is integral to Aquinas' thought that all creatures are needed in order to display most fully divine goodness.[35]

The difference between non-human and human animals for Aquinas lies in the latter's power of universal (abstract) reasoning, so that he is prepared to admit to a degree of rationality in non-humans, but to a lesser extent compared with humans. Judith Barad has also commented on this, comparing the judgements in animals as that arising from natural estimate, rather than deliberation as such.[36] Hence, Aquinas suggests that 'we find that animals, in proportion to their connatural assessment of things, have a certain share of shrewdness with regard to particular activities. But man has – or can have – a universal shrewdness that is the measure of all possible activities.'[37] The difference between animals and humans seems to be the latter's capacity for *abstract* deliberation. He reinforces this in other places by suggesting that animals are restricted to operations of the sensitive appetite, so that they do not have powers of discrimination. For him, the common behaviour of all members of a species suggests that prudence is only partially evident in animals,

---

33 Aquinas, *Summa Theologiae: Volume 19 (1a2ae. 23–30), The Emotions*, trans. Eric D'Arcy, London: Blackfriars, 1967, q. 24.4. Those passages mentioned above that point to Aquinas' interpretation of animals as acting as if they were reasonable, but in reality just according to divine design (e.g. Aquinas, *Summa Theologiae*, 1a2ae, q. 13.2) could perhaps be used as a primary filter here in order to support the notion of animals as automata, but the idea of being subject to higher reason is also a goal of human life, inasmuch as natural law is a participation in the eternal law, hence the much more radical distinction is between God and creatures, rather than between human and non-human animals.

34 Aquinas, *Summa Theologiae: Volume 21*, q. 40.3.

35 Aquinas, *Summa Theologiae: Volume 8 (1a. 44–49), Creation, Variety and Evil*, trans. T. Gilby, London: Blackfriars, 1967, q. 47.1.

36 See J. Barad, *Aquinas on the Nature and Treatment of Animals*, International Scholars Publications, San Francisco: Catholic Scholars Press, 1995, pp. 113–14.

37 Aquinas, *Summa Theologiae: Volume 13 (1a. 90–102), Man Made in God's Image*, trans. Edmund Hill, London: Blackfriars, 1964, q. 96.1.

full practical wisdom or prudence is discovered in a person who has sound judgement about how things should be done, while a partial reflection of this is exhibited by some animals whose particular instinctive manifestations adapt them to tasks similar to those which tax human ingenuity.[38]

According to Aquinas, the least developed forms of prudence included memory, then teachableness, and, finally, its fullest expression is found in human animals.[39]

It is also fair to say that much of human moral deliberation is not the kind of detached reasoning that humans are capable of; rather, humans more often than not behave by acting out of deeply seated emotions that they share with non-human animals. Can we say that only those actions detached from our emotions are moral? I would argue that this is a false view of moral action – action that is moral is that which tends towards the good and avoids evil. This is, of course, the first principle of natural law.[40]

MacIntyre's *Dependent Rational Animals* explores the kind of virtues arising out of human vulnerability and our animal condition. His empha-

---

38 Aquinas, *Summa Theologiae: Volume 16 (1a2ae. 1–5), Purpose and Happiness*, trans. T. Gilby, London: Blackfriars, 1968, q. 3.1.

39 There are plenty of references to this in Aquinas. A particularly useful citation comes from his *Commentary on the Metaphysics*, Book 1, where he claims: 'Again, from the fact that some animals have memory and some do not, it follows that some are prudent and some not ... Now those animals which have memory can have some prudence, although prudence has one meaning in the case of brute animals and another in the case of man. Men are prudent inasmuch as they deliberate rationally about what they ought to do.' *Commentary on the Metaphysics*, trans. John P. Rowan, Chicago, 1961, html-edited by Joseph Kenny OP at <http://www.diafrica.org/kenny/CDtexts/Metaphysics1.htm#1> (accessed 15 April 2007), Book 1, Lectio 1, n. 11. Aquinas also believed that animals shared not only in memory, but at a higher level, namely experience, but only to a limited extent (Book 1, Lectio 1, n. 15). The difference between animals and humans seems to be related to capacity for art and universal reason in the latter, and customary activity and particular reason in the former (Book 1, Lectio 1, n. 16). A full discussion of this aspect of Aquinas' thought is outside the scope of the present work. He also considered that the productive activity of art differed from that of prudence, as is clear from his *Commentary on the Metaphysics*: 'And these also differ; for prudence directs us in actions which do not pass over into some external matter but are perfections of the one acting ... but art directs us in those productive actions, such as building and cutting, which pass over into external matter' (Book 1, Lectio 1, n. 34). In the light of current knowledge of animal behaviour, their ability to reason in a planned way comes close to Aquinas' definition of art. See, for example, Nicola S. Clayton and Nathan J. Emery, 'Canny Corvids and Political Primates: A Case for Convergent Evolution in Intelligence', in S. Conway Morris (ed.), *The Deep Structure of Biology: Is Convergence Sufficiently Ubiquitous to Give a Directional Signal?*, Philadelphia: Templeton Foundation Press, 2008, pp. 128–42.

40 Aquinas, *Summa Theologiae: Volume 28 (1a2ae. 90–97), Law and Political Theory*, trans. Thomas Gilby, London: Blackfriars, 1966, q. 94.1.

sis on human dependence stresses the social character of human life that has some analogies with dependencies in other social animals. He examines the differences between non-human and human animals in the light of ethological studies of animal behaviour. Unlike Martin Heidegger he refuses to lump together all animals under one category as those incapable of relating to something as something; for Heidegger animals are merely captive in their inner worlds. While this tendency to group animals together is also found in Aquinas, at least he was aware that animals are rational to different extents. MacIntyre, in common with animal ethologists, compares animals with children in suggesting that their initial reasoning skill is based on having reasons for acting in a certain way. It is also helpful as a comparison in that we can readily agree that children might be morally culpable, but not yet capable of the kind of sophisticated moral reasoning that matures with time. Eventually we arrive at 'its specifically human state of being able to evaluate those reasons, to revise them or to abandon them and replace them with others'.[41] Virtues, similarly, can be characterized in two different ways.[42] In the first sense, they are qualities shown in response to different situations, such as when to take risks, when to be cautious, when to praise or not, when to be relaxed or demanding, when to show anger or tell a joke, and so on. Virtues are also shown in a second sense as practical reasoning, or prudence, in terms of what action is best to do in given circumstances, according to particular premises about the goods that are at stake and possible harms. The question remains: how far is it helpful to speak of animals as having virtues, that is, habits of mind that lead to particular behaviours that enhance flourishing?

Anthropomorphism: does it help or hinder understanding morality?

Much ink has been spilt on how far non-human animal behaviourists, ethologists and others are committing that fallacy that has been a common tendency for humans, namely, reading into animal behaviour that which is found in human communities. Mary Midgley, in her epic book *Beast and Man*, has correctly alerted us to numerous historical examples where humans projected their frustrations onto animal communities, portraying human evil as a mirror of that found in our beastly cousins.[43] She

---

41 Alasdair MacIntyre, *Dependent Rational Animals*, London: Duckworth, 1999, p. 91.
42 MacIntyre, *Dependent*, p. 92.
43 Mary Midgley, *Beast and Man: The Roots of Human Nature*, London: Routledge, 1995 [1979].

has continued this line of thought in her more recent *The Ethical Primate: Humans, Freedom and Morality*.[44] Here she states that kinship with animals depends on how they are conceived, so that 'at a deep imaginative level, people still tend to see animals as symbols of odious, anti-human qualities', and as a consequence resist the idea of kinship. According to the social contract view, there is virtually no difference between humans and animals; both are egoists, while humans are enlightened and self-aware egoists. The opposite view draws a sharp division between humans and other animals, viewing only humans as capable of possessing mind, that is then inserted into a body characteristic of an 'animal nature' in distinction from 'human nature' that includes mind. Both, she suggests, buy into the mythical view of animals. Yet she does not hold back from suggesting that 'everyone knows that animals are as incapable of vice as they are of virtue'; for her, all such portrayals are symbolizing, not real.[45] Are ethologists committing a category mistake in describing animal emotions, including discussion of emotions such as joy, happiness, embarrassment, hope, grief, despair, and behaviour patterns such as reconciliation, peace-making or love? The difficulty, of course, is how to describe what is observed. Its variety and flexibility does not lend support to the idea of purely innate behaviours supposedly detached from reasoning. Moreover, inasmuch as this language helps as a heuristic tool in understanding animal behaviour then it needs to be welcomed, regardless of the extent to which such behaviour shares an identical biological basis with similar human behaviours.

Insights from archaeologists such as Steven Mithen are helpful in tracing the evolution of cognition in early hominids. He suggests that the early human mind possessed a separate social intelligence and a technical intelligence, like a Swiss army knife, but the modern human mind was able to integrate these, a process known as cognitive fluidity. I have considerable doubts about the validity of the Swiss army knife model, as it presupposes that different mental capacities are evolved traits according to natural selection, whereas the concept of an evolved fluid mind seems far more probable.[46] It was this cognitive fluidity that, according to Mithen, leads to

---

44 Mary Midgley, *The Ethical Primate: Humans, Freedom and Morality*, London: Routledge, 1994, pp. 129–30.

45 Midgley, *Beast*, p. 31. She softens this harder line in her more recent work, by referring to the work of ethologists who have observed the ability of other animals to live together and co-operate, so much so that she suggests that this ability 'has to be their natural disposition to love and trust one another'. *Ethical Primate*, p. 131.

46 The idea of cognitive fluidity may also prove unnecessary, since human minds have simply evolved to be flexible.

anthropomorphic thinking, where non-human animals are treated as more like persons, and totemic thinking, where humans take on characteristics of animals, and appeared in the Upper Palaeolithic groups of humans.[47] For him Neanderthals were capable of music, but not much more, and religion only developed in *Homo* species. He resists the idea that animals have minds that are rather like humans, believing that this is unwarranted anthropomorphism that seems to be built into the way humans, historically, have related to the creaturely world.[48] In other words, he would object to de Waal's portrayal of animals as in some sense sharing moral capacities with humans. He also suggests that unlike humans chimpanzees rely on general intelligence for tool-making, rather than, as in hominids, exhibiting a specialist cognitive capacity for tool-making. Unlike de Waal, he is hesitant to ascribe 'cultural' activities to primates, viewing their tool-making as still showing simple repetitive actions that one would expect if it stemmed from a far more generalized intelligence.[49]

But does the fact that humans have evolved specialist intelligence in tool-making and natural history, if we assume this model is indeed correct, necessarily rule out the possibility that non-human animals do share aspects of the *social* intelligence characteristic of humans? Mithen compares the evolution of human minds with that of a cathedral: even the earliest minds share the great nave of general intelligence. Likening the mind to a cathedral implies a type of 'design' that many other biologists find is much too rigid to be acceptable. Mithen readily admits that even early humans and chimpanzees share a specialist social intelligence, so one might have anticipated a form of morality to develop in this sphere in order to serve that intelligence without needing to invoke the idea that this simply stems from unwarranted anthropomorphism that distorts, rather than illuminates, what is happening in animals. Moreover, ethologists such as Bekoff are quite happy to admit that inasmuch as an anthropocentric reading of animal behaviour takes place, it is useful as a heuristic tool, rather than making any claim that what is observed is identical to that found in humans.[50]

---

47 Steven Mithen, *The Prehistory of the Mind*, London: Pheonix, 1996, pp. 186–7. For dialogue, see also S. Mithen, 'The Evolution of the Religious Mind', and reply C. Deane-Drummond, 'Whence Comes Religion? Mithen on Prehistory and Mind', in N. Spurway (ed.), *Theology, Evolution and Mind*, London: Scholars Press, *in press*.

48 Mithen, *Prehistory*, p. 188. In this respect he relies on the work of J. S. Kennedy.

49 Mithen, *Prehistory*, p. 85.

50 See, for example, discussion in Alexandra C. Horowitz and Marc Bekoff, 'Naturalizing Anthropomorphisms: Behavioural Prompts to Our Humanizing of Animals', *Anthrozoos* 20:1, 2007, pp. 23–35.

Is conscience an evolved capacity?

The crucial question for moral decision-making is how far and to what extent animals might be aware or conscious that an action is wrong or right. In human societies, a person who acts wrongly without sensitivity to the fact is known as someone with a dulled conscience. Is conscience a capacity that has evolved? If so, it is intimately bound up with the evolution of what we might term bad and good behaviours, vice and virtue. This is not, of course, a projection of human values into non-human animal behaviour, for I am not speaking about those predatory behaviours that have sometimes been referred to as 'natural evil'. When humans projected human vices into the behaviour of, for example, wolves, they more often than not focused on their predatory capacity, rather than the social relationships characteristic of wolf societies. Somewhat quaint medieval accounts of animals 'on trial' for various misdemeanours reflect the projection of human vices onto that of other creatures, especially in those instances where the animal was blamed not just in a literal sense, but in a moral sense for an attack on another human being. Rather, what seems to be at stake here are those *social* capacities in animals which seem to present the individual animal with a choice for good or not in relation to their own social worlds. In other words, morality for an animal is what is considered good in terms of their society, that is, what will contribute to its flourishing.

Some interesting research on the common ancestor – that is, common to higher primates (bonobos, gorillas, chimpanzees and humans) – seeks to tease out the evolution of moral behaviour in general and conscience in particular. At this point we might ask how we might be able to go back to the Late Pleistocene past. Anthropologist Christopher Boehm has attempted to do this by assessing 329 foraging societies and eliminating those that were likely to be anomalous with respect to prehistoric societies. This left 154 'Pleistocene-appropriate' mobile hunter-gatherer societies that had also been studied ethnographically. Fifty of these were subject to more intensive analysis, including assessment of 'moral universals' or moral rules. In this respect:

> Typical deviances include being arrogantly overaggressive or stingy; being a thief, cheater, excessive liar or bully; or being an unpredictable recidivist killer. At the same time, active social sanctioning generally includes direct criticism and 'social distancing' (mild ostracism to group

ejection) along with shaming and ridicule, capital punishment and supernatural sanctions.[51]

Co-operative behaviour, on the other hand, led to reproductively significant social rewards. Can this behaviour model that in Late Pleistocene times? Boehm suggests that the answer is yes, for it is known that people were in similarly sized small hunter-gatherer communities. While fascinating, his working assumption seems to be that just because we cannot rule out analogies between suitably selected modern hunter-gatherer societies with late Pleistocene societies, this means that meaningful comparisons can be made. He is certainly able to counter criticisms about the possible lack of diversity of physical environments. It is rather more difficult to justify assumptions about the egalitarian political structure of extant societies. In addition, he also assumes that the earliest human communities mirrored male-dominant societies that, he believes, are characteristic of apes. Such aggressive behaviour was then curbed. However, other scholars have questioned both the extent to which primates can be characterized in this way and the universal, speculative nature of his claims.[52]

Accordingly, in this research, we find group mores that involve internalized values and rules, and what is termed a 'self monitoring conscience based on sympathy . . . and a strong sense of shame'.[53] In order to support

---

51 Christopher Boehm, 'Conscience Origins, Sanctioning Selection, and the Evolution of Altruism in *Homo Sapiens*', *Behavior and Brain Sciences*, submitted for publication July 2008, p. 12. I am very grateful to the author for allowing me access to this article (pp. 1–62). He is acutely aware of the difficulties in using an appropriate present-day example in order to project back in history, but he argues that we can legitimately draw on those groups that *cannot be ruled out* as sharing common features. Also relevant is C. Boehm, 'Conflict and the Evolution of Social Control', in Katz (ed.), *Evolutionary Origins of Morality*, pp. 79–101. Here Boehm argues that the earliest forms of morality were those that were imposed in social hierarchies by individuals tending towards active intervention in the form of consolation, reconciliation and active pacifying behaviour. Once this behaviour became collective and language could track such behaviour, he believes that 'full-blown morality was on its way'. He also suggests that bullying was one of the first forms of behaviour to be labelled as morally deviant. Presumably conscience, as Boehm defines it, reflected accompanying psychological reactions to these newly developed rules. How far such evolutionary development follows Darwinian processes is, of course, still contested. In describing the development of morality more in political terms than in sociobiological terms Boehm avoids some of the fallacies committed by evolutionary psychology, while allowing for lines of continuity between early hominid and modern human societies.

52 See I. S. Bernstein, 'Logic and Human Morality: An Attractive if Untested Scenario', pp. 105–07, and Donald Black, 'On the Origins of Morality', pp. 107–19, in Katz (ed.), *The Evolution of Morality*.

53 Boehm, 'Conscience Origins', p. 14.

these behaviours, collective social sanctions are used as agreed by what is termed 'moralistic gossips'. The moral code includes proscription against murder, incest, boasting, bullying, deception, cheating, theft and lying, as well as mild condemnation of adultery. There are also proscriptions in favour of generosity, co-operativeness and peacefulness within the group as a whole. The locus of brain activity that leads to a sense of conscience is found in the prefrontal cortex. A sense of shame or embarrassment is much more universal compared with a sense of guilt that is more limited in its distribution. Shame as a more universal trait is linked with negative psychological reactions to past, present or anticipated moral malfeasances. Hence, anthropologists define 'conscience' as

> a partly shame-driven means of moralistic self appraisal and self-control, which not only helps in avoiding the bad opinion of one's fellows, but also serves to control many impulses that could have direct negative fitness consequences because of punitive group sanctioning.[54]

Boehm, while broadly sympathetic to the possibility of a sense of 'culpritude' in chimpanzees, holds back on the attribution of this as moral, on the basis that

> It is having a self-judgmental conscience and shameful blushing that makes humans distinctively 'moral', and this brings us back to shame, as a specialized manifestation of conscience. Chimpanzees and bonobos appear to experience neither socially-induced facial flushing nor psychological malaise based on a sense of having broken internalized rules, so I believe that ancestral preadaptations for specifically *moral* emotions cannot be identified.[55]

But is this correct? Marc Bekoff describes several anecdotal stories of apes and rhesus monkeys that suggest that they do feel shame or embarrassment.[56] In spite of the difficulties with such evidence, the possibility cannot be overlooked. In addition, to tie moral behaviour specifically to conscience-laden activity limits the definition of morality, and thereby constitutes a circular argument. For Boehm it is possible to be virtuous without being moral, for he attributes moral feelings specifically to having a self-judgemental conscience. He argues, in particular, that ancestral Pan

---

54 Boehm, 'Conscience Origins', pp. 16–17.
55 Boehm, 'Conscience Origins', p. 20.
56 Bekoff, *The Emotional Lives of Animals*, pp. 77–8.

had a non-moral sense of 'culpritude', which included past offences, but lacked internalization of values which leaded to self-judgement; in other words, it lacked conscience.

Boehm suggests that conscience evolved as a result of selection pressure against greedy and aggressive behaviour, in such a way that coincided with social self-inhibition functions in the brain. In other words, there was a gradual internalization of the external rules that led to social cohesion. It seems to me highly likely that the brain has evolved in such a way that it became more capable of complex self-referential function. I am less sure that we can call this capacity for self-reference *conscience*, which seems to me to be taught, as much as depending on an innate capacity for that internalization. While I would agree that the very general capacity for embarrassment or feeling shame may well be biologically based, this is not the same as a developed conscience, even according to anthropological definitions, that reacts internally to given externally imposed rules and deviations from these rules. We know as much from the education of young children; a sense of shame only arises in relation to knowledge about certain rules and expectations given by the community.

The above suggests that as long as we define morality in terms of judgements about right and wrong, and as long as this is perceived in the context of the *specific* social life of non-human animals, then it is entirely possible to attribute 'morality' of a sort to some animals. Our pre-hominid ancestors may have shared in this form of morality as a precursor to the more developed forms in more sophisticated human societies. Further, the biological basis for developing a capacity for conscience, including the capacity to feel shame, may be present in some animal societies. Other capacities for emotion, along with the ability to exercise reasoned judgement as that expressed in prudence, are also present in some animals, though the power of universal reasoning seems confined to human animals. The difference, in other words, seems to be one of degree, rather than absolute distinction.

Human distinctiveness as *imago Dei*

What are we to make of these intimations towards conscience in rational animals? I suggest that in biological terms the differences between non-human animals and humans is more often than not one of degree. Yet the summation of all these differences does put humanity in a unique position, not least in the potential exercise of human responsibility as a moral agent. The traditional theological way of speaking of human uniqueness is under the category of *imago Dei*, the image of God. In the discussion above it was clear that while Aquinas has been read through the eyes of Descartes, another reading is possible that lends him far more sympathetic to the possibility of reasoning in animals. Aquinas also links the degree of image-bearing with moral agency in humans, and this in turn is connected with the presence of a rational soul.

If we turn to Aquinas' discussion of the topic of human distinctiveness, following Augustine he views the human rational soul as a special creation of God, even though he agrees with Augustine that in general a soul makes a living thing the sort of thing that it is, that is, the actuality of its physical body.[57] The rational soul is closely linked with the image of God in humanity, but the image refers to the way in which a rational soul reflects something of God. Yet it is not a perfect image, which is only found in Christ; rather it is in humanity 'as in an alien nature, like the king's image on a silver coin'.[58] He also considers the possibility that God's image might also be in the universe as a whole, since this was declared 'very good' in Genesis. Instead, he argues for the retention of the term 'image' specifically for rational creatures, while allowing for the possibility of 'likeness' in non-rational creatures. Such a 'likeness of nature' serves to connect all things as beings to the first being, all living things to the first life, and all intelligent beings to the supreme wisdom.[59]

The religious dimension to both image-bearing and moral agency becomes clearer in Aquinas' discussion of the differential use of the image in men and women, where he links moral performance to the bearing of the image. He suggests that there are three stages in image-bearing.[60] The first is a created natural aptitude for loving and understanding God, as an activity of mind shared by men and women. The second stage is the *habitus*, or attitude, of one who loves and knows God, but still imperfectly, so that the image of God is received and re-created through conformity to God's grace, and is found in the just. The third stage is knowing and loving God perfectly, the image through the likeness of glory, which is found only in the blessed. Aquinas incorrectly confines the second and third stages to the male gender, using 1 Corinthians 11.7 to back up his

---

57 Aquinas, *Summa Theologiae: Volume 13*, q. 90.4.
58 Aquinas compares the image with that in the Son, which is an image of nature, like a king in relation to his son. *Summa Theologiae: Volume 13*, q. 93.1.
59 Aquinas, *Summa Theologiae: Volume 13*, q. 93.2. Intelligence is used in a general sense in relation to non-intelligence, rather than in modern usage.
60 Aquinas, *Summa Theologiae: Volume 13*, q. 93.4.

argument that man reflects the glory of God and woman reflects the glory of man. The point to be noted here is that all three stages in the progression of the image are not related simply to the impetus of an intelligent nature, but closely linked with the capacity for knowing God, and its expression in particular ways. It is for this reason that Aquinas can include those whose reasoning is impaired as also bearing the divine image, even though he had to admit that according to his model such an image was 'practically non existent' in those who lack any reason, 'dim and disfigured' in sinners, and 'bright and beautiful' in the just.[61] There is certainly support for the idea that all animals share in the likeness of the divine nature, even non-rational animals. Aquinas also includes all parts of the human body and soul under this category of likeness. Somewhat confusingly, likeness is also the term used to describe the perfection of the image in terms of 'likeness of divine virtue, in so far as it can be in man'.[62] In other words, for Aquinas it is in the practical outworking of the male human as moral agent that human image-bearing becomes most obvious. While we can certainly object to the sexist language used here, what is of interest is the link between image and moral agency, and the link between image-bearing and capacity to know God in a way that seems to be graduated.

If, as I have argued above, non-human animals can be thought of as in some sense sharing in moral agency, whether in a latent sense or through specific behaviour in their own moral worlds, then the question that comes to mind is whether it also makes sense to speak of animals as sharing in the divine image. Specifically, we need to ask whether animals might have a religious sense, bearing in mind the gradation suggested earlier in relation to the capacity to know God. In other words, do animals have the capacity to use their reason to know God in the way that seems to be clear in human beings? Certainly, religious ritual and practices are hallmarks of even the earliest communities of humans. However, in the light of ethological studies I suggest that the jury is out on how far animals may or may not have a religious sense.[63] Just as Aquinas was incorrect to see women as in some sense lacking a full share in the abundance of image-bearing, so, too, I suggest that it is incorrect to exclude the possibility of a form of image-bearing that is suited to particular animal species in relation to their own kinds. It is perhaps akin to an image-

---

61 Aquinas, *Summa Theologiae: Volume 13*, q. 93.8.

62 Aquinas, *Summa Theologiae: Volume 13*, q. 93.9.

63 Space does not permit discussion of this topic here, except so far as to suggest that the observed capacity of animals to experience something like wonder may give us pause for thought.

bearing that reflects their own particular 'nature', rather than necessarily *just* seeing this as the 'lowest' rung of image-bearing characteristic of human religious and moral experience that might follow from consideration of Aquinas' discourse on the image-bearing in men and women. In other words, just as there is a form of 'morality' in animals that could be considered a type of 'latent' morality, which has its analogies in the idea of general likeness and image-bearing in human communities, so there may be a distinct form of image-bearing that is true for that particular species, in so far as it reflects a tendency towards the good, as judged according to their own kind. Like humans, animals also can mirror something of the glory of God, even if they are not religiously self-conscious in the manner of human beings. We may find the concept of 'image-bearing' too anthropomorphic a term to use, but perhaps this gives us a good hint at the kind of capacities that might be present. Overall the discussion so far suggests that not only are animals remarkably similar to human beings, but also, they are striking in their differences, and need to be treated with respect by humans who have a particular vocation to share in the fullest relational sense of what it means to be in the image of God, *imago Trinitatis*.[64] If humans are *imago Dei* in this sense, then they also have a duty to show that capacity through imitation, that is, through giving moral attention to other species, especially those animal kinds that can be regarded as our kin.

---

64 Aquinas affirmed the diversity of creation by suggesting that the glory of God is manifest through the variety of creatures as they express the 'likeness of the Trinity by way of trace'. *Summa Theologiae: Volume 8*, q. 45.7. See also Aquinas, *Summa Theologiae: Volume 10 (1a. 65–74), Cosmogony*, trans. William A. Wallace, London: Blackfriars, 1967, q. 65.2.

Humans, Animals, Evolution and Ends

NEIL MESSER

Introduction

This chapter is an attempt to locate a range of practical moral questions about the human treatment of non-human animals within the framework of one Christian theological tradition, Reformed Protestantism, and to show how they might be constructively addressed within that tradition. An anecdotal observation illustrates the kind of question I have in mind. It involves no great hardship for relatively affluent Westerners to be vegetarian; in such contexts, it is relatively easy to avoid benefiting – directly, at any rate – from the killing of animals for food. In the same contexts, though, it would be much harder to avoid benefiting directly from the killing of animals in medical research, since that would mean refusing much or most of what is on offer whenever one goes to the doctor or is admitted to hospital. Are there limits to the use that humans ought to make of non-human animals, and, if so, where are the limits to be drawn? Is either meat-eating or biomedical research on animals beyond the pale?

The discussion of such practical questions, however, depends on answers to prior questions about how we understand ourselves and non-human animals, our and their places in the scheme of things, and so forth. So the two linked questions in view in this chapter are along the following lines: first, how ought we to understand the relationship between humans and non-human animals? Second, what does this understanding imply about how humans should treat non-human animals? The burden of my argument is that the kind of answer that proves theologically satisfactory will be in some sense teleological, and that the kind of teleology we need must be learned first and foremost through God's self-revelation in Christ.

On the need to learn about ends

How, then, is a theologically satisfactory account of the relationship between humans and non-human animals, and of the proper human treatment of animals, to be developed? What might such an account look like? Two approaches frequently taken in the literature on animals and ethics are unlikely to be satisfactory. The first is an ethic of non-maleficence and beneficence towards animals based on Jeremy Bentham's famous dictum that 'the question is not, Can they *reason?* nor, Can they *talk?* but, Can they *suffer?*'[1] It is not that such an ethic would necessarily be wrong, but that it would be radically incomplete and thin. The problem is that Bentham's dictum is rooted in his version of utilitarianism, in which the pursuit of the good is reduced without remainder to the maximization of happiness, the latter understood as pleasure and the absence of pain. But the maximization of happiness is widely held by theological critics to be an over-thin account of the *human* good;[2] and if we say that, it would seem a little odd if we were prepared to settle for such an account when attempting to speak theologically about the good in respect of God's other earthly creatures.[3]

The second approach that is unlikely to prove satisfactory is to set the discussion up in terms of the *rights* of animals. Apart from the philosophical problems associated with the use of rights language in relation to non-human animals, there is an important question as to how an ethic of animal rights might be located within a theological frame of reference. This problem was acknowledged and a solution attempted in Andrew Linzey's account of 'theos-rights', in which the rights of creatures are derivative of God's rights in the creation.[4] But what is required by the

---

1 Jeremy Bentham, *An Introduction to the Principles of Morals and Legislation*, ed. J. H. Burns and H. L. A. Hart, London: Athlone, 1970 [1789], p. 283.

2 See, e.g., Gerald P. McKenny, *To Relieve the Human Condition: Bioethics, Technology and the Body*, Albany NY: State University of New York Press, 1997, pp. 17–21.

3 Many utilitarians, of course, have attempted to develop accounts of utility richer than Bentham's. One recent example, influential in discussions of animals and ethics, is Singer's account of utility as preference satisfaction: Peter Singer, *Practical Ethics*, 2nd edn, Cambridge: Cambridge University Press, 1993. However, even such elaborations of utilitarian theory, whatever their other merits, offer too reduced a conception of the good to be *theologically* satisfactory accounts (see, further, Andrew Sloane, 'Singer, Preference Utilitarianism and Infanticide', *Studies in Christian Ethics* 12.2, 1999, pp. 47–73, esp. pp. 62–72), and I would think that the critique suggested above applies *mutatis mutandis* to them as well.

4 Andrew Linzey, *Christianity and the Rights of Animals*, London: SPCK, 1987, pp. 68–98; *Animal Theology*, London: SCM Press, 1994, pp. 19–27; *Creatures of the Same God:*

Creator's right must then be filled out with some content. If this is not to be simply a matter of divine *fiat* that lapses into the worst kind of voluntarism (certainly not what Linzey intends), this account must depend on some understanding of what kinds of treatment are congruent with God's good purposes in creating these kinds of creature. Accordingly, in Linzey's account, the proper treatment of animals is determined by God's good purposes for them, which are directed towards an eschatologically realized *telos*. The account for which I shall argue will have a good deal in common with Linzey's. The difference between us is at least partly an argument about language: I am not convinced that rights language is the most helpful for giving this kind of account of the proper human treatment of animals, nor that it is secure against the kinds of confusion and misunderstanding well rehearsed by its critics.[5]

In introducing Linzey's account of animal rights, I have hinted at one of the central claims of this chapter, which bears repeating and emphasizing: a theologically satisfactory account of proper human conduct in respect of non-human animals will have to be teleological in character. It must be shaped and guided by an understanding of our, and their, proper ends: what we, and they, are for.

How (not) to learn about ends

If that is so, how might we learn what those ends are? One obvious source of a Christian teleological account would seem to be Thomas Aquinas, whose account of natural law is based on a threefold scheme of natural ends: first, those common to all beings, for example existing and maintaining their existence; second, those common to all animals, such as procreation and the raising of offspring; third, those peculiar to humans as *rational* animals, such as living in ordered societies and knowing the truth about God.[6] Over and above this threefold scheme of natural ends, of course, humans have the ultimate end of eternal life in God's presence.

Aquinas, influenced by both his reading of Scripture and Aristotelian biology, gives a fairly clear answer to the question of the proper relation

---

Explorations in Animal Theology, Winchester: Winchester University Press, 2007, pp. 35–46, 82–8.

5 See, e.g., Mary Midgley, *Animals and Why They Matter*, Athens GA: University of Georgia Press, 1984, pp. 61–4.

6 Thomas Aquinas, *Summa Theologiae*, ed. and trans. Fathers of the English Dominican Provinces, 60 vols, London: Eyre & Spottiswoode, 1964–76, I-II.94.2. Hereafter cited as *ST*.

between humans and animals – an answer that has been influential on the subsequent Christian tradition and for which he is frequently taken to task by both Christian and secular critics. '[T]he order of things is such that the imperfect are for the perfect', and it is in keeping with this ordering of nature that we kill plants for the benefit of animals and animals for our benefit.[7] Non-human animals are 'devoid of the life of reason whereby to set themselves in motion'.[8] This means that they are 'not competent, properly speaking, to possess good', which is one of three reasons given by Aquinas for holding that 'we cannot have the friendship of charity towards an irrational creature', though we can love such creatures in so far as they glorify God and are of use to our (human) neighbours; God too, according to Aquinas, loves non-human animals for these indirect reasons.[9]

The best science available to Aquinas was Aristotelian, and, as already noted, Aquinas' view of animals depends significantly upon appeals to Aristotelian biology. This seems to make his account vulnerable to the extent that it depends on empirical or theoretical Aristotelian claims discredited by more recent biology. For example, the clear distinction between human and non-human animals, consisting in humans being rational creatures and non-humans being irrational, is called into question both theoretically and empirically by contemporary evolutionary biology.[10] One possible way of addressing such difficulties might be to develop an updated version of natural law theory in which modern science does the work that Aristotelian biology did for Aquinas. For example, let us suppose for the sake of argument that sociobiological accounts of human evolution demonstrate that humans have evolved a disposition to show greater love to kin than to unrelated strangers. Should this, as Stephen Pope suggested several years ago, lead Christian moralists

---

7 Aquinas, *ST* II-II.64.1, citing Aristotle, *Politics*, I.3.
8 Aquinas, *ST* II-II.64.1 ad 2; cf. Aristotle, *Politics*, I.8.
9 Aquinas, *ST* II-II.25.3.
10 See, e.g., Frans B. M. de Waal, *Good Natured: The Origins of Right and Wrong in Humans and Other Animals*, Cambridge MA: Harvard University Press, 1996. This distinction has sometimes been overstated: Aquinas of course recognizes that humans have much in common with non-human animals, as is clear from his presentation of the natural law in *ST* I-II.94.2 and from his frequent use of the term 'rational animal' to describe human beings. It has also recently been argued that for Aquinas, the 'rationality' that distinguishes humans from other animals is not to be seen as an all-or-nothing characteristic, but a matter of degree; such a reading could tend to reduce the distance between Aquinas and modern authors such as de Waal. See Celia Deane-Drummond, *The Ethics of Nature*, Oxford: Blackwell, 2004, pp. 65–77, and John Berkman, 'Towards a Thomistic Theology of Animality', this volume.

to modify their assertions about the universal and indiscriminate claims of neighbour-love, on the grounds that biology shows us a deep-seated aspect of human nature that Christian ethics ignores at its peril?[11]

Two crucial, and related, modern developments make this way of proceeding problematic. One is that whereas Aristotelian science was teleological in character, there was a powerful move in early modernity to exclude teleological thinking from the natural sciences. This non-teleological programme was more easily implemented in the physical than the biological sciences, and, even after Darwin, opinion has been divided as to whether the theory of natural selection supports or disposes of teleological thinking in biology.[12]

However, even if – as Michael Ruse argues[13] – neo-Darwinian evolutionary theory *is* teleological in something like an Aristotelian sense, a second problem comes into play: the problem of 'is' and 'ought'. This problem has bedevilled attempts to draw ethical conclusions from evolutionary biology ever since T. H. Huxley, under the influence of Hume, used it to discredit the evolutionary ethics of Herbert Spencer.[14] Even if neo-Darwinian evolution can be said to give an account of final causes, those final causes are survival and reproductive success. Whereas Aquinas could define the *good* as 'what all things seek after',[15] all that modern biology can say is that 'what all [living] things seek after' is survival and reproductive success. Biology *qua* biology gives no grounds for equating these ends with the good, in any morally informative sense, or for concluding that they are *proper* ends. They may be, but biology cannot tell us that they are. This difficulty is intensified by theoretical and empirical claims that forms of behaviour which no credible ethic would call good

---

11 Stephen J. Pope, *The Evolution of Altruism and the Ordering of Love*, Washington DC: Georgetown University Press, 1994. For a recent, more extensive discussion that takes a more critical stance towards sociobiology, see Stephen J. Pope, *Human Evolution and Christian Ethics*, Cambridge: Cambridge University Press, 2007.

12 See, further, Michael Ruse, *Darwin and Design: Does Evolution Have a Purpose?*, Cambridge MA: Harvard University Press, 2003.

13 Ruse, *Darwin and Design*, pp. 273–89.

14 Thomas Henry Huxley, 'Evolution and Ethics' (The Romanes Lecture, 1893), in *Evolution and Ethics and Other Essays*, Collected Essays, vol. 9, London: Macmillan, 1894, pp. 46–116 (p. 80). Hume's formulation of the problem is in David Hume, *A Treatise of Human Nature*, ed. L. A. Selby-Bigge, rev. P. H. Nidditch, Oxford: Clarendon Press, 1978 (1739–1740), p. 469. See, further, Neil Messer, *Selfish Genes and Christian Ethics: Theological and Ethical Reflections on Evolutionary Biology*, London: SCM Press, 2007, pp. 97–104.

15 Aquinas, *ST* I-II.94.2.

have in some circumstances proved conducive to the survival and reproductive success of humans and our evolutionary relatives.[16]

Christian attempts to incorporate modern biology into a natural law
theory are motivated by the Thomist dictum that 'grace does not destroy
nature but perfects it'.[17] I have no quarrel with that motivation, but much
hangs on what we mean by 'nature' and how we know it when we see it.
For the reasons I have given, it seems clear that an understanding of
'nature' in a morally or theologically significant sense cannot straightforwardly be had from a scientific inspection of the world alone. As
Eugene Rogers argues, a more satisfactory understanding of Aquinas' dictum will recognize that we cannot understand what nature is apart from
its end, which is graciously given by God and made known in Jesus Christ:
'We ought to define nature in terms of grace because it takes Jesus Christ
to tell us what nature is.'[18] Rogers explicitly connects Aquinas' understanding of the relation of nature and grace, so understood, with Karl
Barth's principle that creation is the external basis of the covenant and the
covenant is the internal basis of creation.[19] This link forms part of his
argument that Aquinas' and Barth's theological projects had much more
in common than is customarily recognized either by Thomists or by
Barthians.[20]

If Rogers is right, there is more common ground between Thomist
natural law and Barthian divine command ethics than might at first sight
appear.[21] And that will have significant implications for the present
project to give a teleological account of the proper human treatment of
non-human animals. For Barth, theological ethics is a part of Christian

---

16 See, e.g., Sarah Blaffer Hrdy, *Mother Nature: A History of Mothers, Infants and
Natural Selection*, New York: Pantheon, 1999, and Richard Wrangham and Dale Peterson,
Demonic Males: Apes and the Origins of Human Violence, London: Bloomsbury, 1997.

17 Aquinas, *ST* I.1.8 ad 2; see Pope, *The Evolution of Altruism*, p. 58.

18 Eugene F. Rogers Jr., *Thomas Aquinas and Karl Barth: Sacred Doctrine and the
Natural Knowledge of God*, Notre Dame: University of Notre Dame Press, 1995, p. 190.

19 Karl Barth, *Church Dogmatics*, English trans. ed. Geoffrey W. Bromiley and Thomas
F. Torrance, 13 vols, Edinburgh: T & T Clark, 1956–75, vol. III.1, §41.2, 3. Hereafter cited
as *CD*.

20 In *Human Evolution and Christian Ethics*, Pope articulates an understanding of
nature that appears quite close to Rogers': 'The normative ideal of natural law identifies
certain human capacities from within the larger conglomeration of traits that constitute our
evolved human nature, but it is selected on theological and moral rather than on biological
grounds' (p. 292). This does seem to support the conclusion that we cannot look to biology
to tell us about the proper ends of human (or, by extension, other) creatures.

21 So also Nigel Biggar, *The Hastening that Waits: Karl Barth's Ethics*, Oxford:
Clarendon Press, 1993, pp. 41–2, 49; but for a counter-argument, see David Clough, *Ethics
in Crisis: Interpreting Barth's Ethics*, Aldershot: Ashgate, 2005, pp. 114–18.

doctrine, with the task of '[understanding] the Word of God as the Command of God'.[22] Thus Barth's ethics, like all his theology, is radically Christocentric: it is first and foremost 'Jesus Christ, as he is attested for us in holy scripture' who is 'the one Word of God which we have to hear and which we have to trust and obey in life and in death'.[23] In the threefold scheme sketched in Barth's *Ethics*,[24] and whose full exposition was begun but left unfinished in his *Dogmatics*,[25] the divine command comes to us as the command of the Creator, the Reconciler and the Redeemer. If so, then a theological account of the proper ends of humans and non-human animals, and the proper relation between them, must get its bearings from God's good purposes in creating, reconciling and redeeming the world, as those purposes are disclosed to us in Christ.

It might seem that, in this approach, there is no room for any sort of constructive conversation with the natural sciences; Darwin and his successors, for example, might play the role of 'masters of suspicion', destabilizing unsatisfactory approaches to the theological and ethical questions at issue, but no more than that. However, this would be an over-hasty conclusion, as a comparison with Barth's theological anthropology shows. If we ask what it is to be human, our answer must, of course, be determined from first to last by what is disclosed to us in 'Jesus Christ, as witnessed to in Holy Scripture'. Empirical investigations can, by contrast, only yield at best what Barth calls 'working hypotheses of human self-understanding'.[26] But, critically appropriated to a christologically determined understanding of the human, these 'working hypotheses' have their place. As Nigel Biggar puts it:

> Barth insists that a properly theological anthropology will not simply repudiate 'the phenomena of the human recognisable to every human eye and every thinking mind'. But it will qualify and order such 'general knowledge' with a necessarily theological account of real human being – that is, human being as creature, pardoned sinner, and child of the Father.[27]

---

22 Barth, *CD* III.4, p. 4.

23 *Theological Declaration of Barmen*, May 1934, art. 1, ET online at <http://warc.ch/pc/20th/index.html> (accessed 30 September 2007).

24 Karl Barth, *Ethics*, ed. Dietrich Braun, trans. Geoffrey W. Bromiley, Edinburgh: T & T Clark, 1981.

25 Barth, *CD* II.2, §§36–39, and *CD* III.4; Barth, *The Christian Life*, trans. Geoffrey W. Bromiley, new edn, London: T & T Clark, 2004 [1981].

26 Barth, *CD* III.4, p. 44.

27 Biggar, *Hastening*, p. 156, quoting Barth, *CD* III.2, p. 199.

By analogy – and as Barth emphasizes, we can *only* speak of our responsibilities in respect of animals cautiously and by analogy[28] – in a christologically determined account of God's good purposes in respect of non-human animals, it may be that critically appropriated insights from the biological sciences have their own contribution to make, for example in (almost literally) fleshing out our notions about what kinds of creature we are discussing and in what their good consists. The point is that no area of human understanding can give us knowledge of God, or of ourselves and our fellow creatures in relation to God, that is in principle independent of God's self-revelation in Christ.

Some diagnostic questions

I have argued that a theological account of the proper ends of human and non-human animals, and the proper relation between those ends, must be shaped by an understanding of God's good purposes in creating, reconciling and redeeming the world, as those purposes are disclosed in Christ. Humans are called to live and act in ways that go with the grain of those good purposes of God. If this is so, then one way of theologically assessing any aspect of human practice, including the concrete issues with which I began, is to ask: do our lives and actions *conform and witness to* God's good purposes, in so far as we know of those purposes through Christ; are they *opposed to* God's purposes, serving instead the ends of chaos and destruction; or are they *attempts to substitute for* God's work in Christ? Obviously, the first and third of these alternatives are the most easily confused with one another, and it is between these that the most careful discernment is likely to be needed.

More specification of this general question will be needed, though, if it is to offer helpful practical guidance. Elsewhere, in a different but related context, I have proposed that the Christian narrative of God's creating, reconciling and redeeming work suggests a series of 'diagnostic questions'

---

28 Barth, *CD* III.4, p. 348. This suggests that the charge of anthropocentrism frequently levelled at Barth might be partly misplaced. To be sure, he gives relatively little theological or ethical attention to non-human animals, but part of his reticence on this score is because he thinks that there is relatively little that we have been told about them, and therefore that we are not entitled to say very much. Perhaps unexamined anthropocentric assumptions lead him to be more reticent than he need be; in any event, the argument of this chapter is that his theological method offers resources for going well beyond what he himself says about the human treatment of non-human animals.

that can guide the theological assessment of practical issues.[29] First, *what attitude does the course of action that we have in view manifest towards the material world?* This question is prompted by the fragment of Dietrich Bonhoeffer's *Ethics* entitled 'Ultimate and Penultimate Things'.[30] The 'ultimate' is God's word of salvation in Christ; the 'penultimate' is this-worldly human action that, by God's grace, can lead us to the ultimate. The 'penultimate' cannot save us, but it can prepare the way for God's word. Bonhoeffer identifies two unsatisfactory ways of setting up the relationship between the ultimate and the penultimate. One he calls 'radicalism', by which he means a fanatical desire to do away with the penultimate in the light of Christ's coming: 'The radical cannot forgive God for having created what is.'[31] The other he calls 'compromise', by which he means a total separation between ultimate and penultimate, allowing the ultimate 'no say in the formation of life in the world'.[32] In this light, two opposite kinds of error must be avoided in relation to our question. One is a hatred of the material world, expressed either in attempted escape from the physical or in its violent subjection. The other is to reduce everything to the material, denying that there is more to creaturely life than material existence in this world, in which case the events of the material world and human action in the world must bear the entire burden of our hopes for the future. More satisfactory human action in the world will embody and express a proper respect for the material: it will value the material as good in and for itself, but will refuse to make an idol of it or invest all human hope in it; it will display an honesty about the finitude of the material world, and our embodied existence therein, that points beyond the material to the hope of its ultimate transformation.

Second, *is this course of action an attempt to be like God* (sicut Deus), *or does it conform to the image of God* (imago Dei)? This question, too,

---

29 Messer, *Selfish Genes*, pp. 229–35, from which the following has been taken and adapted. The decision to use 'diagnostic *questions*' as an aid to moral discernment, rather than (for example) attempting to specify a set of ethical principles or 'middle axioms', is a deliberate attempt to avoid interposing any over-elaborate intellectual structure between the biblical witness to God's work in Christ, on the one hand, and our detailed moral reasoning, on the other. The danger of devising a set of principles to do the mediating work is that this would amount to over-confidence about our ability to specify in advance what will constitute faithful response to the command of God the Creator, Reconciler and Redeemer in the face of a particular problem.

30 Dietrich Bonhoeffer, *Ethics*, ET ed. Clifford J. Green, *Dietrich Bonhoeffer Works*, vol. 6, Minneapolis MN: Fortress Press, 2005, pp. 146–70.

31 Bonhoeffer, *Ethics*, p. 155.

32 Bonhoeffer, *Ethics*, p. 156.

alludes to Bonhoeffer, specifically to his reflections on the narrative of the fall (Gen. 3), in which he sets up a sharp contrast between creaturely human existence in the image of God (*imago Dei*) and the perhaps superficially similar, initially attractive, but ultimately destructive, way of being 'like God' offered by the serpent.[33]

My third diagnostic question is: *what attitude does the action that we have in view manifest towards past human failures?* It hardly needs saying that there is much in the world that is damaged and distorted, and much of that damage and distortion is in one way or another the result of human mistakes, failures and wickedness. There is probably no human action in the world that is not affected in some way or another by this damage and distortion, and many of our plans and projects are at least in part attempts to repair the consequences of past failures. The Christian theological perspective I have articulated names this complex mix of distortion, mistake, failure and wickedness as sin, to which the appropriate response is repentance (*metanoia*): a change of heart and mind. When our action in the world is a response to problems that are the product of human sin, the failure to acknowledge the origin of our problems risks replicating them. This is the pathology diagnosed by Karl Barth in his strictures against the kind of human pride that wants to be its own helper and thereby turns away from the true and ultimate source of its help.[34] More satisfactory human action in the world will be characterized by an (explicit or implicit) acknowledgement of past failures and mistakes, an acknowledgement that things will have to be different in the future, and an openness to the kinds of help that will be needed if they are indeed to be different.

The final diagnostic question that I propose is: *is the action that we have in view good news for the poor?* Who stands to gain from it, and at whose expense? Does it unsettle, or further reinforce, relationships of coercion and domination; does it empower, or further disempower, those who are relatively powerless; does it tend to protect those who are vulnerable, or increase their vulnerability; does it draw the marginalized towards the heart of things, or sideline them further?

---

33 Dietrich Bonhoeffer, *Creation and Fall: A Theological Exposition of Genesis 1–3*, ET ed. John W. de Gruchy, trans. Douglas Stephen Bax, *Dietrich Bonhoeffer Works*, vol. 3, Minneapolis MN: Fortress Press, 1997, p. 113.

34 Barth, *CD* IV.1, pp. 458–78.

A worked example

I conclude by returning to the concrete issues with which I began, using them as a 'worked example' to show how this theological approach might guide a particular reading of the Scriptures and the Christian tradition, and how that in turn might suggest specific practical conclusions.

A key text in theological and ethical discussions of non-human animals is the Isaianic vision of the peaceable kingdom (Isa. 11.6–9), one of the texts cited by Barth in his discussion of the human use of animals.[35] Barth describes the history of the world as an 'interim' between the 'pre-historical realm' of creation depicted in Genesis 1 and 2 and the promised eschatological consummation. In the pre-historical realm, creation was in a state of peace in which there was no necessity for humans to kill animals, or animals to kill one another, for food or for any other purpose. By contrast, in the historical realm that we inhabit, this 'peace of creation' is broken by human sin. In this new situation, characterized by the 'struggle for existence',[36] the killing of animals became a possibility 'permitted and even commanded' by God. But the peace of creation depicted in Genesis 1 and 2 is a constant reminder that the present state of affairs 'does not correspond with the true and original creative will of God, and that it therefore stands under a *caveat*'. Texts such as Isaiah 11 are reminders of the promised 'last time . . . when there will be no more question of the struggle for existence and therefore of slaughter between man and beast'.

This, according to Barth, is the perspective in which every practical question about the human use and killing of animals should be considered. On the detailed practical questions themselves he says little. Of vegetarianism, he allows the objection that 'it represents a wanton anticipation' of the new age promised in Isaiah's prophecy, but nonetheless acknowledges its value as a 'radical protest' against the routine exploitation of animals: 'for all its weaknesses we must be careful not to put ourselves in the wrong in the face of it by our own thoughtlessness and hardness of heart.'[37]

---

35 Barth, CD III.4, pp. 348–56. All the quotations in the present paragraph are from p. 356.

36 This seems to be a deliberate echo of Darwin: in German, Barth's phrase is 'der Kampf ums Dasein', the same phrase used in German translations of the *Origin of Species*. See Barth, *Die Kirchliche Dogmatik*, III.4, Zollikon-Zürich: Evangelischer Verlag A. G., 1951, p. 402; cf. Charles Darwin, *Über die Entstehung der Arten im Thier- und Pflanzen-Reich durch natürliche Züchtung*, German trans. H. G. Bronn, Stuttgart: Schweizerbart, 1860, p. 65, online at: <http://darwin-online.org.uk/contents.html> (accessed 15 January 2008).

37 Barth, CD III.4, pp. 355–6.

Taking his cue in part from Barth, Andrew Linzey has also drawn on Isaiah's vision of the peaceable kingdom. However, he is less reticent than Barth in drawing ethical inferences from it, calling on his readers to '[approximate] the Peaceable Kingdom', or seek 'to realize what can be realized in our own time and space of the Messianic Age'.[38] This line of thought leads him to advocate vegetarianism unequivocally, and informs his critique of animal experiments as 'un-godly sacrifices'.[39]

Linzey follows much of Barth's theological method and shares many of his presuppositions, yet comes to rather different practical conclusions. Might the diagnostic questions that I proposed earlier help evaluate Linzey's differences with Barth?

The first of those questions, about our attitude to the material world, suggests the context in which our practical questions should be considered. One way of acting out a hatred of the material creation would be what could be called a pseudo-ascetic flight from it. This suggests, at any rate, that there could be bad reasons for being a vegetarian or refusing the benefits of scientific medicine. If we do conclude that either eating meat or animal experimentation represents unacceptable exploitation of non-human animals, our conclusion must not be motivated by a general disposition to reject the good gifts that God gives us to sustain our creaturely life in the world, gifts such as 'food from the earth, and wine to gladden the human heart, oil to make the face shine, and bread to strengthen the human heart' (Ps. 104.14–15).

Another way of expressing a kind of hatred of the material world would be to treat it as an adversary, a threat to human well-being, which must be subdued for our own protection. Something like this attitude is manifested in what Gerald McKenny has called the 'Baconian project' in biomedicine: seeking mastery over the material world to the ends of relieving suffering and expanding individual choice.[40] But this drive to subdue the world in the service of our own needs and goals comes to seem more urgent if we believe that there is nothing more to human life or the life of the world than the present material reality that we inhabit. If this is all there is, then all human goals and aspirations depend solely on human action in this world. No one will heal or save us if we do not do it for ourselves. Paradoxically, therefore, the second of the erroneous attitudes to the material creation that I identified – the reduction of everything to the

---

38 Linzey, *Animal Theology*, pp. 134, 136.
39 Linzey, *Animal Theology*, pp. 95–113.
40 McKenny, *To Relieve the Human Condition*, pp. 17–24.

material – reinforces the first. There could be elements both of 'radicalism' and 'compromise' (to use Bonhoeffer's terms) at work in much of our human action in the world, including many of our scientific, technological and medical projects.[41]

My second diagnostic question makes use of Bonhoeffer's contrast between the *imago Dei* and the attempt to be 'like God', *sicut Deus*. Bonhoeffer associates the latter with knowledge that does indeed make us (in a sense) like God, but in so doing alienates us *from* God. In alienating ourselves from God, of course, we also become alienated from ourselves, one another and our fellow creatures. Bearing in mind the close and complex relationship between knowledge and power, and the long (not to say problematic) Christian tradition that identifies the *imago Dei* with dominion and stewardship – that is, both authority or power over the created order and accountability to God for its exercise – perhaps the contrast between *sicut Deus* and *imago Dei* could be drawn as a contrast between two opposed ways of exercising power or authority in the created world. (It is almost certainly a fantasy to think that humans could avoid all exercise of power, for good or ill, in the world that we inhabit.) If so, Bonhoeffer points to the kind of power or authority consistent with God's good purposes when he introduces a third term into his discussion: 'Imago dei, sicut deus, agnus dei – the human being who is God incarnate, who was sacrificed for humankind sicut deus, in true divinity slaying its false divinity and restoring the imago dei.'[42] The sacrifice of Jesus, the Lamb of God, for our sakes is a complete inversion of the structures of domination by which alienated humans *sicut Deus* exercise power over one another and the world. *Inter alia*, the sacrifice of the Lamb of God has put an end to animal sacrifices: in God's good future, there will be no need for humans to sacrifice non-human animals in order to heal their own ills or the ills of the world. Andrew Linzey well understands this point, and infers from it that animal experiments are 'un-godly sacrifices'[43] – in my terms, opposed to God's good purposes, or at best a parody of them. Is he right to draw this inference?

It has to be said that much present human use of non-human animals has the appearance of humanity *sicut Deus*: an exercise of raw power that hardly seems to reflect the *imago Dei*. It also has to be acknowledged that much of what the Christian tradition has in the past taken to be proper

---

41 See, further, Messer, *Selfish Genes*, pp. 235–6.
42 *Creation and Fall*, p. 113.
43 Linzey, *Animal Theology*, pp. 103–6.

dominion reflecting the *imago Dei* looks, with hindsight, much more like the kind of domination characteristic of humanity *sicut Deus*. We might say that the tradition has often failed to appreciate the difference made by the *agnus Dei* in this sphere.

However, Barth's diagnosis of the pride that wants to be its own helper reminds us that it is possible to act *sicut Deus* not only in ways that are blatantly opposed to God's good purposes – such as the exercise of raw, dominating and destructive power – but also in more subtle and well-intentioned ways, by confusing the kind of thing that is given to us to do in the world with what can only be done by God: in Bonhoeffer's terms, confusing the penultimate with the ultimate. We are called to live in ways that are congruent with what has been disclosed to us of God's good and loving purposes, and that witness to those purposes – specifically, in this case, to the promise of the peaceable kingdom. But we are *not* called to inaugurate or establish that kingdom; the attempt to do so risks lapsing into a dangerous and potentially inhumane utopianism or fanaticism. Linzey's language of 'approximating' the peaceable kingdom has its dangers, because it tends to obscure this distinction between witnessing to and establishing the kingdom.[44]

In this connection, one useful piece of work that evolutionary biology can do for us is to remind us how distant God's promise of the peaceable kingdom is from our present experience of the world. As Barth says, we learn from the Bible that the 'struggle for existence' is a feature of this fallen world, and is no part of the peace depicted in the creation narratives and promised for the age to come.[45] But life as we know it in the present age has been profoundly shaped by the 'struggle for existence': in this world, lions would not *be* lions if they ate straw like oxen. So if we wish to take seriously the Isaianic promise of a coming age in which lions live at peace with cattle, we shall also have to acknowledge that it is quite beyond our power to imagine what such an age will look like, much less to bring it in or to 'approximate' it.

Another way of putting this is to say that the life of the world is distorted in subtle and complex ways, the product of (*inter alia*) the contingent course of evolutionary history, the choices and actions made by our predecessors and the choices we ourselves make. Elsewhere, I have argued that the traditional Western Christian language of fallenness and original

44 Linzey, *Animal Theology*, p. 134.
45 Barth, *CD* III.4, pp. 353–4.

sin powerfully articulates this condition of distortion and brokenness.[46] If I am right, then the diagnostic question about our attitude to human failure should remind us that we cannot avoid this complex entanglement in human sin and the fallenness of the world. If we think we can save ourselves from this predicament, we are – again – guilty of the self-defeating pride that wants to be its own helper. We can only live in the world in dependence on God's mercy and forgiveness, and this has been so since the very beginning of our history.

According to Barth, one way in which God's mercy is manifested in this situation is in divine permission to use non-human animals – even, sometimes, to kill them – to meet human needs.[47] But as I have already noted, this permission is subject to the *caveat* that such use is no part of God's original good purpose or promised good future. Even in the present age, the permission is strictly limited: no easy compromise with a fallen world is in view. A properly repentant attitude to human sin and the brokenness of the world should lead us to avoid the violent exploitation of non-human animals whenever we can.

Barth, as we have seen, holds that vegetarianism risks being a 'wanton anticipation' of the peaceable kingdom. Stephen Clark remarks: 'the case would be more convincing if it were not so easy for us (I say nothing about lions, nor yet the Inuit) to be vegetarian.'[48] In many Western contexts, Clark's retort to Barth is telling – though as he suggests, there may well be other contexts in today's world in which it is hard enough to get an adequate diet as it is, and would be more or less impossible without eating meat or fish. In such contexts, vegetarianism would hardly be 'good news to the poor'. But for affluent Westerners, it is harder to see why we should *not* be vegetarian.

However, even in relation to this question, and more in relation to animal experimentation, the question about good news to the poor not only illuminates, but also complicates matters. If, as I suggested in framing the question, 'poor' is understood broadly, to mean those in any situation who are weak, vulnerable, marginalized etc., then patients and those whose lives are threatened by disease are clearly included. But in view of the great imbalance of power between humans and non-human animals,

---

46 Messer, *Selfish Genes*, pp. 133–215. My understanding of sin is heavily indebted to Alistair I. McFadyen, *Bound to Sin: Abuse, Holocaust and the Doctrine of Sin*, Cambridge: Cambridge University Press, 2000.

47 Barth, *CD* III.4, pp. 352–6.

48 Stephen R. L. Clark, *Biology and Christian Ethics*, Cambridge: Cambridge University Press, 2000, p. 286.

should the circle of 'the poor' be extended to include non-human animals? Should a Christian imperative to give 'moral priority [to] the weak', as Linzey holds, lead humans to sacrifice their own interests and well-being rather than exploit animals?[49]

These questions seem to require us to balance the conflicting claims of two groups of 'the poor': vegetarianism might be bad news for some poor human populations, but good news for those creatures that they eat; medical research is often good news for patients with life-threatening diseases, but bad news for the non-human animals used. Attempts to resolve these competing claims with general, *a priori* answers risk doing so in one of two unsatisfactory ways. They might fall back on some kind of utilitarian calculus of the harms and benefits to both groups, which I suggested at the beginning of the essay is a theologically unsatisfactory way to approach these questions, or they might resort to circular arguments relying on stipulative definitions of the moral status of humans and animals.

Rather than attempt to settle these questions in general and *a priori*, it might be theologically wiser to recognize that, in each situation, it is a question of the command of God: is the taking of this animal life permitted or commanded? The fact that in the biblical texts cited by Barth, God *does* give humans permission to kill animals, suggests that the answer could sometimes be yes.[50] To rule it out *a priori* would risk attempting a 'wanton anticipation' of God's promised good future. Barth might have been wrong about vegetarianism, at least as far as affluent modern Westerners are concerned, but his argumentation is sound. His point is much more convincing in relation to medical research, and in relation to those contexts in which lives depend on the nutrition to be had from meat or fish. But the *caveat* to God's permission – or to put it another way, the diagnostic question about sin and repentance – should prompt us to seek alternatives to the killing of animals whenever we can. And to the extent that we succeed, the boundary between faithful witness to God's good future and 'wanton anticipation' of it will shift. When aspects of biomedical research, for example, can be done without animals, then avoiding the

---

49 Linzey, *Animal Theology*, pp. 28–44.

50 This is not, of course, a matter of simply reading the command of God off particular texts. If it were, the argument might be vulnerable to the objection that it raises the alarming possibility of acts like child sacrifice conceivably being permitted or commanded (cf. Gen. 22.2). In fact, of course, Barth's hermeneutic is somewhat more sophisticated than that, and well able to resist such dangers. See Biggar, *Hastening*, pp. 97–122; cf. (on Gen. 22), Barth, *CD* III.3, p. 35.

killing of animals becomes a matter of simple faithfulness, not fanaticism.

A final *caveat*: self-interest easily clouds our judgement; it is always tempting to define 'faithfulness' as whatever we find easy, and 'fanaticism' as what we find too hard or uncomfortable. So a measure of suspicion and self-criticism in respect of these practical conclusions is in order. More generally, when one attempts to draw practical moral conclusions about issues such as these, there is inevitably a certain provisionality about them. But because we have to live and act in the world, we cannot endlessly defer decisions about the practical questions; we have to seek at least provisional answers. And even if the practical conclusions I have reached are wrong (which is quite possible), if answers are to be sought in the context of the theological tradition that I have been articulating, then it seems to me that the questions will have to be asked in something like the way that I have proposed.

Part Five

ECOLOGICAL PERSPECTIVES

'They shall not hurt or destroy in all my holy mountain' (Isaiah 65.25): Killing for Philosophy and a Creaturely Theology of Non-violence

MICHAEL NORTHCOTT

The science campus of the University of Edinburgh is located in an Edwardian suburb of the City of Edinburgh on the edge of Blackford Hill, a hill which is crowned by the copper dome of an Edwardian observatory since at one time it was sufficiently far from the smoking chimneys and lights of the city to confer a clear view of the heavens. And it is still possible to observe sheep grazing in the fields from the high-rise blocks on the science site. The science site is more than two miles from the old humanities and social science buildings of the university and this geography helps to sustain the split between science and the arts and humanities that has characterized the intellectual life of the West since the Enlightenment and which is memorialized in C. P. Snow's famous essay 'The Two Cultures'. My work as a moral theologian spans that divide since many of the moral cases on which I work are problems arising from the scientific domination and manipulation of embodied and ecological life. But given the geography of my university I more often read scientific information on anthropogenic climate change, endangered species or threatened habitats on my computer in papers downloaded from journals such as *Nature*, *Science* and *Geophysical Letters* than hear such papers read by scientific colleagues in my own university.

It is, however, my habit twice a year to get on my bicycle and pedal from New College up the hill to King's Buildings – as the science site is known – in order to give two morning sessions on ethics to a group of science postgraduates who are studying for a Masters' degree in Environment and Sustainability. With first degrees in engineering, biology and zoology these students have little facility in the kinds of discourses and discriminations that have made it possible for moderns to make the sharp cultural and moral distinctions between sheep and people that have been the stock in trade of philosophers since Hume and Kant, and that have served as moral veils for the extensive cruelty and suffering systematically visited upon animals in modern industrial farming and pharmaceutical laboratories. Moreover, science graduates find thinking about ethics in the discourse of philosophers hard to engage because it does not present them with the kinds of hard data or heuristic descriptions of the world that they are accustomed to receiving in science lectures.

Dangerous discourse

Science graduates are not alone in finding philosophical discourse difficult and even dangerous. For more than 30 years animal scientists and those involved in the uses of animals in laboratories or farming have found it hard to comprehend or engage the philosophical discourses of animal liberation and animal rights as plied respectively by Peter Singer and Tom Regan and their disciples.[1] This is partly because the writings of animal philosophers often lack the kinds of taxonomic distinctions between kinds – humans, primates, pigs and so on – that are fundamental to the business of animal-keeping and animal science. And it is partly because of the anger and violence that characterizes the campaign for animal liberation. While Singer has criticized the violence of those who have taken up the animal liberation cause he is unable to argue for non-violence as a core ethical value because his philosophy invokes the need, even the right, to kill and be killed. For Singer, the fulcrum of moral value is the capacity to feel pain and experience pleasure. Animals, whether human or non-human, that are sensate, fully conscious and so capable of expressing a preference between being alive and not being alive ought not to be treated instrumentally whatever their kind.[2]

In practice most people, as Stephen Clark points out, are consequentialists when it comes to other animals, and deontologists when it comes to persons.[3] In other words, most people have no difficulty making the

1 David Fraser, 'Animal Ethics and Animal Welfare Science: Bridging the Two Cultures', *Applied Animal Behaviour Science* 65, 1999, pp. 171–89.

2 Peter Singer, *Animal Liberation: A New Ethic for Our Treatment of Animals*, London: Jonathan Cape, 1990, and Tom Regan, *The Case for Animal Rights*, London: Routledge, 1988.

3 Stephen Clark, *Animals and their Moral Standing*, London: Routledge, 1998.

kinds of distinctions between persons and other animals that are part of the common taxonomy of a culture in which animals are regularly abused and killed in the course of meat production and drug testing. This is why Singer's work in particular provokes such incomprehension, for he suggests that there is no clear boundary between humans and other animals and far from invoking a right to life for people and not for animals, as some philosophers do, in reality no being has a *right* to life. Life itself is not the highest good. Instead it is the capacity to live a good life – that is, a pleasurable life free from coerced pain – that is the fulcrum of Singer's moral world. But if there is no boundary line between humans and other animals in this respect then fur-farmers and primate-pharmers are genocidal killers.

Using this logic, prominent individuals in the anti-vivisection movement, though not Singer himself, are prepared to advocate the killing of laboratory scientists, while animal activists have used bombs and other violent tactics against the vehicles and homes of laboratory scientists and animal farmers. Dr Jerry Vlasak, an American trauma surgeon and prominent anti-vivisection campaigner, likens animal experimentation to the Holocaust and argues that killing scientists would be exemplary and would discourage others from continuing in this cruel work: 'I don't think you'd have to kill too many. I think for five lives, 10 lives, 15 human lives, we could save a million, 2 million, 10 million non-human lives.' And this clear utilitarian logic is allied with the argument often used in liberation movements that 'it is inevitable that violence will be used in the struggle and that it will be effective'.[4]

While Singer does not advocate violence against scientists and farmers, intentional killing is a clear consequence of his philosophy when he recommends that doctors may legitimately participate in killing badly deformed children at birth or in assisting consenting adults in ending their lives prematurely. It is therefore unsurprising that his followers use violence in the animal liberation struggle. For Singer the modern moral poverty of human relations with other animals arises not from the propensity of humans to hunt and kill but from speciesism. The fox-hunter, the fur-farmer and the laboratory scientist behave immorally towards animals not because they are violent people but because they do not respect the feelings and sensate experiences of those they maltreat or kill. They may be quite capable of bringing up their own children, or

---

4 Quoted by Jamie Doward in 'Kill Scientists Says Animal Chief', *Observer*, 25 July 2004.

keeping pets, without violence but they are prejudiced against other species and so refuse to validate the conscious lives and sensate feelings of other species. By drawing an analogy with racism Singer is also clearly linking the animal liberation struggle with the struggle against racism or the victimization of innocents because of their skin colour.

In his account of speciesism Singer offers a validation for the use of violence in the defence of innocent mammals, just as the Christian just war tradition legitimizes the use of violence in the defence of innocent humans. For Singer the answer to toxic human–animal relations is not to end killing and violence in such relations but to extend the circle of moral considerability in which moral discernment is required about just violence. It is possible to kill humans and other animals but only when so doing produces a greater number of beneficial consequences than harmful ones; by ending a life afflicted by unendurable pain or a life that lacks the possibility of rich relational flourishing.

The roots of violence

The Old Testament identifies the roots of disordered relations between humans and other animals in a very different place to Singer and other modern animal philosophers. In the story of the Garden of Eden, creation is described as a realm of original peace in which there was no predation and no intentional killing. For the narrator, killing and predation begin not with creation but after the fall of Adam and Eve from original sinlessness. This theological imaginary of life before sin already suggests that violence and predation are a problem in creation and stand in need of redemption. And it does this by imagining the creatures as living in original peace where there are no relations of master and slave, no predation and no violence. Hence, all mammals are idealized by the narrator as vegetarians since the peace of the Garden is not disturbed by killing or predation.

As Marjorie Suchocki has suggested, the Genesis saga describes the fall from grace into sin as a fall into violence.[5] And as the saga proceeds the violence of the children of men increases. In the days of Noah humans are said to be infected by violence and wickedness that originates in part from a confusion and intermingling of kinds between the 'sons of gods' and the

---

5 Marjorie Suchocki, *The Fall to Violence: Original Sin in Relational Theology*, New York: Continuum International, 1995.

daughters of humans (Gen. 6.4). And as the orders of being intermingle, violence grows on earth among all creatures and Yahweh is said to come to regret creating the 'race of men' (Gen. 6.7). The great flood is then described as a divine punishment on human beings for their failure to observe appropriate boundaries between the different orders of being. And the divine intention is revealed to Noah that Noah will be the divine instrument to save species from the judgement that God will visit on human beings.

The ark is in a way a return to Eden for on the ark all the species live together peaceably with Noah and his family, and with each other. On the idealized creaturely community of the ark there can have been no predation and Noah will have had to study the needs of the species he saved in order to provide them with fodder. The pacifist folk art painter Edward Hicks understood this, for in his painting of the animals entering the ark Hicks depicts the animals in the same way as he does in his famous painting of the peaceable kingdom in which the lion and the lamb are lying down together and the child is playing close to a snake. Hicks depicts a striking male lion with an impressive mane in a long line of animals entering the ark. And the lion is looking round rather carefully at a sheep which is standing innocently a short lion's pounce away in the queue. In the wild the lion would eat the sheep but Hicks' lion, while clearly wistful, does not pounce but peaceably stays his predatory instincts. For Hicks the community of animals entering the ark have returned to their Edenic, prefallen state. The ark, like the Garden of Eden, is a peaceable space, a non-predatory place, where there is to be no killing.

Hicks' interpretation of the ark highlights the moral significance of these early chapters of Genesis in framing human relations to animals in Jewish and Christian traditions, and the role of covenant in ordering such relations. The peaceable community of species in Genesis stands as a moral ideal at the beginning of the Old Testament, from which in many respects the sacrificial system of killing is a falling away. After Noah, meat-eating is represented as a divine concession for human sinfulness as 'every creature that lives and moves' is given as food to Noah and his descendants (Gen. 9.3).[6]

This seminal moral community of being between humans and other animals shapes the Jewish and Christian imaginary of species relations. It is also reflected in the Hebrew word *nephesh*, or life-blood, which in

---

6 Andrew Linzey and Dan Cohn-Sherbok, *After Noah: Animals and the Liberation of Theology*, London: Mowbray, 1997, p. 22.

Jewish tradition is sacred, and which must be drained from the flesh before it is eaten. And the subsequent ritualization of killing in the development of the sacrificial system, as described in the remaining books of Moses, has the further effect both of distinguishing between clean and unclean animals and between people permitted to shed blood and the rest of the Israelites. Levites are set apart as ritual killers because they carry the burden of shedding blood first referred to in Genesis. They are consequently ordered to live apart from the people of Israel who are themselves not supposed to engage in butchering, and butchering is only supposed to be undertaken in the temple precincts.[7]

The setting apart of those involved in killing is indicative of a moral sensibility in ancient Israel that humans and other animals share the same biological constitution; they are warm-blooded animals and it is the blood that brings life from the air into their bodies. The Hebrew word for blood, *nephesh*, is also used of breath, wind and spirit. Blood for the Israelites was the spiritual life force and was therefore sacred. This is why the blood had to be poured on the ground rather than eaten. Only meat properly drained of the life-blood was moral meat. And all those involved in dealing with this precious life force had to be set apart for a special kind of holy life or else the violence of regularly shedding blood might infect Israelite society. The sacrificial system expressed reverence for *nephesh*, or the life-blood, as it involved careful and limited ritual slaughter of the animals the Israelites kept in their fields. It also specifically excluded wild animals, including birds and reptiles. It thus enjoined a careful and sacred respect for the lives of animals who might otherwise have been regarded as the property of Israelites to dispose of at will, while at the same time ensuring that wild animals were preserved from hunting, and that the extent of grazing and crop lands were limited by the requirement to give wild animals sufficient habitat.

There is a parallel in some respects between the setting apart of the Levites and the relative secrecy that surrounds animal farms and abattoirs in modern industrial society. Abattoirs and factory farms are places of violence and cruelty and this violence is mostly hidden from consumers of meat, hence the efforts of the animal rights lobby to photograph and publicize the horrific cruelty such places sustain. But animal science, because it is reductionist, is deaf to the claim that participation in abattoirs or farming practices or laboratory experiments that involve cruelty

---

7 Klaus Eder, *The Social Construction of Nature*, London: Sage, 1996, pp. 58–96.

to animals might infect the persons who participate with blood guilt, or that such cruelty, which is far more extreme in modern animal systems than in those of ancient pastoralists, might influence how humans treat other humans in societies that depend upon systematic animal cruelty. In this respect animal science is morally inferior to the Old Testament animal ethic. And the Old Testament ethic is in continuity with Christian attitudes to the treatment of animals. The core argument of Thomas Aquinas against animal cruelty is not that it causes suffering to animals but that it corrupts the character and the virtue of those who participate in it and makes them more likely to express the same kinds of behaviours towards other persons.[8] Singer suggests this gives animals negligible moral consideration but his criticism misses the significance of virtue as the moral fulcrum of Aquinas' thought, which is unsurprising given the irrelevance of questions of character to Singer's utilitarianism.[9] Singer's dismissal of Aquinas also misses the importance of his account of the ends of all created things and the duty of human beings not to frustrate the ends of other orders of creation.[10]

The roots of animal philosophy

Animal philosophers, and Singer in particular, argue that the moral concern of modern utilitarians is unique to modern moral philosophy and indicative of moral progress since the Enlightenment. However, far from making moral progress, modern societies under the guidance of a utilitarian ethic manifest more systematic cruelty towards other animals, and a stronger tendency to instrumentalize animals, than traditional societies. In Christian ethics, at least until the Middle Ages, the source of respect for animals arises from such Christian virtues as compassion, justice and peaceableness. Traditional Christian concern for animal welfare arose from the recognition that right relations between humans and other animals – relations that promote the welfare of other animals – are worthy to be pursued because these kinds of behaviour are intrinsically good, and their absence, or worse their substitution with cruelty and violence, corrodes good character and hence the good society. And animals are *part* of

---

8 Thomas Aquinas, *Summa Contra Gentiles*, I-II 99.1.

9 Peter Singer, 'Animals', in Ted Honderich (ed.), *The Oxford Companion to Philosophy*, Oxford: Oxford University Press, 1995, pp. 35–6.

10 See further Michael S. Northcott, *The Environment and Christian Ethics*, Cambridge: Cambridge University Press, 1996, pp. 128–31.

the good society in premodern ethics, not some other category of being which may for most purposes be excluded from moral considerations. Thus in Christ's teaching, the ritual law of Sabbath observance does not stop a man from rescuing an animal that has fallen into a pit. And for Aquinas cruel actions towards what he calls other animals are morally problematic because they corrupt the virtue of those who engage in them.[11] And his nomenclature is significant here since for Aquinas humans share the same creaturely constitution as *other* animals, and pursue the same natural law. The difference is that animals pursue the natural law by instinct whereas humans pursue it through their powers of reasoning.

Modern animal philosophers such as Singer and Regan do not envisage a moral community of humans and other animals reflecting a more compassionate approach to animal-keeping. Instead they want a society in which animals are no longer subjected to human purposes. Paradoxically at a time when animal cruelty has never been practised on so many animals as it is in modern intensive farming, the philosophy presented to resolve this problem is less invested in animal welfare than the traditional ethics it seeks to outdo. While claiming a greater moral concern for animals than the ancients, many modern animal philosophers exclude animal welfare from moral consideration and would prefer humans not to use animals at all except in some circumstances as domestic pets. Given this position, the welfare of animals who live on farms or pharms is not a matter for moral deliberation by such philosophers. They simply believe they should not *be* in such places and therefore farmers and scientists find little assistance from their writings in thinking about animal welfare.

There have been attempts in the UK to overcome the resultant divide between animal campaigners and animal users, including an informal round table of campaigners and animal scientists convened by Professor Kenneth Boyd of the University of Edinburgh in the mid-1990s.[12] New Home Office guidelines on the approval of experimental procedures were subsequently established and all institutions sponsoring such experiments were required to establish ethical review committees, including universities. However, evidence of systematic cruelty to higher mammals at Huntingdon Life Sciences in the pursuit of xenotransplantation has led

---

11 Aquinas, *Summa Contra Gentiles* I-II, 99.1.

12 See further, 'Ethical review of research involving animals: a role for institutional ethics committees?', The Boyd Group, 1995, at <http://www.boyd-group.demon.co.uk/ethicscomms. htm>. This report led to the adoption of new Home Office guidance on animal ethics committees.

animal rights activists to question the effectiveness of these new procedures.[13]

Besides these procedural moves there has also been an important intellectual development in the last 30 years as a result principally of the work of animal ethologists who through field studies of animals in the wild have begun to challenge conventional taxonomic distinctions between human persons and other animals based on accounts of what is a person, or a 'subject of a life', or a being with moral interests. In the latter part of this chapter I will review the implications of these ethological studies for the ethics and theology of animals. But before so doing it will be useful to recall the reasons that drove Enlightenment philosophers to establish boundaries between humans and other animals as firmly as many of them attempted.

Valuing humans above all things

The crucial move in Enlightenment philosophy to set humans apart from other animals was made by Immanuel Kant who identified what he called the 'categorical imperative' as a new way of enshrining the absolute character of the traditional command ethic, but without reference to revelation of religion. The intention was to ensure that by reasoning alone persons could not be instrumentalized like objects. However, the personalism of Kant's philosophy seems to reduce animals to the status of philosophical objects and this raises the question whether for Kant animals were things. Though we have no precise statement from Kant indicating that animals *are* things he nowhere explicitly says that they are not.[14] Kant's clearest statement about animals indicates that humans have no direct moral duties towards them but only indirect duties. In other words, humans only have duties to animals inasmuch as their treatment of animals affects other humans.[15]

A core motive for Kant's attempt to found moral rationality on a principle that excluded animals from direct moral consideration was Kant's

---

13 Dan Lyons, 'The animal care regulatory system is a sham: inspectors often overrate the value of an experiment and underestimate the pain it causes', Letters in *Nature* 430, 22 July 2004, p. 399.

14 Mary Midgley, 'Are Dolphins Persons?', in *Utopias, Dolphins and Computers*, London: Routledge, 1996.

15 Immanuel Kant, 'Duties to Animals and Spirits', in *Lectures on Ethics*, trans. Louis Infield, New York: Harper & Row, 1963, pp. 239–41.

desire to sheer morality of all those trappings which link moral judgements with the judgements and instrumental techniques of scientists concerning the non-human world. There are, however, a number of problems
with Kant's sheerings for it turns out that what he leaves on the sheering
floor is less epiphenomenal to the moral lives of humans than a coat of
wool to the welfare of sheep in a Prussian summer. Embodiment and
sociability seem to play no part in Kant's categorical imperative. The
imperative is such that it can be recognized in all circumstances by all
reasonable adult individuals. In practice, however, people vary in their
moral perceptions and practices and these variations reflect different
patterns of nurture, different cultural sensibilities and different kinds of
moral development. And so a growing number of philosophers reject the
elegant but reductionist simplicity of Kantian rationalism and have
sought through moral psychology, social ethics, or the language of the
virtues to provide a more holistic account of human moral action and
perception.

It is, however, important to understand clearly Kant's reasons for
attempting to erect a wall between scientific reasoning and moral reasoning, since it is the peculiar animus of modern science not only to know and
describe the natural world but to dominate and subject it to human purposes so as to advance human welfare. The results of such advances are
evident. Human longevity has been extended, and it is no longer a life-
threatening event to give birth to a child in most developed countries. But
recent extensions of the drive to dominate nature indicate that parts of
human identity are also now increasingly being subjected to the instrumental animus, from human embryos and 'foetal matter' to population
groups unwittingly used in drug trials by pharmacology companies in
developing countries. Thus the attempt to build a wall between animals
and humans, while it was intended to preserve human life from the con-
trolling hubris of science, has not preserved humans from instrumentalization by what Jacques Ellul called the 'technological imperative'.[16]

There are two fundamental difficulties with the categorical imperative.
First, Kant took insufficiently into account the extent to which humans
are *sociable* beings and hence depend on one another in the development
of their capacities for moral reasoning. If persons acquire moral capacities
through such dependence, then the sheering of talk about practices, traditions and virtues from the description of the good life begins to look
highly problematic. And, second, Kant insufficiently considered the

---

16 Jacques Ellul, *The Technological Society*, New York: Free Press, 1966.

extent to which human reasoners are *embodied* reasoners. If humans are embodied, and acquire their knowledge of the world through embodied engagements with other bodies, and with other beings in their environment, then an account of moral reasoning that neglects this is also likely to be inadequate.[17]

Now it might be thought that if Kantianism is insufficient in these regards at least utilitarian reasoning is not. Jeremy Bentham, the earliest of the modern hedonists, proposed an extension of his utilitarian logic to all animals that evidently experience pain. However, utilitarians have until recently been no better than Kantians at resisting the kinds of cost benefit logics, and taxonomic distinctions, that have made it possible for animals to be subject to widespread and systematic cruelty in the course of twentieth-century developments in meat production and drug testing. And this is because utilitarians share with Kantians a preference for accounts of moral reasoning that are shorn of reference to embodiment and sociability. Hence while according to Singer a utilitarian is someone who refuses to put the suffering of an animal into a moral calculus alongside the welfare of a person, nonetheless Singer himself gets into the business of aggregating levels of suffering between animals and humans in his comparison of situations where animals or humans might have their lives prematurely terminated. The emphasis of Kant on the right of the individual not to be instrumentalized may be said to better preserve the moral significance of individuals because it is not susceptible to the kinds of aggregate calculations of greater goods and evils, costs and benefits, that the hedonic calculus sustains.

In practice it has not been Kantian propositions but utilitarian judgements that have led the popular turn against the modern instrumentalization of animals. Ask most vegetarians why they do not eat animals and they mostly say because they do not want animals to suffer. The rights language comes later. They may want to ascribe rights to animals but it is the extension of a utilitarian logic that has led them down that path. To this extent it might be said we are all utilitarians now. People who live in cultures dominated by large-scale market logics are inevitably going to resort to consequentialist arguments in their efforts to make moral discriminations because this is how the public culture trains them to behave and to think. When shopping becomes the only kind of politics in which most citizens engage on more than a five-yearly basis then decisions about

---

17 This point is well made in Alasdair MacIntyre, *Dependent Rational Animals*, London: Duckworth Press, 1999.

what to eat or what to wear are the commonest form of public moral deliberation. Given that the price of food and fashion is directly related to the degree to which those involved in its production have been instrumentalized, it is unsurprising that choices against certain kinds of suffering – of farmed animals, farm or sweatshop workers – should become the primary moral drivers in the politics of food and fashion.

As a philosophy, utilitarianism has always been more amenable to concerns about animal suffering than Kantianism. But the political form that utility aggregation takes in modern liberal democracies is cost benefit calculation. And it is this economistic form of the hedonist calculus that has driven down the cost of food while driving up the quantity of suffering involved in its production. Kantianism on the other hand offers a language of duties and responsibilities that at least suggests that farmers and factory workers, if not animals, are due greater moral consideration than they receive in such calculations.

The ethological challenge to animal science

Animal scientists may well at this point call down a plague on both houses since neither philosophical approach consistently presents moral arguments for the appropriate treatment of animals by humans. There is however another way. While claiming an interest in animal welfare and behaviour, Singer's and Regan's interest in animal science does not extend much beyond experiments and observations that prove that animals feel pain and have consciousness. Animal welfare science on the other hand has a rich seam of observation of animals in artificial environments, which complexifies the state of knowledge about animal consciousness and sensibility. Colleagues at Edinburgh, for example, study communication among pigs at the university's agricultural research centre and are developing ways of interpreting meanings indicated by different utterances.[18] But most of this science of welfare is conducted in artificial environments and this may help to explain Singer's and Regan's neglect of it.

Since Singer and Regan wrote their seminal texts far more knowledge has now accrued in animal science about the behaviour of animals in the wild. Some of the innovators of this approach were women and they include such notable individuals as Jane Goodall and Diane Fossey.

---

18 Michael C. Appleby, Daniel M. Weary, Allison A. Taylor and Gudrun Illmann, 'Vocal Communication in Pigs: Who Are Nursing Piglets Screaming At?', *Ethology* 105, 1999, pp. 881–92.

Known as animal ethology, the approach they pioneered is more like field anthropology than traditional zoology in which animal behaviours were more often studied among captive animals. Goodall, Fossey and others suspected that traits that were often to the fore in caged animals – aggression and sexual obsession – were traits that were exaggerated by the artificial environments in which the animals lived. They hypothesized that when studied in the wild it was possible that animals would reveal a richer range of communicative and relational abilities.[19]

In a synthetic work that draws on an extensive range of ethological studies of primates the biologist Frans de Waal shows that these reveal that reciprocal altruism, compassion, empathy, nurture and desire for community are as characteristic of relations between kin, and among friends, in elephants, dolphins, monkeys, and even vampire bats, as they are among humans. In a series of observations of empathy in animal groups, de Waal describes the behaviour of a group of chimpanzees around the body of one of their number who fell from a tree breaking its neck. The male chimpanzees went into a frenzy of wailing and calling around a gully where their companion's body had fallen. Several chimpanzees stopped to stare at the body and one individual sat looking at the body for a whole hour. Other chimpanzees were 'embracing, mounting, touching, and patting one another with big, nervous grins on their faces'.[20]

The expression of empathy and grief in chimpanzees which are genetically and in other ways so close to humans may be less surprising than its existence in other groups of animals more genetically distant from humans. A group of lemurs was observed by another student in the process of helping one of their young who had mounted an electric fence, received a shock and been thrown off. Infant lemurs who do not normally groom one another groomed the injured infant intensively after its injury. Its grandmother, who did not normally allow infants to ride on her back, carried the infant for some time after the incident, and also persuaded its reluctant mother to carry it for longer. De Waal assembles a whole range of accounts of care, empathy and grieving among elephants, dolphins, whales and other mammals. A photograph in the book shows an elephant caressing the skull of its mother at the place where its mother had died 18 months previously. And even more remarkable than these accounts of in-

---

19 A fuller version of what follows can be found in Michael Northcott, 'The Moral Standing of Nature and the New Natural Law', in Nigel Biggar (ed.), *The Revival of Natural Law*, Aldershot: Ashgate, 2000, pp. 262–82.

20 Frans de Waal, *Good Natured: The Origins of Right and Wrong in Humans and Other Animals*, Cambridge MA: Harvard University Press, 1996, p. 56.

species empathy and care are observations of inter-species altruism such as an incident involving an elephant aiding an infant goat threatened by the hooves of a group of adult elephants approaching a tree where the goat had previously been feeding with its parents. Seeing the danger to the goat, the elephant picked it up with its trunk and took it towards the group of goats which had recently left the tree for the larger approaching mammals.[21]

The focus in animal philosophy on sensate capacities misses this larger moral dimension that animal ethology reveals. Ethicists as well as biologists are therefore finding that there is a great deal of common ground between humans and their mammalian relatives in moral behaviour, and that in both cases moral behaviour is essential to the flourishing of the societies in which it is expressed even though for the individuals who express it there may be no direct or obvious short-term pay-backs. De Waal enumerates four key elements in human moral community that ethologists have also found in mammalian groups. These include sympathy and empathy, learning and enforcement of social rules and norms, reciprocal exchange and giving and punishment of individuals who violate reciprocal rules, and peace-making, avoidance of conflict and community concern. Community concern and social restraint on excessive self-interest and aggression are as common among some groups of mammals as among humans. Ethologists observe that in both cases the end result is a collective improvement in welfare and peaceableness: 'the higher a species' level of social awareness, the more completely its members realize how events around them ricochet through the community until they land at their own doorstep.' Such collective concern may sometimes be perceived to be in the interests of the individuals who practise it, particularly in higher mammals, but its widespread expression gives the lie to the moral dualism between personal and subpersonal ethics that Kantianism – even in the form of animal rights – sustains, for as de Waal notes 'conscious community concern is at the heart of human morality'.[22]

The extension of the field in which humans recognize the existence of moral considerability is by no means a uniquely modern project. As we have seen, the ancient Israelites express a much greater sense for the common bonds of life and blood that they shared with other animals than do moderns. This sense of common life bonds is expressed in rituals and taboos found not just among the ancient Israelites but among most primal

---

21 Northcott, *The Environment and Christian Ethics*, p. 251.
22 De Waal, *Good Natured*, p. 208.

peoples around the killing of an animal. These rituals express a sense of reverence for life and a recognition that the taking of life incurs real moral guilt. This reverence for life is also expressed in communal customs that impose limits on hunting in the social systems and rules of most primal peoples. And such limits are not always confined to humans. Ethologists have often observed the tendency of animal predators to hunt older and weaker individuals, perhaps because they are easier targets, perhaps from some deeper instinct that their prey also deserve, as a species, to continue to live.

The scientific recognition of the moral sensibilities and capacities of other than human beings is accompanied by a restatement by some philosophers and others of a moral community between humans and other animals which, while common in primal societies, has largely disappeared in modern societies.[23] These developments suggest that the grounds for ending the vast array of modern practices and behaviours that involve systematic cruelty in other animals are larger than a mere recognition of their sensate capacity to feel pain as we do. De Waal resists ascribing rights to animals because such ascriptions may result in the extension of the recognition of rights to creatures lower down the consciousness scale, from crows to cockroaches, with impossible consequences. However, he does argue that we should either phase out the use of apes in experimentation or take steps to 'enrich and enhance their lives in captivity and reduce their suffering'.[24] However, moral recognition of the rightness of reducing animal suffering and the preparedness of economic corporations, farmers and scientists to make the necessary changes to their behaviours and practices are two very different things and it is precisely the gap between these that Christians call sin, and which motivates some in the animal liberation struggle towards acts of violence that they believe will provoke a more serious change of direction.

The roots of violence

Sin in the Genesis narrative is a dimension of being in which both humans and animals are involved as a result of the primeval fall of creation from original peace. Violence is among the earliest manifestations of sin as described in Genesis, both among humans and between humans and other

---

23 Again, see MacIntyre, *Dependent Rational Animals*, for one of the clearest expositions of this view.
24 De Waal, *Good Natured*, p. 216.

animals. Turning away from violence in human relations and in human–non-human relations is therefore crucial to the recovery of moral community between humans and other animals that ethological studies suggest is a possibility. The Old Testament also witnesses to the possibility of redemption from sin in terms of a restored community between humans and other animals, and between all creatures and the creator. One form of this community is a community of praise. For the psalmist, animals and even non-sensate beings such as trees are capable, alongside humans, of redemptive responses to the Creator in the form of giving praise to God. And some creatures are also said to be capable of prophetic utterance, as in the case of Balaam's ass.

Some of the Hebrew prophets also imagine a redeemed future in which the original absence of killing and predation in the Garden of Eden is recovered by humans and other animals. In third Isaiah the renewed community of shalom will be a place where there is no more predation and the dread that prey feels for predator, memorialized in the Noah saga, will disappear. In that day the lion will be like the lion depicted by Hicks, 'eating straw like an ox' and lying with lambs instead of eating them. Such a place, Isaiah suggests, will be a place where the root of violence is redeemed in all creatures and so 'they shall not hurt of destroy in all my holy mountain' (Isa. 65.25).

Peaceable relations with other animals are not central to Christian ethics in either the early centuries or today. And yet there is a significant stream of Christian living and practice that comes close to realizing Isaiah's vision. It was ascetic monks, and Cistercians in particular, who first introduced novel kinds of animal husbandry into Britain, and especially lamb-keeping.[25] Christian monasticism developed a strongly agrarian shape from the time of Benedict, since the Rule of Benedict presented a vision of work on the land, which along with study and worship was central to the pursuit of holiness and the sanctification of community life. Benedict's Rule represents a monastic realization of Isaiah's vision of a restored and peaceable earth in which work, including work on the land, is no longer seen as a punishment for sin, as it is presented in the Genesis narrative of the fall, but as a source of spiritual fulfilment and hence of holiness. If work on the land in the context of liturgical time and monastic community is healed from its infection from sin then Christian

---

25 On the role of sheep-keeping in the demise of monasticism, and the history of the enclosures, see L. T. C. Rolt, *High Horse Riderless*, London: George Allen & Unwin, 1947.

monasticism can be seen as bringing in the restoration of creation first anticipated in the physical resurrection of Jesus Christ.

But paradoxically the wealth that monastic agrarianism, and lamb-keeping in particular, brought to the monasteries was also the source of their own corruption, and subsequently of their dissolution in England by a cash- and power-hungry monarch. It was also the cash sheep brought to the farmer that was the occasion for the greed that led landowners in the seventeenth-century English parliament to pass successive Acts of Enclosure. These evicted large numbers of peasants and smallholders from common lands and strip farms in early modern England, reducing them to hired servants or vagrants. The later criminalization of vagrancy added insult to injury and many of these people were then sent in waves of migrants to the 'new worlds' of the Americas, Australia, Argentine and New Zealand where they in turn evicted indigenous peoples and native species and introduced cattle and sheep in their place.[26] The roots of the modern world are found once again in Christian history as the corruption of ascetic holiness by animal-related wealth led eventually to the mass eviction of peasants and smallholder farmers by powerful landowners, and to the later genocidal attacks on indigenous peoples of settlers in colo-nial lands. In the present global food economy large food and plantation companies continue this colonial process of eviction to this day in Africa, Asia and Latin America.

If the modern industrial food economy begins in England with the sub-stitution of animals for people on the land then a radical reduction in the number of sheep and cattle on the land in Britain might also be the occa-sion for a more equitable sharing of the land between householders and landowners so that more households have access to land on which they may grow food for themselves and so recover a more sustainable and less destructive and violent relation to the land than that manifest by the industrial food economy. But for a Christian vision of a peaceable king-dom in which violence between creatures is volitionally ended by those capable of ending it something more would be needed than a reduction in animal-keeping. A consistent embrace of the idea that Christians are called to a more perfect way, a higher law than that revealed in the five books of Moses, indicates that Christians will move towards a recovery of a mode of living with animals that does not involve ending their lives prematurely for meat, though it would still involve using animals in

---

26 For the consequences for Aboriginals in Australia, see Tom Kinnealy, *A Common-wealth of Thieves: The Improbable Birth of Australia*, Sydney: Random House, 2005.

appropriate ways. Lamb on this approach might be off a Christian's menu, whereas the occasional leg of mutton or haunch of venison might still have a place. Similarly it might still be possible for a Christian to wear a woollen sweater, or buy leather shoes. But they will want to ensure that the relation between the animal and its keeper was a just and peaceable one and that there was compassion even in the ending of an animal's life. This approach also holds out the possibility for genuine dialogue between those concerned with ethical and peaceable eating and animal-keepers.

13

The New Days of Noah? Assisted Migration as an Ethical Imperative in an Era of Climate Change

CHRISTOPHER SOUTHGATE

Introduction

The relationship between modern *Homo sapiens* and other animals has been a complex one. It has included hunting and being hunted, peaceful coexistence, and that strange form of symbiosis we call domestication (in its various forms). The character of some animals has been enormously altered by human breeding (very strikingly in the breeding of domestic dogs from the Siberian wolf). Some animals have been translocated by humans into environments they would never have occupied.[1] As Mooney and Cleland put it, 'Since the beginnings of the Age of Exploration, humans have purposefully and inadvertently moved biological material across barriers that for recent evolutionary time have separated the unique biotic realms of the continental land masses.'[2] Very many species have been driven to extinction[3] – so much so that it seems now that humans may be the single greatest cause of a sixth great extinction event in the history of the planet.[4]

---

1 The impact of species translocation on a remote volcanic island group such as Hawaii, where every species has been 'introduced', either by wind, bird or human, is particularly striking. Such translocations have often been disastrous, especially in countries with very different indigenous flora and fauna.

2 H. A. Mooney and E. E. Cleland, 'The Evolutionary Impact of Invasive Species', *Proceedings of the National Academy of Sciences* (hereafter, *Proc. Natl Acad. Sci.*) 98:10, 2001, pp. 5446–51, at p. 5450.

3 Michael Boulter, *Extinction: Evolution and the End of Man*, London: HarperCollins, 2003, especially ch. 7. Boulter records how within a few thousand years of humans' arrival in North America 70 per cent of the species of large mammals were extinct (p. 9).

4 Richard Leakey and Roger Lewin, *The Sixth Extinction: Biodiversity and Its Survival*,

This history poses a range of problems for the ethicist. What moral status is to be accorded other animals and on what basis?[5] What moral framework would lead us to halt 'the sixth extinction'? Does that involve extending moral considerability not just to animals presently living but also to future generations of animals? How do these moral claims relate to the needs and aspirations of humans – present and future?

The classic positions in animal ethics explored elsewhere in this volume were formulated before the extent of the present threat of species extinction became quite so evident. The ethics of relating to non-human animals has tended to divide them into either being in the wild (therefore the subject of 'environmental ethics'[6]) or directly the responsibility of humans, because of being kept as pets or zoo animals, for work, food or experimentation. Much work in the area has sought to address the interests of wild nature by calling for it to be left absolutely to its own devices, and of animals under human control by giving them a status as comparable to that of humans as possible.

I hold that to make a sharp distinction between the ethics of wild nature and that of the human sphere has been problematic for some time. In the current situation it breaks down altogether. Human activity is affecting the whole course of planetary evolution,[7] and almost every environment on earth. Our activities continually alter and jeopardize the health of all sorts of ecosystemic contexts. This generates a strong imperative to understand these contexts as fully and accurately as we can, and to take action to maintain the flourishing of creatures. It is ever more unlikely that the action of simply 'letting be' will prove sufficient. This is, first,

London: Weidenfeld & Nicolson, 1996; Norman Myers and Andrew H. Knoll, 'The Biotic Crisis and the Future of Evolution', *Proc. Natl Acad. Sci.* 98:10, 2001, pp. 5389–92, at p. 5389. As Woodruff notes, 'The rate of warming is unusually fast but not without precedent.' However, 'The ability of species to respond to future climatic oscillations by range shifts is greatly reduced by our creation of an inhospitable matrix between the remaining habitat patches.' David S. Woodruff, 'Declines of Biomes and Biota and the Future of Evolution', *Proc. Natl Acad. Sci.* 98:10, 2001, pp. 5471–76, at p. 5472.

5 Approaches here range from the radical anti-speciesism of Peter Singer, the subject-of-a-life approach to animal rights of Tom Regan and the biocentric vision of Paul Taylor, to the 'theos-rights' model of Andrew Linzey. See Lisa Kemmerer, *In Search of Consistency: Ethics and Animals*, Leiden: Brill, 2007, for a recent introduction to these positions.

6 As in the work of Holmes Rolston III, especially his *Environmental Ethics: Duties to and Values in the Natural World*, Philadelphia: Temple University Press, 1988; also Paul W. Taylor, *Respect for Nature: A Theory of Environmental Ethics*, Princeton NJ: Princeton University Press, 1986; Lisa Sideris, *Environmental Ethics, Ecological Theology and Natural Selection*, New York: Columbia University Press, 2003; Andrew Light and Holmes Rolston III (eds), *Environmental Ethics: An Anthology*, Oxford: Blackwell, 2003.

7 Myers and Knoll, 'The Biotic Crisis', p. 5389.

because the pressure of human population and economic activity makes retaining pure wildernesses very difficult, and therefore it tends to be necessary to establish some sort of relation between human flourishing and the 'wilderness' – often through some form of ecotourism. But increasingly also it is because the effects of anthropogenic climate change are non-local – to an ever greater extent it is human action far away beyond the 'reserve' or 'hotspot of biodiversity' that imperils the health of that place. Even the minimum level of likely climate change will eliminate many habitats, particularly in tropical and subtropical zones,[8] so the letting be of wild nature in reserves[9] is no longer an adequate strategy. Climate change, in short, is giving rise to a strikingly new situation in respect of non-human species, one in which it may be necessary to carry out 'Noah-like' activities, preserving species by moving them to new habitats before their existing ranges have disappeared.

I write as a Christian theologian and ethicist, so the third section of this chapter ('Meta-ethical themes from the New Testament') will consider whether a Christian ethical approach makes a distinctive contribution in this area. A few initial markers establish that, at the very least, Christians may not ignore the status of animals. A biblically informed ethic will insist on the value of species to God, as such classic texts as Genesis 1.31 insist, 'God saw all that he had made, and behold it was very good'; cf. also Psalm 24.1, 'The earth is the Lord's and all that is in it.'[10] God's care for God's creatures, and their dependence on divine providence, is a recurrent theme of Psalm 104. The Lord's enigmatic reply to Job out of the whirlwind also implies God's care for all species, even the ugly, the monstrous and the implausible (Job 39—41). Furthermore, the language of divine covenant so powerful in the Hebrew Bible is also extended at Genesis 9.8–17 to guaranteeing the integrity of the non-human creation (cf. also Hos. 2.18). Therefore the non-human creation cannot simply be a commodity, nor should its 'voice' fail to be heard in human deliberations.[11]

---

8 See Myers and Knoll, 'The Biotic Crisis', p. 5390, for the observation that these 'evolutionary powerhouses' may be under particular threat.

9 The proposed strategy of E. O. Wilson in *The Future of Life*, London: Little Brown, 2002, ch. 7.

10 Biblical quotations are from the New Revised Standard Version.

11 An important emphasis of the Earth Bible Project, see, e.g., Norman C. Habel (ed.), *Readings from the Perspective of Earth*, vol. 1 of, *The Earth Bible*, Sheffield: Sheffield Academic Press, 2000. This notion of the 'voice' of the non-human creation needs careful development; at its best it can make helpful connections with the biblical motif of creation's praise of God. (See Christopher Southgate, *The Groaning of Creation: God, Evolution and the Problem of Evil*, Louisville KY: Westminster John Knox Press, 2008, ch. 4.) However, it should not be allowed to lead to a romanticized or inadequately scientific approach.

Tellingly in terms of the present chapter, God charged Noah with the preservation of every species on the earth (Gen. 6.19–20; 7.1–3). In tension with much ecotheological writing, I hold that a Christian ethic will insist on the importance of humans' role and their contribution to the good of the created order.[12] Christianity is in Vischer's helpful terminology an anthropocentric, though not an anthropomonist, religion.[13] It does insist on a special role for humans, though emphatically not that theirs are the only interests to be considered. The human role may be variously conceived – as steward, priest, co-creator, co-redeemer, as the one species able to witness to the glory around us.[14] The concept of stewardship implies that the human role is to ensure that the future is no worse than the present, and this in effect has been the ethos of most conservation biology up to now. That rather cautious ethic does not do justice to the richness of the human calling before God.[15] Climate change, however, is likely to give rise to a future very much worse, in terms of the flourishing of existing species in their present habitats, than the present. It calls therefore for imaginative stewarding on a large scale, for the determined defence of the biodiversity that is under such great threat. As I noted above, the strategy of letting be of wild nature beloved of so much ecotheological writing[16] will not prove adequate. Merely to establish reserves, free of human depredation, in species' present ranges will not be enough. Ingenious co-creatorly activity may be needed to introduce species into loci they have not occupied for many millennia, if at all, and

---

12 Southgate, *Groaning of Creation*, ch. 6.

13 Lukas Vischer, 'Listening to Creation Groaning: A Survey of Main Themes of Creation Theology', in Lukas Vischer (ed.), *Listening to Creation Groaning: Report and Papers from a Consultation on Creation Theology Organised by the European Christian Environmental Network at the John Knox International Reformed Center from March 28 to April 1st 2004*, Geneva: Centre International Réformé John Knox, 2004, pp. 11–31, at pp. 21–2. Vischer's distinction is particularly important in the light of the Earth Bible Team's 'ecojustice principles', which include a profound suspicion of anthropocentrism (see Habel (ed.), *Readings*, pp. 38–53).

14 Cf. Bill McKibben, *The Comforting Whirlwind: God, Job, and the Scale of Creation*, Grand Rapids MI, Eerdmans, 1994, p. 88. See Christopher Southgate, 'Stewardship and Its Competitors: A Spectrum of Relationships between Humans and the Non-Human Creation', in R. J. Berry (ed.), *Environmental Stewardship*, London and New York: T & T Clark/Continuum, 2006, pp. 185–95, for an account of the interplay between these understandings.

15 Southgate, 'Stewardship'; also *Groaning of Creation*, ch. 6.

16 See McKibben, *The Comforting Whirlwind*, and the work of Holmes Rolston, e.g. 'Wildlife and Wildlands: A Christian Perspective', in Dieter Hessel (ed.), *After Nature's Revolt*, Minneapolis MN: Augsburg Fortress Press, 1992, pp. 122–43.

to make sure that the population in the new locus has an adequate gene pool to ensure its long-term viability.[17]

The challenge of climate change

Although the precise unfolding of the detailed patterns of global climate over the next 50 years remains very uncertain, the scientific consensus is clear enough. A rise in global mean surface temperature (GMST) of 2°C now looks almost inevitable, and a greater rise looks likely unless stringent measures are taken to restrict net emissions of greenhouse gasses. It is disturbing how little reference there is in most books on climate change to the levels of extinction that these changes might occasion.[18] The 2006 Stern Report on the economic challenge of climate change mentions almost casually that a rise of 3°C in GMST would be expected to lead to a 20–50 per cent loss of species including 25–60 per cent of all mammals.[19] Human economics, as currently conducted, is not only anthropomonist. It also discounts the future in a way that I shall argue runs counter to an important instinct in Christian ethics.

In contrast, books on extinction major ever increasingly on the impact of climate change.[20] We should be clear as to the irreversibility of bio-

17 These efforts may be helped by strategies still present in the genomes of species that survived the last Ice Age, which would allow them to be moved much nearer the poles than their present ranges, even before the effects of climate change affect their habitats (Jason S. McLachlan, Jessica J. Hellmann and Mark W. Schwartz, 'A Framework for Debate of Assisted Migration in an Era of Climate Change', *Conservation Biology* 21:2, 2007, pp. 297–302, p. 301). However, those same data on 'glacial refuges' may show that previous estimates of the speed of dispersion of those species after the Ice Age were far too high, and therefore that those same species are far more endangered by climate change than had been imagined. (See Jason S. McLachlan, James S. Clark and Paul S. Manos, 'Molecular Indicators of Tree Migration Capacity under Climate Change', *Ecology* 86:8, August 2005, pp. 2088–98.) In a time in which mass extinction is threatened, the boundaries between the debate about the treatment of wild nature and the treatment of animals in human care begin to blur – humanity has all but destroyed wildness. It is my contention therefore that humans must take much greater levels of direct responsibility for the care and conservation of species than was previously necessary.

18 An honourable exception is Michael Northcott's impressive *A Moral Climate: The Ethics of Global Warming*, London: Darton, Longman & Todd, 2007, which promises to be a lasting contribution even to this fast-moving field. See especially pp. 59–63 on extinction.

19 Quoted in Gary Yohe, 'Climate Change', in Bjorn Lomborg (ed.), *Solutions for the World's Biggest Problems: Costs and Benefits*, Cambridge: Cambridge University Press, 2007, pp. 103–24, at p. 106.

20 See, for example, Peter D. Ward, *Under a Green Sky: Global Warming, the Mass Extinctions of the Past and What They Can Tell Us about Our Future*, New York: HarperCollins, 2007; Boulter, *Extinction*.

logical extinction – it is a loss of a whole way of being alive, a whole quality of living experience.[21] Michael Soule has written: 'Death is one thing, an end to birth is something else.'[22] Thomas Berry puts it even more trenchantly:

> Extinction is a difficult concept to grasp. It is an eternal concept. It's not at all like the killing of individual life forms that can be renewed through normal processes of reproduction. Nor is it simply diminishing numbers. Nor is it damage that can somehow be remedied or for which some substitute can be found. Nor is it something that only affects our own generation. Nor is it something that could be remedied by some supernatural power. It is, rather, an absolute and final act for which there is no remedy on earth as in heaven.[23]

The possibility of climate-change-induced loss of habitat on a massive scale is leading to a new debate in conservation biology. As a significant number of present habitats are likely to disappear, could representatives of animal species be moved to new locations where they might thrive? Woodruff, writing as far back as 2001, asserted that 'Bioneering, the interventionist genetic and ecological management of species, communities and ecosystems in a postnatural world, is poised to become a growth industry.'[24] Assisted migration might be effected in two main ways: either by ensuring that corridors exist that would enable species to move gradually to a more favourable habitat, or by physically moving organisms to new environments in which they might be expected to be able to continue to flourish. The subject has recently been explored by McLachlan et al., and at a more popular level by Holmes.[25]

As McLachlan et al. point out, 'Assisted migration is a contentious issue that places different conservation objectives at odd with one another.'[26] 'Conservation ethics are strongly rooted in a sense of place, and a feeling of what belongs where.'[27] Mark Schwartz calls assisted migration 'a man-

---

21 Southgate, *Groaning of Creation*, p. 9; see also pp. 124–32.

22 Quoted in Myers and Knoll, 'The Biotic Crisis', p. 5389.

23 Thomas Berry, *The Dream of the Earth*, San Francisco: Sierra Club Books, 1988, p. 9, quoted in Sean McDonagh sc, *The Death of Life: The Horror of Extinction*, Blackrock, Co. Dublin: Columba Press, 2004, p. 85.

24 Woodruff, 'Declines', p. 5474.

25 McLachlan, 'A Framework'; Bob Holmes, 'Special Deliverance', *New Scientist*, 6 October 2007, pp. 46–9.

26 McLachlan et al., 'A Framework', p. 297.

27 Holmes, 'Special Deliverance', p. 49; cf. also Doug Fox, 'When Worlds Collide', Feature in *Conservation in Practice* 8:1, January–March, 2007.

agement option of last resort . . . all local options for conservation must be exhausted prior to assisted migration'.[28]

As with the new technologies for manipulating genes and embryos, assisted migration would change our sense of what is a 'given' of the natural world and what is properly an object of human manipulation. Many introductions of species have proved very destructive – anyone who has lived in the American South will be familiar with the impact of Japanese knotweed on those ecosystems, and famously Australian eco-systems have been badly damaged by a whole series of introductions of exotic species.[29] The damage may not be immediately evident because of the so-called 'lag effect'.[30] Occasionally, but much less typically, exotic species may prove to be surprisingly beneficial.[31]

It is not necessarily easy to determine in advance what species will prove to be damaging in a new environment. This is all the more so because there will be relatively few cases in which a species could be moved by itself. This may be confined to the cases of top predators being introduced into places with abundant potential prey, and species being reintroduced into contexts from which they had previously been elimin-ated by human action (as in recent experiments with the reintroduction of wolves). It is much more likely that species may need to be moved in clus-ters or 'functional groups'[32] (e.g. in the case of a herbivore with a special-ized diet, which in turn would depend on a certain matrix of other organisms). The sheer complexity of such an operation suggests that wherever possible the approach to assisted migration should be via the provision of corridors that enable species or combinations of species to migrate by themselves, rather than out-and-out translocation (but see the fourth section below, 'A thought-experiment in assisted migration', for a special case where the latter may be the only possibility).

McLachlan et al. helpfully point to three classic positions on this issue, depending on (a) confidence in ecological understanding, (b) perceived risk of no assisted migration, and (c) perceived risk of assisted migra-

---

28 Mark Schwartz, <http://www.des.ucdavis.edu/faculty/mschwartz/website%20 publications/WildEarth.pdf> (accessed 20 February 2008).

29 Reg Morrison, *The Spirit in the Gene: Humanity's Proud Illusion and the Laws of Nature*, Ithaca NY: Cornell University Press, 1999, p. 30.

30 Mooney and Cleland, 'Evolutionary Impact', p. 5446.

31 See Jeffrey Foster and Scott K. Robinson, 'Introduced Birds and the Fate of Hawaiian Rainforests', *Conservation Biology* 21:5, October 2007, pp. 1248–57.

32 David Western, 'Human-modified Ecosystems and Future Evolution', *Proc. Natl Acad. Sci.* 98:10, 2001, pp. 5458–65, at p. 5460.

tion.[33] A balanced approach will want to invoke the precautionary principle in considering any given introduction of species, given that this may well be irreversible. Nevertheless, McLachlan et al. conclude that 'Delays in policy formulation and implementation will make the situation even more urgent . . . we cannot wait for better data.'[34] Despite the disastrous history of species introductions into Australia, the Ecological Society of Australia has issued a position paper on climate change that accepts that translocation or assisted migration of key species may be a necessary part of a response to the crisis.[35]

The classic positions in contemporary animal ethics would all have their different responses to this proposal of assisted migration, depending on the precise way in which they balance the needs and goods of human flourishing against the needs and goods of animal species. But it is the contention of this chapter that the particular crisis occasioned by the present accelerating rates of extinction goes beyond previous work in animal ethics, and calls for new explorations. Extinction is barely mentioned in the classic works of Singer, Regan and Linzey (see note 5). As a Christian ethicist I turn to the resources that might be gained from reinvestigation of the New Testament.

Meta-ethical themes from the New Testament

The New Testament notoriously offers little of direct comfort to the contemporary environmental ethicist. As a result, certain 'mantra-texts', in particular Romans 8.19–23 and Colossians 1.15–20, which seem to draw the non-human creation into the narrative of Christian salvation history, are cited over and over again, though often somewhat uncritically.[36] However, it is worth considering whether a more general consideration of principles arising from New Testament thought might nevertheless have

---

33 McLachlan et al., 'A Framework', p. 298.

34 McLachlan et al., 'A Framework', p. 301.

35 <http://www.ecolsoc.org.au/Position_papers/ClimateChange.htm> (accessed 20 February 2008).

36 I draw in this section on a project being carried out by David G. Horrell, Cherryl Hunt and myself on 'The Uses of the Bible in Environmental Ethics'. Some of this work has already been published: see David G. Horrell, Cherryl Hunt and Christopher Southgate, 'Appeals to the Bible in Ecotheology and Environmental Ethics: A Typology of Hermeneutical Stances', *Studies in Christian Ethics* 21:2 2008, pp. 53–72; Cherryl Hunt, David G. Horrell and Christopher Southgate, 'An Environmental Mantra? Ecological Interest in Romans 8.19–23 and a Modest Proposal for Its Narrative Interpretation', *Journal of Theological Studies* 59 2008, pp. 546–79.

particular application to environmental conundra. In what follows I consider how themes in the Pauline corpus might give rise to principles capable of extension into the sphere of ecological theology. A similar exercise might be attempted from the Johannine writings, or the work of the Synoptists, but the Pauline material offers the most extended focus in the New Testament on how eschatological life is to be framed in the context of Christian worship and in response to the gift of the Spirit. It therefore seems the best place to start on such an exercise. I list three great themes that emerge from such a rereading, and explore how they might be interpreted in ways that are fruitful for considering the ethics of extinction.

The first theme, already identified by Horrell in 2005 as a 'meta-ethical principle' which might overrule other considerations in the Christian response to a particular dilemma, is that of 'other-regard'.[37] The imperative to do good to others goes well beyond the Christian community (1 Thess. 3.12; 5.15; Gal. 6.10; Rom. 12.17).[38] Though there is no indication that this was in Paul's mind, the biblical principles outlined in my first section above clearly indicate God's concern for non-human creatures, and hence the appropriateness of extending human concern and other-regard. Other-regard is underpinned by that resonant language of the Philippian hymn: 'the mind that was in Christ Jesus' (2.5) led him not to snatch at status but to empty himself, taking the form of a servant (2.7–8).

Other-regard, then, has broad application, and carries with it an expectation that it will prove costly and sacrificial. Such an 'ethical kenosis' – of aspiration, appetite and acquisitiveness – is vitally needed in the lives of those whose current affluence and level of consumption is unsustainable.[39] The more general principle, however, is one of costly self-giving – other-regard is expressed through the expenditure of prayerful effort, imagination, care, as well as material resources. And this may well imply, in the sorts of situation now arising in ecosystems, the active consideration of costly assisted migrations, where the alternative is the extremely costly event of a biological extinction (see the section on 'The challenge of climate change' above). Questions as to the balancing of the needs and goods of human populations with those of other species, and the taking of a precautionary view of likely impacts of introductions on ecosystems, remain no less problematic viewed within this Christian ethical frame.

---

37 David G. Horrell, *Solidarity and Difference: A Contemporary Reading of Paul's Ethics*, London and New York: T & T Clark/Continuum, 2005, ch. 7.

38 Horrell, *Solidarity*, pp. 261–7.

39 Southgate, *Groaning of Creation*, ch. 6.

Thus far, then, the radical Christian principle of other-regard gives us an imperative to generosity, indeed to sacrifice, on the part of those capable of making such, but not necessarily any distinctive ethical insight into the issue of assisted migration.

A second key ethical principle to emerge from consideration of the Pauline corpus is the apostle's concern for the poor, a concern which he records sharing with the leaders of the church in Judaea (Gal. 2.10). Indeed it is very striking how much effort he seems to have exerted on the collection for the poor of Jerusalem (Rom. 15.26; 2 Cor. 8—9).[40] That concern for the poor seems to have been a precious common factor between the two great factions of the emerging church. In turn it reflects a strong motif of divine care for the poor, which is threaded through the whole of the Hebrew Bible (cf. Lev. 19; Deut. 10.17–18; 14—15; 25; 2 Sam. 22.28; Job 5.15; Ps. 9.12; 10.12; 34.6; 107.41; 132.15; Isa. 25.4; 49.13; Amos 2.6; 4.1 etc.).

However, the poor are not simply to be equated with those who happen to be materially poor.[41] The underlying condition of the poor is that their future flourishing is threatened, and they lack the power, the voice, to assert themselves and to remedy their situation. Hence the association of the poor in the New Testament with those who hunger, thirst and mourn (Matt. 5.3f, par. Luke 6.20–21), with the blind, the lame, lepers and the dead (Matt. 11.4–5), and with the maimed, the lame, the blind (Luke 14.13, 21) – also the very telling grouping at Revelation 3.17, 'wretched, pitiable, poor, blind and naked' (cf. Matt. 25.34–46 where the hungry, the thirsty, the stranger, the naked and those in prison are all those who are close to Christ in their need).[42] All share this underlying condition of being unable to flourish, or restore their state to one of flourishing, and the biblical tradition constantly asserts God's closeness to them and concern for their restoration.

Here, I submit, is a promising contribution that Christian ethics can make to the new problems posed by climate change. Liberation theolo-

---

40 See Horrell, *Solidarity*, pp. 231–41.

41 Though material deprivation does seem to have been Paul's central concern in respect of the Jerusalem collection.

42 See the analysis of Bruce J. Malina in his *The New Testament World: Insights from Cultural Anthropology*, 3rd edn, revised and expanded, Louisville KY: Westminster John Knox Press, 2001, pp. 99–100, from which the above list of references is drawn. I submit that it is this same underlying condition of being unable to depend on worldly resources that led to the spiritualizing of the concept of 'the poor' as 'the pious' and hence also 'faithful Israel'. We can see this spiritualizing motif in the Matthaean redaction of the first Beatitude (Matt. 5.3, compare Luke 6.20).

gians have already articulated that passionate call for just and equitable treatment of all presently living persons that a follower of Jesus must make,[43] but this call may also be extended to include consideration of future generations. The future generations of humans in communities living in low-lying areas, and in areas especially vulnerable to hurricanes and typhoons, already have their flourishing threatened by the thoughtless – and indeed in a sense oppressive[44] – actions of the presently rich. An argument could well be made that those future generations are the most profoundly voiceless persons affected by the present crisis, and that their flourishing is profoundly at risk – to the extent indeed that some traditional island communities will literally lose the ground on which they are based.[45] But in the light of the very powerful passage quoted from Thomas Berry above I consider the same argument may be pushed yet further. It is not only future human generations, but future generations of non-human species whose flourishing is under profound threat, and whose voice is barely heard when humans are considering their medium-term interest. These too – it might be held – are the new 'poor', the beleaguered, those whose future is proscribed by the actions of the powerful; those, therefore, so the biblical tradition implies, particularly of concern to God.[46]

Robin Attfield, in a recent paper, has argued for this same extension of ethical concern to future generations, human and non-human.[47] He admits the sheer difficulty of giving this effect, though the appointment of proxies to give voice to these interests in current forums of decision-making could be a first step. There is an echo here of Pat Fleming and Joanna Macy's powerful call for a 'Council of All Beings'.[48] Attfield

---

43 Cf. Galatians 3.28 – in the eschatological era inaugurated by Christ the old distinctions that kept persons apart can no longer be maintained.

44 Cf. Northcott, *A Moral Climate*, ch. 3.

45 Indeed, Myers and Knoll estimate that 'the total number of people affected by what we do (or do not do) during the next few decades will be in the order of 500 trillion – 10,000 times more people than have existed until now' ('The Biotic Crisis', p. 5389).

46 For ecotheologians invoking the earth as 'the new poor', see Matthew Fox, *The Coming of the Cosmic Christ*, New York: Harper & Row, 1988, p. 147; Sallie McFague, *The Body of God: An Ecological Theology*, London: SCM Press, 1993, p. 165. See also Northcott, *A Moral Climate*, p. 42, advocating an 'option for the poor', and Neil Messer's ethical criterion, 'Is [a project] good news for the poor?' in this present volume.

47 In his unpublished paper 'Ecological Issues of Justice', cited with permission. Attfield refers to Hans Jonas, *The Imperative of Responsibility*, Chicago and London: University of Chicago Press, 1984, and Kenneth E. Goodpaster, 'On Being Morally Considerable', *Journal of Philosophy* 75, 1978, pp. 308–25, on this issue.

48 Pat Fleming and Joanna Macy, 'The Council of All Beings', in John Seed, Joanna Macy, Pat Fleming and Arne Naess (eds), *Thinking Like a Mountain: Towards a Council of All Beings*, London and Philadelphia: Heretic Books, 1988, pp. 79–90.

makes the interesting argument that the human vocation is to steward-ship,[49] and that therefore the call of those with power and freedom of choice must be to empower the (human) poor to take their part in stewardship and trusteeship of the planet.[50] I noted above the imperative to stewardship that the current crisis forces upon us, but I continue to find it a somewhat cautious and sterile image for the human vocation under God. One might, however, adapt Attfield's insight by calling for those who have power, affluence and freedom of action to empower – through their own self-giving and other-regard – the opportunities for self-giving and other-regard in those whose present focus necessarily needs to be on survival. As I have just indicated, this would include that capacity for other-regard that seeks out particularly the interests of those with even less power, less voice, less opportunity for flourishing. That this is a strong (God-given) human instinct is seen in the strong traditions of hospitality often to be found among very poor human communities.

Which brings me to my third strong emphasis from the ethics of the New Testament. A continual concern of the Pauline writings is *koinōnia*, that fellowship in community that enables the giving and receiving of gifts of all kinds. Contemplation of *koinōnia* reveals how the interdependence of humans in community is underpinned by the work of the Holy Spirit. The making of community, then, is the process of *sunoikesis* of which Bergmann writes,[51] it requires that we find ways to make the Spirit of God at home. The fruit of such a process is the love, joy and peace mentioned in Galatians 5.22.

The language of community has been perhaps too blithely evoked by ecotheological writers, often attracted to the simplicity and cogency of Aldo Leopold's 'land ethic'.[52] The term is not without its problems, and is helpfully discussed by Celia Deane-Drummond.[53] Scientifically, Leopold's formulation is problematic given the modern recognition that 'biotic com-munities' are not static entities – they unfold dynamically around complex

---

49 Robin Attfield, *Creation, Evolution and Meaning*, Aldershot: Ashgate, 2006, chs 9–10.

50 Attfield, 'Ecological Issues'.

51 Sigurd Bergmann, 'Atmospheres of Synergy: Towards an Eco-theological Aesth/Ethics', *Ecotheology* 11:3, September 2006, pp. 326–56, and references to his earlier work therein.

52 'A thing is right where it tends to preserve the integrity, stability and beauty of a biotic community. It is wrong when it tends otherwise.' Aldo Leopold, *A Sand County Almanac: With Essays on Conservation from Round River*, Oxford: Oxford University Press, 1966, p. 262.

53 Celia Deane-Drummond, *The Ethics of Nature*, Oxford: Blackwell, 2004, pp. 32–4.

'attractors' in phase space. Ethically, too strong an emphasis on inter-species community can run into the same type of difficulties as Regan's emphasis on rights for non-human subjects. Human community is full of quasi-contractual mutual obligations – rights interwoven with responsi-bilities. Where a whole range of subjects are accorded rights, without being able to sustain any responsibilities, many understandings of com-munity begin to fail.

However, there is a deep truth in this language of community, in the sense that humans are undoubtedly and inalienably dependent not only on each other but on a whole range of other organisms. It has become increasingly evident that these networks of interdependence include not just our intestinal flora, the crops we might grow and the animals we might keep, but relationships at great distances. To breathe we depend on photosynthesis for our oxygen, to eat protein we are dependent ultimately on the fixation of atmospheric nitrogen by legumes, but far less obviously we are dependent also on the recycling of atmospheric sulphur by marine algae.[54] There are many other examples. Much use of the language of community has been oriented towards conferring moral status on non-human entities. But a recent emphasis in the work of Anne Primavesi is more helpful. She has written extensively of gift and the need to develop a sense of gift exchange.[55] This seems to me to be of the essence of the Christian approach to community. We receive, in all sorts of ways, from the rest of God's creation, and are called to gratitude and reverence in receiving. As Wendell Berry has written:

> To live, we must daily break the body and shed the blood of Creation. When we do this knowingly, lovingly, skilfully, reverently, it is a sacra-ment. When we do it ignorantly, greedily, clumsily, destructively, it is a desecration. In such a desecration we condemn ourselves to spiritual and moral loneliness, and others to want.[56]

Wendell Berry's formulation is important not least because it recognizes the essential element of human *activity*. We do not live merely by receiv-ing – we have to 'do', to break and shed, that is both because of the kind of animals we are and is also our God-given calling. We interact with the

---

54 James Lovelock, *The Ages of Gaia: A Biography for Our Living Earth*, Oxford: Oxford University Press, 1989, pp. 143–5.

55 See, for example, Anne Primavesi, *Gaia's Gift*, London: Routledge, 2003, chs 8–9.

56 Wendell Berry, *The Gift of Good Land: Further Essays Cultural and Agricultural*, San Francisco CA: North Point Press, 1981, p. 281.

environment in order to survive, but also in order to work out our own gifting, to express the co-creatorly capacities that are part of humans' distinctive contribution to creaturely community.

A thought-experiment in assisted migration

I suggested in an earlier section ('The challenge of climate change') that these co-creatorly capacities might, in the face of the impending loss of habitats occasioned by global warming, extend to the assisted migration of species to new loci which they have not occupied for millennia, if at all. There may be a particular need to consider this for 'large species with low population densities and species with poor dispersal abilities across humanscapes'. Western notes that these 'are especially vulnerable to extinction'.[57] It will have been clear from the analysis given above just how difficult, partial and risky such efforts will be. Perhaps initially only 10 per cent of the introductions of species will work[58] (though it is reasonable to suppose that this percentage will increase in the course of such an intensive effort, as more becomes known about what makes for success).

There is much current concern over the plight of the polar bear, which was placed on the US Endangered Species List in May 2008. Consider as a thought-experiment an effort to establish polar bears – a magnificent, iconic species potentially doomed by global warming – in Antarctica. Could they survive such a journey? What would be the carbon cost of flying them there, as almost certainly the only way to deliver healthy animals? Will there be, on the melting fringes of late twenty-first-century Antarctica, sufficiently stable habitats of ice on water, with sufficiently stable sources of food, to enable them to establish themselves? These are huge imponderables.

But I would suggest that the Christian ethical reflection in my third section ('Meta-ethical themes from the New Testament') moves us in the direction of very active consideration of such measures. It insists on an extended other-regard, involving the sacrificial use of resources by those with resources to give. I noted above that this meta-ethical principle does not necessarily tell us which costly choices to make, and this indeed is a characteristic of such principles. But both the general biblical emphasis on

---

57 Western, 'Human-modified Ecosystems', p. 5461.
58 Holmes, 'Special Deliverance', p. 47.

creatures belonging to the Lord, noted in my first section above, and the stress I noted in the third section on the priority of the voiceless and those whose flourishing is most threatened, do add power and poignancy to the crisis of extinction. These emphases resist the discounting of the future on which other systems of valuing are based. They reinforce the principle of other-regard, and draw into its application both future human generations (to whom life with a whole range of other species may be lost if predictions of extinction rates prove accurate), and also the potentially lost generations of non-human creatures. These include those polar bears that may simply never exist as a result of anthropogenic melting of the Arctic ice.

My third principle – the centrality of community, characterized by the interdependence of giftings – argues against any anthropomonist or commodifying calculation of competing values as we respond to the current crisis. That dynamic exchange of giftings in which the Spirit makes her home, of which we read in such passages as Romans 12.4–8 and 1 Corinthians 12.4–31, can reinforce a concern that we not lose opportunities to give to and receive from other creatures. But it will also tend to counsel against despairing of human activity, and towards consideration of expressions of human ingenuity which might make a decisive difference in the saving of species. Polar bears have become dependent on our activities to a new extent, and may need to rely on our ingenuity and giftedness in unprecedented ways.

But the enormous effort and care required of such a project as polar bear relocation, its costliness and precariousness, would have another value. It would not only serve the needs of that species. Whereas Barlow and Martin describe the proposed introduction of the Florida torreya into more northern latitudes as 'easy, legal and cheap',[59] clearly many assisted migrations will be neither easy nor cheap. Great thought-experiments like polar bear relocation, even before they actually came to possible implementation, would act as a rhetorical device to make yet more plain to those who influence the course of the most carbon-intensive economies in the world just how vital a change of overall policy has become. There is a whole complex of measures – economic, fiscal, technological, sociopolitical – that needs to be put in place to mitigate the impact of climate change, and most of these measures will be easier, cheaper and more dependable as means of preventing mass extinction than great projects in assisted migration. To have to think through the latter emphasizes the vital impor-

---

59 McLachlan et al., 'A Framework', p. 297.

tance of the former.[60] As Novacek and Cleland note, 'Recovery [including 'enlightened human intervention'] cannot be decoupled from preventative measures . . . any success in recovery is profoundly dependent on the state of what we have to work with.'[61]

Conclusion

Like many of his critics I am uneasy with the 'rights' language that Andrew Linzey proposes in respect of non-human animals.[62] But I strongly support Linzey's conclusion that Christians should be doing eschatological ethics, and that their care for animals should be informed by the aspiration of Romans 8.21 that other creatures should experience something of 'the freedom of the glory of the children of God'. This passage conveys an implicit sense of the responsibility of humans to co-operate with God in the liberation of creation.[63] We are a long way from being able to carry out our side of such a co-operation (not surprisingly, in the Christian view, since we are so far from claiming the freedom that is open to us in Christ). But the vision of such co-creativity, with the priorities of extended other-regard, concern for the trapped and the voiceless, and the building of authentic community to which I have referred here, should continue to claim a prominent place in the Christian imagination, and be a key part of the Christian contribution to the ethics of climate change.

To return lastly to the Noah myth, which I mentioned above as an index of divine concern for all creatures, it would be tempting, once the possibility of assisted migration is actively being considered, to overstate our Noachic role and suppose that indeed we are in a position to save the creatures as Noah does in the story. However, the profoundly difficult and risky exercise of moving animals from one locus to another should

---

60 Pacala and Socolow suggest a series of 'wedges' to be driven in to stabilize climate and halt the crisis, increasing combinations of which will have increasing effects (S. Pacala and R. Socolow, 'Stabilization Wedges – Solving the Climate Problem for the Next 50 Years Using Current Technologies', *Science* 305 (5686), August 2004, pp. 968–72; and comment in Mark Lynas, *Six Degrees: Our Future on a Hotter Planet*, London: Fourth Estate, 2007, pp. 293–98).

61 Michael J. Novacek and Elsa E. Cleland, 'The Current Biodiversity Extinction Eevent: Scenarios for Mitigation and Recovery', *Proc. Natl Acad, Sci.* 98:10, 2001, pp. 5466–70, at pp. 5466–7.

62 Andrew Linzey, *Animal Theology*, London: SCM Press, 1994.

63 Southgate, *Groaning of Creation*, pp. 95–6 and ch. 7; cf. also N. T. Wright, *The Resurrection of the Son of God*, London: SPCK, 2003, p. 258.

reinforce the point that the earth is our only ark, and the great preponderance of our current creativity and ingenuity must be towards prayerfully and humbly ensuring the continued health of the 'vessel', such that it is no longer necessary to keep displacing its inhabitants.

I thank the Arts and Humanities Research Council for their support of this work under Grant No. AHD001188/1, and Drs David G. Horrell and Cherryl Hunt for many helpful discussions. I also thank Professor Celia Deane-Drummond and the Centre for Religion and the Biosciences at University College Chester for their support of the Colloquium at which these ideas were first discussed, and colleagues there for their most helpful insights. An earlier version of some of this thinking was published as Christopher Southgate, Cherryl Hunt and David G. Horrell, 'Ascesis and Assisted Migration: Responses to the Effects of Climate Change on Animal Species', *European Journal of Science and Theology* 4:2, June 2008, pp. 19–25.

Postscript

DAVID CLOUGH AND
CELIA DEANE-DRUMMOND

As the preceding chapters indicate, to attempt a 'creaturely theology' that is conscious of the theologian's creatureliness, and to take God's other-than-human creatures as a focus of interest, opens up a wide variety of possible methodologies. Most of the chapters here include treatments of the Bible, though sometimes at second hand. Some have engaged significant figures in the Christian tradition – Athanasius, Gregory of Nazianzus, Gregory of Nyssa, Augustine, Maximus the Confessor, Aquinas, Luther, Barth and Bonhoeffer, to name but a few. Others have considered the implications for theology of the work of philosophers such as Kant, Bentham, Alasdair MacIntyre, Peter Singer, Tom Regan, Claude Lévi-Strauss and Leo Strauss, Carol Adams, Mary Midgley, Stephen R. L. Clark, Georgio Agamben, Bruno Latour and John Gray. Scientists such as Frans de Waal and Marc Bekoff have made appearances, together with the odd poet, such as Yeats, Clare and Blake and the novelist Peter Høeg. The subject matter has been equally broad, often focused on human/non-human borderlands, but coming at that ground from a wide range of trajectories. The engagements have clearly been fruitful, providing new insights both for a theology of non-human animals and for the reciprocal implications on what these insights mean for theological anthropology. Equally clearly, these fruits have been widely scattered, and whatever one might say about the diversity of the offerings here, we are therefore not in a position to offer a conclusion setting out the central theses of creaturely theology.

One interpretation of this diversity might be that these essays are united only in their binding. Given that the culpability for such a reprehensible state of affairs would lie most obviously with the editors, the reader will not be surprised to learn that this is a reading we would quarrel with. Our contention is that this is what a new phase of scholarship on a topic looks like in its early stages. To attend with theological seriousness to questions of the commonality and difference between human and non-human creatures, and with attentiveness to modern, philosophical, scientific and artistic developments in the field, is a novel enterprise – not unique and certainly not without precedent, as many of the discussions in this book demonstrate, but little considered and underdeveloped. If readers share the view of the authors collected here that such reflections are fruitful, it may be that in a later phase all sorts of methods and categories and labels may be applied to different strands of theological reflection on human and non-human animals, resulting in more narrowly defined and focused tomes to fill library bookshelves as yet unbuilt. For now, this is where we are with the project of a creaturely theology.

We believe the essays here advance understanding of different aspects of this field in significant ways, but also recognize that perhaps the most important outcome of facilitating and collecting these reflections is to assist the process of compiling a 'to do' list for further research. On a first rough accounting, we see tasks on this list under five headings, as follows.

The first group of tasks concerns reappraisals of the interpretation of scriptural texts in relation to the relative position of human and non-human animals before God and in relation to one another. While some work has been completed in this field, and other projects are underway, different hermeneutical strategies alert to issues of how the human/non-human boundary is construed promise to be revealing both for a theology of non-human animals and for theological anthropology. The significant contribution made to this book by the Jewish scholar Aaron Gross, focused on Christian theology, makes clear the insight that dialogue between readers of texts in different religious traditions can generate in this task.

The second area is to engage in detail with figures in the Christian tradition and its neighbours with attentiveness to the implications of their thought for the construal of what it means to be human and non-human. That is begun in relation to some here, but even for those figures who have been the focus of chapters, there is clearly much more to be said, and there are many more for whom pressing the question of the animal will generate new and interesting readings of their work.

The third group of tasks relates to exploring the implications of modern scientific understandings of the capacities of non-human animals in relation to theological definitions of the human/non-human boundary. Again, essays in this volume have treated different aspects of this topic at points, but the transformation of our understanding of the lives of other animals in the past 30 years places us in a different position from our theological forebears, and the implications of this for our theological understanding is yet to be adequately explored. Traffic here is not one-way: while at times attending to scientific discoveries will demand new theological thinking, at other times there will be theological reasons for challenging the presuppositions or supposed implications of scientific experimentation and results. Research here therefore positions itself at one of the many interfaces between scientific and theological world-views and engages respectfully and with care in both directions, requiring literacy in both disciplines in order to avoid trite judgements and ignorant errors. Theology in this context properly resists overreaching 'scientistic' claims that suppose science the arbiter of theological truths, but also recognizes the integrity and internal logic of the scientific methodologies it engages.

The fourth heading on the list of research to be done in this area concerns the relationship between theology and the growing literature treating new understandings of human and non-human animals in the social sciences and humanities, including, of course, philosophical, feminist and political analysis, some of which is noted at the end of the Introduction to this volume. Feminist scholars in particular have identified some common ground between oppressive treatment of women and non-human animals, and studies here will examine those places where women and animals are found bound together in literary and textual sources, and those forms of essentialism that identify animals, nature and women. There are many hard and searching questions being asked by other disciplines in this field for which theologians will also have to find answers.

The final area of further work this collection shows the need for falls under the heading of the 'pragmatic rigour' in Aaron Gross's categorization in his chapter in this volume. Such pragmatism includes reflection on the varied liturgical practice of the Church from different denominational and contextual starting points. It also overlaps with political questions inasmuch as they impinge on given practices, as demonstrated so clearly in Peter Scott's chapter. Ethical topics have not been entirely absent from the discussions here: in addition to Gross, Neil Messer defends both forms of vegetarianism and certain kinds of medical experimentation on animals; Michael Northcott argues that if guided by the right human/non-human relationships not all meat-eating or use of non-human animals in other ways is necessarily prohibited for Christians; Christopher Southgate argues that Christians should be bold and sacrificial in doing what is necessary to defend other species, and Celia Deane-Drummond approaches the topic from the opposite direction, challenging us to consider that human beings may not have a monopoly on behaving ethically. Other authors would disagree with these conclusions, but all would concur that theologizing about non-human animals is not grounds for deferring questions of how we should treat them. The motivation for many of the essays represented here is pre-existing and on-going commitment to practices that better the lives of other animals, and part of the reason for doing theology about God's creatures is to think in greater depth in dialogue with the Christian tradition about how our relationships with non-human animals should be ordered. The theological ethics of non-human animals, informed by the kind of reflections begun here, is therefore a crucial area of research, and 'creaturely ethics' is both a necessary stimulus for and corollary to the 'creaturely theology' we have engaged in here.

These are signposts towards areas of future work, rather than attempts to specify its detail or parameters. The groups of tasks are clearly not exhaustive or mutually exclusive: the most interesting projects are likely to press at the boundaries of what we have sketched, and to juxtapose and negotiate between two or more of these areas. Setting out this range of questions has the merit, however, of indicating the scope of new research possible in this area, and may serve to provoke those with interests in the field to further reflection. All this must take its place alongside other important theological work, but this book has both argued and exemplified that attention to creatureliness in theological thinking will provoke new questions and insights across a wide range of doctrinal topics, and not least for our understanding of what it means to be human. Given this promising potential, a previous less-than-benign theological neglect of creaturely questions, and the recent attention given to the issue by scholars in other disciplines, this may be the right time for a vigorous and rigorous pursuit of new questions in creaturely theology.

Bibliography

Adams, Carol J., *The Sexual Politics of Meat: A Feminist-Vegetarian Critical Theory*, New York: Continuum, 1990.

—— *Neither Man Nor Beast: Feminism and the Defence of Animals*, New York: Continuum, 1994.

Agamben, Giorgio, *Homo Sacer: Sovereign Power and Bare Life*, Stanford: Stanford University Press, 1998.

—— *The Open: Man and Animal*, trans. Kevin Attell, Stanford CA: Stanford University Press, 2002, ET 2004.

Albertus, Magnus, *On Animals: A Medieval Summa Zoologica*, trans. and annotated K. F. Kitchell and I. M. Resnick, Baltimore: The Johns Hopkins University Press, 1999.

Almond, Philip, 'Adam, Pre-Adamites, and Extra-Terrestrial Beings in Early Modern Europe', *Journal of Religious History* 30, issue 2, 2006, pp. 163–74.

Anatolios, Khaled, *Athanasius: The Coherence of His Thought*, London and New York: Routledge, 1998.

—— *Athanasius*, London and New York: Routledge, 2004.

Anderson, Virginia DeJohn, *Creatures of Empire: How Domestic Animals Transformed Early America*, Urbana and Chicago: University of Illinois Press, 2005.

Animal Studies Group (ed.), *Killing Animals*, Urbana and Chicago: University of Illinois Press, 2006.

Anscombe, Elizabeth, *Intention*, Oxford: Blackwell, 1957.

Appleby, Michael C., Daniel M. Weary, Allison A. Taylor and Gudrun Illmann, 'Vocal Communication in Pigs: Who Are Nursing Piglets Screaming At?', *Ethology* 105, 1999, pp. 881–92.

Aquinas, *Commentary on Aristotle's de Anima*, trans. Kenelm Foster OP and Sylvester Humphries OP, New Haven: Yale University Press, 1951, html edition by Joseph Kenny OP <http://www.diafrica.org/kenny/CDtexts/DeAnima.htm#34> (accessed 1 July 2008).

—— *The Summa Theologica of St Thomas Aquinas (ST)* III Supplement, 2nd and rev. edn, trans. Fathers of the English Dominican Province, 1920. Online edition copyright (c) 2006, Kevin Knight, <http://www.newadvent.org/summa>.

—— *Summa Theologiae*, Chicago: Benziger Bros., 1947.

—— *The Soul [De Anima]*, trans. J. P. Rowan, St Louis: B. Herder, 1949.

—— *Truth [De Veritate]*, questions 21–29, trans. Robert W. Schmidt SJ, Chicago: Henry Regnery Co., 1954.

—— *Commentary on the Metaphysics*, trans. John P. Rowan, Chicago, 1961, html edited by Joseph Kenny OP <http://www.diafrica.org/kenny/CDtexts/ Metaphysics1.htm#1> (accessed 15 April 2007).

—— *Summa Theologiae*, ed. and trans. Fathers of the English Dominican Provinces, 60 vols, London: Blackfriars and Eyre & Spottiswoode, 1964–76.

—— *Summa Theologiae: Volume 13 (1a. 90–102), Man Made in God's Image*, trans. Edmund Hill, London: Blackfriars, 1964.

—— *Summa Theologiae: Volume 21 (1a2ae. 40–48), Fear and Anger*, trans. John Patrick Reid, London: Blackfriars, 1965.

—— *Summa Theologiae: Volume 28 (1a2ae. 90–97), Law and Political Theory*, trans. Thomas Gilby, London: Blackfriars, 1966.

—— *Summa Theologiae: Volume 8 (1a. 44–49), Creation, Variety and Evil*, trans. T. Gilby, London: Blackfriars, 1967.

—— *Summa Theologiae: Volume 10 (1a. 65–74), Cosmogony*, trans. William A. Wallace, London: Blackfriars, 1967.

—— *Summa Theologiae: Volume 19 (1a2ae. 23–30), The Emotions*, trans. by Eric D'Arcy, London: Blackfriars, 1967.

—— *Summa Theologiae, Volume 16 (1a2ae. 1–5), Purpose and Happiness*, trans. T. Gilby London: Blackfriars, 1968.

—— *Summa Theologiae, Volume 17 (1a2ae. 6–17), Psychology of Human Acts*, trans. Thomas Gilby, London: Blackfriars, 1970.

—— *Summa contra gentiles*, trans. Anton C. Pegis, Notre Dame IN: University of Notre Dame Press, 1975.

—— *Commentary on the Metaphysics of Aristotle*, trans. John P. Rowan, Notre Dame IN: Dumb Ox Books, 1995.

—— *Commentary on Aristotle's De anima*, trans. Robert Pasnau, New Haven: Yale University Press, 1999.

—— *Commentaries on Aristotle's 'On Sense and What is Sensed,' and 'On Memory and Recollection'*, trans. Kevin White and Edward M. Macierowski, Washington DC: The Catholic University of America Press, 2005.

Aristotle, 'De Anima', in *The Complete Works of Aristotle: The Revised Oxford Translation*, ed. Jonathon Barnes, Oxford: Oxford University Press, 1984.

Arluke, Arnold, *Regarding Animals*, Philadelphia: Temple University Press, 1996.

Ashley OP, Benedict M., 'Aristotle's *De Sensu et Sensato* and *De Memoria et Reminiscentia* as Thomistic Sources', presented at The University of Notre Dame Thomistic Institute, 14–21 July 2000, available at < http://maritain.nd. edu/jmc/tioo/ashley.htm>.

Attfield, Robin, *Creation, Evolution and Meaning*, Aldershot: Ashgate, 2006.

Augustine of Hippo, *Against Faustus the Manichaean*, in *A Select Library of Nicene and Post-Nicene Fathers of the Christian Church. First Series*, ed. Philip Schaff, Edinburgh: T & T Clark, 1994, vol. 4, pp. 151–346.

Bainton, Roland H., 'Luther's Struggle for Faith', *Church History* 17:3, 1948, pp. 193–206.

Baker, Steve, *The Postmodern Animal*, London: Reaktion, 2000.

Barad, Judith, *Aquinas on the Nature and Treatment of Animals*, San Francisco: International Scholars Press, 1995.

Barnes, Jonathon (ed.), *The Complete Works of Aristotle: The Revised Oxford Translation*, Oxford: Oxford University Press, 1984.

Barth, Karl, *Die Kirchliche Dogmatik* III.4, Zollikon-Zürich, Evangelischer Verlag AG, 1951.

—— *Church Dogmatics*, ET. ed. Geoffrey W. Bromiley and Thomas F. Torrance, 13 vols, Edinburgh: T & T Clark, 1956–75.

—— *Ethics*, ed. Dietrich Braun, trans. Geoffrey W. Bromiley, Edinburgh: T & T Clark, 1981.

—— *The Christian Life*, trans. Geoffrey W. Bromiley, new edn, London: T & T Clark, 2004 [1981].

Basil the Great, *Hexaemeron*, Homily IX, in Philip Schaff (ed.), *Nicene and Post-Nicene Fathers*, series 2, vol. IX.

BBC News, report on BBC Radio 4's *Today* programme, 5 October 2007.

Beers, Diane L., *For the Prevention of Cruelty: The History and Legacy of Animal Rights Activism in the United States*, Athens: Ohio University Press, 2006.

Bekoff, Marc, *The Emotional Lives of Animals*, Novato: New World Library, 2007.

Bentham, Jeremy, *An Introduction to the Principles of Morals and Legislation*, ed. J. H. Burns and H. L. A. Hart, London: Athlone, 1970 [1789].

Bergmann, Sigurd, 'Atmospheres of Synergy: Towards an Eco-theological Aesth/Ethics', *Ecotheology* 11:3, September 2006, pp. 326–56.

Berkman, John, 'Prophetically Pro-Life: John Paul II's Gospel of Life and Evangelical Concern for Animals', *Josephinum Journal of Theology* 6:1, 1999, pp. 43–59.

—— 'The Consumption of Animals and the Catholic Tradition', in Steve F. Sapontzis (ed.), *Food for Thought: The Debate About Eating Meat*, Amherst NY: Prometheus Press, 2004, pp. 198–208.

Berkman, John and Stanley Hauerwas, 'The Chief End of All Flesh', *Theology Today* 49:2, 1992, pp. 196–208.

Berry, Thomas, *The Dream of the Earth*, San Francisco: Sierra Club Books, 1988.

Berry, Wendell, *The Gift of Good Land: Further Essays Cultural and Agricultural*, San Francisco: North Point Press, 1981.

Biggar, Nigel, *The Hastening that Waits: Karl Barth's Ethics*, Oxford: Clarendon Press, 1993.

Boehm, Christopher, 'Conscience Origins, Sanctioning Selection, and the Evolution of Altruism in *Homo Sapiens*', *Behavior and Brain Sciences*, submitted for publication July 2008.

Bonhoeffer, Dietrich, *Christology*, London: Fount, 1978.

—— *Creation and Fall: A Theological Exposition of Genesis 1—3*, ET ed. John W. de Gruchy, trans. Douglas Stephen Bax, *Dietrich Bonhoeffer Works: Vol. 3*, Minneapolis MN: Fortress Press, 1997.

—— *Ethics*, ET ed. Clifford J. Green, *Dietrich Bonhoeffer Works: Vol. 6*, Minneapolis MN: Fortress Press, 2005.

Boulter, Michael, *Extinction: Evolution and the End of Man*, London, Harper-Collins, 2003.

Briggs, Katherine, *The Fairies in Tradition and Literature*, London: Routledge & Kegan Paul, 1966.

Brueggemann, Walter, *Genesis*, Louisville KY: John Knox Press, 1982.

Cairns, David, *The Image of God in Man*, London: SCM Press, 1953.

Calarco, Matthew, *Zoographies: The Question of the Animal from Heidegger to Derrida*, New York: Columbia University Press, 2008.

Calarco, Matthew, 'Deconstruction is Not Vegetarianism: Humanism, Subjectivity, and Animal Ethics', *Continental Philosophy Review* 37 (2004).

Calarco, Matthew and Peter Atterton (eds), *Animal Philosophy: Essential Readings in Continental Thought*, London: Continuum, 2004.

Calvin, John, *Commentaries on the First Book of Moses Called Genesis*, ed. and trans. John King, Grand Rapids MI: Baker Books, 1999.

Casanova, José, 'Rethinking Secularization: A Global Comparative Perspective', *The Hedgehog Review*, vol. 8, nos. 1 and 2, 2006, pp. 7–22.

Cassidy, Rebecca and Molly Mullin (eds), *Where the Wild Things Are: Domestication Reconsidered*, Oxford and New York: Berg, 2007.

Cavanaugh, William T., 'The City: Beyond Secular Parodies', in John Milbank, Catherine Pickstock and Graham Ward (eds), *Radical Orthodoxy: A New Theology*, London and New York: Routledge, 1999.

Cavell, Stanley, Cora Diamond, Ian Hacking, John McDowell and Cary Wolfe, *Philosophy and Animal Life*, New York: Columbia University Press, 2008.

Cekanskaja, Kira V., 'Traditional Veneration of Icons in the Russian Orthodox Church', *Acta Ethnographica Hungarica* 51:3–4, 2006, pp. 265–80.

Chesterton, G. K., *What's Wrong with the World*, London: Cassell & Co., 1910.

—— *Four Faultless Felons*, London: Cassell, 1930.

—— *The Poet and the Lunatics*, London: Darwen Finlayson, 1962 [1929].

—— *The Judgement of Dr. Johnson* [1927]: *Collected Works*, vol. 11, ed. D. J. Conlon, San Francisco: Ignatius Press, 1989.

Clare, John, *Selected Poems*, London: Penguin, 2000.

Clark, Stephen R. L., *Aristotle's Man*, Oxford: Clarendon Press, 1975.

—— *The Moral Status of Animals*, Oxford: Clarendon Press, 1977.

—— *The Nature of the Beast: Are Animals Moral?* Oxford: Oxford University Press, 1982.

—— 'How to Believe in Fairies', *Inquiry* 30, 1988, pp. 337–55.

—— *How to Think about the Earth*, London: Mowbray, 1993.

—— *Animals and Their Moral Standing*, London: Routledge, 1997.

—— *The Political Animal: Biology, Ethics and Politics*, London: Routledge, 1999.

—— *Biology and Christian Ethics*, Cambridge: Cambridge University Press, 2000.

—— 'Posthumanism: Engineering in the Place of Ethics', in Barry Smith and Berit Brogaard (eds), *Rationality and Irrationality: Proceedings of the 23rd International Wittgenstein Symposium*, Vienna: ÖbvetHpt, 2001, pp. 62–76.

—— *G. K. Chesterton: Thinking Backward, Looking Forward*, London: Templeton Foundation Press, 2006.

Clarke, P. and A. Linzey (eds), *Dictionary of Ethics, Theology and Society*, London: Routledge, 1996.

Clough, David, *Ethics in Crisis: Interpreting Barth's Ethics*, Aldershot: Ashgate, 2005.

—— *Faith and Force: A Christian Debate about War*, Washington DC: Georgetown University Press, 2007.

—— 'All God's Creatures: Reading Genesis on Human and Non-human

Animals', in Stephen Barton and David Wilkinson (eds), *Reading Genesis after Darwin*, Oxford and New York: Oxford University Press, forthcoming.

Coetzee, J. M. (ed.), *The Lives of Animals*, Princeton: Princeton University Press, 1999.

Cohen, Jeremy, *Living Letters of the Law: Ideas of the Jew in Medieval Christianity*, Berkeley: University of California Press, 1999.

Conway Morris, S. (ed.), *The Deep Structure of Biology: Is Convergence Sufficiently Ubiquitous to Give a Directional Signal?*, Philadephia: Templeton Foundation Press, 2008.

Cottingham, J., 'A Brute to the Brutes? Descartes' Treatment of Animals', *Philosophy* 53, 1978, pp. 551–9.

Crist, Eileen, *Images of Animals: Anthropomorphism and Animal Mind*, Philadelphia: Temple University Press, 2000.

Crowley, John, *Beasts*, London: Futura, 1978.

Cunningham, David S., *These Three Are One: The Practice of Trinitarian Theology*, Oxford: Blackwell, 1998.

—— *Christian Ethics: The End of the Law*, London and New York: Routledge, 2008.

Dan Lyons, 'The animal care regulatory system is a sham: inspectors often overrate the value of an experiment and underestimate the pain it causes', Letters in *Nature* 430, 22 July 2004, p. 399.

Darwin, Charles, *Über die Entstehung der Arten im Thier- und Pflanzen-Reich durch natürliche Züchtung*, German trans. H. G. Bronn, Stuttgart: Schweizerbart, 1860. Online at <http://darwin-online.org.uk/contents.html> (accessed 15 January 2008).

—— *The Descent of Man*, Princeton: Princeton University Press, 1981 [1871].

Daston, Lorraine, 'Intelligences: Angelic, Human, Animal', in L. Daston and G. Mitman (eds), *Thinking with Animals: New Perspectives on Anthropomorphism*, New York: Columbia University Press, 2005, pp. 37–58.

Daston, Lorraine and Gregg Mitman (eds), *Thinking Animals: New Perspectives on Anthropomorphism*, New York: Columbia University Press, 2005.

Davies, Brian, *Introduction to the Thought of St Thomas Aquinas*, Oxford: Oxford University Press, 1992.

Dawkins, Richard, *The Selfish Gene*, 30th anniversary edition, Oxford: Oxford University Press, 2006.

De Fontenay, Elisabeth, *Le Silence des Bêtes: La Philosophie à L'épreuve*, Paris: Favard, 1998.

de Waal, F., *Good Natured: The Origins of Right and Wrong in Humans and Other Animals*, Cambridge MA: Harvard University Press, 1996.

—— *Our Inner Ape: The Best and Worst of Human Nature*, London: Grant Books, 2006.

—— 'Primate Social Instincts, Human Morality and the Rise and Fall of Veneer Theory', in Stephen Macedo and Josiah Ober (eds), *Primates and Philosophers: How Morality Evolved*, Princeton: Princeton University Press, 2006, pp. 6–7.

Deane-Drummond, Celia, *The Ethics of Nature*, Oxford: Blackwell, 2004.

—— *Genetics and Christian Ethics*, Cambridge: Cambridge University Press, 2006.

—— *Wonder and Wisdom: Conversations in Science, Spirituality and Theology*, London: Darton, Longman & Todd, 2006.

—— *Ecotheology*, London: Darton, Longman & Todd, 2008.

—— 'Shadow Sophia in Christological Perspective: The Evolution of Sin and the Redemption of Nature', *Theology and Science* 6:1, 2008, pp. 13–32.

—— (ed.), *Pierre Teilhard de Chardin on People and Planet*, London: Eqinox, 2006.

Deane-Drummond, Celia and Bronislaw Szersynski (eds), *Reordering Nature: Theology, Society and the New Genetics*, London: T & T Clark, 2003.

Deane-Drummond, Celia and Peter Scott (eds), *Future Perfect: God, Medicine and Human Identity*, London: T & T Clark, 2006.

DeGrazia, David, *Taking Animals Seriously*, Cambridge: Cambridge University Press, 1996.

Derrida, Jacques, *The Animal that Therefore I Am*, trans. David Willis, New York: Fordham University Press, 2008.

Derrida, Jacques, '"Eating Well" or the Calculation of the Subject', in Elisabeth Weber and Peggy Kamuf (eds), *Points, Interviews, 1974–1994*, Stanford: Stanford University Press, 1995.

—— 'The Animal that Therefore I Am (more to follow)', trans. David Willis, *Critical Inquiry* 28:2, 2002, p. 418.

Diamond, Cora, *The Realistic Spirit*, Cambridge MA: MIT Press, 1991.

Doward, Jamie, 'Kill Scientists Says Animal Chief', *Observer*, 25 July 2004.

Dupré, J., *Humans and Other Animals*, Oxford: Clarendon Press, 2002.

Dyson, Freeman, 'The Darwinian Interlude', *Technology Review*, March 2005 <http://www.technologyreview.com/read_article.aspx?id=14236&ch=biotech>.

Ecoffey, Chloé Bregnard, 'Asylum in Switzerland: A Challenge for the Church', unpublished MA dissertation, University of Manchester, 2007.

Ecological Society of Australia, <http://www.ecolsoc.org.au/Position_papers/ClimateChange.htm> (accessed 20 February 2008).

Edwards, Denis, *The God of Evolution: A Trinitarian Theology*, New York: Paulist Press, 1999.

—— *Breath of Life: A Theology of the Creator Spirit*, Maryknoll NY: Orbis Books, 2004.

—— *Ecology at the Heart of Faith*, Maryknoll NY and Edinburgh: Orbis Books, 2006.

—— (ed.), *Earth Revealing – Earth Healing: Ecology and Christian Theology*, Collegeville MN: Liturgical Press, 2001.

Edwards, Denis and Mark Worthing (eds), 'Biodiversity and Ecology: An Interdisciplinary Challenge', *Interface* 7:1, 2004.

Eliot, T. S., *Complete Poems and Plays*, London: Faber & Faber; New York: Harcourt Brace and World, 1969.

Ellul, Jacques, *The Technological Society*, New York: Free Press, 1966.

Evans-Wentz, W. Y., *The Fairy Faith in Celtic Countries*, London and New York: H. Frowde, 1911.

Fabre-Vassas, Claudine, *The Singular Beast: Jews, Christians and the Pig*, vol. *European Perspectives*, trans. Carol Volk, New York: Columbia University Press, 1997.

Farrow, Douglas, *Ascension and Ecclesia: On the Significance of the Doctrine of the Ascension for Ecclesiology and Christian Cosmology*, Edinburgh: T & T Clark, 1999.

Fellenz, Marc R., *The Moral Menagerie: Philosophy and Animal Rights*, Urbana and Chicago: University of Chicago Press, 2007.

Filler, Aaron G., *The Upright Ape: A New Origin of the Species*, Franklin Lakes NJ: New Page Books, 2007.

Firey, Abigail, 'The Letter of the Law: Carolingian Exegetes and the Old Testament', in Jane Dammen McAuliffe, Barry D. Walfish and Joseph W. Goering (eds), *With Reverence for the Word: Medieval Scriptural Exegesis in Judaism, Christianity, and Islam*, New York: Oxford University Press, 2003, pp. 204–24.

Fitzmyer, Joseph, 'Pauline Theology', in Raymond E. Brown, Joseph A. Fitzmyer and Roland E. Murphy (eds), *The New Jerome Biblical Commentary*, London: Geoffrey Chapman, 1990, pp. 1397–401.

Fleming, Pat and Joanna Macy, 'The Council of All Beings', in John Seed, Joanna Macy, Pat Fleming and Arne Naess (eds), *Thinking Like a Mountain: Towards a Council of All Beings*, London and Philadelphia: Heretic Books, 1988, pp. 79–90.

Foot, Philippa, *Natural Goodness*, Oxford: Oxford University Press, 2001.

Foster, Jeffrey and Scott K. Robinson, 'Introduced Birds and the Fate of Hawaiian Rainforests', *Conservation Biology* 21:5, October 2007, pp. 1248–57.

Fox, Doug, 'When Worlds Collide', Feature in *Conservation in Practice* 8:1, January–March, 2007.

Fox, Matthew, *The Coming of the Cosmic Christ*, New York: Harper & Row, 1988.

Franklin, Adrian, *Animals and Modern Cultures: A Sociology of Human–Animal Relations in Modernity*, London: Sage, 1999.

Fraser, David, 'Animal Ethics and Animal Welfare Science: Bridging the Two Cultures', *Applied Animal Behaviour Science* 65, 1999, pp. 171–89.

Fudge, Erica, *Perceiving Animals: Humans and Beasts in Early Modern English Culture*, Basingstoke: Macmillan, 1999.

—— (ed.), *Renaissance Beasts: Of Animals, Humans, and Other Wonderful Creatures*, Urbana, IL: University of Illinois Press, 2004.

Gaita, Raimond, *The Philosopher's Dog*, New York: Random House, 2002.

George, Marie, 'Thomas Aquinas Meets Nim Chimpsky: On the Debate about Human Nature and the Nature of Other Animals', *Aquinas Review* 10, 2003, pp. 1–50.

Gibbons, Ann, *The First Human: The Race to Discover our Earliest Ancestors*, New York: Doubleday, 2006.

—— 'Hominid Harems: Big Males Competed for Small Australopithecine Females', *Science*, 1363, 07/11/30, 2007, p. 1443.

Gilhus, Ingvild Sælid, *Animals, Gods, and Humans: Changing Attitudes to Animals in Greek, Roman, and Early Christian Ideas*, London and New York: Routledge, 2006.

Golding, William, *The Inheritors*, London: Faber, 1955.

Goodpaster, Kenneth E., 'On Being Morally Considerable', *Journal of Philosophy* 75, 1978, pp. 308–25.

Gray, John, *Straw Dogs: Thoughts on Humans and Other Animals*, London: Granta Books, 2002.

Gregersen, Niels Hendrik, 'The Cross of Christ in an Evolutionary World', *Dialog: A Journal of Theology* 40:3, 2001, pp. 192–207.

Gregory the Dialogist, St, *Epistle to Bishop Serenus of Marseilles*, in Philip Schaff (ed.), *Nicene and Post-Nicene Fathers*, series 2, vol. XIII, Edinburgh: T & T Clark, 1980, p. 53.

Gregory of Nazianzus, 'Oration 28: On the Doctrine of God', in Frederick W. Norris (ed.), *Faith Gives Fullness to Reasoning: The Five Theological Orations of Gregory Nazianzen*, trans. Lionel Wickham and Frederick Williams, Supplements to *Vigiliae Christianae*, 13, Leiden: E. J. Brill, 1991, pp. 224–44.

Grier, Katherine C., *Pets in America: A History*, Chapel Hill NC: University of North Carolina Press, 2006.

Gunton, Colin E. (ed.), *The Doctrine of Creation: Essays in Dogmatics, History and Philosophy*. London: T & T Clark, 2004.

Habel, Norman C., *The Book of Job*, London: SCM Press, 1985.

—— (ed.), *Readings from the Perspective of Earth*: vol. 1 of *The Earth Bible*, Sheffield: Sheffield Academic Press, 2000.

Habel, Norman C. and Shirley Wurst (eds), *The Earth Story in Genesis*: vol. 2 of *The Earth Bible*, Sheffield: Sheffield Academic Press; Cleveland: Pilgrim Press, 2000.

Hall, Douglas John, *Imaging God: Dominion as Stewardship*, Grand Rapids: Eerdmans; New York: Friendship Press, 1986.

Ham, Jennifer and Matthew Senior, *Animal Acts: Configuring the Human in Western History*, London: Routledge, 1997.

Hanssen, Beatrice, *Walter Benjamin's Other History*, Berkeley: University of California Press, 2000.

Haraway, Donna, *Simians, Cyborgs and Women: The Reinvention of Nature*, London: FAB Books, 1991.

—— *The Companion Species Manifesto: Dogs, People, and Significant Otherness*, Chicago: Prickly Paradigm Press, 2003.

Harpur, Patrick, *Daimonic Reality*, London: Arkana, 1994.

Høeg, Peter, *The Woman and the Ape*, London: The Harvill Press, 1997.

Hoffmann, Paul, 'Aquinas on the Halfway State of Sensible Being', *Philosophical Review* 99, 1990, pp. 73–92.

Holmes, Bob, 'Special Deliverance', *New Scientist*, 6 October 2007.

Horowitz, Alexandra C. and Marc Bekoff, 'Naturalizing Anthropomorphisms: Behavioural Prompts to Our Humanizing of Animals', *Anthrozoos* 20:1, 2007, pp. 23–35.

Horrell, David G., *Solidarity and Difference: A Contemporary Reading of Paul's Ethics*, London and New York: T & T Clark/Continuum, 2005.

Horrell, David G., Cherryl Hunt and Christopher Southgate, 'Appeals to the Bible in Ecotheology and Environmental Ethics: A Typology of Hermeneutical Stances', *Studies in Christian Ethics* 21:2, 2008, pp. 53–72.

Hrdy, Sarah Blaffer, *Mother Nature: A History of Mothers, Infants and Natural Selection*, New York: Pantheon, 1999.

Hull, David L. (ed.), *Darwin and His Critics*, Chicago and London: University of Chicago Press, 1983.

Hume, David, *A Treatise of Human Nature*, ed. L. A. Selby-Bigge, rev. P. H. Nidditch, Oxford: Clarendon Press, 1978 [1739–1740].

Hunt, Cherryl, David G. Horrell and Christopher Southgate, 'An Environmental Mantra? Ecological Interest in Romans 8.19–23 and a Modest Proposal for Its Narrative Interpretation', *Journal of Theological Studies* 59, 2008, pp. 546–79; doi: 10.1093/jts/fln064.

Hursthouse, Rosalind, *On Virtue Ethics*, Oxford: Oxford University Press, 1999.

Huxley, Thomas Henry, 'Evolution and Ethics', The Romanes Lecture, 1893, in *Evolution and Ethics and Other Essays*, Collected Essays, vol. 9, London: Macmillan, 1894. pp. 46–116.

—— *Evolution and Ethics*, Princeton: Princeton University Press, 1989 [1894].

Ickert, Scott, 'Luther and Animals: Subject to Adam's Fall?', in Andrew Linzey and Dorothy Yamamoto (eds), *Animals on the Agenda: Questions About Animals for Theology and Ethics*, London: SCM Press, 1998, pp. 90–9.

Ingold, Tim (ed.), *What Is an Animal?*, London: Unwin Hyman, 1988.

Ingold, Tim, 'Hunting and Gathering as Ways of Perceiving the Environment', in Roy Ellen and Katsuyoshi Fukui (eds), *Redefining Nature*, Oxford: Berg, 1996.

—— *Perception of the Environment: Essays on Livelihood, Dwelling and Skill*, London and New York: Routledge, 2005.

Irvine, Leslie, *If You Tame Me: Understanding Our Connection with Animals*, Philadelphia: Temple University Press, 2004.

Jaspers, Karl, *The Origin and Goal of History*, trans. Michael Bullock, London: Routledge & Kegan Paul, 1953 [1949].

Jonas, Hans, *The Imperative of Responsibility*, Chicago and London: University of Chicago Press, 1984.

Kant, Immanuel, 'Duties to Animals and Spirits', in *Lectures on Ethics*, trans. Louis Infield, New York: Harper & Row, 1963.

Katz, Leonard D. (ed.), *Evolutionary Origins of Morality: Cross-Disciplinary Perspectives*, Thorverton: Imprint Academic, 2000.

Kaufman, Gordon D., 'A Problem for Theology: The Concept of Nature', *Harvard Theological Review* 65, 1972, pp. 337–66.

Kemmerer, Lisa, *In Search of Consistency: Ethics and Animals*, Leiden: Brill, 2007.

Kennedy J. S., *The New Anthropomorphism*, Cambridge: Cambridge University Press, 1992.

Keselopoulos, Anestis, G., *Man and the Environment: A Study of St Symeon the New Theologian*, trans. Elizabeth Theokritoff, Crestwood NY: St Vladimir's Seminary Press, 2001.

Kete, Kathleen, *The Beast in the Boudoir: Pet-Keeping in Nineteenth-Century Paris*, Berkeley and Los Angeles CA: University of California Press, 1994.

Keynes, G. (ed.), *Complete Writings of William Blake*, Oxford University Press: London, 1966.

Kinnealy, Tom, *A Commonwealth of Thieves: The Improbable Birth of Australia*, Sydney: Random House, 2005.

Klaus Eder, *The Social Construction of Nature*, London: Sage, 1996.

Kuzniar, Alice A., *Melancholia's Dog: Reflections on Our Animal Kinship*, Chicago and London: University of Chicago Press, 2006.

Latour, Bruno, *We Have Never Been Modern*, New York: Harvester Wheatsheaf, 1993.
—— 'Is There a Cosmopolitically Correct Design?', lecture given at the University of Manchester, 5 October 2007.
Lawlor, Leonard, *This Is Not Sufficient: An Essay on Animality and Human Nature in Derrida*, New York: Columbia University Press, 2007.
Leakey, Richard and Roger Lewin, *The Sixth Extinction: Biodiversity and Its Survival*, London: Weidenfeld & Nicolson, 1996.
Leopold, Aldo, *A Sand County Almanac: With Essays on Conservation from Round River*, Oxford: Oxford University Press, 1966 [1949].
Leslie, John, *The End of the World: Science and Ethics of Human Extinction*, London: Routledge, 1996.
Lévi-Strauss, Claude, *The Savage Mind*, Chicago: University of Chicago Press, 1973.
Levinas, Emmanuel, *Nine Talmudic Readings*, trans. A. Aronowicz, Bloomington: Indiana University Press, 1990.
—— *Totality and Infinity: An Essay on Exteriority*, trans. A. Lingis, Pittsburgh: Duquesne, 1990.
—— 'The Name of a Dog; or, Natural Rights', in *Difficult Freedom*, trans. Seán Hand, Baltimore: John Hopkins, 1997.
Lewis, C. S., *Studies in Words*, Cambridge: Cambridge University Press, 1960.
—— *The Discarded Image: An Introduction to Medieval and Renaissance Literature*, Cambridge: Cambridge University Press, 1964.
Light, Andrew and Holmes Rolston III (eds), *Environmental Ethics: An Anthology*, Oxford: Blackwell, 2003.
Linzey, Andrew, *Animal Rights: A Christian Assessment*, London: SCM Press, 1976.
—— *Christianity and the Rights of Animals*, London: SPCK, 1987.
—— *Animal Theology*, London: SCM Press, 1994.
—— 'Animal Rights', in Paul Barry Clarke and Andrew Linzey (eds), *Dictionary of Ethics, Theology and Society*, London: Routledge, 1996, pp. 29–33.
—— 'Introduction: Is Christianity Irredeemably Speciesist?', in Andrew Linzey and Dorothy Yamamoto, *Animals on the Agenda: Questions About Animals for Theology and Ethics*, London: SCM Press, 1998.
—— *Animal Gospel: Christian Faith as if Animals Mattered*, London: Hodder & Stoughton; Louisville: Westminster John Knox Press, 1999.
—— *Animal Rites: Liturgies of Animal Care*, London: SPCK, 1999.
—— *Creatures of the Same God: Explorations in Animal Theology*, Winchester: Winchester University Press, 2007.
—— 'The Conflict between Ecotheology and Animal Theology', in *Creatures of the Same God: Explorations in Animal Theology*, Winchester: Winchester University Press, 2007, pp. 49–71.
Linzey, Andrew and Tom Regan (eds), *Animals and Christianity: A Book of Readings*, London: SPCK, 1989.
Linzey, Andrew and Dan Cohn-Sherbook, *After Noah: Animals and the Liberation of Theology*, London: Mowbray, 1997.
Linzey, Andrew and Dorothy Yamamoto (eds), *Animals on the Agenda:*

Questions About Animals for Theology and Ethics, London: SCM Press, 1998.

Lippit, Akira Mizuta, *The Electric Animal: Toward a Rhetoric of Wildlife*, Minneapolis: University of Minnesota Press, 2000.

Lisska, Anthony J., 'Thomas Aquinas on Phantasia: Rooted in but Transcending Aristotle's *De anima*', presented at the University of Notre Dame Thomistic Institute, 14–21 July 2000, available at <http://maritain.nd.edu/jmc/tioo/stier.htm>.

Lovejoy, Arthur O., *The Great Chain of Being: A Study of the History of an Idea*, Cambridge MA: Harvard University Press, 1942.

Lovelock, James, *The Ages of Gaia: A Biography for Our Living Earth*, Oxford: Oxford University Press, 1989.

Lovibond, Sabina, 'Practical Reason and its Animal Precursors', *European Journal of Philosophy* 14:2, August 2006, pp. 262–73.

Lukac de Stier, Maria L., 'Aristotle's *De anima* as Source of Aquinas' Anthropological Doctrine', presented at the University of Notre Dame Thomistic Institute, 14–21 July 2000, available at < http://maritain.nd.edu/jmc/tioo/stier.htm>.

Luther, Martin, *D. Martin Luthers Werke: Kritische Gesamtausgabe, Tischreden*, 6 vols, Weimar: Hermann Bölhaus Nachfolger, 1912.

—— *Luther's Works*, ed. Helmut T. Lehmann and Jaroslav Pelikan, Philadelphia: Muhlenberg Press, 1958.

—— *The Letters of Martin Luther*, ed. Margaret A. Currie, London: Macmillan & Co., 1908.

Lütticken, Sven, 'Unnatural History', *New Left Review* 45, 2007, pp. 115–31.

Lynas, Mark, *Six Degrees: Our Future on a Hotter Planet*, London: Fourth Estate, 2007.

Mabey, Richard, *Nature Cure*, London: Pimlico, 2006 [2005].

MacIntyre, Alasdair, *Three Rival Versions of Moral Enquiry*, South Bend IN: University of Notre Dame Press, 1990.

—— *Dependent Rational Animals*, London: Open Court Press, 1999.

Mahoney, Edward P., 'Sense, Intellect, and Imagination in Albert, Thomas, and Siger', in Norman Kretzmann, Anthony Kenny and Jan Pinborg (eds), *The Cambridge History of Later Medieval Philosophy*, Cambridge: Cambridge University Press, 1982, pp. 602–22.

Maimonides, Moses, *The Guide of the Perplexed*, trans. Shlomo Pines, Chicago: University of Chicago Press, 1963.

Malamud, Randy, *Poetic Animals and Animal Souls*, New York: Palgrave Macmillan, 2003.

Malina, Bruce J., *The New Testament World: Insights from Cultural Anthropology*, 3rd edn, revised and expanded, Louisville KY: Westminster John Knox Press, 2001.

Mallet, M. L. (ed.), *L'animal Autobiographique: Autour de Jacques Derrida*, Paris: Galilée, 1999.

Manning, Aubrey, and James Serpell (eds), *Animals and Human Society: Changing Perspectives*, London: Routledge, 1994.

Marion, Jean-Luc, '*Mihi magna quaestio factus sum*: The Privilege of Unknowing', *Journal of Religion* 85:1, 2005, pp. 1–24.

Marshall, Bruce, *Trinity and Truth*, Cambridge Studies in Christian Doctrine, ed. Colin Gunton and Daniel W. Hardy, Cambridge: Cambridge University Press, 2000.

Martin, Dale, *The Corinthian Body*, New Haven and London: Yale University Press, 1995.

Mayor, Adrienne and Michael Heaney, 'Griffins and Arimaspeans', *Folklore*, vol. 104, no. 1/2, 1993, pp. 40–66.

McCabe, Herbert, *The Good Life*, New York: Continuum, 2001.

McDaniel, Jay, 'Practicing the Presence of Animals: A Christian Approach to Animals', in Paul Waldau and Kimberley Patten (eds), *A Communion of Subjects: Animals in Religion, Science and Ethics*, New York: Columbia University Press, 2006, pp. 132–45.

McDonagh SC, Sean, *The Death of Life: The Horror of Extinction*, Blackrock, Co. Dublin: Columba Press, 2004.

McFadyen, Alistair I., *Bound to Sin: Abuse, Holocaust and the Doctrine of Sin*, Cambridge: Cambridge University Press, 2000.

McFague, Sallie, *Models of God: Theology for an Ecological, Nuclear Age*, London: SCM Press, 1987.

—— *The Body of God: An Ecological Theology*, London: SCM Press, 1993.

McKenny, Gerald P., *To Relieve the Human Condition: Bioethics, Technology and the Body*, Albany NY: State University of New York Press, 1997.

McKibben, Bill, *The Comforting Whirlwind: God, Job, and the Scale of Creation*, Grand Rapids MI, Eerdmans, 1994.

McLachlan, Jason S., James S. Clark and Paul S. Manos, 'Molecular Indicators of Tree Migration Capacity under Climate Change', *Ecology* 86:8, August 2005, pp. 2088–98.

McLachlan, Jason S., Jessica J. Hellmann and Mark W. Schwartz, 'A Framework for Debate of Assisted Migration in an Era of Climate Change', *Conservation Biology* 21:2, 2007, pp. 297–302.

Meeks, M. Douglas, *God the Economist: The Doctrine of God and Political Economy*, Minneapolis: Fortress Press, 1989.

Messer, Neil, *Study Guide to Christian Ethics*, London: SCM Press, 2006.

—— *Selfish Genes and Christian Ethics: Theological and Ethical Reflections on Evolutionary Biology*, London: SCM Press, 2007.

Middleton, J. Richard, *The Liberating Image: The Imago Dei of Genesis 1*, Grand Rapids MI: Brazos Press, 2005.

Midgley, Mary. *Beast and Man: The Roots of Human Nature*, Ithaca: Cornell University Press, 1978.

—— *Animals and Why They Matter*, Athens GA: University of Georgia Press, 1983.

—— *The Ethical Primate: Humans, Freedom and Morality*, London: Routledge, 1994.

—— *Beast and Man: The Roots of Human Nature*, London: Routledge, 1995 [1979].

—— 'Are Dolphins Persons?', in *Utopias, Dolphins and Computers*, London: Routledge, 1996.

Miller, Geoffrey David, 'Attitudes Toward Dogs in Ancient Israel: A Reassessment', *Journal for the Study of the Old Testament* 32:4, 2008, pp. 487–500.

Mithen, Steven, *The Prehistory of the Mind*, London: Pheonix, 1996.

—— *The Singing Neanderthals: The Origins of Music, Language, Mind and Body*, London: Weidenfeld & Nicolson, 2005.

Mooney, H. A. and E. E. Cleland, 'The Evolutionary Impact of Invasive Species', *Proceedings of the National Academy of Sciences* 98:10, 2001, pp. 5446–51.

Morrison, Reg, *The Spirit in the Gene: Humanity's Proud Illusion and the Laws of Nature*, Ithaca NY: Cornell University Press, 1999.

Morwood, Mike and Penny van Oosertzee, *A New Human*, New York: Smithsonian Books, 2007

Muers, Rachel, *Keeping God's Silence: Towards a Theological Ethics of Communication*, Oxford: Blackwell, 2004.

—— 'Setting Free the Mother Bird: On Reading a Strange Text', *Modern Theology* 22:4, 2006, pp. 555–76.

—— *Living for the Future: Theological Ethics for Coming Generations*, London: T & T Clark, 2008.

Muers, Rachel and David Grumett (eds), *Eating and Believing: Interdisciplinary Perspectives on Vegetarianism and Theology*, London: T & T Clark, 2008.

Myers, Norman and Andrew H. Knoll, 'The Biotic Crisis and the Future of Evolution', *Proceedings of the National Academy of Sciences* 98:10, 2001, pp. 5389–92.

Northcott, Michael S., *The Environment and Christian Ethics*, Cambridge: Cambridge University Press, 1996.

—— 'The Moral Standing of Nature and the New Natural Law', in Nigel Biggar (ed.), *The Revival of Natural Law*, Aldershot: Ashgate, 2000.

—— 'Do Dolphins Carry the Cross? Biological Moral Realism and Theological Ethics', *New Blackfriars* 84, 2003.

—— *A Moral Climate: The Ethics of Global Warming*, London: Darton, Longman & Todd, 2007.

Novacek, Michael J. and Elsa E. Cleland, 'The Current Biodiversity Extinction Event: Scenarios for Mitigation and Recovery', *Proceedings of the National Academy of Sciences* 98:10, 2001, pp. 5466–70.

Nussbaum, Martha Craven, *Aristotle's De Motu Animalium*, Princeton NJ: Princeton University Press, 1978.

—— 'Beyond Compassion and Humanity: Justice for Non-Human Animals', in Cass R. Sunstein and Martha Nussbaum (eds), *Animal Rights: Current Debates and New Directions*, Oxford: Oxford University Press, 2005, pp. 299–320.

—— *Frontiers of Justice: Disability, Nationality, Species Membership*, Cambridge: Belknap/Harvard University Press, 2006.

O'Keefe, John J. and R.R. Reno, *Sanctified Vision: An Introduction to Early Christian Interpretation of the Bible*, Baltimore and London: The Johns Hopkins University Press, 2005.

O'Rourke Boyle, Marjorie, 'Luther's Rider-Gods: From the Steppe to the Tower', *Journal of Religious History* 13:3, 1985, pp. 260–82.

Osborne, Catherine, *Dumb Beasts and Dead Philosophers: Humanity and the Humane in Ancient Philosophy and Literature*, Oxford: Clarendon Press, 2007.

Pacala, S. and R. Socolow, 'Stabilization Wedges – Solving the Climate Problem for the Next 50 Years Using Current Technologies', *Science* 305:5686, August 2004, pp. 968–72.

Page, Ruth, 'The Human Genome and the Image of God', in Celia Deane-Drummond (ed.), *Brave New World? Theology, Ethics, and the Human Genome*, London and New York: T & T Clark, 2003.

Pasnau, Robert, *Theories of Cognition in the Later Middle Ages*, Cambridge: Cambridge University Press, 1997.

—— *Thomas Aquinas on Human Nature*, Cambridge: Cambridge University Press, 2002.

Patterson, N., D. J. Richter, S. Gnerre, E. S. Lander and D. Reich, 'Genetic Evidence for Complex Speciation of Humans and Chimpanzees', *Nature* 441, 2006, pp. 1103–08.

Patton, Kimberley, '"Caught with Ourselves in the Net of Life and Time": Traditional Views of Animals in Religion', in Paul Waldau and Kimberley Patton (eds), *A Communion of Subjects: Animals in Religion, Science, and Ethics*, New York: Columbia University Press, 2006.

Pettersen, Alvyn, *Athanasius*, London: Geoffrey Chapman, 1995.

Philo, Chris and Chris Wilbert, *Animal Spaces, Beastly Places: New Geographies of Human–Animal Relations*, vol. Critical Geographies, London: Routledge, 2000.

Philo, *De opificio mundi*, in *Philo I*, Loeb Classical Library, trans. F. H. Colson and G. H. Whitaker, London: Heinemann, 1929.

Planalp, S., *Communicating Emotion: Social, Moral and Cultural Processes*, Cambridge: Cambridge University Press, 1999.

Plumwood, Val, *Feminism and the Mastery of Nature*, London: Routledge, 1993.

Poliakov, Léon, 'Humanity, Nationality, Bestiality', in Elisabeth Weber, *Questioning Judaism*, Stanford: Stanford University Press, 2004.

Pope, Stephen J., *The Evolution of Altruism and the Ordering of Love*, Washington DC: Georgetown University Press, 1994.

—— *Human Evolution and Christian Ethics*, Cambridge: Cambridge University Press, 2007.

Primavesi, Anne, *Gaia's Gift*, London: Routledge, 2003.

Quenot, M., *The Resurrection and the Icon*, Crestwood NY: St Vladimir's Seminary Press, 1997.

Rasmussen, L. L., *Earth Community, Earth Ethics*, New York: Orbis Books, 1996.

—— 'Luther and a Gospel of Earth', *Union Seminary Quarterly Review* 51:1–2, 1997, pp. 1–28.

Reed, Esther D., *The Ethics of Human Rights: Contested Doctrinal and Moral Issues*, Waco TX: Baylor University Press, 2007.

Regan, Tom, *The Case for Animal Rights*, London: Routledge, 1988.

—— *The Thee Generation*, Philadelphia: Temple University Press, 1991.

Regan, Tom and Peter Singer (eds), *Animal Rights and Human Obligations*, Englewood Cliffs: Prentice Hall, 1976.

Roberts, Mark S., *The Mark of the Beast: Animality and Human Oppression*, Indiana: Purdue University Press, 2008.

Rogers, Jr, Eugene F., *Sexuality and the Christian Body: Their Way into the Triune God*, Oxford: Blackwell, 1999.

—— *Thomas Aquinas and Karl Barth: Sacred Doctrine and the Natural Knowledge of God*, Notre Dame IN: University of Notre Dame Press, 1995.

Rohan, Michael Scott, *The Winter of the World*, London: Macdonald: London, 1986–9.

Rolston, Holmes, *Environmental Ethics: Duties to and Values in the Natural World*, Philadephia: Temple University Press, 1988.

—— 'Wildlife and Wildlands: A Christian Perspective', in Dieter Hessel (ed.), *After Nature's Revolt*, Minneapolis MN: Augsburg Fortress Press, 1992, pp. 122–43.

—— *Genesis, Genes and God: Values and Their Origins in Natural and Human History*, Cambridge: Cambridge University Press, 1999.

Rolt, L. T. C., *High Horse Riderless*, London: George Allen and Unwin, 1947.

Rosenzweig, Franz, *The Star of Redemption*, trans. Barbara E. Galli, Madison: University of Wisconsin Press, 2005.

Rothfels, Nigel, *Representing Animals*, Bloomington: Indiana University Press, 2002.

Royce, James, *Man and His Nature*, New York: McGraw Hill, 1961.

Ruse, Michael, *Darwin and Design: Does Evolution Have a Purpose?*, Cambridge MA: Harvard University Press, 2003.

Russell, Norman, *The Doctrine of Deification in the Greek Patristic Tradition*, Oxford: Oxford University Press, 2004.

Santmire, H. Paul, *The Travail of Nature: The Ambiguous Ecological Promise of Christian Theology*, Minneapolis: Fortress Press, 1985.

Santmire, H. Paul and John B. Cobb Jr, 'The World of Nature According to the Protestant Tradition', in Roger S. Gottlieb (ed.), *The Oxford Handbook of Religion and Ecology*, Oxford: Oxford University Press, 2006, pp. 115–46.

Sarmiento, Esteban, G. J. Sawyer and Richard Milner, *The Last Human: A Guide to Twenty-two Species of Extinct Humans*, New Haven and London: Yale University Press, 2007.

Sawyer, Robert, *Hominids*, New York: Tom Doherty Associates, 2002.

Sax, Boria, *Animals in the Third Reich: Pets, Scapegoats and the Holocaust*, London: Continuum, 2000.

Schmeichen, Peter, *Saving Power: Theories of Atonement and Forms of the Church*, Grand Rapids MI: Eerdmans, 2005.

Schmemann, Alexander, *The Eucharist: Sacrament of the Kingdom*, Crestwood NY: St Vladimir's Seminary Press, 1988.

Schwager, Raymund, *Jesus in the Drama of Salvation: Towards a Biblical Doctrine of Redemption*, New York: Crossroad, 1999.

—— *Banished from Eden: Original Sin and Evolutionary Theory in the Drama of Salvation*, Leominster: Gracewing, 2006.

Schwartz, Mark, 'Conservationists Should Not Move *Torreya taxifolia*' <http://www.des.ucdavis.edu/faculty/mschwartz/website%20publications/Wil dEarth.pdf> (accessed 20 February 2008).

Scott, Peter, *Theology, Ideology and Liberation*, Cambridge: Cambridge University Press, 1994.

—— *A Political Theology of Nature*, Cambridge: Cambridge University Press, 2003.

Scott, Peter and William T. Cavanaugh (eds), *The Blackwell Companion to Political Theology*, Malden MA and Oxford: Blackwell, 2004.

Sherrard, Philip, *Human Image, World Image: The Death and Resurrection of Sacred Cosmology*, Cambridge: Golgonooza Press, 1992.

Sideris, Lisa, *Environmental Ethics, Ecological Theology and Natural Selection*, New York: Columbia University Press, 2003.

Silver, Carole G., *Strange and Secret Peoples: Fairies and Victorian Consciousness*, New York: Oxford University Press, 2000.

Singer, Peter, *Animal Liberation: A New Ethic for Our Treatment of Animals*, London: Jonathan Cape, 1990.

—— *Practical Ethics*, 2nd edn, Cambridge: Cambridge University Press, 1993.

—— 'Animals', in Ted Honderich (ed.), *The Oxford Companion to Philosophy*, Oxford: Oxford University Press, 1995.

Sloane, Andrew, 'Singer, Preference Utilitarianism and Infanticide', *Studies in Christian Ethics* 12:2, 1999, pp. 47–73.

Smirnova, Engelina, *Moscow Icons: 14th–17th Centuries*, trans. Arthur Shkarovsky-Raffé, Oxford: Phaidon, 1989.

Smith, J. Z., 'I am a Parrot (Red)', in *Map Is Not Territory*, Chicago: University of Chicago Press, 1978.

Smith, Neil, 'Nature as Accumulation Strategy', in Leo Panitch and Colin Leys (eds), *Coming to Terms with Nature*, London: Merlin Press, 2006, pp. 16–36.

Soper, Kate, *What Is Nature?*, Oxford: Blackwell, 1995.

Sorabji, Richard, *Animal Minds and Human Morals: The Origins of the Western Debate*, Ithaca NY: Cornell University Press, 1993.

Southgate, Christopher, 'God and Evolutionary Evil: Theodicy in the Light of Darwinism', *Zygon* 37, 2002.

—— 'Stewardship and Its Competitors: A Spectrum of Relationships between Humans and the Non-Human Creation', in R. J. Berry (ed.), *Environmental Stewardship*, London and New York: T & T Clark/Continuum, 2006, pp. 185–95.

—— *The Groaning of Creation: God, Evolution and the Problem of Evil*, Louisville KY: Westminster John Knox Press, 2008.

Southgate, Christopher, Cherryl Hunt and David G. Horrell, 'Ascesis and Assisted Migration: Responses to the Effects of Climate Change on Animal Species', *European Journal of Science and Theology* 4:2, June 2008, pp. 19–25.

Southgate, Christopher et al. (eds), *God, Humanity and the Cosmos*, Edinburgh: T & T Clark, 2nd edn, 2005.

Spurway, N. (ed.), *Theology, Evolution and Mind*, London: Scholars Press, 2008, forthcoming.

Steeves, H. Peter (ed.), *Animal Others: On Ethics, Ontology, and Animal Life*, Albany NY: State University of New York Press, 1999.

Stefanatos DVM, Joanne, *Animals Sanctified: A Spiritual Journey*, Minneapolis MN: Light and Life Publishing Company, 2001.

Steiner, Gary, *Anthropocentrism and Its Discontents: The Moral Status of Animals in the History of Western Philosophy*, Pittsburgh: University of Pittsburg Press, 2005.

Stiassny, Melanie L. J. and Axel Meyer, 'Cichlids of the Rift Lakes', *Scientific American*, February, 1999, pp. 44–9.

Strauss, Leo, *Natural Right and History*, Chicago: University of Chicago Press, 1965 [1953].

Striffler, Steve, *Chicken: The Dangerous Transformations of America's Favourite Food*, New Haven and London: Yale University Press, 2005.

Stuart, Tristram, *The Bloodless Revolution: A Cultural History of Vegetarianism from 1600 to Modern Times*, New York and London: W. W. Norton & Co., 2006.

Suchocki, Marjorie, *The Fall to Violence: Original Sin in Relational Theology*, New York: Continuum International, 1995.

Symeon the New Theologian, St, *The First-Created Man: Seven Homilies by St Symeon the New Theologian*, trans. Fr Seraphim Rose from the Russian edition of St Theophan the Recluse, Platina CA: St Herman of Alaska Brotherhood, ET 2001.

Tappert, Theodore G. (ed.), *The Book of Concord: The Confessions of the Evangelical Lutheran Church*, Philadelphia: Fortress Press, 1959.

Taylor, Paul W., *Respect for Nature: A Theory of Environmental Ethics*, Princeton NJ: Princeton University Press, 1986.

Theological Declaration of Barmen, May 1934, ET online at <http://warc.ch/pc/20th/index.html> (accessed 30 September 2007).

Thompson, Robert (ed. and trans.), *Athanasius: Contra Gentes and De Incarnatione*, London: Oxford University Press, 1971.

Ticciati, Susannah, *Job and the Disruption of Identity: Reading beyond Barth*, London: T & T Clark, 2005.

Torrell OP, Jean-Pierre, *Saint Thomas Aquinas: The Person and His Work*, trans. Robert Royal, Washington DC: Catholic University of America Press, 1996.

Tradigo, Alfredo, *Icons and Saints of the Eastern Orthodox Church*, trans. Stephen Sartarelli, Los Angeles CA: The J. Paul Getty Museum, 2006.

van Huyssteen, J. Wentzel, 'Human Uniqueness and the Image of God', in *Alone in the World? Human Uniqueness in Science and Theology*, Grand Rapids MI: Eerdmans, 2006.

Veyne, Paul, *Did the Greeks Believe in Their Myths? Essay on the Constitutive Imagination*, Chicago: University of Chicago Press, 1988.

Vialles, Noélie, *Animal to Edible*, Cambridge: Cambridge University Press, 1994.

Vidal, John, untitled article, *Guardian*, 4 August 2007, pp. 29–30.

Vischer, Lukas, 'Listening to Creation Groaning: A Survey of Main Themes of Creation Theology', in Lukas Vischer (ed.), *Listening to Creation Groaning: Report and Papers from a Consultation on Creation Theology Organised by the European Christian Environmental Network at the John Knox International Reformed Center from March 28 to April 1st 2004*, Geneva: Centre International Réformé John Knox, 2004, pp. 11–31.

Waldau, Paul, 'Seeing the Terrain We Walk: Features of the Contemporary Landscape of "Religion and Animals"', in Paul Waldau and Kimberly Patton (eds), *A Communion of Subjects: Animals in Religion, Science, and Ethics*, New

York: Columbia University Press, 2006.

Waldau, Paul and Kimberley Patten (eds), *A Communion of Subjects: Animals in Religion, Science and Ethics*, New York: Columbia University Press, 2006.

Ward, Nicholas, *Before the Dawn: Recovering the Lost History of Our Ancestors* New York: Penguin, 2005.

Ward, Peter D., *Under a Green Sky: Global Warming, the Mass Extinctions of the Past and What They Can Tell Us About Our Future*, New York: HarperCollins, 2007.

Webb, Stephen H., *Of God and Dogs: Christian Theology of Compassion for Animals*, Oxford: Oxford University Press, 1997.

—— *Good Eating: The Bible, Diet and the Proper Love of Animals*, Grand Rapids: Brazos Press, 2001.

Webb, Stephen, *If the Universe Is Teeming with Aliens . . . Where Is Everybody? Fifty Solutions to Fermi's Paradox and the Problem of Extraterrestrial Life*, New York: Copernicus Books, 2002.

Western, David, 'Human-modified Ecosystems and Future Evolution', *Proceedings of the National Academy of Sciences* 98:10, 2001, pp. 5458–65.

Williams, Raymond, *Problems in Materialism and Culture*, London: Verso, 1980.

Williamson, Jack, *Darker than You Think*, London: Gollancz, 2003 [1948].

Willmer, Haddon, 'Images of the City', in Anthony Harvey (ed.), *Theology in the City*, London: SPCK, 1989, pp. 32–46.

Wilson, E. O., *The Future of Life*, London: Little Brown, 2002.

Winslow, Donald F., *The Dynamics of Salvation: A Study of Gregory of Nazianzus*, Cambridge MA: The Philadelphia Patristic Foundation, 1979.

Woese, Carl, 'A New Biology for a New Century', *Microbiology and Molecular Biology Reviews* 68:2, June 2004, pp. 173–86.

Wolch, Jennifer and Jody Enmel, *Animal Geographies: Place Politics and Identity in the Nature-Culture Borderlands*, London and New York: Verso, 1998.

Wolfe, Cary, *Animal Rites: American Culture, the Discourse of Species and Posthumanist Theory*, Chicago and London: University of Chicago Press, 2003.

—— (ed.), *Zootologies: The Question of the Animal*, Minneapolis: University of Minnesota Press, 2003.

Wolfson, Elliot, *Venturing Beyond: Law and Morality in Kabbalistic Mysticism*, Oxford: Oxford University Press, 2006.

Wolfson, Harry Austryn, 'The Internal Senses in Latin, Arabic, and Hebrew Philosophic Texts', in Harry Wolfson, *Studies in the History of Philosophy and Religion*, ed. I. Twersky and G. H. Williams, Cambridge MA: Harvard University Press, 1973, pp. 250–314.

Wood, Bernard, 'Hominid Revelations from Chad', *Nature* 418, 11 July 2002, pp. 133–5.

Woodruff, David S., 'Declines of Biomes and Biota and the Future of Evolution', *Proceedings of the National Academy of Sciences* 98:10, 2001, pp. 5471–76.

Wrangham, Richard and Dale Peterson, *Demonic Males: Apes and the Origins of Human Violence*, London: Bloomsbury, 1997.

Wright, N. T. *The Resurrection of the Son of God*, London: SPCK, 2003.

Wright, Tamara, Peter Hughes and Alison Ainley, 'The Paradox of Morality: An Interview with Emmanuel Levinas', in Robert Bernasconi and David Wood (ed.), *The Provocation of Levinas*, London: Routledge, 1988.

Wynn, M., 'Aquinas's Appropriation of the Dominion Tradition', in D. Horrell, et al. (eds), *Towards an Ecological Hermeneutic: Biblical, Historical, and Theological Perspectives*, forthcoming.

Yazykova, I., 'The Theological Principles of Icon and Iconography', in Lilia Evseyeva et al., *A History of Icon Painting*, trans. Kate Cook, Moscow: Grand-Holding Publishers, 2007.

Yeats W. B., *Selected Poetry*, London: Pan, 1974.

Yohe, Gary, 'Climate Change', in Bjorn Lomborg (ed.), *Solutions for the World's Biggest Problems: Costs and Benefits*, Cambridge: Cambridge University Press, 2007, pp. 103–24.

Index of Names and Subjects

Adams, Carol, 9, 138, 266
Agamben, Giorgio, 66, 68, 73–7, 133–4, 182–3, 266
Alexander of Hales, 27
altruism, 93, 193, 243–4
Anatolios, 84–90
angels, 1, 65, 75
anima, 25, 26, 32
animal studies, 14, 121, 136
animalization, 123
'animal', definition of, 2
animals
  as agents of justice, 5
  as pets, 6, 178, 183, 234, 238, 250
  campaigners, 198, 238
  celebration of, 5
  commodification of, 172, 178, 180, 183
  cruelty towards, 128, 232, 236–8, 241, 245
  ethological account of, 12–3, 34, 197, 201, 209, 239, 243, 246
  flourishing of, 6, 38, 66, 93, 98, 176, 182, 201, 204, 234, 244, 250–2, 256, 258, 259, 260, 263
  liberation of, 4, 12, 70, 81, 91, 93, 95, 99, 174–5, 177, 232–5, 264
  medical use of, 3–4, 12, 183, 187, 211, 223, 226, 268
  redemption of, 8, 81–3, 88, 90–4, 97–9, 116, 174–5, 234, 246
  sociability of, 177, 240, 241
  suffering of, 3, 4, 70, 94–5, 138,

165–6, 222, 232, 237, 241–2, 245
  wild, 13, 42, 47, 97, 106, 140, 143, 151, 165, 178, 183, 235–6, 239, 242–3, 250–3
anthropocentrism, 8, 15, 24, 42, 43, 46, 49, 58–9, 66, 70, 173, 184–6, 203, 218, 252
anthropomorphism, 180, 203
anti-human, 10–11, 171–2, 177, 182–7, 202
anti-materialism, 12
anti-vivisection, 233
appetites, 7, 21, 28–9, 34
Aquinas, 7, 21–38, 68, 102, 104, 108, 134, 197–201, 207–10, 213–16, 237, 238, 266
argumentum e silentio, 106
Aristotle, 6, 22–3, 25–9, 32, 36–8, 47, 102–3, 134, 198, 214
ascension, 11, 172, 184–5
assisted migration, 13, 249, 254–64
Athanasius, 8, 82–98, 266
Attfield, Robin, 259–60
Augustine, St, 1, 9, 133, 147–9, 207, 208, 266
australopithecine, 152, 157
Averroes, 27
Avicenna, 27

baboon, 157
bacteria, 91, 163
Barad, Judith, 7, 199
Barth, Karl, 12, 109, 216–26, 266

basar, 114
Basil the Great, 68
battery cages, 175
Behemoth, 143–5
Bekoff, Marc, 11, 195–6, 203, 206, 266
Benedict, Rule of, 23, 246
Bentham, Jeremy, 212, 241, 266
Bergmann, Sigurd, 260
Berry, Thomas, 254, 259
Berry, Wendell, 104, 261
Biggar, Nigel, 216–7, 226, 243
biodiversity, 98, 163, 251–2, 264
biomedical research, 11, 211, 226
birds, 2, 7, 24, 31, 53–60, 65, 73, 97, 105, 106, 113, 115, 128, 164, 236
Blake, William, 165–7, 266
Boehm, Christopher, 204–6
Bonhoeffer, Dietrich, 4, 12, 174, 219, 220, 223–4, 266
bonobos, 36, 158, 204, 206
Boulter, Michael, 249, 253
Brueggemann, Walter, 60
butchering, 236

Cairns, David, 108
Calvin, 58, 108–9
Casanova, José, 188
categorical imperative, 239–40
Chesterton, G.K., 161–3, 167
chicken, 175, 180–1
chimpanzee, 1, 39, 159, 190
Christ the Pantokrator, 75
Christology, 86, 116, 174
Chryssavgis, John, 75–6
citizenship, 11, 182–7
Clark, Stephen R. L., 5, 176, 225, 266
Cleland, Elsa E, 249, 255, 264
climate change, 13, 61, 231, 249, 251, 253, 256, 258, 263, 264
cloning, 181
Clough, David, 1, 7, 13, 41, 102–4, 116, 125, 138, 145–6, 216, 266
cockles, 181
cockroaches, 245

cognition, 27, 32, 40, 202
Cohn-Sherbok, Dan, 5
Columba, St, 2, 254
commonality, 8, 11, 49, 50, 51, 180, 186, 187, 267
compassion, 6, 11, 49, 94, 155, 167, 237, 243, 248
conscience, 11, 190, 193, 204, 205, 206, 207
consequentialism, 3
conservation, 13, 99, 187, 252, 253, 254, 255, 260
Copernicus, 103, 161
cosmology, 72, 184
cosmos, 69, 72, 116
crabs, 176
creation, 1, 2, 7, 8, 13, 22–4, 42, 44–5, 51–64, 68–107, 113–7, 127, 136, 144, 147–8, 164–75, 184–5, 208, 210, 212, 216, 221–4, 234, 237, 245, 247, 249, 251, 256, 261, 264
creaturely theology, 1, 117, 121, 122, 126, 137, 266, 267, 269
Crowley, John, 164
crows, 245
Cyril of Alexandria, 88

Darwin, Charles, 7, 51, 102–3, 152, 156–7, 159, 162, 192, 193, 215, 217, 221
Daston, Lorraine, 180
Dawkins, Richard, 192
De Grazia, David, 6
de Waal, Frans, 11, 13, 192–7, 203, 214, 243–4, 266
deification, 83, 87–90
deliberation, 6, 30–2, 199–200, 238, 242
Derrida, Jacques, 124, 128, 131
desires, 28, 29, 30, 31, 84
dogs, 33, 39, 44, 48, 53–4, 60, 92, 124–5, 132, 142, 158, 176, 198, 249
dolphins, 26, 39, 82–3, 97–8, 193, 239, 243

domestication, 249
dominion, 44–7, 54, 58, 59, 106, 112, 223–4
donkey, 49, 143
Dyson, Freeman, 163–4, 167

eagles, 43, 92, 166
Ecoffey, Chloé Bregnard, 183
ecotourism, 251
Eden, Garden of, 46, 50, 71, 75, 92–3, 234–5, 246
Eder, Klaus, 236
elephants, 39, 65, 193, 243–4
Ellul, Jacques, 240
embarrassment, 202, 205–7
emotional contagion, 194
empathy, 54, 58, 154, 180, 194, 196, 243–4
ensoulment, 7
eschatology, 61, 74
estimative sense, 25–30, 32, 35, 198
ethology, 34, 243–4
evolution, 11, 163, 192, 193, 202–4, 214–5, 249–50, 255
experimentation, 3, 5, 12, 14, 222, 225, 233, 245, 250, 268
exploitation, 5, 11, 182, 221–2, 225
extinction, 13, 95, 249–64

Fabre-Vassas, Claudine, 135, 146
factory, 128, 136, 165, 180, 236, 242
fall, doctrine of the, 42–6, 58, 70, 85, 91, 108, 116–7, 220, 224–5, 234, 245–6
farming, 3, 99, 127, 165, 176, 180, 232, 236, 238
Farrow, Douglas, 184
fish, 73, 81, 104–6, 115, 167, 225–6
Flack, Jessica, 195, 197
Fleming, Pat, 259
flesh, 4, 8, 67–70, 76, 83–101, 114–7, 124–9, 140, 148, 166, 174, 176, 185, 236
Fossey, Diane, 242–3
Francis of Assisi, St, 2

Fraser, David, 232
free will, 112
freedom, 31, 82, 90, 95, 173–4, 187–8, 260, 264

Gaita, Raimond, 40
geeps, 164
generosity, 4, 84, 91, 174, 205, 258
Genesis, 12, 42–60, 91, 94, 102, 104–110, 125, 135, 155, 165, 191, 208, 220–1, 234–6, 245–6, 251
genome, 155, 159, 163
George, Marie, 33–5
Gilhus, Ingvild, 146, 148
Golding, William, 154
Goodall, Jane, 242–3
gorilla, 157
Gray, John, 7, 61–2, 74, 77, 173, 185, 266
Gregory of Nazianzus, 69, 71, 112, 266
Gregory of Nyssa, 63–4, 75, 266
Gunton, Colin, 41, 46, 107

Habel, Norman, 105, 144, 251, 252
Hall, Douglas John, 186
Haraway, Donna, 177
Harvey, William, 104
Hegel, 109
Heidegger, Martin, 124, 201
hens, 3, 57
Herder, 109
Hesychasm, 72
hippopotamus, 144, 196
Hobbes, Thomas, 104
Høeg, Peter, 172, 266
hominid, 10, 152, 154–9, 164, 204
Horrell, David G., 68, 249, 256–8
horses, 92
human-animal studies, 121
Humane Slaughter Act, 123
humanism, 61, 131, 186
Hume, David, 191, 215, 232
hunting, 4, 5, 26, 54, 55, 95, 204, 236, 245, 249

Huntingdon Life Sciences, 238
Huxley, T. H., 215

iconography, 62–4, 70, 71, 74
icons, 7, 8, 62,–76
imago Dei, 8, 62, 69–76, 100–1,
    106–17, 190, 207, 210
imago Trinitatis, 210
incarnation, 4, 8, 60, 82– 98, 104,
    116–17, 174, 185
incarnational theology, 82–3, 86,
    97–8
Ingold, Timothy, 122–3
insects, 81
instinct, 31, 140, 161, 195, 198–9,
    238, 245, 253, 260
intelligence, 26, 36, 39, 98, 202–3
interdependence, 92, 117, 260–3

justice, 11, 44–5, 60, 92, 193, 196,
    237, 252

kangaroos, 82–3
Kant, Immanuel, 12, 232, 239–41,
    266
Katz, Leonard, 192, 195–7, 204–5
Kaufman, Gordon, 173, 175
Kesekopoulos, Anestis G., 69
kingdom of heaven, 72, 89
kinship, 71, 114, 147, 202
koinōnia, 260
kookaburras, 82–3
Kummer, Hans, 197

lambs, 9, 148–9, 246
Latour, Bruno, 176, 182, 189, 266
Leakey, Richard, 249
lemurs, 243
Leopold, Aldo, 260
Levinas, Emmanuel, 9, 121–37
Levi-Strauss, Claude, 134–5
Lewin, Roger, 249
liberation, 4, 12, 70, 81, 91–9, 174–7,
    232–4, 245, 264
Linzey, Andrew, 3–6, 12, 46, 52, 116,

174, 198, 212–3, 222–4, 226, 235,
    250, 256, 264
Locke, John, 104
logos, 63, 71–6, 88–90, 116, 126,
    130, 174
love, 28, 83, 92–8, 141, 155, 166,
    184, 196, 202, 214, 260
Lovejoy, Arthur O., 111
Lovelock, James, 261
Lovibond, Sabina, 40
Luther, Martin, 7, 41–60, 108, 266
Lütticken, Sven, 186–7

Mabey, Richard, 179–80
macaques, 35, 158, 194
MacIntyre, Alasdair, 33–4, 38–40,
    197, 200–1, 266
Macy, Joanna, 259
Magnus, Albertus, 22
Maimonides, Moses, 60
mammals, 234, 238, 243–4, 249, 253
Marshall, Bruce, 107, 111, 116
Marx, Karl, 104
Maximus the Confessor, 69, 71, 266
McCabe, Herbert, 31–2
McFadyen, Alistair I., 225
McFague, Sallie, 174, 259
meat, 4, 5, 11, 12, 46, 121, 149, 211,
    222, 225–6, 233, 235–6, 241, 247,
    268
memory, 22, 26, 29, 36, 84, 96, 99,
    111, 152–3, 157, 200
Middleton, Richard, 107, 109, 113
Midgley, Mary, 6, 9, 13, 121, 140–9,
    201–2, 213, 239, 266
Mithen, Steven, 154, 202–3
monkeys, 158, 194–5, 206, 243
Mooney, H.A., 249, 255
moral agency, 207–9
Morrison, Reg, 255

natural law, 28, 199, 200, 213, 214,
    216, 238
natural order, 65, 102, 110
natural right, 11, 135, 186–8

natural selection, 93–4, 97, 192, 202, 215

nephesh, 235–6

New Jerusalem, 67–70, 75

New Testament, 81–2, 87, 102, 106, 114–5, 146, 256, 258, 260

Northcott, Michael, 12–4, 97–8, 115, 231, 237, 243–4, 253, 259, 268

Novacek, Michael J., 264

Nussbaum, Martha, 6

Old Testament, 54, 64, 106, 109, 114, 125, 147, 234, 235, 237, 246

original sin, 92–3, 234

other-regard, 257–64

ox, 53, 143–4, 246

parsimony, principle of, 38–9

patristics, 68

Patton, Kimberly, 124, 127, 136

peaceable kingdom, 12, 221–5, 235, 247

Pettersen, Alvyn, 83–4

pigs, 9, 44, 146–9, 232, 242

Planalp, S., 190

Plato, 25, 47, 166

Plumwood, Val, 173

polar bear, 13, 262–3

Poliakov, Léon, 123

political practices, 99

pongids, 157, 159

Pope, Stephen, 215

power relations, 178

pragmatism, 268

predation, 92, 95, 234–5, 246

prey, 26, 35, 54, 95, 245–6, 255

Primavesi, Anne, 261

production line, 181

prudence, 11, 26, 198–201, 207

Ptolemy, 103

rational soul, 21, 207–8

rationality, 7, 21, 29–40, 58, 76, 103, 108, 199, 214, 239

reading strategies, 63–4

reconciliation, 15, 74, 76, 81–2, 177, 195, 202, 204

redemption, 8, 81–3, 88, 90–9, 116, 174–5, 234, 246

Reformation, 108, 153

Regan, Tom, 3–4, 6, 12, 232, 238, 242, 250, 256, 261, 266

Reno, R. R., 63

repentance, 57, 220, 226

resurrection, 68, 70–3, 81–7, 92–8, 177, 185, 247

rights, animal, 3–4, 6, 12, 136, 190, 198, 212–3, 232, 236, 239, 244, 250

ritual slaughter, 236

Rogers, Eugene, 216

Rohan, Michael Scott, 154

Rolston, Holmes, 94, 191, 193, 250, 252

Rosenzweig, Franz, 126, 127

Ruse, Michael, 215

Russell, Norman, 87

sacrifice, 46, 47, 82, 87, 91, 122, 186, 223, 226, 258

salvation, 7, 61, 64, 67–8, 72, 75, 81–93, 98, 174, 219, 256

Santmire, Paul, 44, 56, 58

sarx, 88, 114, 116

Sax, Boria, 141

Schmeichen, Peter, 82

Schmemann, Alexander, 96

Schwager, Raymund, 92–3

Schwartz, Mark, 254, 255

Scott, Peter, 10, 177, 268

Sen, Amartya, 6

senses, 25–9, 32, 34–5, 43, 100, 108, 130, 146

sentience, 94

shame, 205–7

sheep, 26, 29–32, 146, 181, 231–2, 235, 240, 246, 247

sinfulness, 58, 235

Singer, Peter, 3, 12, 102, 212, 232, 237, 250, 266

slaughterhouses, 128
Smith, Neil, 178, 179, 180
sociability, 177, 240, 241
sola scriptura, 62
Soper, Kate, 178–9
Sophronius, St, 70
Soule, Michael, 254
souls, 6, 21–2, 25, 29, 55, 66, 83–4
Southgate, Christopher, 13, 98, 249, 251–7, 264, 268
speciesism, 3, 233–4
Spencer, Herbert, 215
Spirit, Holy, 89, 90, 93, 260
Stefanatos, Joanne, 73
stewardship, 13, 223, 252, 260
Stoicism, 141, 146
Strauss, Leo, 182, 188, 266
Suchocki, Marjorie, 234
suffering, 3, 4, 70, 94–5, 138, 165, 166, 222, 232, 237, 241, 242, 245
superiority, human, 47, 58, 141
syggenes, 71
symbolism, 6, 65
Symeon the New Theologian, St, 69, 73, 74
sympathy, 7, 55, 124, 176–7, 193, 205, 244

teleology, 211
telos, 21, 24, 213
theological anthropology, 8, 15, 58, 217, 266, 267
theology
 apophatic, 73, 100
 cataphatic, 73
 creaturely, 1, 2, 5, 15, 52, 60, 86, 117, 121, 122, 126, 137, 150, 174, 184–5, 203, 219, 220, 222, 235, 238, 262, 266, 267, 269
 sacramental, 51, 58, 83
theosis, 71, 72
theos-rights, 4, 174, 212, 250
tortoise, 196
transformation, 67, 81–2, 87–8, 96, 219, 267
translocation, 249, 255–6
Troeltsch, 109

utilitarianism, 5, 212, 237, 242

vampire bats, 243
vegetarianism, 12, 14, 131–2, 139, 221–2, 225–6, 268
Veyne, Paul, 153
violence, political, 12
Virgin Mary, 67, 73–6
virtue ethics, 196–7
Vischer, Lukas, 252
Vlasak, Dr Jerry, 233

Waldau, Paul, 124, 127
Webb, Stephen, 6, 141
welfare, animal, 232, 237–44
Williams, Raymond, 171, 178
Williamson, Jack, 154
Wisdom, 67, 81–98
wolves, 48, 55, 140, 142, 146, 193, 195, 204, 255

xenotransplantation, 238

zoos, 165